Peronism Without Perón

JAMES W. McGUIRE

Peronism Without Perón

Unions, Parties, and
Democracy in Argentina

STANFORD UNIVERSITY PRESS

STANFORD, CALIFORNIA   1997

Stanford University Press
Stanford, California
©1997 by the Board of Trustees of the
Leland Stanford Junior University

Printed in the United States of America

CIP data appear at the end of the book

To
My Parents

Preface

Peronism, the Argentine political movement created by Juan Perón in the mid 1940s, has revolved since its inception around a personalistic leader, powerful and autonomous union organizations, and weak and disarticulated party structures. This study analyzes the relationships among these components of Peronism and links them to the vicissitudes of Argentine democracy. It argues that deliberate actions by Peronism's personalistic leaders, together with turf battles among its trade unionists, have undermined attempts by secondary Peronist figures to institutionalize its party structures, and that the failure of these party-building projects has impeded the consolidation of democracy in the broader political system. By exploring the forces and conditions that promoted and undermined these Peronist party-building projects, and by showing how their collapses have shaped Argentina's experience with democracy, the study seeks to illuminate opportunities and constraints that political actors face, in Argentina and elsewhere, in their efforts to build democratic political regimes.

Underpinning the study are two convictions. The first is that procedural democracy—fair elections, real power for elected officials, and basic human and civil rights—is worth pursuing. By deterring the abuse of political power, by allowing the exercise of popular sovereignty, and by making it easier for the disadvantaged to influence and benefit from public policy, democracy promotes the free development of human capabilities. The second conviction behind the study is that social structures, historical legacies, and political arrangements can be changed by acts of human will. Political choices matter, and they will matter even more if those who make them understand the opportunities and constraints their predecessors have faced. A grasp of these opportunities and constraints can help such actors identify, and thus more easily overcome, obstacles that might otherwise overwhelm them.

Argentina captured my interest a decade ago, for the same reason it has caught the attention of many other political scientists: I wanted to understand how a country that had become more and more prosperous and democratic from 1880 to 1930 could subsequently have been drawn into a descending spiral of sometimes weak, sometimes overbearing civilian governments alternating with periods of increasingly harsh military rule. I focused my research on Argentine trade unions partly because of their centrality in Argentine politics, and partly because of my experience organizing in 1980 with the New York local of the International Typographical Union. Also contributing to my interest in Argentine politics was the opportunity I had in 1982 to translate from Spanish to English Guillermo O'Donnell's *El estado burocrático-autoritario*, whose account of conflict and collaboration among political forces deepened my interest in the subtleties of Argentine politics.

The book that has grown out of these convictions and influences reflects the inspiration and help of persons and institutions too numerous to acknowledge in a few paragraphs. I shall therefore restrict myself to mentioning, more briefly than they deserve, those whose contributions have shaped the best facets of this study. Above all I would like to thank my parents, whose love and guidance have been at the core of my personal and intellectual development, and whose comments on and suggestions about this study have helped greatly to improve it.

This project could not have been completed without the contributions of those who supervised my doctoral dissertation (political science, Berkeley, 1989), which treated the role of unions in Argentine politics from 1955 to 1966 and introduced the distributive conflict–party institutionalization approach that guides the present analysis. I am deeply indebted to David Collier, the chair of my dissertation committee, for fifteen years of friendly support, sage advice, and intellectual stimulation. David Collier's work with Ruth Berins Collier on the interactions among unions, parties, and regime dynamics in Latin America provided inspiration for this work. Tulio Halperín Donghi helped guide the analysis with his deep understanding of Argentine history; I am particularly grateful to him for encouraging me to examine how conflicts within the Peronist movement have shaped conflicts between Peronism and other political forces in Argentina. Jack Citrin gave advice on quantitative analysis and made useful critiques of arguments in several parts of the book.

Outside of the committee itself, Guillermo O'Donnell, who was partly responsible for my initial decision to focus my work on Argentina, has given me years of warm friendship and close intellectual guidance, not to mention some crushing defeats in eight-ball in a certain pool hall in Mishawaka, Indiana. Marcelo Cavarozzi, whose work on Argentine political parties has profoundly shaped the analysis in this book, has contributed to my work, both intellectually and practically, by inviting me to undertake research in the congenial and stimulating environment of the Centro de Estudios de Estado y Sociedad (CEDES) in Buenos Aires, where I spent most of 1986, and to which I have returned on each of three subsequent research visits to Argentina. The distributive conflict–party institutionalization approach used in this book to analyze the vicissitudes of Argentine politics may be viewed in part as a synthesis and extension of O'Donnell's and Cavarozzi's pioneering work, informed by the comparative analyses of David Collier and Ruth Berins Collier and the historical insights of Tulio Halperín Donghi. I am also deeply indebted to William Smith, not just for producing the important studies of Argentine political economy on which this study has drawn, but also for his close reading and incisive critique of an earlier draft of the manuscript, which helped greatly to improve the final version. Two outstanding teachers of political science, Christopher Achen and Kenneth Sharpe, deepened my understanding of methodological and theoretical issues pertinent to this study.

This research would not have been possible without the supportive working environment I enjoyed in 1986 as a visiting scholar at CEDES. Also of invaluable assistance to my research in Buenos Aires were the archives and staffs of the Centro de Estudios sobre Estado y Administración (CISEA), Centro de Estudios Unión para la Nueva Mayoría, Centro de Estudios y Información Laboral (CEIL), Consejo de Investigaciones Técnicas, Instituto Torcuato di Tella, Ministerio de Trabajo de la República Argentina, *La Razón*, Partido Justicialista (Capital Federal), Servicio de Documentación e Información Laboral (DIL), and the Sindicato de Luz y Fuerza.

I also owe an enormous personal and intellectual debt to the many people with whom I discussed various aspects of this work. In Argentina, I would like especially to thank the scholars at CEDES, including Carlos Acuña, Beatríz Cappelletti, Liliana de Riz, Roberto Frenkel, Monica Gogna, Alejandro Lamadrid, María Matilde Ollier, Vicente Palermo, Leonor Plate, Catalina Smulovitz, and Andrés Thompson.

I am also grateful to others in Argentina who contributed in various ways to making this study possible, including Rubén Heguelein, Fredy Kofman, Miguel Llanos, Ronaldo Munck, Héctor Palomino, Mariano Plotkin, María Laura Rodríguez Mayol, Stephen Rasmussen, Julio Rodríguez Morano, Ricardo Santos, Alberto Serú García, Kathryn Sikkink, Elizabeth Station, María Eugenia Streb, and Rubén Zorrilla.

In the United States, I learned especially from discussions with Scott Mainwaring, J. Samuel Valenzuela, and other faculty, fellows, staff, and students associated in 1988 with the Kellogg Institute of International Studies at the University of Notre Dame; with Daniel James, Margaret Keck, María José Moyano, Sylvia Maxfield, and Yossi Shain of Yale University; and with Ronald Archer, Leslie Armijo, Alasdair Bowie, Ruth Berins Collier, María Lorena Cook, Giuseppe Di Palma, Francisco Durán, Serge Halimi, Wendy Hunter, John Gerring, Donald Green, Kenneth Jowitt, Richard Keiser, Steven Levitsky, Victor Magagna, James Mahon, Deborah Norden, Pierre Ostiguy, Anthony Pickering, Ben Schneider, Timothy Scully, John Seery, Richard Stahler-Sholk, Arun Swamy, Kathe Thelen, Daniel Unger, and Deborah Yashar, all of the University of California, Berkeley. I am also indebted to Alex Dupuy, Nancy Gallagher, Russell Murphy, Peter Rutland, Nancy Schwartz, David Titus, and Ann Wightman of Wesleyan University, each of whom commented helpfully on portions of this work. The comments of Samuel Amaral, Luigi Manzetti, Gerardo Munck, and María Victoria Murillo also helped to improve the work. Grant Barnes, Peter Dreyer, John Feneron, Norris Pope, and others at Stanford University Press have been helpful throughout the editorial process.

My research in Argentina in 1986 was funded by a Fulbright-Hays Doctoral Dissertation Research Abroad Fellowship and a Social Science Research Council International Doctoral Research Fellowship. A U.C. Berkeley Center for Latin American Studies/Tinker Foundation Travel Grant allowed me to conduct research in Argentina in 1985, and a University of California Regents' Fellowship, followed by a Visiting Assistant Faculty Fellowship at the Kellogg Institute, supported my writing in 1987 and 1988. A Wesleyan University Project Grant and an American Political Science Association Research Grant provided funding for research trips to Argentina in 1989 and 1991, and a visiting appointment at U.C. Berkeley's Institute of Industrial Relations facilitated my research and writing in 1992. I am deeply indebted to each of these institutions for their very generous support.

I have drawn material from the following articles and chapters:

"Union Political Tactics and Democratic Consolidation in Alfonsín's Argentina, 1983–1989," *Latin American Research Review* 27 no. 1 (1992): 37–74; "Perón y los sindicatos: La lucha por el liderazgo Peronista," in Samuel Amaral and Mariano Ben Plotkin, eds., *Perón: Del exilio al poder* (San Martín [Buenos Aires]: Editorial Cántaro, 1993), 171–217; "Interim Government and Democratic Consolidation: Argentina in Comparative Perspective," in Yossi Shain and Juan J. Linz, eds., *Between States: Interim Governments and Democratic Transitions* (Cambridge: Cambridge University Press, 1995), 179–210; "Political Parties and Democracy in Argentina," in Scott Mainwaring and Timothy R. Scully, eds., *Building Democratic Institutions: Party Systems in Latin America* (Stanford: Stanford University Press, 1995), 200–246; "Strikes in Argentina: Data Sources and Recent Trends," *Latin American Research Review* 31, no. 3 (1996): 127–50.

The purpose of this work is to advance the understanding of twentieth-century Argentine politics in a way that illuminates options available to those who struggle for democracy and social justice. To the extent that this goal has been achieved, the individuals and institutions mentioned in the preceding paragraphs deserve a large share of the credit. I alone am responsible for any errors of fact or interpretation.

J.W.M.

Contents

Tables and Figure

Abbreviations

"15"	Grupo de Quince ("Group of 15," a conciliatory Peronist union faction formed in 1987)
"25"	Grupo de Veinticinco ("Group of 25," a combative Peronist union faction formed in 1977)
"32"	Treinta y Dos Organizaciones Democráticas ("32 Democratic Organizations," an anti-Peronist union faction formed in 1957)
"62"	Sesenta y Dos Organizaciones ("62 Organizations," a Peronist union faction formed in 1957)
ANSSAL	Administración Nacional del Seguro de Salud (National Administration of Health Insurance)
AOT	Asociación Obrera Textil (Textile Workers' Association)
APRA	Alianza Popular Revolucionaria Americana (American Popular Revolutionary Alliance)
ATE	Asociación Trabajadores del Estado (State Workers' Association)
CGE	Confederación General Económica (General Economic Confederation)
CGEC	Confederación General de Empleados de Comercio (Commercial Employees' Confederation)
CGT	Confederación General del Trabajo (General Labor Confederation)
CTA	Congreso de Trabajadores Argentinos (Argentine Workers' Congress)
CTERA	Confederación de Trabajadores de la Educación de la República Argentina (Education Workers' Confederation)
DGI	Dirección General Impositiva (National Tax Board)

DIL	Documentación e Información Laboral
ENTel	Empresa Nacional de Telecomunicaciones (National Telecommunications Enterprise)
FATLyF	Federación Argentina de Trabajadores de Luz y Fuerza (Light and Power Workers' Federation)
FGPIC	Federación Gremial del Personal de la Industria de la Carne y sus Derivados (Meatpackers' Federation)
FIEL	Fundación de Investigaciones Económicas Latinoamericanas
FIEL/CEA	Fundación de Investigaciones Económicas Latinoamericanas/Consejo Empresario Argentino
FOETRA	Federación de Obreros y Empleados Telefónicos de la República Argentina (Telephone Workers' Federation)
FONIVA	Federación Obrera Nacional de la Industria del Vestido y Afines (Garment Workers' Federation)
FOTIA	Federación Obrera Tucumana de la Industria Azucarera (Tucumán Sugar Workers' Federation)
FREJULI	Frente Justicialista de Liberación (Justicialist Front for Liberation)
FREPASO	Frente del Pais Solidario (Front in Solidarity for the Country)
GDP	Gross Domestic Product
GNP	Gross National Product
GOU	Grupo de Oficiales Unidos (United Officers' Group)
GyT	Comisión Gestión y Trabajo (Labor Action Commission)
IAPI	Instituto Argentino para la Promoción del Intercambio (Argentine Institute for Trade Promotion)
INDEC	Instituto Nacional de Estadística y Censos (National Statistical and Census Institute)
MID	Movimiento de Integración y Desarrollo (Movement of Integration and Development)
MON	Movimiento de Opinión Nacional (Movement of National Opinion)
MPM	Movimiento Popular Mendocino (Mendoza Popular Movement)
MSMP	Mesa Sindical Menem Presidente (Union Board for Menem for President)
MTA	Movimiento de Trabajadores Argentinos (Movement of Argentine Workers)

PAIS   Política Abierta para la Integridad Social (Open Politics
            for Social Integrity)
PAMI   Programa Asistencial Medical Integrada (Integrated
            Medical Assistance Plan)
PI   Partido Intransigente (Intransigent Party)
PJ   Partido Justicialista (Justicialist Party)
SIDE   Secretaría de Informaciones del Estado (State
            Intelligence Service)
SMATA   Sindicato de Mecánicos y Afines del Transporte
            Automotor (Auto Workers' Union)
SOMISA   Sociedad Mixta Siderurgia Argentina (Argentine Steel
            Company)
SRA   Sociedad Rural Argentina (Argentine Rural Society)
SUPE   Federación de Sindicatos Unidos Petroleros del Estado
            (State Oil Workers' Federation)
UCeDé   Unión del Centro Democrático (Union of the
            Democratic Center)
UCR   Unión Cívica Radical (Radical Civic Union; Radical
            Party)
UCR-JR   Unión Cívica Radical–Junta Renovadora (Radical Civic
            Union–Renovation Board)
UCRI   Unión Cívica Radical Intransigente (Intransigent Radical
            Civic Union)
UCRP   Unión Cívica Radical del Pueblo (People's Radical Civic
            Union)
UIA   Unión Industrial Argentina (Argentine Industrial Union)
UOCRA   Unión Obrera de la Construcción de la República
            Argentina (Construction Workers' Union)
UOM   Unión Obrera Metalúrgica (Metalworkers' Union)
YPF   Yacimientos Petrolíferos Fiscales (State Petroleum
            Corporation)

Peronism Without Perón

Chapter 1

Peronism, Party Institutionalization, and Democracy

Peronism is strong as a collective identity, but weakly institutionalized as a political party. Ever since Juan Perón founded the Peronist movement in the mid 1940s, top Peronist leaders, including Perón and Carlos Menem, have neglected or undermined the parties connected to Peronism. Using Philip Selznick's definition of institutionalization, Peronist leaders have never moved far toward infusing their party organization with value.[1] Those who have spoken for the Peronist movement, beginning with Juan Perón himself during his 1946–55 presidency, have repeatedly insisted that Peronism is a national movement committed to real democracy, not a political party preoccupied with formal democracy. The movement might be associated with a party, but the party is primarily a concession to those preoccupied with the formalities of electoral competition. The basic goal of the movement is to put into power a Peronist who will enact policies pursuant to social justice, economic independence, and national sovereignty. This goal can be achieved by party-mediated electoral participation, but also (especially when the electoral route is blocked) by an alliance with sympathetic military officers or by an insurrectionary general strike. The plebiscitarian leader and the trade unions, not party organization, have always been the core, indispensable embodiments of Peronism.

This study examines the origins of Peronism's weak party institutionalization, explores why Peronism continued to be weakly institutionalized as a party after Perón was overthrown in 1955, and suggests some ways in which this weak party institutionalization may have impeded the consolidation of Argentine democracy. Special attention is devoted to two periods, 1962–66 and 1984–88, when some Peronist union leaders and politicians tried, but failed, to create a better-institutionalized Peronist party. By identifying the forces that led to these efforts at party institutionalization and by analyzing the counterforces that thwarted them, the study will direct attention to obstacles and opportunities that Peronists have faced in seeking to create a better-institutionalized party—and thus to one set of obstacles that Argentines have faced in consolidating democracy. The decision to focus on these "missed opportunities" to forge a better-institutionalized Peronist party reflects a conviction that social science research is most useful when it identifies critical points at which social actors can intervene to redirect the course of events from channels to which historical legacies might otherwise confine them.

In twentieth-century Argentina, sectoral elites representing workers, urban business interests, and the export-oriented landowners of the Pampas region have been powerful and politicized. The power and politicization of these sectoral elites, given their often competing interests, has accentuated conflict over the distribution of wealth and income. This conflict has been expressed to some extent through political parties, but more continuously and forcefully through nonparty vehicles like lobbies, media pronouncements, demonstrations, urban uprisings, and labor, management, or investment strikes. Some of these vehicles for political expression have tended to create a climate of instability conducive to military coups. Moreover, because sectoral elites have tended to neglect party activity, they have acquired a reduced stake in the survival of electoral and legislative institutions.

Party institutionalization is crucial to democratic stability. By investing resources in parties, by getting used to making demands through party channels, and by infusing parties with value, sectoral elites gain an instrumental stake in the survival of democracy—over and above any principled commitment they may have to democracy itself. Whereas nonparty vehicles of political influence (lobbying, disinvestment, strikes, demonstrations, insurrection) can be effective under authoritarian regimes, parties (defined, in Giovanni Sartori's sense, as "parts" of the polity) can be effective only under democratic ones.[2] In the absence of fair elections and a reasonably vigorous legislature, parties become empty shells. People who come to value party activity thus acquire a more direct and salient instrumental stake in the survival of elections and legislatures than do people who subordinate party activity to pressure through class organizations, to wheeling and dealing with government officials, or to an "anything goes" approach to empowering a plebiscitarian leader. People who acquire a stronger stake in the survival of such institutions are, in turn, more likely to defend them when they are threatened. Perceiving this possibility, actors discontented with democracy will be less likely to try to destroy it.

The literature on the relationship between parties and democracy in Latin America has paid more attention to party systems than to individual parties.[3] It may be useful to restore the balance. Larry Diamond and Juan Linz note that "our understanding of democracy in many Latin American countries is handicapped by a lack of systematic knowledge of some of the parties." Summarizing the contributions to *Democracy in Developing Countries: Latin America* (1989), Diamond and Linz stress that "all of our cases call attention to the institutional strength or weakness of parties as a determinant of success or failure with democracy, and each of them grapples with the problem of institutionalization." Referring to Carlos Waisman's chapter on Argentina, Diamond and Linz add that "the extraordinary incoherence of the Peronist Party, containing mutually contradictory tendencies, has been especially damaging [to competitive politics], and its recent evolution of a more democratic structure and commitment is an encouraging sign."[4] Although this trend toward Peronist party institutionalization was coming to a halt just as Diamond and Linz were writing their essay, these authors were right about the need to understand more about Latin America's individual parties, to relate their levels of institutionalization to the prospects for democracy, and to explore the role that party organization has played in the Peronist movement. The purpose of this study is to make some headway toward meeting these needs.

Movementism and Its Consequences for Democracy

Argentina has been democratic since 1983, but preceding years were marred by electoral proscription, political violence, or military dictatorships—the last of which, from 1976 to 1983, was responsible for the "disappearance" of thousands of persons. From 1955, when Perón was ousted and exiled, to 1983, when Raúl Alfonsín was elected president, Argentina experienced a descending spiral of often unfairly elected civilian governments alternating with periods of increasingly harsh military rule. Peronism's self-definition as a movement rather than a party helped to perpetuate this spiral.

Two impediments to democratic consolidation follow from the idea that Peronism is a national movement rather than a political party.[5]

First, a "party," as Sartori has pointed out, portrays itself as a "part" of a "polity conceived as a pluralistic whole."[6] The leaders and members of a party recognize that other parties have a rightful, or at least enduring, place in the polity. No party contests elections with the intention of losing, but all recognize that party competition is legitimate, or at least inevitable. The leaders and members of a national movement, by contrast, think it desirable, and potentially feasible, to establish full and permanent control of the polity. Whereas party leaders view the ideal polity as one in which their organizations win repeated victories in free and fair elections in competition with other parties, movement leaders view the ideal polity as one in which opposition withers away. For much of its history, Peronism has been marked by the hegemonic vocation that characterizes movements and distinguishes them from parties. Given Peronism's centrality in the political system, its hegemonic vocation has tended to reinforce values and practices that have impeded the consolidation of democracy.

Another implication of the idea that Peronism is a national movement rather than a party is that many routes to power, not all of them electoral, may acceptably be explored. A party is confined to electoral competition, but a movement that defines its own interests as inseparable from those of the nation has a duty to advance those interests as soon and as fully as possible. If the electoral road is blocked, or even if it looks unpromising, those who see the movement as uniquely capable of embodying the highest interests of the nation will find little to deter them from calling for mass insurrection or from piggybacking on a coup led by apparently sympathetic military officers. Should they attain office, leaders of such a movement will find it easy to justify keeping themselves there and forcing through their policies by manipulating or abusing electoral procedures, by stacking the judicial system with their allies, or by using unwarranted executive decrees to circumvent congress.[7] This eclectic view of permissible ways to acquire and retain power, which is rooted in a broader subordination of means to ends, is not easy to reconcile with the values that support a stable procedural democracy.

Peronism's weak party institutionalization has also impeded democratic consolidation through its effects on the union leadership. Partly because Peronist party organization has been weakly institutionalized, Peronist union leaders have tended to express their broad political demands through nonparty channels like mass demonstrations, factory-occupation campaigns, politically aimed general strikes, thunderous condemnations of government policy in the mass media, and direct negotiation with members of the national executive.[8] Trade unions around the world employ these vehicles, and their right to do so is a cornerstone of democracy. Used extensively in a country where the military has intervened in the recent past, however, veto politics opens political space for those who claim that a "strong hand" is needed to eradicate a national "climate of instability."[9] Such a climate, generated in part by veto politics, preceded the 1966 and 1976 coups in Argentina.

Peronism's weak party institutionalization has also reduced the stake of union leaders in the survival of the electoral and legislative institutions that parties require in order to be effective. Party activity requires a democratic regime; syndical activity does not. General strikes, mass rallies, and bargaining with the national executive are more difficult under military rule, but they are not impossible, as Argentina's unions have demonstrated. By devoting most of their resources and energy to veto politics and to wheeling and dealing with government officials, Peronist union leaders have acquired a weaker stake in the survival of democratic electoral and legislative institutions than would have been the case had they devoted more resources and energy to party activity. This relatively weak stake in the survival of electoral and legislative institutions (paradoxical in view of the fact that military governments have repeatedly repressed workers and union leaders) has helped make some union leaders sympathetic to overtures by military leaders promising, as in 1966, a "union of the people and the armed forces." Such promises were attractive to certain labor leaders who associated a close union-army relationship with the 1943–46 period, when Perón, an army colonel serving as labor secretary in a military government, reached out for labor support. Many (though not all) Peronist union leaders supported the 1966 coup, and many resigned themselves to the 1976 intervention.

Union leaders have been tied to a weakly institutionalized Peronist party since Perón created one in 1946. In previous years, although some union leaders supported a socialist party, most stayed away from parties altogether. In this respect, union leaders resembled agrarian elites and business leaders. During most of the twentieth century, neither agrarian elites nor business leaders have forged strong ties to a party (or parties) capable of winning fair elections. Agrarian elites have been isolated from party politics partly because they have suffered from a lack of electoral clout. The powerful landowning class of the Pampas region is numerically small, and its electoral viability is further diminished by the absence of a large sedentary peasantry of the kind long coerced or cajoled into delivering votes to landowner-dominated parties in countries such as Chile. Beginning in 1912, when blatant electoral fraud was eliminated, and more completely in the 1920s, when agrarian elites lost influence in Radicalism, the powerful Pampean landowners have remained largely indifferent or hostile to party politics. A similar detachment from parties has characterized industrialists. During the early decades of the twentieth century, industrialists had weak incentives to establish ties to parties, because many of them, like many workers, were immigrants who lacked the right to vote. The proportion of native-born industrialists eventually rose, and some of them backed Perón, but many soon abandoned him, and Peronism in any case failed to create an enduring party organization. Reinforcing the weakness of ties between these sectoral elites and parties, each has evolved a set of powerful interest associations to express its political demands. Just as workers have used the Confederación General de Trabajo (CGT), Argentina's umbrella labor confederation, to mobilize strikes and demonstrations, organize factory occupations, and support or denounce the government in the mass media, agrarian and business elites have used a panoply of organizations, the most important being the ranchers' Sociedad Rural Argentina (SRA) and the big industrialists' Unión Industrial Argentina (UIA), to lobby the government, influence public opinion, and thwart a variety of government policies.[10] Weak ties between sectoral elites and parties have reduced the stake of such elites in the survival of the electoral and legislative institutions that parties require to be effective.

Sectoral Elites, Party Institutionalization, and Democracy

The term *sectoral elite* as used in this study is derived from a definition proposed by Michael Burton, John Higley, and Richard Gunther, who view elites as

persons who are able, by virtue of their strategic positions in powerful organizations, to affect national political outcomes regularly and substantially. . . . "regularly" in that their individual points of view and possible actions are seen by other influential persons as important factors to be weighed when assessing the likelihood of continuities and changes in regimes and policies . . . [and] . . . "substantially" in the sense that without their support or opposition, an outcome salient to their interests and locations would be noticeably different . . . a lone political assassin can affect outcomes substantially but not regularly, and a citizen casting votes in democratic elections can affect outcomes regularly but not substantially.[11]

A sectoral elite is an elite that speaks for workers, urban business, or landowners. Peronist trade union leaders constitute an elite because they occupy strategic positions in Argentina's powerful labor organizations, and because influential members of the armed forces regard their views and possible actions as important factors to be weighed when deciding whether to launch a coup. To the extent that Peronist union leaders view party organization as expendable to advancing their political ends (and to the extent that military elites recognize that they hold this view of party organization), military elites will feel freer, and be freer, to abolish electoral and legislative institutions.

The term *political party* is used in this book to refer to an organization whose leaders and members seek to control the state exclusively through elections involving competition with other parties.[12] This usage, which excludes "vanguard parties" and would-be majoritarian movements, is consistent with the etymology of a word that refers to organizations whose leaders and members perceive themselves as a "part" of a polity in which other parties have a rightful, or at least enduring, place.

The term *political movement* means, by contrast, a set of people who share a common political identity and whose leaders aspire to full and permanent control of the state through the most readily available means, electoral or not. Peronism long had the hegemonic vocation and eclectic view of permissible roads to power that characterize political movements and distinguish them from political parties. These tendencies became attenuated during the 1980s but returned during the early 1990s.

Party organizations can be more or less institutionalized. Institutionalization involves a combination of attitudes, predispositions, and effects on behavior. A party (or any organization or procedure) is more or less institutionalized to the extent that the individuals who operate within it infuse it with value, take it for granted, and behave in accordance with its incentives and sanctions. Institutionalization thus has three dimensions: conscious valuation, preconscious supposition, and behavioral influence. Institutionalization is best regarded as a continuum, rather than as a dichotomy. One might reasonably make the continuum into a dichotomy by establishing a minimum threshold for institutionalization, but to specify where that threshold lay would be difficult, because conscious valuation, preconscious supposition, and behavioral influence are relatively autonomous from one another. Organizations or procedures with varying mixes of value-infusion, taken-for-grantedness, and behavior-shaping capacity might reasonably be regarded as equally institutionalized. Nonetheless, among the three dimensions, value-infusion has a certain causal primacy. Value-infusion helps an organization survive long enough to become taken for granted, and both value-infusion and taken-for-grantedness enhance an organization's capacity to shape and constrain behavior over an extended period of time. Conversely, an organization deficient in value-infusion is less likely to become taken for granted, and an organization deficient in value-infusion or taken-for-grantedness is less likely to be able to influence behavior over a sustained period. Philip Selznick has made a particularly explicit case for the primacy of value-infusion within the concept of institutionalization:

In what is perhaps its most significant meaning, "to institutionalize" is to *infuse with value* beyond the technical requirements of the task at hand . . . the test of infusion with value is expendability. If an organization is merely an instrument, it will be altered or cast aside when a more efficient tool becomes available. Most organizations are thus expendable. When value-infusion takes place, however, there is a resistance to change. People feel a sense of personal loss; the "identity" of the group or community seems somehow to be violated . . . organizations become infused with value as they come to symbolize the community's aspirations, its sense of identity.[13]

Other writers consider value-infusion to be only one aspect of institutionalization. Samuel Huntington defines institutionalization as "the process by which organizations and procedures acquire value and stability," but adds that "the level of institutionalization of any particular organization or procedure can be measured by its adaptability, complexity, autonomy, and coherence."[14] Huntington refers to value-infusion in his more detailed discussion of adaptability, complexity, autonomy, and coherence, but as only one subindicator (along with chronological age and generational age) of adaptability. In discussing the relationship between value-infusion and adaptability, however, Huntington arrives at a notion of institutionalization that closely resembles Selznick's:

Usually an organization is created to perform one particular function. When that function is no longer needed, the organization faces a major crisis: it either finds itself a new function or reconciles itself to a lingering death. An organization that has adapted itself to changes in its environment and has survived one or more changes in its principal function is more highly institutionalized than one that has not. Functional adaptability, not functional specificity, is the true measure of a highly developed organization. Institutionalization makes the organization more than simply an instrument to achieve certain purposes. Instead its leaders and members come to value it for its own sake, and it develops a life of its own quite apart from the specific functions it may perform at any given time. The organization triumphs over its function.[15]

Other writers on institutionalization make no reference at all to value-infusion. According to Ronald Jepperson, organizations are institutionalized to the extent that they display a high degree of taken-for-grantedness and to the extent that they empower and constrain the actors who operate within them.[16] It may seem at first glance that an organization cannot simultaneously be valued and taken for granted, but the conflict between Selznick's and Jepperson's notions of institutionalization, each of which seems to capture an important aspect of the process, is only apparent. To take something for granted is to maintain a preconscious impression that it will persist, not to express a conscious belief that it is valueless. Indeed, members of an organization who have come to take it for granted may often value it in a latent sense, such that they would come readily to its defense if it were threatened. Moreover, it is unlikely that an organization could survive long enough to achieve a state of taken-for-grantedness had its leaders and members (or their predecessors) not infused it with value at some time in the past. Rethinking Jepperson's definition in light of Selznick's, institutionalization might best be conceptualized as consisting of stages, with value-infusion coming early in the process and taken-for-grantedness (incorporating latent value-infusion) coming later. Initial value-infusion encourages an organization's leaders and members to invest resources in it, to become habituated to acting through it, and ultimately to take it for granted. Both value-infusion and taken-for-grantedness, in turn, improve the organization's capacity to shape and constrain the behavior of the individuals who operate within it.

Peronist party organization never experienced this initial infusion with value. From the outset, Peronists felt more allegiance to Perón or to the Peronist-led unions than to the movement's party structures, which Perón created almost as an afterthought. Because they invested few resources in these structures and did not become habituated to expressing political demands through the party organization,

Peronists, including Peronist union leaders, acquired a relatively weak instrumental stake in the survival of the electoral and legislative institutions. Lacking a strong instrumental stake in the survival of such institutions, union leaders tended to express their broad political demands through massive strikes and demonstrations, and some of them remained available for an alliance with military officers promising a "union of the people and the armed forces."

It is instructive to juxtapose this value-infusion definition of party institutionalization to a multidimensional definition of party strength. In an article on Colombian parties, Ronald Archer measured party strength along four dimensions: (1) electoral (the party's ability to win elections and to control policy-making positions), (2) affective (the scope and intensity of commitment displayed by the party's supporters), (3) organizational (the party's ability to mobilize supporters for elections or for defense against a threat to the party's existence), and (4) representational (the party's ability to channel major social divisions or cleavages through existing institutions).[17] On these dimensions, the Partido Justicialista (PJ; Justicialist Party), the party representing the Peronist movement, would have to be considered very strong in electoral terms. The PJ won a plurality of votes in five consecutive nationwide congressional elections between 1987 and 1995, sponsored the candidacies of a majority of legislators and governors, and contributed to Carlos Menem's election as president in both 1989 and 1995. The PJ could also be considered fairly strong in organizational terms. Despite assertions to the effect that Peronist party organizations are characterized by "extraordinary incoherence," "tremendous organizational weakness," "low visibility," and "weak and unstable structures,"[18] the PJ has statutes, parliamentary groups, paid professionals and employees, and thousands of basic units (local party offices) around the country, making it reasonably well equipped to mobilize supporters for electoral or other purposes. PJ organizations in the provinces of Buenos Aires and Mendoza are particularly well equipped to mobilize votes.

Archer's affective and representational dimensions of party strength are where the PJ is weak. Archer's concept of affective strength resembles this study's notion of party institutionalization, which the PJ lacks. Many Peronists are, of course, deeply devoted to the Peronist movement—especially to its pantheon of plebiscitarian leaders, which now includes Carlos Menem as well as Juan and Eva Perón. They are much less intimately committed, however, to the

PJ, which is only one component of the movement. Since Juan Perón first rose to prominence in the mid 1940s, the labor elites and ordinary citizens who have identified with the Peronist movement have had stronger affect for its union and leadership components than for its party organization. The PJ's weakness on the affective dimension has, in turn, weakened it on the representational dimension. Because Peronists have never moved far toward infusing their party organization with value, that organization has never played a major part in channeling their broad political demands through electoral and legislative institutions. As a result, Peronists have developed a weaker stake in the survival of electoral and legislative institutions than would otherwise be the case.

Until one specifies the analytical goal it is meant to serve, one definition is as good as another. If our concern were to assess the PJ's chances in the next election, it might be appropriate to assign more weight to its organizational or electoral strength than to its affective or representational strength. This analysis is specifically concerned, however, with the aspects of party strength most immediately relevant to democratic consolidation. The electoral and organizational dimensions of party strength are relevant to democratic consolidation, but their relevance resides mainly in their role as inputs to the party's affective strength, and thus to its representational strength. In other words, parties that have enough organizational strength to produce a high degree of electoral strength are likely to acquire affective strength and thereby representational strength, which is the dimension most immediately relevant to democratic consolidation. But organizational and electoral strength do not guarantee affective or representational strength. If those who share a distinctive political identity view their party as an intermittently useful but ultimately dispensable instrument for achieving political power, the party can acquire organizational and electoral strength without acquiring commensurate affective or representational strength. Peronist party organizations have typically achieved significant organizational and electoral strength without developing significant affective or representational strength, with deleterious consequences for the consolidation of democracy.

By almost any definition, the PJ is stronger or better institutionalized than parties in some other Latin American countries. Few contemporary Brazilian parties existed before 1979, and Brazilian legislators are notorious for switching from party to party in search of patronage resources. In Ecuador, voters frequently shift their partisan preferences, and few parties have any ties whatsoever to sectoral elites.[19] Here again, however, it is important to remember that the specific concern of this study is with aspects of party strength or institutionalization that bear directly upon the problem of democratic consolidation. Despite the weakness of most parties in Brazil and Ecuador, in neither of these other countries does one find a weakly institutionalized party serving as the main electoral expression of a political identity that is deeply held by a powerful sectoral elite. This juxtaposition of factors, not the weak institutionalization of the PJ per se, is what makes democratic consolidation difficult in Argentina, and what provides the intellectual puzzle that this study addresses. The weak institutionalization of political parties in Brazil and Ecuador has impeded democratic consolidation in these countries as well, but via different mechanisms than have been at work in Argentina.

A third key term that requires definition is *democracy*. Universal agreement on what democracy means is probably impossible—and may not even be desirable, for the polity may be improved by holding it up to a variety of standards.[20] But for meaningful communication and empirical research, it is necessary to build a working definition of democracy. Such definitions generally fall into one of two categories. Democracy is sometimes viewed in continuous terms, as an abstract ideal approximated more or less closely by actual political arrangements, and sometimes in discrete terms, as a set of political arrangements either present or absent. The discrete view of democracy is usually formulated in minimalist or threshold terms, and permits actual political arrangements to be characterized, with inevitable qualification, as democratic or undemocratic.

It may initially seem more plausible to view democracy as a continuum than as an either-or concept. The continuous view of democracy runs into trouble, however, when it confronts the notions of democratic stability and democratic breakdown. In the continuous view, democratic breakdown would best be described as a precipitous drop in the quality of democracy. It would be absurd, however, to describe Argentina's 1976–83 military regime as a democracy of unusually low quality. To avoid such a conclusion while retaining the plausibility of the notion that there are high-quality and low-quality democracies, the most useful way to conceptualize democracy is to view it in both discrete and continuous terms.[21] A regime may be considered undemocratic up to a threshold constituted by a procedural minimum, and then as more or less democratic according to the breadth, depth, and range of participation it embodies. For a regime to be considered democratic, it must, at minimum, have the following characteristics: (1) leaders must be chosen in fair and periodic competitive elections in which virtually all adult citizens have the right to vote and to stand for office, (2) nonelected agents (like military officers, guerrilla groups, or foreign governments) must not be able to veto policy decisions made by elected officials; and (3) citizens must be granted in principle, and not systematically denied in practice, basic civil rights like freedom from physical abuse by agents of the state, freedom of speech and the press, freedom of association and assembly, and the right to petition the government.[22] Regimes that meet this procedural minimum can become more democratic along the dimensions of breadth (with more people participating in a greater variety of ways), depth (with people participating in a better-informed, more thoughtful, and more autonomous fashion), and range (with the extension of democracy to subnational and nonstate institutions).[23]

It is no easier to set an empirically applicable threshold for minimalist democracy than it was for institutionalization. Were elections fair in the United States prior to 1965, when the Voting Rights Act began to dismantle severe effective restrictions on black electoral participation in many southern states? Was the United States a democracy when, during the Iran-Contra years in the 1980s, shadowy figures with military and intelligence connections ran their own secret, and often illegal, policy toward Central America? Are violations of basic rights by police officers in many U.S. cities sufficiently severe, widespread, and systematic to drop the United States below the threshold of minimalist democracy? Taken literally, the minimalist criteria are extremely demanding. No country has completely fair elections, complete freedom from reserved domains and tutelary powers, or complete respect for basic rights. It would be convenient to have an a priori line of demarcation that would tell us when, for example, a country's elections were fair enough to qualify as having met the fair elections criterion, but no one has yet proposed one. Rough-and-ready distinctions are possible, however. Precisely because some polities approximate the ideals fairly closely, their citizens may criticize them—often on the grounds that they have not lived up to their ideals. Indeed, a democracy might well be defined as a regime whose democratic status is contested. At any rate, all regimes whose democratic status is not contested are easily classifiable as nondemocracies.

A democracy may be viewed as consolidated when its quality exceeds the procedural minimum and when it has achieved a fair degree of institutionalization. A useful shorthand definition of democratic consolidation is that of Juan Linz, who, stressing the taken-for-granted-ness and behavioral-influence dimensions of institutionalization, views democracy as consolidated when it has come to be regarded as "the only game in town."[24] Consolidated democracies are not perfect democracies. They may be improved in a variety of ways—for example, along the dimensions of breadth, depth, and range. An adequate level and more equitable distribution of economic, educational, and informational resources would certainly help to enlarge the breadth, depth, and range of democracy. It would be a mistake, however, to write social justice into the definition of democracy. In addition to greatly restricting, perhaps to zero, the number of democratic regimes available for analysis, defining democracy as social justice would tend to block off critical questions about the causal relationships that may exist between democracy and social justice.[25] In different contexts, in different ways, and to different degrees, social justice may be a condition, concomitant, cause, and/or consequence of democracy. It is not, however, a component of democracy.

Generative Causes of Peronism's Weak Party Institutionalization

Peronism became weakly institutionalized as a party primarily because Perón, during his initial 1946–55 presidency, neither wanted nor needed a strongly institutionalized party. Perón did not want such a party because he admired Mussolini's vision of a partyless society organized along corporatist lines; because he had become skeptical of parties and politicians during the 1932–43 period of backroom deals and electoral fraud; and because he did not want to provide potential rivals with an organizational base. Perón did not need such a party because the personal popularity he had gained as labor secretary in the 1943–46 military government sufficed to carry him to the presidency in the February 1946 elections, and because he was able to rely subsequently on nonparty institutions—the unions to mobilize the vote and the Eva Perón Foundation to dispense patronage—to undertake tasks that might have helped to institutionalize the party. Angelo Panebianco has underscored the importance of a party's origins to its future organizational characteristics:

A party's organizational characteristics depend more upon its history, i.e. on how the organization originated and how it consolidated, than upon any other factor. The characteristics of a party's origin are in fact capable of exerting a weight on its organizational structure even decades later. Every organization bears the mark of its formation, of the crucial political-administrative decisions made by its founders, the decisions which "molded" the organization.[26]

As Panebianco suggests, the prospects for party institutionalization depend heavily on the way in which the party originated. Peronism originated partly as a charismatic movement, and partly, albeit ephemerally, as a labor-based political party. Although Peronist allegiances focused more on Perón himself than on a party organization, Perón won the 1946 presidential election thanks partly to the backing of the Partido Laborista (Labor Party), which was founded by pro-Perón union leaders shortly after they led the 17 October 1945 demonstration that freed Perón from a brief imprisonment and paved the way for his presidential candidacy. Peronism's charismatic side has always existed in an uneasy tension with its labor-based side. Before his inauguration, turning a deaf ear to the protests of prominent union leaders, Perón dissolved the Partido Laborista and replaced it with a highly personalized organization that came to be known, appropriately, as the Partido Peronista (Peronist Party). Perón carefully guarded his personal control over Peronism and tried to establish a direct relationship with his followers unmediated by party organization. This initial plebiscitarian configuration has served ever since as a significant impediment to the institutionalization of a Peronist party.[27] But because union leaders have a strong interest in expressing their broad political demands through electoral and legislative institutions, Peronism has also embraced a strong (albeit never fully realized) drive toward party institutionalization. Max Weber's analysis of the routinization of charisma provides a good starting point for understanding how this tension evolved, particularly after Perón was overthrown and exiled in 1955.

Charisma is a type of authority based on the shared belief that a certain person has extraordinary insight into the right way to live and to organize the community. Of Weber's three types of authority— charismatic, traditional, and rational-legal—charismatic authority is the most fertile and most unstable. When a charismatic leader dies or is displaced, the charismatic community, which forged its identity around the leader and typically has not contemplated the problem of succession, is thrown into crisis. Either the community disappears, or charisma becomes routinized into one of the other forms of authority. Routinization is a process whereby secondary leaders, guided by the message of the original leader, develop regular ways of administering the community and of organizing its interaction with the outside world, transforming what was originally a direct, unmediated relationship between leader and followers into a rule-based organization. In the context of mass politics, routinization means the transformation of a leader-centered mass movement into an institutionalized political party.

Routinization began in Peronism shortly after the 1955 coup that ended Perón's presidency and sent him into an eighteen-year exile. Given that the movement survived, routinization was to be expected once Perón had left the country. What was unusual about the process is that, after making significant progress, it disintegrated. This study will attempt to unravel and expose the forces that promoted Peronism's routinization, to explain why the process has repeatedly collapsed, and to indicate some ways in which these collapses have affected the evolution of Argentine politics. Its main conclusions are that the material interests of secondary Peronist leaders, particularly union leaders, promoted the movement's routinization; that deliberate action by Perón (and later Menem), together with the disintegrative effects of internal conflict within the trade union leadership, halted momentum toward routinization in the mid 1960s and mid 1980s; and that the failure of the routinization process to sustain itself has been an impediment to democratic consolidation. The Peronist case shows that charismatic leaders who physically survive displacement, or new personalist leaders thrown up by the movement, may be able to reverse routinization even after it has gathered considerable momentum; that the routinization process favors some secondary leaders over others; and that out-of-favor secondary leaders interested in protecting their turf can help to undermine the process.

Peronism is often described as a charismatic movement.[28] It began, indeed, as a leader-centered movement lacking formal procedures for leadership rotation. But charisma is an ideal type, a heuristic construct to which actual social phenomena cannot be expected to conform precisely. Underscoring this ambiguity, Weber himself refers in some places to charismatic authority, in others to charismatic communities, and in still others to charismatic leaders. It is not always clear in Weber's work, or in the work of others, what sorts of nouns the adjective *charismatic* may appropriately modify. Even within the category of charismatic leaders, Weber's own examples are rather diverse, ranging from Teddy Roosevelt to the Nordic berserker who "bit into his shield and all about himself, like a mad dog, before rushing off in a bloodthirsty frenzy."[29] In view of the ambiguity in Weber's own work, it is not surprising that Perón as a leader and Peronism as a political movement should differ in important respects from other charismatic phenomena. These differences must be duly noted, although they do not detract from the utility of Weber's notion of routinization for analyzing Peronism's internal dynamics.

One important difference between Peronism and the ideal-typical charismatic community lies in the forces that led to Peronism's emergence. In analyzing the formation of charismatic communities, Weber highlights the need to relieve psychic distress as an important factor predisposing followers to support the leader. In line with Weber's analysis, writers often assign a crucial role in Perón's initial support coalition to migrants from the countryside to the cities who were experiencing psychic distress. There is, in fact, strong evidence that recent migrants to Buenos Aires and to other big cities made up a significant proportion of Perón's initial followers.[30] However, it has also been shown that many of Perón's initial supporters were long-term city dwellers. Equally important, it is far from clear that the migrants were experiencing psychic distress, or that they supported Perón exclusively because of preconscious or compensatory motives. Like the long-term city dwellers, the migrants also had good instrumental reasons to support Perón, who was personally and plainly responsible for a sudden rise in the wealth, power, and prestige of Argentina's poor. In addition, the notion that migrants were experiencing psychic distress is based on the assumption that they had developed patron-client normative frameworks while living in rural areas, and that these normative frameworks were wrenched apart during or after their migration to the cities.[31] Casting doubt on this assumption, it has been shown that many rural migrants came from areas of fairly modern agriculture, that others may have adjusted while migrating in "steps" (living in smaller cities before moving to bigger ones); and that many "rural" migrants came from counties with cities with populations over 20,000.[32]

A second difference between Peronism and a charismatic community involves the leader-follower relationship. In a charismatic community, this relationship is typically direct and unmediated. In Peronism, by contrast, the leader-follower relationship was partly mediated, at least in the case of workers, by a set of relatively autonomous union organizations. By the time Perón appeared on the scene, 50 years of organization and struggle had allowed the Argentine unions to develop considerable power and autonomy. One analysis suggests that Argentina already had Latin America's strongest trade unions in 1943, before Perón enacted any reforms whatsoever.[33] Unlike the CGT labor confederation, which Juan Perón and Eva Perón staffed with handpicked sycophants, the individual national-level unions retained a degree of autonomy throughout Perón's presidency. This independence was visible in the early 1950s, when dissidents won leadership struggles in several unions. The autonomy that the unions preserved during Perón's presidency provided the seed around which routinization later crystallized. And ironically, given his opposition to the process, Perón's own economic and labor policies provided a catalyst for routinization. Perón greatly increased the state's role as an employer, regulator of economic variables, participant in collective bargaining, and overseer of union finances and elections. Because the state remained active in all of these areas after Perón was overthrown, union leaders had strong incentives to participate in electoral politics—whether or not Perón wanted them to. Hence, it is not surprising that the first stage of the routinization process took the form of a party-building project sponsored by a Peronist union leader.

Sustaining Causes of Peronism's Weak Party Institutionalization

In the early 1960s, a Peronist union leader, Augusto Vandor, began to shift the movement's center of gravity toward a political party independent of Perón. Setting aside the traditional hostility between unionists and politicians, Vandor and his union allies, who were based in the Buenos Aires region, began to forge alliances with "neo-Peronist" politicians who led patronage-based party organizations, notably in interior provinces, that claimed continuity with the Peronist tradition but refused to submit to Perón's supervision. Vandor enjoyed a steady flow of financial resources, thanks to a provision in the 1945 Law of Professional Associations that required employers to withhold union dues from workers' pay. The neo-Peronists, meanwhile, had access to the material resources of the provincial governments they controlled. Both the unionists, who needed labor ministry recognition in order to collect dues, and neo-Peronist politicians, whose provincial governments depended on central government allocation of tax revenue, had a strong material interest in being allowed to compete for state power. This material interest, as Weber might have predicted, was important in activating the routinization process.

Unwilling to be marginalized by Vandor's initiative, Perón began a campaign to undermine it. Two factors enabled him to succeed. First, many of Perón's followers continued to revere him. This reverence derived from a partly idealized, partly accurate memory of how much better his 1946–55 government had been for them than previous or subsequent governments. Because of their deep loyalty to the exiled leader, most of Perón's supporters obeyed his instructions to vote against Vandor's proxy candidate in the pivotal 1966 elections for the governorship of Mendoza. Vandor's defeat in this election dealt the fatal blow to his party-building project. Second, Perón was able to forge alliances with anti-Vandor factions among Peronism's union and political personnel, who opposed Vandor's initiative because it threatened to marginalize them as well. Had it not been for the organizational resources these anti-Vandor Peronists supplied, it is possible that Perón's continued personalistic appeal would not have sufficed to derail the powerful political machine that Vandor and the neo-Peronist politicians were building.

The failure of this first cycle of routinization helped precipitate the 1966 coup. Vandor's initiative represented a way out of what Guillermo O'Donnell has called the "impossible game,"[34] at the core of which was a dilemma: the military could live neither with nor without the electoral restrictions imposed on Peronism after the 1955 coup. The military could not live with the restrictions because disputes over how strong to make them were destroying the institutional cohesion of the armed forces, and because many officers feared that Peronism, kept permanently from electoral competition, might turn to the left. But the military could not live without the restrictions either, because few officers were willing to contemplate a new edition of the 1946–55 government, especially if it meant Perón's return to power.[35]

Had Vandor managed to strip Perón of effective leadership of the Peronist movement, the military would no longer have faced the specter of a return to the 1946–55 years. Moreover, had Vandor, a pragmatic anticommunist, won effective control of Peronism, his victory would have diminished military fears that the movement might turn to the left. And had Vandor combined these achievements by creating a firmly anticommunist "Peronism without Perón," hard-line anti-Peronists might well have become more receptive to the movement's participation in electoral politics, eliminating the issue dividing the armed forces.

In the end, however, Vandor's initiative succumbed to Perón's efforts to undermine it. When Perón's proxy candidate beat Vandor's in the closely watched April 1966 Mendoza gubernatorial election, key military officers realized that any attempt to bring Perón's followers into the mainstream of civilian politics would require negotiations, not with Vandor, but with Perón himself. Whereas many officers would have accepted electoral participation by a neo-Peronist party under Vandor's hegemony, no important military figure was willing to negotiate with Perón. The defeat of Vandor's project helped precipitate the 1966 coup by making military leaders more skeptical of the alternative scenario of continued civilian rule.

The second cycle of routinization began shortly after the Peronist candidate Italo Luder lost the October 1983 presidential election, which followed seven years of harsh military rule. During the 1983 electoral campaign, the PJ was tightly controlled by Lorenzo Miguel, Vandor's successor as leader of the metalworkers' union. Miguel's prestige dropped precipitously after Luder lost the election to the candidate of the Unión Cívica Radical, Raúl Alfonsín, and by late 1984, many Peronist leaders were demanding changes in the party, including Miguel's resignation as party vice president, more open competition for party candidacies and leadership posts, and reorganization of the party to increase its autonomy from the unions. Miguel and his allies fought back, defending their heavy-handed political style and tradition of backroom deals. Those demanding change became known as the renewal wing; those favoring the status quo became known as the orthodox wing. The renewal wing included urbane politicians and intellectuals, provincial notables with clientelistic followings, and the "Group of 25": leaders of smaller unions who had organized general strikes toward the end of the 1976–83 dictatorship. The orthodox wing featured union leaders in Lorenzo Miguel's "62 Organizations," its own provincial notables, and political bosses from the industrial suburbs of Buenos Aires.

Apart from reverence for Perón, the orthodox and renewal sectors of Peronism had little in common. Under the Alfonsín government, most renewal Peronists favored prosecuting military leaders accused of human rights violations, legalizing divorce, condemning U.S. aid to the Nicaraguan Contras, and calling a moratorium on payment of the foreign debt, whereas most orthodox Peronists opposed these initiatives. Factions of the Peronist movement have always taken contradictory ideological and programmatic positions. What was novel about the situation was that each group—even Lorenzo Miguel and his allies, who explicitly supported Peronism's configuration as a national movement (controlled implicitly, with Perón having died in 1974, by their faction of the union leadership)—were fighting for space within the PJ, implying that each had come to see the party at least as an important base from which to advance their interests. If to institutionalize, following Selznick, is to "infuse with value beyond the technical requirements of the task at hand," then the PJ, in terms of what was implied by the behavior of the orthodox and renewal sectors, was beginning to move toward institutionalization during the Alfonsín presidency. Peronism was becoming more a party and less a movement.

Some developments in Peronism under the 1983–89 Alfonsín government were less conducive to party institutionalization. In 1985, the struggle for the PJ was upstaged by the rise of Peronist union leader Saúl Ubaldini, head of the nominally nonpartisan CGT. Instead of competing for control of the party, Ubaldini tried to make the CGT the main pole of opposition to the Alfonsín government. To this end he began a campaign of general strikes, demonstrations, and thunderous criticism of the government. The resulting three-way polarization between the renewal-linked, orthodox-linked, and pro-Ubaldini unionists raised an issue relevant to democratic consolidation. Despite their differences, the "Group of 25" and the "62 Organizations" were committed to the survival and effective operation of the PJ and, consequently, acquired an instrumental stake in the survival of elections and legislative activity. By contrast, although Ubaldini's commitment to democracy was beyond serious dispute, his tactics tended to marginalize parties, elections, and the legislature as arenas for political conflict.

The orthodox wing of Peronism never recovered from the 1983 electoral defeat, but it hung on to the formal party machinery until 1987, when the renewal wing took control behind Antonio Cafiero, the newly elected Buenos Aires governor. Under Cafiero, the PJ moved farther toward institutionalization than at any time in its history. But even as Cafiero assumed the party presidency and the governorship of the key province of Buenos Aires, Peronism was shaken by the rise of a new political figure: Carlos Menem. The flamboyant governor of La Rioja made no secret of the fact that he planned to compete against Cafiero in Peronism's first-ever direct presidential primary, scheduled for July 1988. Although Menem had originally belonged to the renewal wing, his main links by the time of the primary were to a new Peronist union leader faction called the "Group of 15" and, more ambiguously, to the orthodox wing of the party. Personal popularity, support from the large and wealthy "15" unions, and Cafiero's inability to distinguish his policy proposals from Alfonsín's enabled Menem to win the primary and become Peronism's nominee in the May 1989 elections, which he won by 47 to 34 percent over the Radical candidate, Eduardo Angeloz.

Upon taking office in July 1989, Menem reversed the earlier trend toward the institutionalization of the PJ. The new president filled the government with extraparty technocrats, erstwhile anti-Peronists committed to liberalizing the economy, and personal favorites with few ties to the party. PJ activity declined at the local level, and few stepped forward to criticize Menem's free-market economic policies or pardons of military leaders convicted of human rights violations. An important symbolic step toward party deinstitutionalization came in August 1990, when Antonio Cafiero resigned as party president and opened the way for Menem to take over and neutralize the party apparatus. The eclipse of the PJ under Menem marginalized the sector of Peronism with the strongest stake in the continuity of electoral and legislative activity.

Menem's presidency also resounded with strong echoes of movementism. In addition to bypassing the PJ, the government arranged a constitutional reform to permit Menem's reelection, floated incessant proposals for self-serving electoral reform, used hundreds of presidential decrees to circumvent the legislature, stacked the supreme court, and was accused of tolerating and even inciting dozens of attacks on antigovernment journalists. Although Menem seemed committed to elections and to recognizing the legitimacy of other parties as permanent contenders for power, aspects of movementism pervaded his first (1989–95) presidency.

Whereas this study contends that Peronism's weak party institutionalization has stemmed mainly from Perón's, and later Menem's, desire and capacity to maintain personal control of the Peronist community, other analyses have attributed this weak party institutionalization to the electoral restrictions imposed on Peronism from 1957, when General Pedro Aramburu's interim military government restored electoral activity, to 1966, when more thoroughgoing military intervention ended electoral activity for all parties. An understanding of this alternative "proscription" explanation requires a brief summary of the events that followed Perón's overthrow. Shortly after the September 1955 military coup, Perón was exiled, Peronist leaders were jailed, the original Partido Peronista was dissolved, and a law was passed aimed at discouraging the party's reincarnation under a new label. To back up this legislation, the military imposed an implicit veto on the right of Peronists to contest or assume the presidency or the governorships of major provinces. This veto was firmly enforced for the next eight years, but was loosened after October 1963, when Arturo Illia became president.

It is sometimes claimed that the legal restrictions on Peronist competition for major elective office, backed by the implicit military veto on such participation, was the main factor underlying Peronism's failure to develop stronger party organization in the post-1955 period.[36] In some ways, proscription did make it harder for a Peronist party to institutionalize. However, proscription was not the root cause of this problem. Peronism was poorly institutionalized as a party *before* proscription was imposed in 1955. The proscription and anti-Peronist repression of the 1955–58 years precipitated the collapse of the original Partido Peronista, but the party's highly personalized character made this repression much easier to carry out. Because the Partido Peronista was so strictly Perón's creature, it never generated a resilient organization or an independent cadre of leaders capable of bargaining for survival with the 1955–58 military government (along the lines of what APRA had done after the 1948 coup in Peru) or of forging an effective clandestine organization (along the lines of what Acción Democrática had done after the 1948 coup in Venezuela). APRA and Acción Democrática survived repression as harsh or harsher than that which precipitated the demise of the original Partido Peronista in part because the Peruvian and Venezuelan "populist" parties each had strong organizations, already tested by years of repression and opposition, by the time each acquired a share of state power in 1945. The Partido Peronista, by contrast, was a weak organization constructed almost as an afterthought by an incumbent president. As a result of their pre-existing strength as organizations, the Venezuelan and Peruvian "populist" parties were better equipped than the Partido Peronista to survive decrees abolishing their formal structures and to withstand repression resulting in the exile and imprisonment of their leaders. The list of parties forged in hostile environments that later succeeded in surviving some sort of proscription could be expanded to include the German Social Democrats (1878–90) and, closer to home, the Yrigo-yenist wing of Argentina's Unión Cívica Radical (1932–35).

A second consideration warranting reevaluation of the notion that proscription was the key factor preventing Peronism's survival (or re-organization) as a party in the decade after Perón's overthrow is that Peronism did not have much success in developing a party organi-zation in the years after proscription ended. Between 1973 and 1976, the Peronists' newly unbanned Partido Justicialista was subordinate first to Perón, then to the López Rega clique, and finally to the Peron-ist union leadership. Between 1984 and 1988, the PJ did become more strongly institutionalized, but the process was abruptly reversed in the latter year, after Carlos Menem outpolled Antonio Cafiero in the Peronist presidential primary. Peronism was thus poorly institution-alized as a party after 1973, when proscription ended, just as it was prior to 1955, before proscription was imposed. This longitudinal com-parison, like the cross-national comparison of Peronism with Acción Democrática and APRA, suggests that proscription was at most one of several factors inhibiting Peronist party institutionalization.

A third consideration that makes it advisable to reevaluate the pro-scription argument is that important political actors of the 1963–66 period, both Peronist and non-Peronist, do not seem to have viewed proscription as an insurmountable impediment to the formation of a viable Peronist party. Prior to 1963, electoral restrictions on Peronism probably were too severe for formal party structures to have devel-oped. By the time of Illia's October 1963 inauguration, however, the implicit military veto on Peronist electoral participation, the real force behind the formal restrictions, had been weakened by three factors: a fear that Peronism kept permanently from electoral competition might "turn to the left," a perception that Perón was losing his personal sway over his followers, and concern that the unresolved "Peronist Ques-tion" was dividing the armed forces. Vandor would only have tried to build a party representing "Peronism without Perón" had he believed that proscription after 1963 contained enough "loopholes" to give his initiative some chance of success.[37] And had Perón or the Illia govern-ment been convinced that the military would finally block Vandor's initiative, they would not have worked so diligently to undermine it.

Fourth, and perhaps most instructively, it is important to consider a counterfactual scenario: what would Peronism's formal party struc-tures have looked like in the absence of proscription? The answer would certainly be: similar to how they appeared while Perón was president. By preventing Perón or his closest collaborators from occupying political office, proscription actually *removed* an obstacle to the emergence of a better-institutionalized Peronist party. It was only within the "political space" created by proscription that Vandor, in alliance with neo-Peronist politicians from the interior provinces, could seek to build a labor-based political party representing Peronism without Perón. Far from undermining Vandor's party-building project, proscription created the conditions that made the initiative possible. Paradoxically, the highly undemocratic electoral restrictions on Peronism paved the way for a party-building project whose success might well have improved the chances for democratization. Had his party-building project remained viable, Vandor and other unionists would have been less inclined to collaborate with military officers holding out the temptation of a "union of the people and the armed forces." Unionists would also have gained an alternative mode of political expression to the politically aimed strikes and factory occupations that helped create the climate of instability propitious for the 1966 coup.

Perón's efforts to maximize his personal control of the Peronist movement, together with the legacy his personalism left after his death in 1974, have been the most important factors obstructing Peronist party institutionalization in the post-1955 era. Proscription did, of course, have negative as well as positive effects on Peronist party institutionalization. So did other environmental factors. Repeated periods of extended military rule have impeded the institutionalization not only of Peronism but also of other political parties. When parties cease to be effective vehicles of political influence, people are less likely to infuse them with value. Here it is important to distinguish generative from sustaining causes. Extended military rule did indeed sustain Peronism's weak party institutionalization, but Peronism's weak party institutionalization preceded, and helped pave the way for, extended military rule itself.

Apart from proscription (with its contradictory effects on party institutionalization) and military rule (with its largely negative effects), a third sustaining cause of Peronism's weak party institutionalization has been the recurrent tendency of factions of the Peronist union leadership to undermine the party-building projects produced by the fitful routinization process. Conventional analysis holds that Peronist union leaders sort themselves into factions according to whether each prefers cooperation or confrontation with the government in office.[38]

Such motives for factional affiliation may well have prevailed during the presidencies of Arturo Frondizi (1958–62), Juan Carlos Onganía (1966–70), and Carlos Menem (1989–95), but during other key periods, the issue of union leaders' cooperation with the government seems to have been much less relevant to factional affiliation. During Arturo Illia's presidency (1963–66), when the Peronist union leadership was as divided as it has ever been, no faction favored cooperating with the government (Chapter 5). Under Raúl Alfonsín (1983–89), it is noteworthy that the combative stance favored by the CGT secretary-general, Saúl Ubaldini, and his followers happened to be the one most compatible with the preservation of Ubaldini's otherwise precarious leadership of the confederation (see Chapter 7). Although students of Argentine unionism have often argued that factions in Peronist unionism *result* from arguments over how closely to cooperate with the government in office, rivalries among unionists may well *cause* some of them to tailor their views on cooperation with the government to the position they expect will best preserve or enhance their power against rivals.

More attention needs to be paid to turf battles among Argentine union leaders in interpreting the political stances they have taken under various governments since 1955. During both periods of incipient party institutionalization examined in this study, one faction of the Peronist union leadership allied with Peronist politicians to spearhead a party-building project that seemed briefly to have possibilities of success. But as soon as the party-building project acquired a certain momentum, other union leaders, predicting that the advance of Peronist party institutionalization would eclipse their own status and power, mobilized against the initiative. Under the Illia government, four mutually hostile factions of the union leadership managed to suppress their differences long enough to help Perón crush Vandor's party-building project. Under the Alfonsín government, union leaders with little in common joined Carlos Menem in undermining the renewal-sector project. In each case, antiparty union leaders gave crucial organizational support to personalistic Peronist leaders seeking to thwart party institutionalization.

The actions of union leaders who stood to lose from these successive party-building projects can be elucidated with reference to the model of "balancing behavior" proposed by Kenneth Waltz in his theory of international relations. This theory contemplates an asymmetrical bipolar situation, where one great power is stronger than the other, and seeks to explain the conditions under which weaker peripheral states will engage in "bandwagoning" behavior (siding with the stronger great power) versus "balancing" behavior (siding with the weaker great power). Assuming that the main goals of the peripheral states are (1) to defend their national identities and (2) to advance their interests in the international arena, Waltz argues that they should engage in "balancing" behavior when the first goal is considered paramount (they retain greater independent bargaining leverage when they side with the weaker of the two great powers), and in "bandwagoning" behavior when their national integrity is sufficiently assured to permit them the luxury of giving primacy to advancing their secondary interests in the international arena.[39]

The analogous situation in the Peronist movement during the 1963–66 period would represent Vandor, with his formidable union machine, as the stronger great power, the distant Perón as the lesser great power, and the four minor union leader factions as the key peripheral states (this characterization is defended in Chapter 5). Given Vandor's enormous advantage over the four minor factions in power resources (such as the capacity to mobilize, finance, and intimidate), each of the four minor factions came eventually to feel its survival threatened and found a convenient rallying point in Perón. The balancing-behavior model explains this "four against one" pattern of cleavage in the Peronist trade unions better than a variety of alternative models and also helps to explain why a diversity of Peronist union leaders turned against the renewal Peronists in the 1980s and threw in their lot with Menem. In each case, "out" union leader factions sided with the charismatic leader to thwart a party-building project supported by an "in" union leader faction in conjunction with a heterogeneous array of Peronist politicians. The situation in Peronism resembled the classic characterization of the situation in Argentina itself, where no sectoral elite has been strong enough to establish hegemony but each has been strong enough to prevent its adversaries from doing so.[40]

Plan of the Study

It has been argued thus far that Waltz's theory of balancing behavior provides a key to understanding the factional struggles in the Peronist trade union movement, and that Weber's writings on the routinization of charisma and Panebianco's theory of party organizational dynamics shed light on the Peronist party's weak institutionalization. These objects of explanation are linked: struggles among Peronist unionists, along with the power-preservation and power-enhancement interests of Peronism's plebiscitarian leaders, have contributed to Peronism's weak party institutionalization. The latter, in turn, has been an impediment to democratic consolidation. Chapter 9 develops this assertion by elaborating a distributive conflict–party institutionalization approach to democratic consolidation, by contrasting it to other approaches to explaining Argentina's democratic instability, and by applying it to an assessment of the prospects for democratic consolidation in the 1990s. The intervening chapters explore the historical processes and events introduced in the present chapter. It is argued in Chapter 2 that many of the social-structural constraints, historical traditions, and political practices that pervaded Argentine politics in the post-1955 era—notably the power of key sectoral elites, the weakness of their ties to political parties, and the crystallization of political identities as national movements—can be traced to the late nineteenth and early twentieth centuries. Chapter 3 examines the origins of Peronism's weak party institutionalization and the new power resources and policy-influencing incentives Perón gave to unions. Chapters 4 and 5 explore the emergence and collapse of Vandor's party-building initiative, while Chapters 7 and 8 discuss the rise and fall of the renewal Peronist project. The intervening Chapter 6 describes the evolution of Peronism under the military governments of 1966–73 and 1976–83, and analyzes a less promising Peronist party-building project during the 1973–76 period of Peronist government.

Chapter 2

Sectoral Elites and Political Parties Before Perón

From 1880 to 1943, Argentina experienced a rise in male electoral participation, the intensification of political competition, and some diffusion of democratic values. At the same time, it saw the growth of political traditions—movementism, skepticism about party politics, and intolerance of political opponents—that persisted into the latter part of the twentieth century. The plebiscitarianism of Roca and Yrigoyen foreshadowed that of Perón, and Roca's Partido Autonomista Nacional (PAN) and Yrigoyen's Unión Cívica Radical (UCR) acquired a hegemonic vocation and eclectic view of appropriate roads to power long before Perón announced that his followers constituted a movement rather than a party. Skepticism about party politics arose with the electoral abuses of the 1880–1912 and 1930–43 eras, and intolerance of political opponents expressed itself in the early decades of the twentieth century in the violent acts of anarchists and of reactionary terror groups. Peronism was a political watershed, but to understand the vicissitudes of democracy during the post-1943 era, it is important to recognize that movementism, skepticism about party politics, and intolerance of political opponents had gained a foothold long before Perón came to power. Similarly, the 1880–1943 period also saw the emergence of powerful sectoral elites with weak ties to political parties, a phenomenon that has impeded democratic consolidation throughout the twentieth century.

Argentina Under Oligarchic Rule, 1880–1916

Argentina grew 5 percent per year in the half-century after 1860, primarily by exporting grain and livestock products to Britain and other European countries. By 1913, Argentina was one of the richest countries in the world, with a per capita GNP higher than that of Sweden or Switzerland.[1] What made Argentina's exports competitive in Europe despite the great distances involved was not, as in the case of other Latin American countries, the superexploitation of labor. Grain and livestock are among the least labor-intensive primary products, so there were no dense concentrations of rural workers to exploit. Rather, Argentina's advantage came from the fertility and benign climate of the Pampas region, the grassy plain to the south and west of the city of Buenos Aires that produces most of Argentina's cattle and export crops.[2] These products made up 90 percent of exports in 1913, 85 percent of which went to western Europe.[3]

Paving the way for the export boom was the consolidation of internal peace. During much of the nineteenth century, Argentina was plagued by wars among *caudillos* (warlords) of various provinces. As exports became more important in the latter part of the century, the Pampean elite gained primacy over the traditional elites from the interior, who produced mostly for local consumption. The turning point in this process came in 1880, when landowners from the Pampas in effect bought off their counterparts from the interior by agreeing to share the customs revenues collected at the port of Buenos Aires with them. In return the provincial caudillos agreed to stop their uprisings, and the stage was set for the expansion of international (as well as internal) trade. On the demand side, the export boom was fueled by the movement of Britons and northern Europeans from agriculture to industry, and by their gradual emergence from destitution. These trends created mass demand for the kind of low-quality, low-cost foodstuffs that Argentina exported. On the supply side, Argentina met this demand through frontier expansion and technological innovation. Cattle and sheep producers acquired new land through General Julio Roca's 1879 "Conquest of the Wilderness," which took the lives of thousands of Tehuelche and Araucanian Indians.[4] As livestock moved south and west, ranches close to railway lines and urban areas switched to grain production, often by tenant farmers. Meanwhile, agricultural and livestock productivity grew as railway trackage expanded and as barbed-wire fencing, pedigreed breeding stock, alfalfa for cattle feed, and new methods of refrigeration were introduced.

Gauchos (cowherds), ox-cart drivers, and others expelled by these modernizing changes streamed into Buenos Aires and other cities, where they converged with a flood of new arrivals from Europe. From 1870 to 1930, Argentina absorbed more than 6 million immigrants, mainly from Italy and Spain. About half of these immigrants eventually returned to Europe, but the demographic impact of the 3 million who stayed was enormous in a country whose population in 1869 was only 1.7 million.[5] Britain was the main source of capital and technology for railway building, port excavation, meat packing, and other industries crucial to the transport and processing of exports, but Argentine nationals controlled the actual production of the main export commodities. Accordingly, export revenue contributed more to domestic capital accumulation in Argentina than in countries like Chile or Peru, where foreigners dominated the production as well as the transport and processing of key export products.[6]

The main beneficiary of the export boom was a landed, commercial, and professional elite, known colloquially as the oligarchy, structured around the largest ranchers of Buenos Aires province. Some elite families had inherited land from the colonial era, but most had received it thanks to the policies of various nineteenth-century presidents. A law enacted by President Bernadino Rivadavia in 1826 gave the state title to vast tracts of new land, which its agents then leased out in huge parcels at a fraction of the value declared by the lessee (and hence at an even smaller fraction of the land's real value). When these leases expired in 1836, General Juan Manuel de Rosas, who extended his control outward from the key province of Buenos Aires from 1829 to 1852, gave families who had benefited from the 1826 law title to the lands they had been leasing. At the same time, he dispensed to political and military allies new land that his armies had wrested from the indigenous people to the south. The government of Domingo Sarmiento (1868–74) further concentrated land ownership by introducing the *cedula*, which gave already-landed purchasers of new land credit for up to one-half of the value of their existing holdings. In 1879, the "Conquest of the Wilderness" by General Roca and his troops allowed 381 persons to gain control of 8.5 million hectares.[7] Further land concentration took place at the close of the nineteenth century, when land values skyrocketed in response to the export boom.

The primary source of the Pampean elite's power was its control of a productive export economy, which allowed for early domestic capital accumulation in both domestic and foreign currency. Reinforcing its economic strength, the oligarchy was unusually cohesive. In contrast to countries like Peru and Brazil, where economic diversity and spatial dispersion contributed to the formation of distinct and often competing regional export elites, Argentina produced on the Pampas a landowning elite that was sufficiently homogeneous in economic activity and geographical concentration to allow it directly to constitute a national state as opposed to a set of regional fiefdoms.[8] Adding to the cohesion of the oligarchy was its cultural homogeneity: most of its members came from a small set of family groups, went to the same schools, belonged to the same clubs, and shared certain rules of behavior.[9] The geographic and cultural cohesion of the Pampean elite was expressed and reinforced by the powerful Sociedad Rural Argentina (SRA), which was founded in 1866 to aggregate and promote the interests of the biggest landowners of the Pampas. During the late nineteenth century, the SRA acted as a "virtual ministry of agriculture until (through its initiative) the latter was created."[10] The SRA remains today one of Argentina's most powerful peak sectoral organizations.

Argentina's first major political party, the Partido Autonomista Nacional (PAN), dominated the political system that emerged under the hegemony of the Pampean elite. The PAN was founded in 1874 from the fusion of two other recently formed organizations, one representing politicians from the interior and the other representing a faction in Buenos Aires province.[11] Its initial goals were to federalize the city of Buenos Aires, to ease restrictions on maritime trade, and to nationalize the customs revenues of the port of Buenos Aires. Around 1880, having achieved these goals, the leaders of the PAN came under the sway of the Pampean elite, whose socioeconomic power had soared with the export boom. In Maurice Duverger's terms, the PAN was a cadre party: a fluid, loosely organized clique of notables that chose its candidates through informal negotiation and settled disputes over credit and railway access through backroom deals called *acuerdos*.[12] Having settled these internal conflicts, the PAN leaders doctored voting lists, bought votes, and used intimidation (taking advantage of the absence of a secret ballot) to undermine candidates running under ephemeral opposition labels.[13] Universal male suffrage had existed since 1857 (longer than in most European countries), but turnout was extremely low, ranging from 10 to 25 percent of eligible voters.[14] The PAN existed nominally until 1909, when it split into a multitude of conservative provincial parties beholden to local landowners and allied professional and commercial groups.[15]

Instead of a system of party competition, Argentina developed a series of incumbent-party hegemonies: the PAN after 1880, Radicalism after 1916, and Peronism after 1946. The origins of this pattern of political development can be illuminated by comparing Argentine political life in the late 1800s to that of Chile and Uruguay, neighboring countries that did develop effective systems of party competition in the early twentieth century—and later sustained periods of competitive politics that were long by European as well as Latin American standards. Party competition was implanted shallowly in late nineteenth-century Argentina in part because parties that lost elections (or, prior to 1880, battles) evaporated or were absorbed by the winning party. In late-nineteenth-century Uruguay and Chile, by contrast, losing parties maintained their partisan identities and incipient party organizations and resumed their challenges after recovering from defeat. This difference, whatever its complex causes, set Argentina on a different path from Chile or Uruguay.

After 1880, whoever controlled the executive branch of the Argentine national state controlled military and political power throughout the country.[16] In Uruguay, by contrast, the Partido Colorado, unable to inflict a decisive military defeat on the opposing Partido Nacional (known colloquially as the Partido Blanco), relinquished control of *jefaturas* (governorships) in some interior provinces in exchange for a Partido Blanco promise not to rebel. Such bargains allowed the Partido Blanco to survive despite its lack of direct control over the national executive, and eventually fostered provisions for losing-party participation in government that helped sustain party competition into the twentieth century. In Chile, a semiparliamentary form of government existed from 1891 to 1925, in contrast to Argentina's highly centralized presidential system. By making political power more divisible, parliamentary power reinforced Chile's incipient multiparty system, whereas the overwhelming predominance of the national executive in Argentina made it easier for the PAN to portray itself as a national movement embodying all that was good about Argentina, rather than as part of a polity in which opposition forces had a rightful (or at least enduring) place.[17] In Chile and Uruguay, by contrast, the "in" political force could neither destroy nor absorb its adversaries. In these countries, the strength and tenacity of the opposition promoted the rise of a political culture in which more value was placed on the right to opposition—a crucial precondition for democracy.[18]

Electoral fraud during the era of PAN hegemony also fostered skepticism that party activity could bring control of state resources. Accordingly, Argentina's first reform alliance opted for armed revolt. In 1889, upper-class university students in Buenos Aires formed the Unión Cívica de la Juventud to protest what they felt was the PAN

government's corruption and shift toward Córdoba in the distribution
of jobs and patronage. In 1890, the organization changed its name to
Unión Cívica, and the university students were joined by new groups:
dissident members of the Pampean elite like General Bartalomé Mitre,
urban politicians like Leandro Alem, believers alienated by PAN secu-
larism, and disaffected army officers. When Mitre and Alem fell out
in 1890 after the Unión Cívica's unsuccessful armed rebellion, Alem's
followers adopted the name Unión Cívica Radical (UCR), which remains the official name of today's Radical Party.[19] Despite Mitre's exit
from the organization, other Pampean landowners dominated the UCR
leadership for the next thirty years. In 1916, the UCR elected officials
included a higher proportion of big landowners and persons with university educations than did the leadership of the Partido Conservador
de Buenos Aires.[20]

When the initial UCR leader, Leandro Alem, committed suicide in
1896, his nephew, Hipólito Yrigoyen, took over. Yrigoyen, the son of
an impoverished Basque immigrant, seldom appeared in public and
cultivated an air of mystery about his person. Until 1912, Yrigoyen
pursued policies of "intransigence" and "abstention," under which the
Radicals rejected the electoral path to government in favor of armed
insurrection. The UCR stood initially for "free suffrage, honest elections, provincial autonomy, and municipal home rule" and later for a
strong peso and a halt to government land sales to the rich.[21] This program was designed to attract middle-class citizens, but to ensure that
the party had the widest possible appeal, its goals were never made
more explicit, with the result that its doctrine and ideology became
"little more than an eclectic and moralistic attack on the oligarchy, to
which was appended the demand for the introduction of representative government."[22] Despite the amorphousness of their program, the
Radicals were "intransigent" in its defense, ready to risk their lives in
armed rebellion rather than participate in fraudulent elections. Intransigence was in part a response to the fact that the PAN gave opposition candidates little hope of success, but it also reflected the view
that the UCR was a movement, not a party. As Yrigoyen insisted, "the
Unión Cívica Radical is not properly speaking a party in the militant sense; it is a conjunction of forces emerging from the opinion of
the nation."[23] And as José Luis Romero has pointed out, the Radicals'
policy of intransigence and abstention was partly "the product of a
fixed conviction that the people had aspirations that the oligarchy was
unable to satisfy and demands that could only be fulfilled by total vic-

tory. The idea gained momentum that the Radical Civic Union was an exceptional political movement—the true embodiment of the popular majority and, therefore, its authentic political representative."[24] This Radical self-perception recalled that of the PAN, prefigured that of the Peronists, and underscored the fragility of the notion of legitimate political opposition in the political culture then prevailing.

As the PAN and UCR counterposed their respective versions of movementism, the urban working class entered the political scene. Worker organization in Argentina dates back to 1877, when Buenos Aires printers formed a union. In 1878, this union launched the country's first strike. Unionization and strikes continued as industrial employment rose, and the Argentine Workers' Federation, Argentina's first umbrella labor confederation, was founded in 1901.[25] Meanwhile, European immigration contributed to the diffusion of socialist, anarchist and syndicalist ideologies. A socialist party was formed in 1894, but because nearly two-thirds of the working class, having been born outside the country (mainly in Italy or Spain), lacked the right to vote, the Socialists had little chance of winning enough seats to push through pro-labor legislation they advocated.[26] Although the Socialists managed to become the majority party in a few working-class districts in the federal capital, electoral abuses made it hard for them to retain this status. The Socialist Alfredo Palacios won the La Boca national deputy seat in 1904, but lost it in 1908 when conservatives changed the electoral law to his disadvantage.[27] In the 1910 Buenos Aires municipal elections, in which the Socialists had no success, the voter registry included Michelangelo and Jesus of Nazareth.[28]

It was not socialism but anarchism, whose insurrectionary tactics did not require citizenship or fair elections, that became the dominant force in the labor movement during the first decade of the twentieth century. Rejecting parties and parliament, the anarchists tried to organize workers to prepare for a revolutionary general strike that would usher in a stateless society. Although some highly skilled groups, like the engineers and stokers in the Railway Brotherhood (La Fraternidad), stayed in the socialist camp, most workers rejected the party and parliamentary route in favor of the "direct action" tactics favored by the anarchists. The anarchists' goals bore little resemblance to those of unionists later in the century, but their skepticism about using the means of party and parliamentary activity foreshadowed the stance of such unionists as José Alonso in the 1960s and, in a different way, Saúl Ubaldini in the 1980s.

The anarchist-led working class launched massive strikes and demonstrations that deeply unsettled conservatives. In August 1902, when the newly formed FOA labor confederation organized the country's first general strike, it was rumored in Buenos Aires that 30,000 armed workers had taken to the streets, and "the fear of social revolution hung in the air."[29] The conservative government responded to the strike by enacting the Ley de Residencia (Residency Law), which allowed the deportation of any foreigner "whose conduct compromises national security or disturbs public order" (many union activists were foreign-born). Despite the Residency Law, strikes and demonstrations continued for the rest of the decade. In May 1904, a clash between workers and police at a rally in Buenos Aires left two dead and fifteen injured. A similar confrontation in May 1909 left twelve dead and eighty injured, whereupon the unions paralyzed the city for a week.[30]

In 1910, an anarchist killed the police chief of Buenos Aires with a bomb. The assassin was sentenced to life in prison, and for the first time since 1900, the government imposed a state of siege. Union locals were closed, the right to assembly was curtailed, and a wave of deportations occurred under the Residency Law. In May 1910, the FORA, a new, exclusively anarchist confederation, called a demonstration to protest these measures and threatened to follow it up with a general strike during the upcoming celebration of the centennial of Argentine independence. To forestall the strike, the government declared another state of siege and arrested several union leaders. This response was too tepid for some members of the oligarchy. Foreshadowing the events of the 1919 Semana Trágica (Tragic Week), mobs of upper-class youths swarmed through the streets of Buenos Aires, sacking the offices of the leading socialist and anarchist newspapers, destroying the headquarters of several unions, and smashing windows and attacking pedestrians in neighborhoods they characterized as "Jewish."[31]

By generating fear that social mobilization could not be contained by existing political institutions, the anarchists' direct action tactics and the Radicals' intermittent attempts at armed rebellion helped shift the initiative toward the reformist faction of the oligarchy, one of whose members, Roque Sáenz Peña, became president in 1910.[32] Two years after taking office, Sáenz Peña introduced a set of electoral reforms that transformed Argentina's political regime from one of fraud, intimidation, backroom deals, and voter apathy to one of honest voter registration, fair vote-counting, compulsory voting, and the secret ballot. The reforms also introduced an incomplete-list electoral system whereby parties could present candidates, and voters cast ballots, for only two-thirds of the vacant seats for presidential electors and national deputies. The effect of this system, which prevailed in the chamber of deputies for most of the next half-century (until proportional representation was definitively introduced in 1962), was usually to give a province's most popular party two-thirds of the vacant seats, leaving the remaining third for the second-most popular party. As the 1912 reforms approached, the conservatives were confident that they would win two-thirds of the seats almost everywhere,[33] with the Radicals coming in second in most provinces (except perhaps the federal capital, where the Socialists had a good chance of outpolling them). The 1912 electoral reforms were not a complete break with the past (foreign-born inhabitants still could not vote), but they sparked a surge in voter participation, which rose from 21 percent of eligible voters in 1910 to 69 percent in 1912.[34] Party competition also began to flourish. The Radicals abandoned their policy of abstention, strengthened their organization in the interior provinces, and increased food handouts and other forms of patronage.[35] As the 1916 presidential elections neared, the UCR was getting ready to replace the PAN as Argentina's hegemonic political movement.

Workers and Radical Governments, 1916–1930

The UCR candidate, Hipolíto Yrigoyen, won the 1916 presidential election with 46 percent of the popular vote, prevailing by a wide margin over a conservative opposition split between the Partido Conservador de Buenos Aires (which had replaced the PAN as the main electoral vehicle of the Pampean elite), the Partido Demócrata Progresista (strongest in Córdoba and Santa Fe), and a multitude of mostly conservative provincial parties. Each of these forces won 13–15 percent of the vote; the Socialists got the remaining 9 percent, almost exclusively in the federal capital.[36] Three specifically political factors help explain the conservatives' electoral defeat. First, the Sáenz Peña reforms ended many of the fraudulent practices on which conservative electoral hegemony had been based. Second, with the demise of the PAN, the Buenos Aires landholders lost the backing of their counterparts in other provinces, many of whom now supported the Partido Demócrata

Progresista or one of the provincial parties. Third, the UCR improved its vote-getting apparatus between 1912 and 1916, increasing its ability to compete with conservative parties for clientelistic support.

In addition to these political factors, a peculiarity of Argentina's rural social structure helps to explain the conservatives' electoral demise. Because cattle-ranching and grain-growing, the country's main agricultural activities, are land-intensive rather than labor-intensive, Argentina lacks a large sedentary peasantry—a class that long supplied "captive" votes to conservative parties in countries like Chile and Brazil.[37] By depriving the oligarchy of a mass electoral base, the absence of a large sedentary peasantry reduced the stake of this powerful sectoral elite in the survival and effective operation of parties and elections. Through local bosses like Alberto Barceló of Avellaneda, the Partido Conservador de Buenos Aires became adept at using patronage to generate political support, but the lack of a large peasantry ultimately limited its electoral base. With the conservative defeat in the 1916 elections, Pampean landowners, still the country's dominant social class, gained a strong incentive to try to exert influence outside of the party and electoral arenas, especially after their influence in the UCR declined in the late 1920s.

The Argentine case suggests a broader proposition. Barrington Moore and others have claimed that labor-intensive agriculture impedes an initial transition to democracy by making landed elites less willing to cede state power, which they need to control a large and exploited labor force.[38] But labor-intensive agriculture may well promote the subsequent consolidation of democracy by giving landed elites a "captive" peasantry whose votes they can funnel to a conservative party (or parties) representing their interests.[39] The lack of such a peasantry in Argentina, while facilitating an initial transition to (proto) democracy, probably jeopardized the stability of the post-1916 political regime. If conservative parties have little hope of winning fair elections, those otherwise inclined to support such parties will acquire a diminished instrumental stake in the survival of electoral and legislative institutions. As Edward Gibson has noted, "no stable democracy anywhere . . . lacks a conservative party (or grouping of parties) capable of attaining national power through the ballot box."[40] Torcuato di Tella has expressed a similar view: "If the economic Right does not have access to the electoral field—that is, if it cannot hope to win an election—it will try to redress things in its favor via the armed forces."[41]

The importance to democratic consolidation of ties between sectoral elites and political parties depends heavily on the strength of the sectoral elites. If union leaders, urban business elites, or landowner representatives have little capacity to disrupt, or if the armed forces can afford to ignore them when contemplating a coup, the strength of their ties to parties will matter little for democratic consolidation. But if their capacity to disrupt is high, or if the armed forces cannot afford to ignore their possible response to a coup attempt, the strength of their ties to parties will be crucial. Here again Chile provides an instructive contrast. Like Argentina, Chile has long had a powerful landed elite, particularly in the central valley. For much of the twentieth century, these landowners, in conjunction with other elites, retained influence in the legislature through electorally successful Conservative and Liberal parties. What kept these Chilean right-wing parties viable long after Argentine conservatism became electorally bankrupt was the presence of numerous peasants and rural workers engaged in labor-intensive fruit, vegetable, wine, and dairy farming, as well as in land-intensive grain production and cattle-raising. As Brian Loveman has argued, "control over the votes of rural labor assured the Conservative and Liberal parties, along with some Radicals, of enough congressional seats to retain important veto power over presidential programs."[42] By coercing, cajoling, or buying the votes of the rural poor, Conservative and Liberal leaders, representing big landowners and other traditional elites, were able to return a sizable bloc of legislators to congress, giving them a stake in the survival of competitive politics. It was precisely when electoral reforms in the late 1950s weakened landowners' grip on the rural vote that the Chilean right began to move toward antiparty politics, removing a bulwark of the country's competitive political system.[43] In its impact on the attractiveness of party politics to the conservative rural elite, the Chilean electoral reform of 1958 had much in common with the Argentine electoral reform of 1912.

By making it hard for conservative parties to win elections, the 1912 reforms made party activity less attractive to landowners. On the other hand, by giving nonconservative parties a chance of winning, the reforms made party activity potentially more attractive to workers and union leaders. Anarchism still discouraged party activity, but began to lose strength in 1910, when members of congress, in response to a bomb explosion in the Colón opera house, passed the Ley de Defensa Social, which barred the immigration of known anarchists, forbade "subversive" activity, and restricted the right to public assembly. Over the next five years, the Ley de Defensa Social, the deportation of foreign-born militants under Ley de Residencia, intermittent police repression, and growing worker frustration with the slow pace of labor gains allowed syndicalism to supplant anarchism as the dominant force in the labor movement.[44] Syndicalism differed from anarchism in both goals and methods. Both doctrines promised a utopian society, but whereas the anarchists envisioned one made up of decentralized workers' cooperatives, the syndicalists foresaw one run by a centralized corporatist state. Both movements rejected party and parliamentary activity in favor of organizing a revolutionary general strike, but the anarchists wanted the strike at the earliest possible moment, whereas the syndicalists were willing to devote their attention to bread-and-butter issues while waiting for the contradictions to sharpen.

The syndicalists had largely supplanted the anarchists by 1915, but their rising prominence brought them into sharper confrontation with the Socialists. Because the Radicals were also competing with the Socialists for control of the labor vote in the federal capital, and because the syndicalists were willing to focus on bread-and-butter issues for the time being, the stage was set for Radical–syndicalist collaboration. Accordingly, when the syndicalist-led maritime workers struck in 1916 and 1917, Yrigoyen took the unprecedented step of intervening on the union's behalf. This response raised fears among the rich that Yrigoyen was weakening on the domestic labor front at a time when the Bolsheviks were taking over in Russia. In 1918, when railway workers launched a series of strikes and fear of a general strike mounted, landowners and industrialists formed the Asociación de Trabajo to recruit and defend strikebreakers in industrial disputes. The formation of this organization was an early sign that the oligarchy, devoid of its own electorally viable parties, would begin to look for extraparty and extra-constitutional ways to exercise political influence.[45]

In January 1919 came an even more ominous sign that the oligarchy had decided to take labor matters into its own hands. In December 1918, a strike broke out at the British-owned Vasena metal works in Buenos Aires. When the strikers sabotaged the factory, the government intervened against them, and several lives were lost in a series of confrontations between strikers and police. The violence subsided, but in the prevailing climate of fear and uncertainty, middle- and upper-class civilians, many apparently recruited by UCR committees, unleashed five days of terror on Buenos Aires, coordinated by navy officers and supported by police.[46] As in May 1910, most of the violence was directed not at workers but at Jews, who were stigmatized collectively as "Russian agitators." One band of civilians "boast[ed] that they had dispatched forty-eight Jews in a single day during the crisis,"[47] and a member of the military told the U.S. ambassador that Russian Jews made up 179 of the 193 workers whose bodies had been identified.[48] The Semana Trágica remains one of the most deadly expressions of hatred and intolerance in a century of intermittent anti-Jewish violence in Argentina.[49] It also showed that conservatives, made fearful by an international climate colored by the Russian Revolution, were willing to take direct action to stifle dissent.

A second step taken by upper-class civilians and navy officers to counter the perceived threat from labor and the left was to form the Liga Patriótica Argentina to instill "respect for the law, the principle of authority, and the social order" and to "cooperate in the repression of all movements of anarchistic character."[50] The Liga performed social and welfare functions, but its main activities between 1919 and 1922 involved the repression of strikes, including those of taxi drivers in the federal capital, rural laborers in Entre Rios, plantation workers in Chaco, and wool workers in Patagonia.[51] The massacre of workers on the sheep ranches of Patagonia between August 1921 and March 1922 claimed more than a thousand lives. Most of the deaths were attributable to the army rather than to the Liga Patriótica, but the latter played a very visible role in the repression.[52] The Pampean elite played a less prominent role in the Liga Patriótica than it had in the Associación de Trabajo, but big landowners were among the Liga's top leaders and could generally count on the organization to support their interests. Many army officers also joined the Liga, solidifying an alliance with the landowning elite that would be consummated after the 1930 coup.[53]

Conservative violence and increased government sensitivity to military unrest caused the Radicals to halt their overtures to labor and turn to solidifying their middle-sector support, especially through public employment. From 1919 to 1922, the Radicals directed only tepid legislative initiatives toward workers, all of which languished in congress.[54] Far from provoking renewed labor protest, the Radicals' drift to the right during the 1920s coincided with a sharp drop in strike activity, a reduction in membership in the major union confederations, and a turn toward negotiation and dialogue on the part of powerful unions like the railway workers. Much as had happened after the repression of 1910, the Semana Trágica contributed to a reduction in labor militancy. This time, however, the oligarchy's violence also put a halt to Yrigoyen's tentative efforts to tie an important segment of the labor movement to the UCR. The conservative reaction to Yrigoyen's overtures ended an important effort by Argentine elites to incorporate workers into party politics.[55] The next attempt did not come until the mid 1940s, by which time the urban working class had grown much larger and more powerful.

Because Argentina's presidents had been constitutionally barred since 1853 from serving two consecutive presidential terms, Yrigoyen anointed Marcelo T. de Alvear, a prominent cattle rancher, as the UCR candidate in the 1922 presidential elections.[56] Alvear won 48 percent of the vote; no other single party exceeded the Socialists' 9 percent. Once again the conservative forces split; the Partido Demócrata Progresista, Partido Conservador de Buenos Aires, and Concentración Nacional each took between 7 and 8 percent of the vote, with the remainder going to provincial parties. The fragmentation and decline of the conservative parties limited their usefulness as vehicles for access to state power, but some managed to survive. Equally important, the oligarchy remained prominent in the UCR itself. In 1916, more Radical than conservative leaders had big landholdings and university educations, and 48 percent of UCR deputies entering the national congress in 1916 were classified as "aristocrats."[57] Five of the eight cabinet ministers in Yrigoyen's 1916–22 administration belonged to the SRA, and Alvear himself, along with four of his eight cabinet ministers, belonged to the organization.[58] The UCR advocated neither land reform nor the abandonment of liberal free-trade policies, and generally enacted policies consistent with the interests of the Pampean elite. The Yrigoyen administration took pro-landowner measures (like helping to suppress an uprising of tenant farmers in the province of La Pampa), but the Alvear government took even more. Twice as many pro-rancher bills were introduced into congress during the Alvear presidency as during Yrigoyen's term, more than half of them sponsored by the UCR.[59] Had Alvear's tendency prevailed, the UCR might well have replaced the PAN as the main electoral vehicle of the landowning elite, increasing its stake in the survival of competitive elections.

Alvear's tendency did not prevail. Tensions between Alvear and Yrigoyen were apparent from the early days of the new president's administration, which centered initially around an eight-member cabinet that included, to the ex-president's dismay, only one of Yrigoyen's close allies. Alvear and Yrigoyen soon fell out, and in 1924, the

UCR split. Alvear's tendency called itself the Unión Cívica Radical–Antipersonalista, while Yrigoyen's retained the UCR label. After the split, the antipersonalist Radicals allied with the conservative parties, opposing the Yrigoyenist Radicals in legislative battles over committee appointments and economic policy. The antipersonalist Radical–conservative alliance solidified prior to the 1928 election, when conservative parties, after uniting in an electoral front, refrained from nominating a presidential candidate so that the antipersonalist Radical nominee, Leopoldo Melo, would have a better chance of beating Yrigoyen.[60] The strategy proved inadequate. Yrigoyen won the 1928 presidential election in his biggest landslide yet, gaining 57 percent of the vote against 30 percent for Melo. To members of the oligarchy who had counted on either the conservatives or antipersonalist Radicals to represent them in electoral politics, Yrigoyen's victory seemed to portend an endless string of defeats. The oligarchy's stake in electoral politics had declined to an all-time low.

Had elite groups retained a foothold in the personalist wing of the UCR, they might have found Yrigoyen's victory less devastating. But persons identified as aristocrats, who had made up 48 percent of UCR deputies in 1916, comprised only 19 percent of the Yrigoyenist deputy bloc by 1928.[61] The class composition of Yrigoyen's support had also changed. Between 1916 and 1928, Yrigoyen's vote share in the federal capital rose in poor districts but fell in wealthy ones.[62] Hence, although Yrigoyen's policies toward labor and foreign capital were more congenial to elite interests during his second administration than during his first,[63] the landed elite no longer saw its members heavily represented in government. To make matters worse, Yrigoyen used the presidential faculty of intervention—the appointment of trustees to replace elected provincial officials—to gain control of four provinces that his party had lost at the ballot box. Because national senators during Yrigoyen's term were elected by provincial legislatures,[64] these interventions threatened to change the balance of forces in the senate, the last redoubt of the conservative opposition (the personalists controlled the chamber of deputies).[65] Together with Yrigoyen's physical and mental deterioration, intimations of economic decline after the 1929 stock market crash, and Yrigoyen's injection of patronage and partisanship into the military promotion process, the denial of space to the conservative opposition was crucial in triggering the 1930 coup.[66]

Stepping back from the causes of the coup in particular, the main structural factors leading to the breakdown of the post-1912 competitive regime were the lack of a sedentary peasantry (which deprived conservative parties of a big electoral base in the countryside), the fragmentation of the conservative vote, and the growing predominance in Radicalism of the interests of the urban middle class over those of the rural elite. From 1928 on, Argentina's most enduring political party, the UCR, primarily represented the country's most heterogeneous and fragmented social sector, the middle class. No electorally viable party emerged to represent either the landowners or urban business interests (which became stronger during the 1930s), and Peronism, with its weak party institutionalization, eventually claimed the allegiance of workers. In short, Argentina's least cohesive and least-organized social class became the one most fully incorporated into party politics, whereas its most cohesive and best-organized social classes were the least fully incorporated into party politics. The disparity between degree of class cohesion and organization and degree of incorporation into party activity impeded democratic consolidation for the rest of the century.

Conservative Rule and Industrial Growth, 1930–1943

The 1930–43 period in Argentina brings to mind three images, the first called up by the phrase "oligarchic restoration." After losing ground to the middle classes in the late 1920s, the big landowners of the Pampas region—and above all the cattle fatteners who controlled the SRA—came again to be represented heavily among the holders of formal political power and the shapers of government policy.[67] The second image of the 1930–43 years, the one responsible for the period being called the "infamous decade," is of a time when extraordinary concessions were made to British economic interests. Epitomizing these concessions was the 1933 Roca-Runciman pact, which gave Argentine ranchers a guaranteed share of the British beef market—in return for which Argentina agreed to minimize tariffs on coal and other British imports and to give privileged treatment to British capital in the meat-packing and transport industries.[68] Later concessions gave British investors control of the Buenos Aires tramways. The third image associated with the 1930–43 period is that of "patriotic fraud." In order to perform their patriotic duty of shaping the national destiny, the politicians of the three-party Concordancia coalition, which represented the interests of the Pampean elite, kept themselves in power by resorting to electoral abuses reminiscent of the pre-1912 era. The notion of "patriotic fraud" harked back to the movementism of the PAN.

General José F. Uriburu headed Argentina's first military government (1930–32), which "was based on a clear-cut alliance between the aristocracy and the military."[69] An admirer of fascism, Uriburu envisioned a polity in which corporatist representation of functional groups (the army, the Church, business, landowners, and labor) would replace parties, elections, and legislatures. To stifle dissent, Uriburu created a special section of the Federal Police to arrest and intimidate political opponents.[70] When his health failed and his corporatist vision was challenged by a stronger army faction led by General Agustín P. Justo, Uriburu called a new presidential election. Setting a precedent for the post-1955 proscription of Peronism, Alvear, who after reconciling with Yrigoyen had returned to the main trunk of the Radicals (bringing about half of the antipersonalists with him), was banned from the November 1931 contest, ostensibly because he had not waited the constitutionally required six years to elapse since the end of his last presidential term.[71] After Alvear's nomination was blocked, the Radicals returned to electoral abstention and launched two unsuccessful military rebellions against the Justo government. The Radical withdrawal also paved the way for the presidential victory of General Justo, an antipersonalist who presented himself as a national rather than military figure.[72] Backing Justo was the three-party Concordancia coalition comprising the UCR–Antipersonalista, the Partido Demócrata Nacional (a newly unified conservative party), and the Partido Socialista Independiente (a conservative offshoot of the Partido Socialista). The losing ticket included Lisandro de la Torre of the Partido Demócrata Progresista and Nicolás Repetto of the main trunk of the Partido Socialista.

Although the losing coalition accused the Concordancia of electoral fraud, Justo owed his victory in the 1931 presidential elections primarily to the proscription of Alvear and the consequent Radical abstention. When Alvear ended Radical abstention in 1935, however, the Concordancia resorted in earnest to fraud. The November 1935 gubernatorial election in the province of Buenos Aires, won by Manuel Fresco of the Partido Demócrata Nacional, was "one of the most fraudulent and irregular in Argentine history."[73] Fraud also guaranteed the victory of the antipersonalist Roberto Ortiz, the Concordancia nominee, over the Radical candidate, Alvear, in the 1938 presidential election. But if Justo had been elected relatively cleanly (except for the proscription of the Yrigoyenist Radicals) before presiding over fraudulent elections, Ortiz, elected by fraud, tried to move back toward clean elections. His health soon deteriorated, however, and in 1940 Ortiz left the presidency to his vice president, Ramón F. Castillo, who resumed the electoral fraud that had characterized the Justo era. The return to fraud came at a time when the military was becoming increasingly worried that electoral abuses, in the context of communist gains in the labor movement, might radicalize the workers, and when a critical mass of military officers had begun to favor a more aggressive program of industrialization.[74] These tensions soon boiled over, and on 4 June 1943, Castillo was overthrown in a military coup.

The 1930–43 period was indeed an era of "patriotic fraud" and, for nationalists, an "infamous decade," but it represented an "oligarchic restoration" in only a qualified sense. The policies of the 1930s favored the landed elite, and the cabinets of the era included numerous SRA members, but a similar situation had prevailed for much of the 1920s. Moreover, industrial production, especially of textiles but also of chemical, metal, and electrical products, grew significantly during the 1930s, not only because of the world depression (which caused a foreign-exchange shortage and consequent drop in import capacity), but also owing to initiatives taken deliberately by increasingly autonomous government policy makers.[75] Finally, economic policy makers during the 1930s began to develop a measure of autonomy from class forces of all types.[76]

Although the onset of rapid industrialization in the mid 1930s did not radically reduce the economic and political clout of the Pampean landowners, industrialists did gain strength relative to this previously dominant group. As new organizations emerged to represent agrarian sectors marginalized by the SRA, weakening the cohesion of the rural interests, the Unión Industrial Argentina (UIA), representing big industrial entrepreneurs, expanded its membership from 300 firms in the early 1930s to 3,000 by 1946.[77] But the UIA spoke only for a sector of industry. Dominated by big food-processing exporters and recently arrived subsidiaries of multinational corporations, it paid little attention to the concerns of smaller-scale enterprises or manufacturers from the interior of the country.[78] Linguistic and cultural divisions also split the urban entrepreneurial class; as late as 1935, native Argentines accounted for only 39 percent of owners of industrial establishments.[79] As with workers, the immigrant status of many industrialists complicated their insertion into party politics.[80] Like agrarian elites, however, industrialists enjoyed extraparty modes of political influence ranging from interest-group pressure to informal lobbying to contacts and expertise, and they used these resources to vault themselves into government policy-making positions.[81] Industrialists never developed the class cohesion that the Pampean elite enjoyed, but from the 1930s onward, they exercised growing political influence, albeit only minimally through political parties.

In addition to making urban entrepreneurial elites more influential political actors, industrialization produced a labor movement of formidable size and strength. By the 1920s, Argentina already ranked higher on factory employment, urbanization, and labor scarcity—all factors conducive to the development of a strong labor movement— than did Brazil, Chile, Colombia, Mexico, Peru, Uruguay, or Venezuela.[82] Industrialization during the 1930s and early 1940s augmented this preexisting strength. Whereas the industrial census of 1936 recorded 438,000 industrial workers, by 1943 the number had increased to 820,000. Many were drawn from the nearly one million internal migrants who moved to big cities between 1936 and 1947.[83] Meanwhile, the number of union members registered by the National Labor Department rose from 287,725 in 1936 to 528,523 in 1945.[84] Another important boost to trade union power came in 1930, when socialist and syndicalist unionists came together to form the Confederación General del Trabajo (CGT), Argentina's umbrella trade union confederation. The CGT founders saw the organization as a vehicle for lobbying for social and labor reforms, but distinguished carefully between lobbying the government and endorsing specific political parties. The 1930 CGT statutes put the new confederation above partisan and ideological disputes by declaring it to be "independent of all political parties and of all ideological, religious, or philosophical currents."[85]

During the Uriburu dictatorship (1930–32) and somewhat more mildly under the Justo government (1932–35), the executive met worker demands largely with repression.[86] Congress, however, paid more attention to union leaders advocating social and labor reforms, in part because the abstention of the Yrigoyenist Radicals allowed the Socialists to win an unprecedented 43 of the 158 seats in the chamber of deputies.[87] Between 1932 and 1935, congress passed 27 new social and labor laws, including such significant advances as the *sábado inglés* (half a day's work on Saturdays), vacations, advance notification of layoffs, severance pay, and maternity insurance.[88] After 1935, economic recovery and the return of Yrigoyenist Radicalism to the electoral arena (which reduced the number of Socialists in congress) diminished legislative attention to workers' concerns, and only five social and labor laws were passed between 1936 and 1939.[89] But in a reversal of the situation that had prevailed earlier in the decade, reduced congressional concern with social and labor problems was accompanied by a new role for the executive branch in industrial relations as the National Labor Department began to mediate in collective bargaining and industrial disputes.[90]

Increased congressional attention to social and labor problems in the early 1930s and the executive's expanding role in labor relations later in the decade gave the unions new incentives to try to influence government policy. But these new incentives also heightened tensions in a labor movement whose leaders disagreed with one another on the appropriate direction of union political action. For example, socialist labor leaders who saw the sábado inglés as a triumph for their strategy of parliamentary action were ridiculed by the syndicalists, who pointed out that many employers had responded to the law by increasing the length of the working day between Monday and Friday. The syndicalists suggested that a more effective approach would be to demand that the National Labor Department pay unionists to help enforce existing laws.[91] As industrialization continued in the post-1935 period, such conflicts at the leadership level were superimposed on new base-level tensions created by the diversification of the industrial workforce. Communist labor leaders were particularly successful at organizing the internal migrants and others who were finding jobs in the expanding industrial sector. The growth of the four largest communist-led unions accounted for 95 percent of the increase in total union membership between 1936 and 1941, and communist-led industrial unions led most of the strikes of the era.[92] The Socialists and syndicalists continued to control the more extensively organized transport and communications sectors, above all the dominant railway workers' union.

When World War II broke out, Socialists, syndicalists, and Communists closed ranks in support of the Allied cause, but they could agree on little else, and the CGT split in two at its 1942 congress. The more conservative CGT-1, made up largely of syndicalist and socialist leaders, was militantly anticommunist, dominated by transport and service-sector unions, and relatively cautious about taking positions on domestic and international political affairs. The more radical CGT-

2, which included communist and some socialist leaders, was dominated by industrial unions and aired its views energetically on political
issues.[93] But as if to underline the degree to which the union movement
as a whole was becoming more politicized, even the CGT-1 leader José
Domenich, who in 1937 had written articles opposing union political involvement, was by 1943 protesting restrictions on union political
action embodied in the recently enacted Law of Professional Associations.[94]

Between 1930 and 1943, as legislators and cabinet ministers were
taking more interest in industrial relations, union leaders were thus
becoming increasingly conscious of the need to involve themselves in
politics, whether through parliamentary activity or through participation in state agencies. In this sense, the stage was set for someone
like Perón to solidify the institutional links between the state and the
unions. In 1932, the CGT had delivered to the chamber of deputies a
program that called for a minimum wage, shorter working hours, paid
vacations and holidays, severance compensation, retirement pensions,
maternity leave, and accident insurance. The program had also called
upon the state to supply aid to families with dependent children, to
provide lay public education free of charge, and to give the CGT
participation in the National Labor Department and in state agencies
dealing with health, immigration, railways, and ports.[95] Few of these
demands had been met by 1943, so social and labor reforms were overdue. Economic expansion and Perón's search for labor support permitted many of them to be carried out, boosting the wealth, power,
and status of the workers and propelling Perón to the presidency.

Chapter 3

Peronism and Its Legacy

The 1943–55 period in Argentina saw the formation of a new collective identity, Peronism, and of its antithesis, anti-Peronism. Workers came to support Perón not, as is sometimes claimed, because his charisma appealed to psychologically dislocated migrants from the countryside to the city, but rather because he was plainly responsible for a large and sudden increase in the wealth, power, and status of the urban working class. Perón was able to keep worker support focused on himself, rather than on the institutions with which he was associated, in part because his pro-labor stance stood out against the largely anti-labor orientation of the military government that propelled him to prominence, and in part because he made little use of party organization in acquiring or retaining power. By increasing the power and politicization of the Argentine labor movement, Perón exacerbated distributive conflict in the post-1955 era, and by cultivating direct affective links to his followers, while neglecting party activity, he perpetuated the hiatus between workers and parties that had persisted since the end of the nineteenth century. Perón's plebiscitarian style of rule was not the only factor that made it hard for parties to organize and channel distributive conflict in the post-1955 period, but its legacy was important and persistent enough to warrant a careful analysis of its origins and implications for party institutionalization.

Material Benefits and Support for Perón

A variety of domestic and international developments came together around 1940 to make military officers anxious about Argentina's near-term future. On the domestic front, accelerated industrial growth had increased the strength of the labor movement at a time when communism was becoming more influential in many unions. On the international scene, the depression had highlighted Argentina's vulnerability to international economic shocks, while the rise of fascist models in Europe increased the plausibility, and for some the attractiveness, of a radical break with economic and political liberalism. As the outbreak of World War II and Brazil's decision to side with the Allies exacerbated the resulting tensions, many officers began to doubt that the governing Concordancia politicians were competent to handle the new threats and opportunities facing the country. In February 1943, military impatience with the Concordancia took a quantum leap upward as rumors began to circulate that President Ramón Castillo had tapped Robustiano Patrón Costas, one of the country's largest sugar growers, as his preferred successor. Patrón Costas's harsh labor practices evoked an image of backwardness at a time when many officers thought it critical to modernize the country.[1] Moreover, Castillo intended to secure Patrón Costas's victory by any means necessary, and growing numbers of officers were reluctant to endorse another fraudulent election, partly because they wished to avoid public expressions of protest at a time of international uncertainty. Finally, some officers were troubled by Patrón Costas's reported, though far from unambiguous, sympathy for the Allies in World War II.[2] On 4 June 1943, these tensions boiled over and Castillo was overthrown. After a brief power struggle, General Pedro Ramírez became president.

An important force behind the June 1943 coup was the Grupo de Oficiales Unidos (United Officers' Group; GOU), an influential cohort of 20 or so officers united by anticommunism, support for industrialization, and advocacy of an implicitly pro-Axis neutrality in World War II.[3] The GOU was not alone in organizing the coup, but its influence soared after General Ramírez, the new president, appointed its leaders to government posts. Among them was Colonel Juan Domingo Perón, who received a top position in the war ministry. In October 1943, as the GOU officers consolidated their position at the expense of a pro-Allied faction, Perón was named to head the National Labor Department, which in December 1943 was upgraded to cabinet status and renamed the Secretariat of Labor and Social Security. From this post, Perón recruited the labor support that would carry him to the presidency.

Soon after taking power, the military government abolished the leftist CGT-2, removed the leaders of the powerful railway workers' union, and imposed the 1943 Law of Professional Associations, which prohibited union participation in politics and restricted other union activities. Numbed at first by this onslaught, labor leaders soon began to demand the restitution of their unions, freedom to organize throughout the country, wage hikes, the expansion of pension and social security coverage, and a ministry of labor to oversee industrial relations and enforce labor laws.[4] Breaking with the anti-labor stance of many of his military colleagues, Perón supported many of the union leaders' demands. Several considerations moved Perón to side with workers and union leaders in their struggles with employers and anti-labor government officials. First, by his own account, Perón developed a special concern with the welfare of workers and the poor during his early days in the army, when he met ill-clad, barefoot, and undernourished recruits and saw the miserable living conditions prevailing in many parts of the country.[5] Second, Perón and his colleagues in the GOU were concerned with preventing a workers' revolution, a possibility that became more salient in the mid 1930s as communist labor leaders won control of important industrial unions.[6] Third, Perón hoped to make Argentina an "organized community" in which a paternalistic state would act to cushion social conflict. Harmonizing labor and capital became a cornerstone of *justicialismo*, the official Peronist ideology.[7] Fourth, Perón had political ambitions and recognized that labor was a potential support group.

Central to Perón's winning the support of labor was his dispensation of legal and organizational support to unions and of material and symbolic benefits to workers. In December 1943, Perón suspended the recently enacted Law of Professional Associations, winning the applause of unionists.[8] He then began to give legal and technical assistance to unions, to consult labor leaders on social and labor legislation, and to enforce existing labor laws, particularly in the interior of the country. He also generalized paid holidays and vacations to the entire labor force; shortened the working day in various industries; created a system of labor courts to handle worker grievances; restricted the conditions under which workers could be fired; and forced employers to improve working conditions and to provide accident compensation and severance pay.[9] He insisted that employers bargain with government-recognized unions, and often intervened on the workers' behalf when the bargaining broke down.[10] He helped sugar, wine, lumber, and migrant workers organize; presided over a large increase in rural wages; froze rural rents; and passed a law providing minimum wages, maximum hours, and vacations for rural workers.[11] Although

few new social and labor laws were passed after 1946,[12] legislation that
had gone on the books in 1944 and 1945 was extended to new segments
of the labor force. Between 1946 and 1951, the number of Argentines
covered by social security more than tripled, so that in 1951, more than
5 million Argentines—70 percent of the economically active population—had social security coverage.[13] Health insurance also spread to
new industries, including metalworking and banking.[14]

Between 1943 and 1946, real wages rose only about 4 percent,[15] but
in 1945, Perón created two institutions that would later boost wages:
the National Institute of Compensation, which implemented a minimum wage and collected data on wages, prices, and living standards,
and the *aguinaldo*—a bonus that gave each worker a lump sum at
the end of the year amounting to one-twelfth of the annual wage.[16]
After Perón became president, moreover, workers' incomes soared.
Between 1945 and 1949, real wages rose 22 percent, while labor productivity rose only 6 percent.[17] Wages fell between 1949 and 1952, but
rose again between 1953 and 1955, ending up at least 30 percent higher
than in 1946.[18] In proportional terms, wages increased from 41 percent of national income in 1946–48 to 49 percent in 1952–55.[19] Several
factors contributed to these trends. By increasing union bargaining
power, the post-1946 broadening and deepening of labor organization
helped to stimulate real wage growth. Also, industry expanded so
rapidly between 1946 and 1948 that even massive migration to indus-
trialized areas could not supply the factories with needed labor power,
and the intense demand for labor drove wages up. Perón accentuated
this labor demand with deliberate policies of financing industry with
rural exports and of extending credit preferentially to the smallest and
most labor-intensive sectors of industry.[20] Moreover, the government
boosted workers' real incomes by enforcing minimum wage laws, controlling the prices of food and other basic consumption items, and
extending housing credits to workers.[21]

In addition to granting these material benefits, Perón was the first
Argentine leader to recognize workers as major contributors to the
welfare of the nation and as full-fledged members of the political community. To show solidarity with the *descamisados* (shirtless ones, a term
he used affectionately to refer to his working-class supporters), Perón
spoke to unionists in an open-necked white shirt.[22] His speeches, moreover, echoed a theme in the preamble to the decree-law creating the
Secretariat of Labor and Social Welfare, which stated that the new
agency would seek "to bring about the practical recognition in all sec-

tors of the country of the supreme dignity of labor."[23] Perón named several figures associated with the labor movement to his first cabinet, and many unionists were given choice places on Peronist congressional slates. In 1946, 11 percent of national legislators, all Peronists, had previously held blue-collar or low-status white-collar occupations.[24] Significant numbers of unionists were elected to both houses of congress in 1952 and 1955,[25] including José Alonso and Amado Olmos, who went on to become top union leaders in the post-1955 period. Given the scope of material and symbolic benefits Perón extended to labor, it is not surprising that many workers became Peronists.

The Personalization of Peronism

To explain why workers supported Perón is one thing, but to explain why Perón was able to keep the focus of this support on himself—even during the latter part of his presidency, when he moved away from pro-labor policies—is another. Peronism revolved from the outset around Perón himself, rather than around the doctrines or policies for which he stood. Perón's slogan "social justice, economic independence, and national sovereignty"[26] embraced a bewildering range of policies. Social justice for Perón included policies ranging from the aguinaldo, the mandatory wage bonus paid once (later twice) a year, to the two-year wage freeze that accompanied the 1952 economic stabilization plan. Economic independence and national sovereignty embraced both the nationalization of British-owned railways (1947) and the signing of oil exploration contracts with U.S. petroleum giants (1954). As is evident from Perón's high level of electoral support throughout his 1946–55 presidency, most Peronists were content to leave to their Supreme Chief (Jefe Supremo) the choice of specific actions that would realize his expressed ideals.

Some have argued that Perón was able to personalize his rule because many of his initial supporters were migrants from the countryside to the cities whose values and experiences predisposed them to a personalistic idea of authority, or whose psychic dislocation during or after the migration process made them susceptible to Perón's charisma.[27] Recent migrants did make up a significant proportion of Perón's original supporters. However, many who voted for Perón in 1946 were long-term city dwellers.[28] It is far from clear, moreover, that the migrants' conception of authority was significantly different from that of established urban workers. Many migrants came from areas of relatively modernized agriculture or from districts including cities with more than 20,000 inhabitants, and others lived in smaller cities before moving on to bigger ones. Moreover, migrants to cities in other Latin American countries do not seem to have experienced any particular disorientation, casting doubt on the notion that those in Argentina suffered psychic distress.[29]

Problems with the internal migrants thesis notwithstanding, Perón's personal appeal, which was strong enough to influence persons of diverse social origins and states of mind, did help him establish direct, plebiscitarian links with his followers. Even more significant, however, was the route he took to the presidency. Perón came to public attention in the context of a largely anti-labor military government. Because his reformism stood out against the anti-labor stance of his colleagues, everyone knew that he—rather than the government, the military, or a political party—was personally responsible for labor's gains. A single, pivotal event early in Perón's political career was crucial in reinforcing this perception. In October 1945, Perón assigned the directorship of the post office to a man who had helped his companion, Eva Duarte, in her years of poverty. This appointment brought to the boiling point the opposition of officers who had long resented "that woman," who disagreed with Perón's social and labor policies, or who were jealous of Perón's popularity and power.[30] These officers forced Perón to resign from the government on 9 October, but before he left office, Perón got permission from his fellow officers to make a "farewell address" on state radio the next day. During the broadcast, Perón "cleverly planted a verbal time bomb by saying he hoped the new administration would implement the substantial wage hike he had just signed."[31] This remark so angered his military rivals that they threw Perón in jail and then confined him on the island of Martín García, where he remained for several days, reportedly contemplating leaving politics altogether, before an army captain persuaded him to return to Buenos Aires for treatment of a feigned health problem.[32]

When the new government failed to organize itself effectively, Perón's supporters decided to take matters into their own hands. In the industrial suburbs of Buenos Aires and in the meat-packing plants farther down the coast in Berisso, union leaders began to prepare a mass demonstration on 17 October 1945, which became a pivotal moment in Argentine history. In the words of one of its important organizers, the meat packers' leader Cipriano Reyes, it represented "the certificate of political adulthood for the laboring masses."[33] As 300,000 workers poured into the Plaza de Mayo in the center of Buenos Aires, Perón was summoned from the hospital in which he was "recovering" to ask the workers to disperse peacefully, a request to which they assented. Rather than ask to be reinstated to his former posts, Perón began to prepare his presidential candidacy.[34] The demonstration of 17 October seemed to show that the only support Perón needed was that of the common people, who, with some organizational help from the unions, could take the streets when necessary to force Perón's opponents to allow him to carry out his programs. It is significant that neither of the key events that paved the way for Perón's rise to the presidency—the June 1943 military coup and the October 1945 demonstration—involved a political party. Parties were organized to support Perón's electoral bid for the presidency in February 1946, but before they had a chance to become more fully institutionalized, Perón disbanded them.

The Peronization, Power, and Politicization of the Unions

Although a great many workers and union leaders came over to Perón during the 1943–46 period, some communist, socialist, and syndicalist unionists did not. Crucial to eliminating these competitors was the 1945 Law of Professional Associations. Although less restrictive than the 1943 version that Perón had suspended, the new labor code placed several constraints on labor organization.[35] It provided that the government would recognize only one union in a given area of economic activity and only one central trade-union confederation, the CGT. Unrecognized unions, although not forbidden to operate, would not be allowed to call strikes or to bargain collectively.[36] Because multiple unions existed in many industries at the time that the law was adopted, the new labor code stated that the largest union in each economic sector would be recognized as the "most representative" one—unless a smaller union's "contributions to the defense and protection of occupational interests" warranted otherwise.[37] The "most representative" clause allowed Perón to grant or withhold recognition from a union according to his own evaluation of whether the union was doing a good job of "protecting occupational interests." When two or more unions competed for recognition, Perón could use this provision to recognize the most sympathetic one, even if its rival was larger or longer-established.[38] If he later decided that the union was doing a

poor job of "protecting occupational interests," he could revoke its recognition or replace its leaders with government trustees. In the end,
unionists who refused to come over to the Peronist camp either lost
the support of most workers in their unions or found themselves marginalized by the "most representative" clause.

In addition to paving the way for the "peronization" of the labor
movement, the 1945 Law of Professional Associations increased union
power by codifying the right to organize, by establishing a centralized
union structure, and by improving union finances through automatic
payroll deductions of union dues. Once this new legal framework
went into effect, union membership skyrocketed. In 1945, Argentina
already had 529,000 union members. This number increased to 877,000
in 1946, 1,532,000 in 1948, 1,992,000 in 1950, and 2,257,000 (43 percent
of wage earners) in 1954.[39] Membership in the metalworkers' Unión
Obrera Metalúrgica, a fast-growing industrial union, rose from 6,000
in 1945 to 108,000 in 1948.[40] The state boosted union membership both
indirectly, by forcing employers to accept new unions and by passing
laws that made organization easier, and directly, by making it mandatory after 1950 for state employees to join unions.[41] Beyond the increase in membership, union organization deepened in the workplace.
In 1947, bargaining agreements began to provide for union workplace
commissions, which oversaw employer compliance with labor laws
and contracts and provided a forum in which ordinary workers, base-
level delegates, and union leaders could discuss work-related matters.
The government took special precautions to protect these commissions from employer persecution. A law was passed providing that
shop stewards could not be fired without due cause, and that due
cause would be judged by the labor ministry. If the ministry upheld the
firing, the shop steward received three times normal severance pay.[42]

As workers became Peronist and as unions became more powerful,
Perón changed the relationship between unions and the state in ways
that made unions more vulnerable to changes in government policy.
This vulnerability politicized the union leadership, in the sense that
it produced new incentives for union leaders to try to exert political
influence. The interests of workers as producers and consumers, and
of union leaders as an elite, became increasingly tied up with government policy as Perón expanded the state's role as an employer, as a
manipulator of economic variables, as an arbiter of industrial relations,
and as an overseer of union finances and elections. During Perón's
presidency, union leaders had little actual influence over government

policy. And willing as they apparently were to leave the deciding to
Perón, most union leaders during the 1946–55 period do not seem even
to have tried very hard to shape such policy. Only after Perón's 1955
overthrow did the new policy-influencing incentives come into play.

The growth of state intervention in the economy and in labor relations antedated Perón. During the 1930s, the state had begun to expand its role as a manipulator of economic variables, making workers'
material fortunes more dependent on the decisions of government
policy makers. In 1932, the Justo government introduced an income
tax, and in 1933, it created a central bank, which, although run by
private (including foreign) banking interests, paved the way for increased government control over credit and the exchange rate. Later in
the decade, institutions were created to redistribute foreign exchange
to priority economic sectors, and regulatory boards were placed in
charge of controlling the production and domestic prices of cereals,
meat, milk, cotton, and wine.[43] World War II greatly increased the
state's economic role. As tensions mounted in Europe, military officers
began to see state-led investment in medium and heavy industry as
crucial to Argentina's war readiness, especially as Argentina adopted
a vaguely pro-Axis neutrality while neighboring Brazil sided openly
with the Allies.[44] In the eyes of government officials, an expanded role
for the state in promoting industry could also help insulate Argentina
from the negative effects of two possible postwar scenarios: a foreign
exchange shortage if postwar Europe proved unable to afford Argentine exports, and a cutoff of imports if war broke out between the
United States and the Soviet Union.[45] After the 1943 coup, accordingly,
the state took full control of the central bank, expanded credit to industry, raised tariffs, nationalized foreign trade, and directed foreign
exchange to industry through a state agency called the Argentine Institute for Trade Promotion (IAPI).[46]

After 1946, Perón further tightened the relationship between government policies and worker well-being by doubling public employment. Between 1945 and 1955, the national civil service expanded from
203,300 to 394,900, while the creation of state-owned steel mills, oil
refineries, shipyards, and armaments plants helped boost the number
employed in state enterprises and autonomous agencies from 109,000
to 148,300.[47] With railway, telephone, post office, and other public-
sector workers already unionized, the growth in the civil service and
in state enterprises made for a truly formidable public-sector unionism, especially after Perón decreed in 1950 that all state employees

would henceforth have to join unions. Because the state directly controlled wages, working conditions, and job security in the public sector, unionists in the civil service and in state-run corporations had special incentives to try to gain input into government policy.

The state's role in matters of special interest to union leaders became much more pronounced after the passage of the 1945 Law of Professional Associations, which gave government policy makers an unprecedented capacity to decide which unions would be able to bargain collectively and collect dues via employer withholding. A union that got on the wrong side of the government was subject to "intervention," which meant that its leaders were replaced by government-appointed trustees, that it lost the right to sign new collective contracts or to go to court to enforce existing ones, that employers no longer had to withhold dues and social security contributions, that shop stewards lost their job security, and that the union's bank accounts were frozen, making it impossible for the union to pay its employees, rent, or bills.[48] After 1946, moreover, Perón increased the state's control over unions by giving the labor ministry power to declare strikes legal or illegal. Strikes during the Peronist period were declared legal only if they were launched against employers who refused to abide by agreements reached through the official conciliation procedure.[49] If a strike was declared legal, the employer often had to give workers back pay for each day they had been on strike.[50] If a strike was declared illegal, employers were usually not obligated to reimburse workers for lost wages, and the union could be intervened.[51] According to the CGT statutes, strikes were extreme actions to be taken only when all other measures had failed. Virtually all of the country's largest national-level unions were put under CGT trusteeship between 1946 and 1954, despite the fact that the CGT until 1950 lacked the statutory power to intervene them. In the late 1940s, the CGT even intervened two unions not affiliated with the confederation.[52]

Perón and Political Parties

Perón's relationship to party organization was always tenuous. From the outset, he saw the political party as a "circumstantial" and "obsolete" organization that was destined to wither away—unlike the union, which he viewed "as an organization which, like the family, springs almost from natural law."[53] Moreover, Perón was reluctant to create a pool of organizational resources that potential rivals might use to challenge his leadership. In addition to not wanting a strong party organization, Perón did not need one. He used the CGT and the national-level unions to mobilize support for elections and demonstrations, and the state rather than a party to dispense welfare benefits and patronage. Perón's reluctance to create a potentially autonomous party organization proved to be of lasting importance for the long-term evolution of Peronism and of Argentine politics.

When Perón began his rise to power, he initially sought the support of the Radicals.[54] Although most Radical leaders rebuffed his efforts, a few proved sympathetic. In December 1945, these leaders broke away from the main trunk of the UCR and formed a new organization, the Unión Cívica Radical–Junta Renovadora (UCR–JR), which nominated Perón as its presidential candidate. The UCR–JR was not the only group of traditional politicians to rally behind Perón: he was also supported by a loose coalition of conservative party offshoots known as the Centros Independientes.[55] As it turned out, the UCR–JR and the Centros Independientes played only subsidiary roles in the party coalition that supported Perón. A week after the demonstration on 17 October 1945, Cipriano Reyes of the meat packers, Luis Gay of the telephone workers, and other union leaders (many formerly affiliated with the Socialist Party) took an important but short-lived step toward greater worker participation in party politics by founding the Partido Laborista (Labor Party), whose purpose was to "defend the conquests achieved during the two and a half years of revolutionary government" and to give the workers their first political party channel for participating in national decisions.[56] The Partido Laborista's 1946 platform called for women's suffrage, the elimination of large land-holdings, the nationalization of public services and strategic mineral deposits, the socialization of medical care, and union participation in efforts to resolve the fundamental problems facing the country.[57] The party committed itself publicly to free and fair elections, both internally and for the country as a whole. As in the British Labour Party, on which it was explicitly modeled, individual members of unions affiliated with the party automatically received membership, unless they expressly requested otherwise.[58] The Partido Laborista supplied the majority of Perón's votes in the February 1946 election,[59] but for the UCR–JR and Centros Independientes, which also sponsored Perón's candidacy, lack of independent support turned out to be an asset for getting nominated for high government office. Wary of giving the independent-minded Partido Laborista officials too much power, Perón gave choice candidacies to the more docile Radical and conservative dissidents. After they won, he used their dependence on his continued support to control them.[60] For the next thirty years, Perón would repeat this balancing act by supporting the weakest factions among his supporters against stronger and potentially more autonomous groups.

The outcome of the February 1946 election surprised everyone, including the victorious Peronists.[61] Perón ran against the Unión Democrática, an unlikely coalition that joined conservatives and Radicals with Socialists and Communists who opposed Perón's implicitly pro-Axis neutrality and resented his support from workers. Taking advantage of U.S. Ambassador Spruille Braden's indiscreet support for José Tamborini, the Unión Democrática candidate, Perón played on nationalism to bolster his presidential bid. In the final tally of an election that observers acclaimed as the fairest to date in Argentine history, Perón outpolled Tamborini by 52 to 43 percent. The parties under whose labels Perón had run did not have long to savor his triumph, however. On 23 May 1946, claiming that internal conflict was threatening the unity of the movement, Perón ordered the three party organizations that had backed his presidential candidacy to dissolve themselves. On 13 June 1946, nine days after assuming the presidency, he replaced them with a new organization, the Partido Unico de la Revolución (Single Party of the Revolution).

Whereas UCR–JR politicians abandoned their organization and rushed to claim places in the Partido Unico,[62] the union leaders in the Partido Laborista initially resisted the call to "unity" and criticized the Partido Unico for "lacking an organic charter, lacking principles, lacking convictions, and lacking the right of self-determination."[63] Under pressure from Perón, however, most soon agreed to join the new organization.[64] To explain the demise of the Partido Laborista, Walter Little has pointed to the ideological immaturity of its leaders, to the indifference workers showed to the party's survival, and to Perón's hostility, coupled with his presidential powers.[65] Just as important, however, may have been the fact that many Partido Laborista leaders, particularly former syndicalists, had little prior experience with parties. The UCR–JR and Centros Independientes were easily dissolved for a different reason: despite their own partisan affiliations, many politicians from these organizations viewed parties as elements of "bankrupt liberalism" or as threats to the organic unity of the community.[66] In short, although the main reason why Peronism did not produce a well-institutionalized party was that Perón neither needed nor wanted one, another factor behind Peronism's weak party institutionalization was that many of the original Peronist politicians were unfamiliar with or hostile to parties.

In July 1947, on the advice of leaders who pointed out that "Unico" lent a totalitarian tinge to the party name, Perón gave his permission to rechristen the organization the Partido Peronista (Peronist Party).[67] From the outset, the Partido Peronista was a monolithic entity controlled strictly by Perón. The party constitution approved in December 1947 empowered the movement's Supreme Chief to "modify decisions of [party] organs," to set the agenda for meetings at all levels of the party, to supervise the selection of party leaders, and to oversee the choice of candidates for elective office. A new charter approved in January 1954 augmented Perón's personal control of the organization by permitting him to "modify or annul the decisions of party authorities" and to "inspect, intervene and replace" its constituent bodies.[68] Another feature of the party that concentrated power in Perón's hands was its division into "union" and "political" branches. Just as he had used the UCR–JR to offset the power of the potentially more autonomous Partido Laborista, Perón used the political branch of the party, whose handpicked leaders were heavily dependent on his personal backing, as a counterweight to the union branch, whose leaders were more likely to have organizational, financial, and prestige resources of their own. The division of the Partido Peronista into political and union wings, formally institutionalized in the party's 1947 charter, was reflected at the local level, where in each jurisdiction ordinary basic units were kept separate from labor basic units.[69] By 1950, the CGT, which had once proclaimed itself to be "independent of all political parties or ideological groupings," had become formally synonymous with the union branch of the Partido Peronista.[70]

A separate women's branch of the Partido Peronista was created in July 1949, two years after women won the right to vote. By 1952, the women's branch had half a million members and more than 3,000 basic units.[71] Eva Perón, the first president of the women's branch, ran the organization as her personal political machine. No party congresses were held in the women's branch during Juan Perón's term in office,[72] and when Eva died in 1952, it was Perón, not one of Eva's subordinates, who succeeded her as president of the women's branch (although

Perón soon turned the organization over to Delia Parodi, one of Eva's trusted intimates). The party's 1954 charter provided at all levels for separate agencies for the men's, women's, and union branches.[73] The personal control that Perón exercised over the party was evident in the fact that direct elections of party leaders were held only at the level of the basic units.[74] According to Oscar Albrieu, a party leader who had once belonged to the now-extinct UCR–JR, elections were spurned at the higher levels in order to prevent the "initiatives of individuals or particular provinces" from presenting an "impediment to the works of the government."[75] As with party authorities, Peronist candidates for electoral office were selected by informal methods in which Perón, or Eva Perón in the case of the women's branch, played a pivotal role. Alberto Iturbe, another former UCR–JR member who served as governor of Jujuy before becoming Perón's last interior minister, reports that Peronist gubernatorial candidates were chosen at meetings with Perón in Buenos Aires, during which "some but not all" of the province's prominent CGT leaders and Peronist politicians would give their opinions about which candidates the party faithful supported. "From all the opinions [given in] this conclave, as we might call it, over which Perón himself presided, the [gubernatorial candidates] were chosen."[76]

Customarily, each of the three branches of the Peronist movement was entitled to its *tercio*—that is, to the right to nominate one-third of the Peronist candidates for national deputy seats and for other posts allocated on a proportional basis. According to Delia Parodi, "the [women's] *tercio* was drawn up by Eva Perón. This was an untouchable, untransferable thing, a right, something that she was always entitled to do."[77] Eva Perón's unilateral role in selecting the women's branch candidates indicates that this sector of the movement was even more authoritarian and personalistic than the men's branch, whose leaders Juan Perón at least consulted when it came time to fill party posts and candidacies.

With authority concentrated almost exclusively in the hands of the Supreme Chief, it is not surprising that a strong leadership cadre failed to emerge in the Partido Peronista. In addition to this weakness at the leadership level, the party was characterized by a low level of mass involvement. The Peronist activist was not necessarily a party member,[78] and the vote was mobilized through the unions as much as through the party. As Perón himself pointed out: "Nowadays you win elections like ours with the unions, not the political parties. You can say to me:

'But you have the political parties as well as the unions.' That's because I'm on top of how things are evolving. I can't dispense with political parties; they are a prejudice beyond which we have not evolved."[79]

Another reason for the low level of mass involvement in the party was that the expansion of the welfare functions of the state, the Eva Perón social welfare foundation, and the unions made the party superfluous from the standpoint of patronage. If Perón's personal control of the party apparatus inhibited the development of a well-entrenched bureaucracy with a strong esprit de corps, the role of nonparty institutions in dispensing social welfare benefits made it unlikely that the party would develop a strong clientelistic organization.[80]

Public employment was one source of patronage that the party did control. One of the few incentives to join the party was that civil service jobs were reserved for party members, a custom that, in Alberto Iturbe's opinion, made it impossible to calculate accurately the real strength of the party in a given electoral district: "It was necessary to be a party member to hold public office. This was . . . a big mistake, because it meant that you never knew how much support you really had or your true political capability. People joined the party just by filling out a form, not because they agreed with [its] ideology."[81]

The Partido Peronista's weakness as an organization was influenced not only by the fact of Perón's personal control but also by how the Supreme Chief chose to exercise his authority. For all his talk about organizing the masses and the organized community, Perón neglected organization-building in favor of direct appeals to the masses and ideological indoctrination. Perón's intention all along was to create a movement, not a party. "The Peronist movement is not a political party; it represents no political grouping," he said. "It is a national movement. . . . we represent only national interests."[82] Perón reiterated this theme in a 26 June 1951 speech at the Olivos presidential residence.

We have said that in our organization, Peronism is not a party: it is a movement, and it is a movement because it does not have an orthodox organization like the ones used by other political parties. . . . Ours is not a conglomerate of men and women lined up behind a political banner. The Peronist movement is a movement of national opinion that follows a doctrine, a doctrine that has pointed out the great objectives we want to achieve for the country and that has pointed out the route we must follow to achieve them.[83]

Perón saw his own role as that of one who mainly "educates, teaches and molds," and viewed the main function of the party as that of "[inculcating] in the people this [Peronist] style of life and this Peronist mystique."[84] For Perón, the Partido Peronista's primary mission was to engender a "spiritual state" of belonging to the Peronist movement. As he put it in 1947,

The first aspect of this organization [the party] is organically to give spirit to the movement, with its mystique and its principles, by laying down the great standards to be fulfilled. This will form what we might call a spiritual state of the movement, which is sometimes understood and sometimes felt. Blessed is whoever can both understand and feel it! And those who can only feel it, let them study, work, and contemplate so they can also understand it. And those who can only understand it, let them pray to God for the privilege of feeling it.[85]

Perón's attitude toward organization-building is summed up in his 1953 confession that "we have kept all of our movement in a state of disarray for the last seven years. Now we have begun to organize ourselves. . . . When one organizes, the first thing one has to do is create a common doctrine, a common way of seeing things. . . . For that reason I did not bother with organization [previously]. . . . almost nine years after we began we have [just been able] to say 'This is the year of Organization!' "[86] This stress on doctrine at the expense of organization distinguished Perón from other populist leaders like Peru's Haya de la Torre and Venezuela's Betancourt, as well as from revolutionaries like Mao and Lenin. Each of these other leaders was more balanced than Perón in attending to these two key dimensions of party building, and each created an organization capable of withstanding repression as harsh, or harsher, than that which the Partido Peronista experienced after 1955.

Perón's inattention to the organizational aspect of party building resulted partly from his skepticism, shaped by the international political climate of the 1930s, about the usefulness and future of parties as political institutions. But it also derived from the situation in which he operated. Urban workers, Perón's main support base, were already organized into unions before the Partido Peronista was created, and Perón used the unions more than the party to mobilize the vote. Moreover, the Partido Peronista was created, as Walter Little has noted, "to retain rather than achieve power."[87] The Aprista (Peru) and Acción Democrática (Venezuela) experiences each suggest that strong party identification and an effective organizational structure, with explicit chains of command and strong esprit de corps, are more likely to develop when a party struggles to attain power than when it is created by a head of state intent on remaining in power. In Argentina itself, the UCR, born in conditions of opposition and repression, developed a more resilient organization and, despite its own movementist tendencies, a greater sense of itself as a party than did the Partido Peronista, which was created by an incumbent president.

Perón's personalization of party authority, his views on how best to exercise that authority, and his organization of the party from the top down were reflected in three dimensions of the Partido Peronista's organizational weakness. First, the party played a relatively minor role in mobilizing voters and dispensing patronage. Second, subaltern party leaders never developed the commitment or capacity to manage the organization on their own. Third, party members and supporters evolved a stronger commitment to Perón himself than to the party organization. These aspects of organizational weakness help explain why the Aramburu government (1955–58), which largely failed in its efforts to eradicate Peronist influence in the unions, was able to dissolve the party with relative ease.

The Decline and Fall of Perón's Government

In July 1952, Eva Perón died of cancer at age 33. She had played a prominent role in the government. In addition to being Juan Perón's main liaison with organized labor, she had been head of the huge Eva Perón social welfare foundation and president of the women's branch of the Partido Peronista.[88] On hearing of her death, the government stopped work for two days, the CGT declared a two-day halt in all but the most essential industries, and two million people joined her funeral procession.[89] The massive outpouring of grief showed workers' great affection for Eva, who had referred to herself as the "bridge of love" between Juan Perón and the workers. Armando Cabo, a leader of the metalworkers' union, reported that he and Perón both considered Eva Perón's death a prime factor behind the weakening of the CGT leadership, and that both viewed the weakening of the CGT leadership as a major reason for Perón's downfall.[90] Yet Eva Perón's presence probably contributed more than her absence to weakening the CGT leadership. After 1946, Eva and Juan Perón turned the CGT into an instrument of government policy. In January 1947, the confederation's newly elected secretary-general, the former Partido Laborista president Luis Gay, was arrested on charges of "collaborating" with labor leaders visiting from the United States. Gay's successor Aurelio Hernández, hand-picked by the Peróns, turned the CGT into a de facto arm of the government, but within a few months, he had fallen out with Eva Perón, who had him replaced by José Espejo, a truck driver for a baking company. Few of the CGT leaders who confirmed Espejo in his post had ever heard of him. Espejo made the CGT even more beholden to the government. At its 1950 congress, the CGT gave up its last shred of independence by rewriting its statutes to proclaim allegiance to Perón.[91]

In 1952, Perón put the CGT in a tough position by launching an economic stabilization program. Aimed at reducing inflation and heading off a foreign-exchange crisis, the program included a two-year wage freeze, a reduction in public spending, and limitations on the domestic consumption of exportables.[92] Price controls and a prior 40 to 80 percent nominal wage hike above 1949 levels helped to offset some of the regressive effects of the plan, and real wages, which had dropped 18 percent in 1949–52, recovered 14 percent in 1953–55.[93] Yet real wages in 1955 were still below their 1948 levels, and the government repressed all strikes for higher wages between March 1952 and March 1954.[94] Moreover, Peronist officials began to throw their weight behind long-standing employer demands for productivity incentives, reduced restrictions on firings and transfers, and curtailment of the power of union factory commissions.[95]

Far from protesting the stabilization plan, CGT chief Espejo announced his support for the government's productivity drive. In response, workers whistled him down at the 1952 "loyalty day" (17 October) demonstration. Rank-and-file dissatisfaction with the stabilization plan was directed not just at the CGT leaders, but also at the leaders of individual unions. Although Perón exercised heavy control over the CGT, it was harder for him to dominate individual unions. In 1953 and 1954, dissident Peronists in the bakers', printers', construction, footwear, telephone workers', and textile workers' unions were able to twist the arm of the labor ministry into backing their electoral bids by hinting that rank-and-file rebellions might be launched against incumbents who limited wage demands to meet the requirements of Perón's stabilization program. Andrés Framini, who had failed in several previous bids to unseat the incumbent leadership of the textile workers' union (AOT), used this argument in 1953 to get labor ministry support for his successful candidacy for the union's secretary-generalship.[96] Augusto Vandor of the metalworkers later called Framini a "great leader" for having "rebelled victoriously against the handpicked leadership of his union."[97]

Not all collaborationist union leaders who lost their posts did so through elections. The metalworkers' UOM exemplifies a more unruly process, one that foreshadowed the violence that would plague the union after 1955. In 1946, Hilario Salvo replaced Angel Perelman as head of the UOM. Unlike Perelman, whose parallel union Perón had sponsored against an existing communist-led metalworkers' union, Salvo was a Peronist dissident. He had opposed the dissolution of the Partido Laborista in 1946, and had objected a year later when Luis Gay was expelled as CGT secretary-general. During the early years of Salvo's leadership, the UOM had called several important strikes, one of which is reported to have involved Argentina's first case of strikers refusing to leave the workplace.[98] Salvo resigned from the CGT's central committee in 1949, but continued as head of the UOM until challenged by Abdala Baluch, a unionist who favored stricter adherence to Perón's orders. Baluch finally unseated Salvo in the 1952 UOM elections, but not before a battle that left eight dead and thirteen wounded. Salvo received a national deputy seat in compensation, but lost it in 1954 after being expelled from the Partido Peronista.[99]

Abdala Baluch had little time to savor his victory. In 1954, the metals industry recovered from a lengthy recession and began to grow at rates unmatched since the 1943–48 period, when production in the sector had doubled.[100] When a strike broke out during contract negotiations in May and June 1954, Baluch found himself in an uncomfortable position: the wage guidelines in Perón's stabilization plan clashed head-on with rank-and-file demands for a big wage hike. When Baluch decided to accept a 12 to 25 percent wage rise and to agree to the employers' demand that the workers not be paid for the two weeks they had been on strike, UOM members protested by marching on the Government House in downtown Buenos Aires, clashing with police along the way. Forty-eight were injured in the protest and three were killed, including Roberto Ruíz, the assistant secretary-general of the national UOM.

The government blamed the violence on "communist agitators" and arrested dozens of suspects.[101] In fact, however, the protest was motivated neither by communist agitators nor by the Baluch-Salvo dispute (Salvo was whistled down when he attempted to put himself at the head of a column protesting Baluch's settlement). Rather, it was a base-level revolt against a disappointing wage rise and the introduction of incentive schemes.[102] The protest provoked a reshuffling of the union leadership, in the course of which Paulino Niembro, a former collaborator of Salvo's, helped to forge an agreement whereby Augusto Vandor was appointed secretary-general of the federal capital section of the UOM.[103] Prior to 1954, Vandor had been a relatively unknown factory delegate, although his name had appeared in press accounts of the 1951 Baluch-Salvo dispute.[104] By 1957, he would be the most powerful union leader in Argentina.

Other signs of increased worker protest and of an incipient reassertion of union autonomy in the waning years of Perón's presidency come from data on labor disputes and union meetings. The number of participants in strikes, sit-down strikes, slowdowns, and work-to-rule protests all took a sharp jump upward in 1954, and the number of participants in union meetings, after declining from 1946 to 1951, rose steadily between 1952 and 1954.[105] Protest took the form of wildcat strikes and the ouster of incumbent union leaders, rather than expressing itself in an organized campaign to change the government's policy, partly because employers and handpicked union leaders like Espejo and Baluch served as lightning rods for worker frustration with the stabilization plan. Moreover, concerted opposition to government policy would have required coordination by the CGT, which remained under the control of subservient union leaders until the 1955 coup.

Workers' willingness to vote for Perón does not seem to have been reduced by the post-1946 clampdown on strikes or by the imposition of monolithic state control on the CGT. Quantitative analyses of the 1951 presidential election show no appreciable decline in the tendency of residents of working-class districts to vote for Perón.[106] These electoral statistics are, it must be noted, imperfect measures of labor support: if the 1946 elections had been the freest in Argentine history, the 1951 elections were characterized by electoral fraud, flagrant gerrymandering, denial of media access to opposition parties, repression of non-Peronist political gatherings, and jailings of opposition candidates.[107] Union activists also used questionable tactics to mobilize the labor vote, as when delegates were sent to union locals with blank forms on which members were invited to promise, in writing, to vote for Perón.[108] If these electoral irregularities concealed a decline in the scope of Perón's labor support, however, it must have been minimal. Workers continued to pay homage to the presidential couple, and union support played a central part in the campaign leading up to the 1951 election.[109] Nor was worker disaffection manifested in the results of the 1954 vice-presidential and congressional contests. The Peronists won 62.5 percent of the vote in 1954, almost exactly the same proportion they had obtained three years earlier when Perón was reelected for a second six-year term.[110]

This continued labor support may be attributed in part to workers' appreciation of Perón's past achievements and to the absence of a preferable alternative to his government. But if the breadth of labor support for Perón remained unchanged, its intensity probably diminished. UOM leader Cabo viewed the death of Eva Perón, the CGT's transformation into a tool of the government, and the 1952 stabilization plan as factors that contributed to workers' largely apathetic response to the 1955 coup.[111] It is possible that the military officers who launched the coup would not have acted had they felt that worker support for Perón was as enthusiastic as ever, or that the unions were relatively free of internal strife and prepared to resist a coup attempt. Changes between 1952 and 1955 in Perón's relations with labor may in this sense have helped to create conditions propitious for the coup. It is notable that the unions, which had stopped an anti-Perón coup on 17 October 1945, put up little coordinated resistance when the military ousted Perón ten years later.

Changes in Perón's relations with industrialists do not seem to have contributed to the 1955 coup. Industrialists were less closely aligned with Perón than scholars once thought,[112] but there is no evidence that they made a concerted effort to overthrow him. The UIA opposed Perón in the 1946 elections, but Perón closed it down shortly after taking office.[113] The General Economic Confederation (CGE), created by Perón in 1952, made no move to conspire against the government on whose sponsorship it depended.[114] The 1952 austerity measures created hardship in the flour-milling, textiles, and metals industries, but industrialists in these sectors did little more than grumble.[115] Industrialists, unlike workers, can destabilize regimes through individual acts (e.g., of disinvestment), but there is little evidence that they did so: manufacturing output rose at an annual rate of 7 percent from 1953 to 1955.[116] The initial Peronist regime was based on a populist class compromise that remained truly viable only during the boom years of 1945–48.[117] Had Perón responded to the breakdown of the compromise by moving to the left, industrialists might have had more incentives to destabilize his regime. By moving to the right, Perón did more to defuse than to exacerbate this potential opposition.

Export-oriented landowners had even more reason than industrialists to oppose Perón, who made the "oligarchy" a main target of his verbal attacks. In 1946, moreover, Perón began to transfer resources from agricultural exporters to industrialists and urban workers by empowering the Argentine Institute for Trade Promotion (IAPI) to act as the sole agent for foreign sales of beef and grain. Using this monopsony, the IAPI bought these commodities from domestic producers at artificially low prices and sold them at the high prices then prevailing on the world market, using the resulting windfall to subsidize social welfare, public employment, and industry. Moreover, Perón froze tenancy contracts and raised rural labor costs by enforcing the Statute of the Peon, which protected landless agricultural laborers. But partly because Perón never followed through on a promise to carry out land reform, and partly because overt opposition was dangerous, the SRA did not go beyond guarded criticism during the 1946–52 period.[118] Moreover, the 1952 stabilization plan, which gave rural producers price incentives and easier credit, boosted agricultural output by 11 percent per year from 1952 to 1955.[119] It also seems to have improved relations between Perón and the Pampean elite: the SRA leaders paid homage to the late Eva Perón in August 1952, praised Perón's economic policies at the 1954 cattle show, and donated to the Eva Perón social welfare foundation in 1955.[120] Although the SRA leaders welcomed the anti-Peronist Aramburu government (1955–58) and awarded Admiral Isaac Rojas, Aramburu's virulently anti-Peronist vice president, an honorary membership in the organization,[121] they do not seem to have mounted a concerted effort to overthrow Perón.

Apparently, then, concerted opposition from industrialists or landowners played no major role in Perón's overthrow. Moreover, although the economic challenges of the early 1950s eroded the populist class compromise that had muted opposition during the prosperous 1940s, they do not seem to have contributed directly to the 1955 coup. Especially by the standards of post-1955 programs, the 1952 stabilization plan proved to be quite successful: the trade balance turned positive, annual inflation averaged only 7 percent, and GNP growth averaged 5.5 percent between 1953 and 1955.[122] One aspect of Perón's post-1952 economic policies may, however, have moved the country closer to military intervention. One goal of the 1952 stabilization plan was to attract foreign investment, and this reversal in Perón's attitude toward foreign capital may have alienated some of his elite supporters. Military and civilian nationalists who had initially supported the regime reacted with surprise when Perón gave Milton Eisenhower, the U.S.

president's brother, a warm reception during his 1953 trip to Argentina.[123] Later in 1953, congress passed a law removing restrictions on foreign investment, and in ensuing months the U.S. Export-Import Bank loaned Argentina $60 million to build a state-owned steel works. The government invited foreign manufacturers to build auto and tractor plants near Córdoba, and in 1955, in a gesture that infuriated many economic nationalists, it signed petroleum exploration contracts with Standard Oil of California.[124]

For the most part, however, it was noneconomic factors that set the stage for the 1955 coup. Among the most important were signs of government corruption and Perón's retreat from his presidential duties. Even the huge sector of the population that in any country pays little or no attention to politics, thereby constituting an important base of tacit support for whoever happens to be head of state, would have found it hard to avoid stories of government malfeasance, especially after Juan Duarte, Perón's private secretary and Eva Perón's brother, died suddenly during a 1953 investigation into his business activities. Nor were even the politically uninvolved likely to have missed lurid tales of liaisons between Perón and the teenage girls with whom he now shared the Olivos presidential estate, part of which he had turned into an athletic facility for female secondary-school students.[125] But of all the factors that formed the background to Perón's overthrow, perhaps the most important was the government's failure to leave space for political opposition. A similar failure was among the factors that contributed to Yrigoyen's overthrow in 1930.[126] The existing regime left no end in sight for Perón's rule. Opposition activities were restricted by election rigging, arrests of Perón's political opponents, official control of the mass media, and the absorption of legislative power into the executive. Meanwhile, intra-Peronist debate was eliminated in accordance with the principle of verticalism.[127] Procedural democracy and civil liberties were challenged by Perón's doctrine of the organized community, which blurred distinctions between the state, the governing party, and interest groups; conflated the resulting juggernaut with the national interest, and subordinated it to the wishes of the Supreme Chief. In accordance with the organized community principle, education became a vehicle for Peronist indoctrination. Adolescents were "organized" into an officially sponsored Union of Secondary-School Students, and Eva Perón's ghost-written *La razón de mi vida* became obligatory reading in public schools. In seeking to capture the hearts and minds of youth, Peronism was encroaching on the territory of one of the few institutions that had hitherto eluded its control: the Catholic Church.

The Church had initially been friendly to Perón. It had supported his candidacy for the presidency in 1946, partly because the opposing Unión Democrática coalition included the Communists and campaigned to legalize divorce, and in 1951, after Perón ratified a decree establishing religious instruction in public schools. In the early 1950s, however, relations between Perón and the Church began to cool. The religious hierarchy opposed Perón's enfranchisement of women and saw many of its own charity and social welfare functions taken over by the Eva Perón Foundation. After the death of his wife, Perón's reported affair with a fourteen-year-old participant in the Olivos athletic camp further antagonized the Church, as did indications that the government was attempting, through the Union of Secondary-School Students, to replace the Church as molder of the values of Argentine youth. In late 1954, Perón received reports that Catholic priests were trying to make inroads into the unions, contemplating the formation of a Christian Democratic party, and founding youth groups to compete with the officially sponsored student organization. After launching a verbal tirade against the Church, Perón withdrew subsidies for Catholic schools and proposed legislation to legalize divorce and prostitution.[128] According to Hilario Salvo and Juan Carlos Loholaberry, prominent leaders respectively of the metalworkers' and textile workers' unions, many unionists were dismayed by Perón's anticlerical crusade.[129]

In response to Perón's attacks, the Church in June 1955 organized a mass demonstration that drew an estimated 100,000 participants, including many nonbelievers who rallied solely to express their opposition to the government.[130] Alleging that the protesters had burnt an Argentine flag, the government "deported" two native Argentine priests who had helped to organize the march. Two days later, the Vatican excommunicated all who had played a role in expelling the priests, leaving Perón's inclusion ambiguous.[131] These events catalyzed discontent in the armed forces. Although most officers had preoccupied themselves with professional concerns immediately after Perón's election, many had begun around 1949 to question Eva Perón's role in the government and Perón's personalization of power. From this point on, military opposition became an ongoing concern for Perón. Perón's conflict with the Church was especially important in alienating nationalist army officers with strong religious convictions. Such officers had previously been Perón's main backers within the armed forces, although their support had been eroding since 1953 because of the government's invitations to foreign investors, its increasingly arbitrary promotion policy, and its decision to have the army raise its own food and livestock, something many officers considered unfit for a military institution. Most navy officers, who tended to identify with what Perón termed the "oligarchy," had never been friendly to the president, although a few of their number, ideologically isolated from their fellows, held high positions in his government. On several occasions after 1950, navy officers had tried to persuade army officers to help them overthrow Perón, and after Perón's attack on the Catholic Church, they convinced General León Bengoa, a key nationalist army officer, to help them prepare a coup. Bengoa dropped out when the plot was discovered, but the navy decided to act immediately.[132]

On 16 June 1955, navy planes bombed the Government House and adjoining Plaza de Mayo in an unsuccessful effort to assassinate Perón. Bombing and strafing continued all afternoon, killing hundreds of unarmed civilians. Lacking effective army support, the rebels were forced to surrender. That night, Peronist militants roamed throughout Buenos Aires burning churches and assaulting priests.[133] Sobered by the violence of the coup attempt, Perón decided to adopt a more conciliatory posture. "I cease to be the head of a revolution and become the president of all Argentines, friends and adversaries," he declared on 15 July.[134] Underscoring this declaration, Perón permitted opposition parties to make radio broadcasts for the first time since 1946 and reshuffled his cabinet to include figures more acceptable to the Church and opposition political parties. These conciliatory gestures were not enough for UCR leaders and other members of the civilian opposition, who demanded more thoroughgoing reforms and continued their efforts to incite a military uprising.[135] In response to this intransigence, Perón reverted dramatically to confrontation. On 31 August 1955, he resigned from the presidency. The CGT immediately called a mass demonstration to persuade him to rescind his decision, which Perón did, but not before delivering the most incendiary speech of his political career. "The watchword for every Peronist, whether alone or within an organization, is to answer a violent act with another more violent. And whenever one of us falls, five of them will fall," Perón proclaimed, reportedly turning as he said this to look directly at a group of officers seated near him on the podium.[136] A few days later

Hugo Di Pietro, the new CGT secretary-general, offered to put volunteer workers at the disposal of the army.[137] Perón declined, but the offer raised the possibility that he might seek to arm the workers, as the CGT had tried tentatively to do during the navy bombardment on 16 June, and as Eva Perón had long advocated.

On 16 September 1955, the army and navy began an uprising that resulted in Perón's overthrow on 23 September and the inauguration of General Eduardo Lonardi as provisional president of Argentina. The coup began when 4,000 rebellious army troops commanded by Lonardi took over important army garrisons in Córdoba. Within a few days, Lonardi's troops were surrounded by a far larger force of loyalists, but the navy was by then advancing up the coast toward Buenos Aires. On 19 September, the navy commanders announced that if Perón did not resign, they would begin bombing the huge Eva Perón oil refinery in the city of La Plata. Perón, unwilling to carry through on the threat in his "five for one" speech to save his government through civil war, responded to the navy ultimatum with an ambiguous statement that left unclear whether or not he had resigned. The next day, however, he abandoned the presidential palace for a Paraguayan gunboat anchored in the Rio de la Plata, from which he embarked on a long exile through several Latin American countries and finally to Madrid. The next time Perón touched Argentine soil was in 1972, a year before he returned to the presidency.

The Legacy of Peronism

By Latin American standards, Argentina had a large and well-organized trade union movement in 1943. But powerful conservative elites had so constrained government policy during the first half of the twentieth century that a large backlog of unaccomplished social and labor reforms had accumulated by the time Perón began to court labor. Perón recognized the disparity between the strength of the labor movement and the relative backwardness of Argentina's social and labor laws. Aided by favorable economic conditions from 1944 to 1948, he attracted labor support by extending material benefits, supporting unionization, and deepening a sense of dignity among workers. The strength of the labor movement gave Perón a formidable power resource with which to propel himself to the presidency, but it also gave workers and union leaders the capacity to extract real benefits from him—concessions that made the labor movement's emergence as an important political actor all the more dramatic and threatening to elite groups accustomed to a more restricted political arena.

Between 1944 and 1948, the working class made unprecedented gains in wealth, power, and social status. Living standards rose dramatically, and union power was institutionalized. Workers for the first time became identified with the nation, rather than being counterposed to it as their immigrant predecessors had been.[138] Because previous governments, controlled or constrained by the powerful oligarchy, had done so little to advance the quality of life and labor for Argentine workers, the sudden improvements introduced by Perón were etched all the more indelibly into workers' memories. Correspondingly, with Perón's rise to the presidency, the dominant classes for the first time faced real challenges to their share of the national income, to their control of the workplace, and to their influence over the political system. Moreover, the state and its resources were placed at the disposal of a man who thumbed his nose at upper-class notions of morality and publicly ridiculed the idea that Argentina's *gente bien* (well-born) were somehow naturally suited to rule over less refined members of society.

The suddenness, breadth, and depth of Perón's pro-labor reforms won him strong support among the workers and equally strong, although for many years muted, opposition from conservative elites. This strength of feeling both for and against Perón had important implications for Argentina's post-1955 political culture. For Peronists, the 1943–55 period represented the triumph of the common people, ending half a century of oppression by the oligarchy. For anti-Peronists, the period saw the defeat of the country's cultured "democratic" forces by a demagogic leader who built a totalitarian regime on the basis of his appeal to the gullible and uneducated. Invidious distinctions between common people and oligarch, totalitarian and democrat, were superimposed on a more basic cleavage between Argentina's poor and rich. These overlapping cultural, political, and economic antagonisms created a political polarization that persisted long after the 1955 coup.

From the perspective of post-1955 Argentine politics, the 1943–55 Peronist period was significant in part for the way it rearranged society's basic power relations. Perón raised the standing of the working class with respect to elite groups, but he did little to diminish the fundamental power resources of landowners or industrialists. Although the state appropriated a share of the foreign-exchange earnings that would otherwise have gone to the Pampean elite, no major land reform was undertaken during Perón's presidencies. And although industrialists could no longer set wages and working conditions as unilaterally as in the past, Perón protected industries from foreign competition, channeled resources from agriculture to industry, and backtracked in 1954 on union control in the workplace. Labor's share of the national income rose from 41 percent in 1946–48 to 49 percent in 1952–55, but landowners retained and industrialists gained enough economic power that the trend was reversed once state resources came under the control of a less pro-labor government. By increasing the power of the labor movement without really reducing that of its class adversaries, Perón set the stage for the political and economic stalemate in the post-1955 period, in which no social sector was strong enough to impose its own project but each had sufficient power to block the projects of its rivals.[139]

In addition to changing the country's basic power relations, the Peronist period affected Argentina's political culture. Peronists and anti-Peronists alike justified their refusal to recognize the legitimacy of the other side by creating "political myths": embellished recollections of a "golden age" in which the other side was not an effective power contender. The predominantly working-class Peronists exalted the 1945–48 period of full employment, soaring real incomes, advances in unionization, and burgeoning worker pride, overlooking the later years of Perón's rule with their authoritarianism, economic ups and downs, and revelations of Perón's personal weaknesses. Anti-Peronists, by contrast, exalted the pre-1930 period, which they remembered as a prosperous era when the lower classes had known their place. After Perón was forced from office in 1955, these idealized memories generated a peculiarly nostalgic political culture in which Peronists and anti-Peronists alike sought to "restore" situations that had never really existed.[140]

These changes in power relations and political culture increased the intensity of post-1955 conflict among Argentina's major social actors. But equally important in contributing to political turbulence was the Peronist period's institutional legacy, which made the post-1955 political system less able to organize and channel this heightened conflict. An important aspect of this institutional legacy involved Perón's reluctance to create a party better able to withstand the post-1955 anti-Peronist repression. This reluctance stemmed from the fact that a well-institutionalized party was not strictly necessary for Perón to retain political power. When the Partido Peronista was created in 1946, Perón already controlled the presidency and knew he could rely on the unions to mobilize support during future elections. Hence, although the party was useful to Perón in spreading his doctrines and in legitimating his rule, it was not indispensable from the standpoint of winning and retaining political power. Moreover, beyond not needing a stronger and more independent party, Perón hesitated to create one for fear that it would give potential rivals an organizational base from which to challenge his capacity to control his followers. As a result, the Peronist party that existed from 1946 to 1955 was little more than an instrument for reinforcing and legitimating Perón's rule.

The Partido Peronista's weak institutionalization had important implications for the post-1955 structure of the Peronist movement. First, because most of the top party leaders had been chosen by Perón, anti-Peronists who held Perón personally responsible for his movement's allegedly pernicious effects on Argentine society saw few reasons to spare what they viewed as a group of handpicked underlings from the kinds of repressive measures that they directed against Perón himself. Hence, the post-1955 anti-Peronist repression was aimed not only at Perón and the most visible symbols of his government but also at the leaders of the Partido Peronista. Second, because the party leaders were so thoroughly dependent on Perón, the overthrow and exile of the Supreme Chief, by decapitating Peronism's entire political apparatus, created apathy and confusion that made it difficult for the deposed party leaders either to bargain with the anti-Peronist Aramburu government for the organization's survival (as APRA had done after the 1948 coup in Peru) or to forge an effective clandestine organization capable of surviving the anti-Peronist repression (as Acción Democrática had done after the 1948 coup in Venezuela). Making the party officials even less able to weather the conservative reaction was the fact that, as leaders of an organization created by an incumbent president, they had no experience in surviving a hostile political environment or in seeking to win or regain political power. Finally, Perón's low opinion of "politicians" and "politicking," together with his continued references to his followers as constituting a "movement" rather than a party, not only sapped strength from the original Partido Peronista, but also made it difficult for Peronists who sought to create a new Peronist party in the post-1955 period to show that their endeavors did not contradict Peronist doctrine. This absence of doctrinal support, combined with Perón's efforts from exile to preserve his control of the movement by resisting the institutionalization of a free-standing

Peronist party, played a major role in ensuring that there would continue to be a hiatus between workers and party activity.

In short, the labor movement during the 1943–55 period became much more powerful and politicized, and emerged for the first time as a major power contender on the political stage. At the same time, most Argentine workers came to identify with the Peronist movement without becoming integrated into a well-institutionalized Peronist party. Perón's reluctance to create such a party while president, his subsequent opposition to Peronist party-building efforts, and the legal restrictions imposed after 1955 on Peronist political activity all combined to deprive the labor movement of a party vehicle for political influence. Without such a vehicle, workers and union leaders expressed themselves politically through large-scale strikes and demonstrations, which, when used under the precarious civilian governments of the 1955–66 period, helped to create a climate of instability inimical to democratic consolidation. Moreover, Peronist union leaders, lacking a strong stake in the party system, became an attractive target for military officers seeking civilian support for a long-term dictatorship.

Chapter 4

Peronism, Proscription, and the Rise of Augusto Vandor

Argentine politics revolved from 1955 to 1966 around a con- flict between Peronism and anti-Peronism. On one side, at least one-third of the electorate, including most urban workers, main- tained allegiance to Peronism. On the other side, powerful civilian and military elites stood firmly against Perón's return to political life and, more broadly, against the installation of any government resem- bling Perón's. Internal struggles were nonetheless crucial in shaping the political strategies of each side. In the anti-Peronist camp, the split in the Unión Cívica Radical in 1957, as well as conflict between hard-line and soft-line military anti-Peronists, changed the dynamics of party politics and affected the stability of the political regime. Simi- larly, internal Peronist conflict helps to explain phenomena that, from the standpoint of "Peronism vs. anti-Peronism," seem paradoxical, like Perón's efforts to thwart his followers' return to electoral competi- tion under rules devised by anti-Peronists but eventually accepted by many Peronist leaders in Argentina.

Peronism Responds to Proscription

From 1955 to 1958, Argentina experienced military rule. The first military president, General Eduardo Lonardi, criticized Perón's leader- ship but left the CGT in Peronist hands, allowed the Partido Peronista to reorganize itself under new leaders, and preserved Perón's social and labor legislation.[1] Two months later, in November 1955, General Pedro Aramburu, a hard-line anti-Peronist, ousted Lonardi and took a far more radical course. Aramburu's government purged the armed forces of suspected Peronist sympathizers; prohibited the use of Peron- ist slogans and symbols; outlawed the Partido Peronista; took over the

CGT; arrested or barred from union office thousands of Peronist labor leaders; and let non-Peronist unionists seize union locals by force. Moreover, in March 1956, the government decreed that no one who had held an elective or high appointive post at the national, provincial, or municipal level between June 1946 and September 1955, or had served as an official of the Partido Peronista, would be eligible to run for elective office.[2] A few months later, the government set the stage for a more institutionalized ban on Peronism by decreeing a new Statute of Political Parties. This decree gave formal recognition to all previously existing "democratic" parties, leaving the judiciary (advised by a government-appointed "Committee for the Defense of Democracy") to decide which ones met this condition. The decree also stipulated that no party could use a personal name or designation (such as "Peronista") and that no parties could receive support from foreign organizations.[3] Backing this legislation was an implicit veto by the military, with a degree of civilian support that varied partly according to the changing strategic calculations of non-Peronist parties, on the right of Perón, and of Peronists regarded merely as his mouthpieces, to contest or assume the presidency or the governorships of major provinces. The proscription of Peronism thus involved the formal dissolution of the Partido Peronista; the decree forbidding former Peronist officials to run for elective office; the 1956 Statute of Political Parties, which contained provisions that made it illegal for Perón or his immediate collaborators to form a new party controlled by the exiled leader; and the implicit military veto that put teeth into all of this legislation.

Perón responded to these measures by urging his followers to engage in sabotage and to try to mount a "revolutionary coup" against the regime.[4] In June 1956, pro-Peronist military officers led by recently retired General Juan José Valle attempted a coup. The government found out about the conspiracy beforehand, declared martial law, and executed without trial 27 persons accused of participating in the attempt.[5] This harsh reaction intensified the antagonism between Peronists and anti-Peronists and extinguished all hope of military backing for Perón's return. At this point, the focus of opposition shifted to the unions.

Aramburu and his allies based their labor policies on the assumption that workers had been tricked or coerced into supporting Perón. They felt that workers, freed of their "authoritarian" Peronist leaders, would switch their allegiance to non-Peronist parties and adopt a bread-and-butter unionism concerned exclusively with wages and working conditions. This assumption proved to be wrong: few workers were prepared to abandon a leader who had done more for them than anyone else in Argentine history. Instead, Peronist workers and union leaders launched the Resistance, a prolonged campaign of strikes, sabotage, and bombings aimed at securing immediate economic gains and at creating a climate of social ferment that would force the government to let Perón return. By attacking the symbols and institutions in which the Peronist identity was embedded, Aramburu and his allies generated a climate of siege and struggle that reinforced this identity and strengthened the union factory commissions that led the Resistance.[6]

By issuing anti-Peronist propaganda and skewing the rules for internal elections, the government tried to bring the unions under non-Peronist control, but here again it failed. When union elections were held in 1956 and 1957, Peronists won in most of the industrial unions. Non-Peronists took the national secretariats of many transport and service-sector unions, but Peronists kept control of many locals, and by 1960, they had regained control of the state workers' and telephone workers' unions. The government's decision to ban old-line Peronist union leaders backfired: discredited by their passivity during Perón's waning years in power, many veteran unionists found themselves displaced by better-respected Peronist successors.[7] The transition to a "new generation" of Peronist union leaders was less than complete, however. An August 1956 decree reportedly rehabilitated thousands of banned unionists,[8] and each of the four main post-1955 Peronist union leaders—Augusto Vandor (metalworkers), Andrés Framini (textile workers), José Alonso (garment workers), and Amado Olmos (private hospital workers)—rose to prominence while Perón was still president.

Of the four key post-1955 unionists, Vandor was by far the most important. Born in 1923 in Bovril, Entre Rios, to a family that operated a small fruit orchard, Vandor received a sixth-grade education before moving to the Once district in the federal capital. In 1950, after a six-year stint in the navy, Vandor used the classifieds to find work as a machinist in a federal capital factory belonging to the Dutch-owned Philips corporation, where he began his union career as a factory delegate. In 1954, Vandor became secretary-general of the federal capital branch of the Unión Obrera Metalúrgica (UOM) as the indirect result of a rank-and-file revolt against a UOM leader who backed Perón's efforts to cap wages and weaken the union factory commissions. After

the 1955 coup, Vandor took an active part in the resistance, helping to organize a major strike in the Philips factory in January 1956
and spending several months in prison.[9] In mid 1957, he was elected
secretary-general of the national UOM, joined in subaltern posts by
Lorenzo Miguel, Jose Rucci, Paulino Niembro, Rosendo García, and
Armando Cabo. Within this cohort Vandor, Niembro, and Cabo had
held high union office before 1955.[10]

The other three main post-1955 unionists were even better known
than Vandor while Perón was president. Andrés Framini, Vandor's
main antagonist in the early 1960s, was a prominent figure in the
textile workers' union (AOT) as early as the late 1940s, and was
elected its secretary-general in 1953.[11] José Alonso, CGT secretary-
general from 1963 to 1966, helped to found the garment workers' federation (FONIVA) in 1943 and became its secretary-general in 1949.
During Perón's presidency, Alonso served on the CGT's central confederal committee, on the Argentine delegation to the annual meeting
of the International Labor Organization in Geneva, and on the editorial boards of the newspapers *La Prensa* and *El Líder*. Elected to
the chamber of deputies in 1951, Alonso helped to draft major laws
involving collective bargaining and social security.[12] Amado Olmos
was a founder and early secretary-general of the national-level health
workers' federation, and was elected to the chamber of deputies in
1954.[13]

The post-1955 Peronist union leaders faced conflicting imperatives.
Keeping the support of the rank and file meant, on the one hand, delivering economic gains and, on the other, obeying Perón's orders, which
many workers viewed as sacrosanct. Union leaders who thought that
the best way to win economic gains was to negotiate, using strikes primarily as an instrument of economic pressure, faced a dilemma when
Perón urged all-out struggle to create the conditions for his return to
Argentina. This dilemma was particularly acute for Vandor and for
other leaders of unions whose size or strategic position made negotiation a particularly attractive strategy. It was generally leaders of
large and strategically positioned unions like the metalworkers, meat
packers, oil workers, and bus drivers who opted to negotiate with governments against which Perón had declared all-out war, and who were
quickest to diverge from Perón in developing their own views about
the role that Peronist unionism should play in Argentine society.

As part of its program of "normalizing" the unions, the Aramburu government convened a congress in May 1957 to replace the

CGT's military trustees with an elected secretariat. In the hope that non-Peronists would gain control of the confederation, the government approved exaggerated membership figures submitted by non-Peronist unions. When the Peronists questioned their credentials, the non-Peronists walked out and formed a group called the "32 Organizations of the Democratic Majority." The Peronists, along with some leftist union leaders who remained at the congress, formed a rival group called the "62 Organizations," which counted Augusto Vandor and Amado Olmos among its initial leaders. After the leftists broke away from the "62" in December 1957, the group began to call itself the "political arm of Peronist unionism." The "62" subsequently served as the chief policy-making body for Peronist unions and as an important point of contact between Peronist union leaders, politicians, and Perón.[14] As the "32" and "62" began to operate informally, the CGT went back under government trusteeship, where it remained until it was returned to a group of 20 union leaders in 1961.

Labor support for Perón had come primarily from the bottom up. The Partido Peronista, by contrast, had been created from the top down. This difference helps explain why the Aramburu government, which largely failed in its efforts to eradicate Peronist influence in the unions, was able to outlaw the Partido Peronista with relative ease. By banning the Partido Peronista and prohibiting the formation of new parties under Perón's direct control, the Aramburu government paved the way for the rise of neo-Peronist parties. These parties gave broad approval to Perón's doctrine and policies but did not put themselves under the former president's guidance or supervision, enabling them to conform to the 1956 Political Party Statute. The Aramburu government tolerated the neo-Peronist parties partly because it hoped that they would help to fragment the Peronist vote. The Unión Popular, founded by Juan Bramuglia in December 1955, was destined to become the most important and durable of the neo-Peronist parties. It was initially among the most orthodox: whereas several neo-Peronist parties competed in the elections for the 1957 constituent assembly, the Unión Popular seconded Perón's instructions to cast blank ballots.[15] In the early 1960s, however, the Unión Popular became the main vehicle for Vandor's challenge to Perón.

In addition to fostering neo-Peronist parties, the restrictions on Peronist electoral participation divided Argentina's main non-Peronist party, the Unión Cívica Radical. On one side were UCR leaders like Arturo Frondizi, who began to court the Peronist vote as soon as Perón went into exile. Frondizi favored preserving Perón's social and labor laws and denounced the Aramburu government as "anti-popular." On the other side were explicitly anti-Peronist Radicals like Ricardo Balbín, who wanted to repeal some of Perón's legislation, and who supported most of Aramburu's efforts to de-Peronize Argentine society.[16] In February 1957, the UCR split. The Frondizi faction called itself the Unión Cívica Radical Intransigente (UCRI), while the strongly anti-Peronist Balbín faction adopted the name Unión Cívica Radical del Pueblo (UCRP).

Frondizi soon concluded that he would need Perón's endorsement in order to win the presidency. To get it, he reportedly agreed in January 1958 to drop legal charges against the former president, to legalize the Partido Peronista, to adopt policies similar to those Perón had enacted, and to call new elections within two years.[17] The pact with Frondizi was Perón's first important effort to thwart the routinization of Peronism. Many Peronist political and union leaders had come by 1958 to favor contesting elections through neo-Peronist parties.[18] Perón seemed at first to support this change in strategy, but on February 10, 1958, barely two weeks before the elections, he dispatched the oil workers' leader Adolfo Cavalli to Buenos Aires with an order to vote for Frondizi.[19]

Perón's decision to back Frondizi seems to have been motivated primarily by his desire to minimize the gains of the neo-Peronist parties.[20] Perón had three options in the 1958 elections: he could have directed his followers to participate through neo-Peronist parties, ordered them to cast blank ballots, or instructed them to vote for Frondizi. Participation through the neo-Peronist parties raised the specter of giving irreversible momentum to a "Peronism without Perón," whereas a blank balloting order might well have been disobeyed by Peronists who recognized that a vote for Frondizi was a vote against Ricardo Balbín, a candidate closely identified with, and supported by, Aramburu's military government.[21] Supporting Frondizi exposed Perón to the danger that the UCRI leader, once president, might be able to use state resources to win the workers' allegiance, but perhaps Perón foresaw that the military would never allow Frondizi to enact the kinds of policies that could sway Perón's supporters permanently toward the UCRI camp. Whatever his reasoning, Perón's decision to back Frondizi seems to have been the option most consistent with preserving his influence over his followers.

Although many Peronist union leaders were reluctant to support

Frondizi, they had some good reasons to do so, including the UCRI candidate's sympathetic attitude toward Perón's labor legislation, his stated commitment to normalizing the CGT, and his generally support-ive stance toward Peronist union leaders in their rivalries with the self-proclaimed "democratic" unionists.[22] In the end, the election results showed that most Peronists had followed Perón's instructions. The UCRI obtained 45 percent of the vote, more than twice its share in the 1957 constituent assembly elections. The UCRP won only 29 percent. Blank ballots, cast mostly by Peronists, accounted for 9 percent, while ten neo-Peronist parties won a combined total of less than 3 percent.

The Frondizi government spent its first three months on a honey-moon with the Peronists. It enacted wage increases, legalized Peron-ist symbols, and repealed the ban on Peronist politicians and labor leaders. Perhaps most important, it restored the main provisions of Perón's Law of Professional Associations, which provided for a cen-tralized, hierarchical, and well-financed trade union movement. On 30 December 1958, however, beset by a foreign-exchange crisis, Fron-dizi enacted a tough economic austerity plan and announced the priva-tization of a meat-packing plant. The meat packers occupied the plant, and the leaders of the "62" called a general strike in sympathy, but the government crushed both strikes and arrested many union leaders. These events and the ensuing recession initiated, as Daniel James has argued, a period of profound change in Peronist unionism. Workers lost virtually all of the major strikes of 1959, and by 1960, many union activists had become demoralized by economic adversity and government repression. Strike activity tailed off dramatically, and the metalworkers, textile workers, and other big industrial unions were forced into give-backs involving control of the workplace and work process. These give-backs, combined with the arrest and blacklisting of base-level militants, weakened the union factory commissions and paved the way for the consolidation of monolithic union leadership structures.[23] The reinstituted Law of Professional Associations, which allowed the national-level unions to regain the institutional recogni-tion and financial security they had enjoyed during the Perón years, also helped shift power from the factory commissions to the national union secretariats.

In addition to consolidating power in their own organizations, the national-level Peronist union leaders expanded their influence at the expense of non-Peronist unionists. By 1960, even the main unions still outside the "62"—the retail clerks, locomotive drivers, railway workers, light and power workers, and construction workers—were cooperating informally with the Peronist leaders.[24] One development, however, bucked the trend toward internal hierarchy and political homogenization: the emergence of factions within the "62" itself. In later years, as hope for Perón's return dimmed and as Peronist union leaders began to exert more influence over the neo-Peronist parties, factional conflict stemmed increasingly from a struggle between those who favored and those who opposed the movement's routinization. But while Frondizi was in office, the main issue dividing the Peronist union leaders was whether to cooperate with the government.

At one end of the Peronist union leadership during the Frondizi government were the hard-liners (*duros*), who favored creating a climate of ungovernability that would force the military and the government to permit Perón's return. The hard-liners came mainly from smaller unions with little bargaining power vis-à-vis employers or the state. Despite Peronism's traditional anticommunism, the hard-liners endorsed a program calling for the "expropriation of the landowning oligarchy" and "establishment of workers' control over production."[25] Amado Olmos of the hospital workers, Roberto García of the leather workers, Jorge DiPasquale of the pharmaceutical workers, and Ricardo de Luca of the naval engineers were among the main left-leaning hard-liners. Andrés Framini of the textile workers was another important hard-liner, but his association with this faction derived more from personal loyalty to Perón, who supported the hard-liners in their struggle against the more conciliatory (and stronger) currents of the Peronist union leadership, than from any commitment to goals such as expropriating land or nationalizing industry.[26]

At the other end of the factional spectrum were the integrationists, Peronist unionists willing to accept Frondizi's invitation to "integrate" their organizations into a new state-sponsored political movement. Unionists like Manuel Carulias of the bus drivers, Eleuterio Cardoso of the meat packers, and Pedro Gomis of the state petroleum workers were inclined to cooperate with Frondizi partly because they wanted to avoid the fate of the unions that had been put under trusteeship and partly because they felt that Frondizi's "developmentalist" economic program, which stressed heavy industry and foreign investment, harked back to the types of policies Perón had advocated toward the end of his own presidency.[27] Because the integrationist faction was tied so closely to Frondizi's project, it did not survive the 1962 coup that deposed him.

The third and most important group of Peronist union leaders was called the "Vandorist" current after its main representative, Augusto Vandor of the metalworkers' union. Vandorist unions in the early 1960s included the metalworkers, hotel and restaurant workers, food workers, garment workers, and glass workers. Insofar as they had an identifiable social and economic program, the Vandorists advocated a nationalist version of capitalist development with more immediate advantages for organized workers than the one Frondizi was proposing. Adopting the slogan "Golpe y negociar" ("Punch and bargain"), the Vandorists criticized the integrationists for refusing to "punch"— that is, for selling out to employers and the government in exchange for privileges for their unions. On the other side, the Vandorists accused the left-leaning hard-liners of betraying Peronism's traditional anticommunism. While criticizing the other factions, the Vandorists worked closely with each, using the integrationists to gain access to state policy makers and working closely with hard-liners on the executive board of the "62." By emphasizing their differences with the left-leaning hard-liners, the Vandorists sought to portray themselves to the government and the armed forces as a barrier against communism. At the same time, the Vandorists employed large and well-organized strikes to give them a combative image, drawing on the traditions of the Resistance to attract to their side unionists who preferred a more confrontational posture. Their ability to work with both the integrationists and the hard-liners, their close contacts with non-Peronist or "non-aligned" leaders of unions like the retail clerks, light and power workers, railway workers, and paper workers, and their self-portrayal to the armed forces as a "barrier against communism" allowed the Vandorists to occupy a strategic place at the center of the labor movement from which they could organize and coordinate strategy for unionism as a whole.[28]

In the context of the rivalries in Peronist unionism, the weakness of the hard-liners vis-à-vis the Vandorists helped them gain Perón's backing. To prevent a challenge to his leadership, Perón supported the hard-liners against the more conciliatory but more powerful Vandorist current. Perón's views about the type of social change appropriate for Argentina were closer to those of the Vandorists than to those of the hard-liners, but this ideological divergence was overshadowed by his preference for groups and individuals whose status depended heavily on his continued personal backing. The hard-liners constituted such a group, and from 1962 onward Perón began to play them off against the Vandorists, especially after Vandor began to make inroads into the neo-Peronist Unión Popular party. Beginning with his decision to support Frondizi, Perón always fashioned his electoral strategy with an eye toward undermining his strongest potential rivals.

The conflict between Perón and Vandor became more explicit as the 1962 gubernatorial and legislative elections approached. A coalition of neo-Peronist parties was planning to contest the elections, opening the way for Vandor, with his extensive organization, skill at backroom bargaining, and capacity to mobilize thousands of workers on a few hours' notice, to extend his influence over the political wing of Peronism. As the elections drew near, the Vandorists agreed to lend their powerful vote-getting apparatus to the neo-Peronist Unión Popular in exchange for the party's key nominations in the federal capital and the province of Buenos Aires. The prospect of a good showing by a Vandorist-dominated Unión Popular put Perón in a tough position. If the elections allowed Vandor to display his candidacy-dispensing and vote-mobilizing abilities, Perón might well begin a one-way journey toward becoming a symbolic figurehead. Blank balloting, on the other hand, would deprive Vandor of a golden opportunity to increase his power and prestige.

Given this constellation of interests, it is not surprising that, with the election still a few months off, Vandor and his allies in the "62" began to hear rumors that Perón was considering ordering his followers to cast blank ballots.[29] Taking a delegation of "62" leaders with him, Vandor traveled to Madrid to try to persuade Perón to endorse the Unión Popular, and returned with the impression that the general had endorsed the neo-Peronist strategy.[30] Subsequent events suggested, however, that Perón was not fully committed to this course of action. In January 1962, he proposed that Andrés Framini, the hardline, unswervingly loyal leader of the textile workers' union, be the Unión Popular's candidate for governor of the key province of Buenos Aires—and nominated himself as the candidate for vice-governor.[31] Because it was common knowledge that the military would never tolerate Perón's candidacy, his decision to run for vice-governor of Buenos Aires may well have been an attempt to provoke the proscription of all Unión Popular candidates.[32] If so, the tactic failed. The military vetoed Perón's candidacy, but allowed the other Unión Popular nominees to continue their campaign.

With the obstacle of Perón's candidacy out of the way, the "62" took control of the candidate-selection process. Setting aside the custom that gave each branch of the movement (union, men's, and women's) the right to nominate one-third of the Peronist candidates, the unionists demanded fully half the Unión Popular's nominations for elective posts in the key provinces of Buenos Aires and Córdoba.[33] In Buenos Aires, for every six candidates nominated by the "62," it was "agreed" that Perón would select two and that one each would go to the women's branch, Unión Popular, Partido Laborista (another neo-Peronist party), and Partido Justicialista (an "orthodox" Peronist party that had operated fitfully since 1959, when its application for legal status had been denied).[34] In the capital, the first five slots on the Unión Popular's list of national deputy candidates were filled by unionists, with the top one occupied by Paulino Niembro, the head of the federal capital metalworkers' union and a close ally of Vandor's.[35] The Unión Popular ran an active campaign in the province of Buenos Aires, financed and run primarily by the unions and above all by Vandor's UOM.[36] The campaign was successful—too successful, it turned out. The Unión Popular won the governorship of Buenos Aires with 37 percent of the vote to 23 percent for its nearest rival, the UCRI. In the final tally nationwide, the Unión Popular polled 17 percent of the vote, and the rest of the neo-Peronist parties grouped in the Frente Justicialista obtained a total of 15 percent. This combined 32 percent of the national vote substantially exceeded the UCRI's 25 percent and the UCRP's 20 percent. The Peronist candidates-elect were never allowed to take office, however. On 28 March 1962, Frondizi was ousted in a military coup triggered by the Peronists' electoral success.

Because Frondizi's vice president had resigned in 1959 and had never been replaced, the presidency passed to José María Guido, president of the senate. The military, however, was the real power behind Guido's eighteen-month presidency. It was obvious that the armed forces would brook no compromise with Perón himself, so Peronists who valued access to the state began to distance themselves from the exiled leader. Marking a new stage in the routinization of Peronism, formerly "orthodox" Peronist politicians like Oscar Albrieu and Alejandro Leloir began to create new neo-Peronist parties, and veteran neo-Peronists strengthened their parties in Jujuy, Mendoza, Neuquén, Salta, and other interior provinces.[37] Vandor joined the Peronist politicians in projecting a moderate image for himself and his followers, arranging meetings with Church officials, leaders of non-Peronist political parties, and even the U.S. ambassador.[38]

Not all sectors of Peronism moved away from Perón or tried to portray themselves as moderates. The textile workers' leader Andrés Framini, increasingly overshadowed by Vandor, fell back on his close association with Perón as his main power resource. Perón and Framini enjoyed a symbiotic relationship: Perón helped Framini keep a power base in the unions, while Framini helped Perón fend off pressure for routinization coming from Vandor and the neo-Peronist politicians. As Framini himself put it,

I was a sort of antibody that Perón created when he wanted to prevent some-one from flying too high: I was the antibody to Vandorism. I represented the masses, the workers; I had a lot of support from the working people, but to Perón I could offer nothing—he already had the masses. My job was to guard Perón at the leadership level, above all from the union leaders and from the big unions, which supported Vandor. I had to make sure they did not get away from [Perón].[39]

Far from portraying Peronism as less obedient to Perón and more moderate than in the past, Framini kept up a stream of attacks on the government, made well-publicized visits to Madrid to consult with Perón, and raised fears in conservative sectors that Peronism was taking a "turn to the left." In July 1962, Framini and Olmos organized a "62" plenary session in Huerta Grande, Córdoba, that adopted a program calling for radical social changes like worker control over production, the nationalization of basic industries, and the expropriation without compensation of the landed oligarchy.[40] By Framini's own account, it was Perón who ordered the "turn to the left" expressed in the Huerta Grande program.[41] Because the program's goals were far to the left of anything Perón had previously advocated, it seems reasonable to accept Alejandro Lamadrid's conclusion that the "turn to the left" was more an effort by Perón to thwart the growing autonomy of Vandor than an expression of any real commitment by Perón to lead Argentina into socialism.[42] Once again Perón's tolerance, and even encouragement, of the left within his movement served to counter the strength of potentially more autonomous sectors whose growing prominence threatened to make him a symbolic figurehead.

In March 1963, the courts rewarded the neo-Peronists and Van-dorists for their moderation and ruled that the Unión Popular could participate in the July 1963 elections. This time the neo-Peronist party arranged to be part of a coalition, the Frente Nacional y Popular, with the UCRI and several smaller parties. The conciliatory posture taken by Vandor and the neo-Peronists facilitated the decision to permit the Unión Popular to run, but equally important was the position taken by key figures in a faction of the army known as the *legalistas*. Many *legalistas* hoped that the neo-Peronist parties would provide the key to coaxing Perón's followers back into the political system while eroding Perón's personal influence and, in the words of Lt. Gen. Benjamín Rattenbach, "preventing a large part of *justicialismo* from turning to the left, toward communism."[43] In the wake of the Cuban revolution, the latter consideration had become particularly acute. Rattenbach further emphasized that "the Army made a distinction between Peronismo, a group of men addicted to Perón, and Justicialismo—a body of ideas held by men for whom the army had great affection, and who should participate in Argentine political life."[44]

Perón was not so easily pushed aside. In May 1963, he announced that he would support Vicente Solano Lima, head of the tiny Partido Conservador Popular, as the presidential candidate of the Frente Nacional y Popular. It was widely believed that Perón had picked Solano Lima because, if elected, the minor party leader would be entirely beholden to him.[45] The "62" were reluctant to support Solano Lima, a conservative business leader devoid of links to labor and identified with the electoral fraud and proscription of the 1930s.[46] But without a better alternative, and with Perón having already publicized his preference, the "62" sent 300 delegates to the interior provinces to drum up support for Solano Lima.[47] Their efforts were in vain. Solano Lima had announced that, if elected, he would permit Perón to return to Argentina, and just two weeks before the election, his candidacy was disallowed. Perón, the "62," and leaders of the Unión Popular called for blank ballots, enabling Arturo Illia of the UCRP to win the presidency with a scant 25 percent of the vote.[48] Blank ballots accounted for 19 percent, and the UCRI, whose majority faction had exited the FNP coalition after Solano Lima's nomination, won 16 percent. No other party got more than 5 percent. Contradicting Perón's orders, several neo-Peronist parties (but not the banned Unión Popular) participated in the elections, taking more than 3 percent of the presidential elector vote and an unprecedented 7 percent of the national deputy vote.

The return to civilian rule in 1958 thus marked the beginning of a process of routinization in Peronism. Neo-Peronist political machines sank roots in interior provinces, Vandor gained momentum in the unions, and the chances of Perón's return came to seem increasingly remote. By the time Illia assumed the presidency, these developments had begun to remove the rationale for the electoral restrictions on

Peronism. The emergence of neo-Peronist parties influenced by anti-communist union leaders who paid only lip service to Perón dovetailed nicely with the anti-Peronists' main concerns: to keep Perón out of Argentine politics; to keep the unions from turning to the left; and to preserve the military's cohesion by reducing tensions between hard-line and soft-line anti-Peronists. Ultimately, Peronism's routinization was thwarted not by anti-Peronists but by Perón and Peronist union and political leaders jealous of Vandor's rise.

Augusto Vandor and the Power Structure of Argentine Unionism

A power broker is someone whose consent is indispensable to the successful mobilization of a constituency. In the early 1960s, Augusto Vandor, the secretary-general of the metalworkers' union (UOM), be-came power broker for Argentina's unions. He also began to challenge Perón for the right to act as power broker for the Peronist vote. This section argues that Vandor become power broker for the unions by achieving and maintaining control of three organizations: the UOM, the "62 Organizations," and the CGT. It also contends that by con-trolling these organizations, whose resources greatly exceeded those of the scattered cohorts of Peronist politicians, Vandor found himself uniquely positioned to challenge Perón for control of the Peronist vote.

Vandor maintained control of the UOM in part by leading it compe-tently. Under Vandor's leadership, the UOM performed fairly well on bread-and-butter issues like wages, working conditions, and job secu-rity. In 1964, workers in the industrial sectors organized by the UOM earned an average hourly wage of 94 pesos (about $2.50 in 1995 U.S. dollars). One could compare this average hourly wage to that of the chemical workers (117 pesos per hour) or garment workers (58 pesos per hour), but such nominal wage comparisons would reveal little about whether Vandor "deserved" support on the basis of his union's wage performance. Such "desert," let us stipulate, is a function of a "union wage effect"—the "extra" wages that a union's members re-ceive exclusively because of its leaders' mobilizational and bargaining skills. To approximate this effect, it is necessary to correct statisti-cally for the influence of such extra-union determinants of wages as labor productivity, metropolitan location, male/female balance, and average workplace size in the industrial sectors a union organizes. Taking the universe of 39 industrial unions reporting 1,000 or more members to the CGT in 1966, ordinary least squares multiple regression was used to remove the wage effect of the four abovementioned nonunion variables. Taking into account the joint effect of these variables, metalworkers, who earned an average of 94 pesos per hour in 1964, were paid about 3.5 pesos per hour more than they "should have been" paid under the assumption that the only factors influencing wages were the four variables included in the regression. This 3.5 peso figure reflects various influences, but it is probably not misleading as a measure of the ability of its leaders to boost wages above the levels predicted by the variables included in the regression. Among six industrial unions reporting more than 25,000 members to the CGT in 1966 (metalworkers, textile workers, meat packers, garment workers, state oil workers, and wood workers), only the metalworkers earned an hourly wage above that predicted by the four "nonunion" variables. Hence, taking into account the structural characteristics of the industry, the UOM under Vandor "delivered" wages better than comparable unions.[49]

The UOM may have been more successful at boosting wages than at improving working conditions. In many of the large factories organized by the UOM, working conditions were harsh. At La Cantábrica, a steelworks employing 4,800 in the Buenos Aires suburb of Morón, few days passed in the late 1950s without a serious accident. La Cantábrica workers who purified scrap iron labored in rat-infested areas on slippery floors amid clouds of dust and iron oxide. In the section where steel was laminated, slag was chipped from the inner walls of the furnaces by one worker shouldering an iron bar several feet in length and holding it against the residue while another pounded from behind with a heavy sledgehammer—which sometimes missed its mark. The vehicle-storage and power-generation area lacked adequate ventilation: workers inhaled exhaust and paint fumes and were regularly exposed to noxious gases emitted by electrical transformers.[50] In 1958, La Cantábrica factory delegates made some progress in ameliorating the worst of these conditions, but in 1959, amid a sudden severe recession, the UOM lost a 53-day nationwide strike. When the new collective contract was signed, the union was forced to give ground on workplace control, production speeds, and grievance procedures. Because of these givebacks, it is unlikely that working conditions in the early 1960s improved much in UOM-organized factories. However, a probable degeneration of already-poor working conditions in the early 1960s was not unique to the UOM. The metalworkers' concessions in

1959–60 were no greater than those made by the textile workers and seem to have been considerably less severe than those made by the meat packers.[51]

The early 1960s were also a time when many metalworkers were unemployed. According to figures compiled by the National Development Council, employment in the metalworking sector dropped from 309,000 in 1959 to 252,000 in 1962, and by July 1963, the unemployment rate in the metals industry had reached 18 percent. But like difficult working conditions, high levels of unemployment during the 1962–63 recession were not unique to the UOM. The July 1963 unemployment rate for metalworkers was below that for wood workers (40 percent), textile workers (26 percent), construction workers (25 percent), and rubber workers (23 percent).[52] In terms of wages, working conditions, and job security, then, Vandor delivered the goods at least as well as the leaders of other major industrial unions. Not all UOM members were in a position to compare their fortunes explicitly to those of workers in other unions, but the evidence suggests that Vandor, of all leaders of major industrial unions, was in the best position to *claim* support for his organization's performance on the issues of greatest material concern to his constituents.

Not all of Vandor's personal qualities marked him as a successful union leader. An infrequent public speaker, he did not inspire great devotion among workers outside the UOM.[53] A public opinion survey indicated that in the closing months of 1965, at the peak of Vandor's influence, only 4 percent of Peronists chose Vandor as a Peronist leader whom they "particularly admired." This proportion was inferior even to the 7 percent who named Andrés Framini, whom Vandor had easily defeated at the leadership level in the "62 Organizations" and the Justicialist Party, and well below the 26 percent who named Raúl Matera, whose decision to run for president in 1963 without Perón's permission had gotten him expelled from the Peronist movement.[54] On the other hand, Vandor had legendary skill at backroom alliance-building, arm-twisting, and negotiation. Even Framini, who was often at odds with Vandor, described the metalworkers' chief as "the most clear-headed backroom union leader I have ever known."[55] Vandor claimed to be a serious student of leadership techniques, once telling a reporter that the only books he read were about great leaders ("I'm not interested in their ideologies but in the mechanics of leadership, whether it be Churchill, Mussolini, Zapata, or Clemenceau"). In his exercise of leadership, Vandor moved very carefully. Even when he knew that he could count on 1,100 of the UOM's 1,200 officeholders to support his positions unquestioningly, he would spend hours discussing strategy with his collaborators before every union meeting.[56]

Vandor's attention to leadership helped maintain an effective chain of command in the UOM, as is evidenced in the response of UOM factory delegates to a 1959 decree revoking automatic union dues withholding. In 1959, Frondizi's economy minister, Alvaro Alsogaray, decreed that union dues, in accordance with the newly revised Law of Professional Associations, henceforth could be withheld only from workers who signed a statement confirming that they desired to be members of the union that represented their branch of economic activity. Vandor telephoned managers in the big industrial plants to ask if they intended to implement the decree. In Avellaneda, an industrial suburb of Buenos Aires, a management representative in one big consumer durables plant responded that the law was the law: he could not do otherwise. Vandor said fine. At 3:00, the factory came to a complete stop. A few minutes later, more than 500 workers had lined up in front of the plant manager's office to sign statements confirming their membership in the UOM. Taken aback, the manager telephoned Rosendo García, the head of the UOM's Avellaneda local, and asked him to request that the workers return to their jobs. García obliged, and he and the manager worked out procedures for distributing the membership confirmation forms, which eventually were signed by virtually every worker in the plant.[57] The UOM's capacity to mobilize on a moment's notice was a source of great pride for Vandor. "If to mobilize a union you need to start acting ten days in advance, it is obvious that there is no union leadership. We can mobilize the 300,000 [metal]workers throughout the country in one hour," Vandor boasted to a reporter.[58]

Although Vandor put himself in a position to claim voluntary support by delivering on bread-and-butter issues and by projecting the image of a strong and competent leader, there was also a strongly coercive side to his leadership. The UOM had dissidents, but they failed to make much headway against Vandor, who used various means to narrow the space for opposition. Vandor and his allies were accused of conniving with employers to secure the firing of dissidents.[59] Moreover, the national UOM leadership had broad powers to expel recalcitrant local leaders and to replace them with their own trustees. Article 9 of the UOM statutes permitted the national leaders to remove any local union official who, in their judgment, had engaged in the "undue use, to the detriment of the organization, of the representa-

tion and faculties granted to him."[60] The UOM's financial system provided the national leadership with another instrument of control over
the locals. The UOM is organized as a single nationwide union rather
than as a federation of local unions. In centralized national unions like
the UOM, employers transfer the union dues and social-service fees
they withhold from workers' paychecks directly into the bank account
of the national union, which then dispenses funds to the locals as its
leaders see fit. In federations like those of the meat packers or light
and power workers, by contrast, dues and social-service fees are paid
directly to the union locals, which then donate a part of their income
to the national organization.[61] Local leaders thus have a wider scope
for dissidence in federations than in centralized national unions.

Characteristics of the UOM's internal elections also helped narrow the space for opposition. A study of 175 union elections between
1957 and 1972 found only two in which an opposition grouping had
defeated an incumbent leadership, and neither was in the UOM.[62] Indirectness was one aspect of UOM elections advantageous to incumbents. Elections took place in three stages: workers elected delegates
to local congresses, who elected delegates to a national congress, who
elected the union's new secretariat and directive commission. This
three-step process facilitated backroom deals at all levels and reduced
the significance of the ordinary worker's vote.[63] By contrast, members
of the textile workers' union—which, like the UOM, is organized as a
single nationwide union rather than as a federation of local unions—
voted directly in their workplaces for lists of candidates seeking as a
bloc to become the union's new directive commission.[64] Besides being
indirect, UOM elections after 1961 were often tainted by ballot-box
stuffing, voting by ineligible workers, collaboration with employers to
dismiss opposition militants, the use of union funds to finance the campaigns of incumbents, and the stacking of electoral oversight commissions by the incumbent leadership.[65] Indirectness and electoral abuses
kept voter participation low. In the UOM's federal capital local, only
26 percent of an estimated 65,000 eligible voters cast ballots in 1961.[66]
Only 27 percent of 58,000 voted in 1965, against a national average
of 49 percent for all union elections; and although turnout rose to 37
percent of 45,000 eligible voters in 1968, this figure was still below the
national average of 45 percent.[67]

No analysis of the ways in which Vandor exercised power in the
UOM would be complete without a discussion of the use of violence
and intimidation. To ensure a smooth flow of proceedings at UOM

assemblies, Vandor and his collaborators organized gangs of street toughs who stifled dissent in exchange for a meal, a few drinks, and a night of camaraderie. In an even more sinister vein, Vandor recruited an "apparatus" of bodyguards and enforcers, including persons on the edge of the law.[68] By the mid 1960s, Vandor was reported to have enjoyed the collaboration of 40 such individuals.[69] One member of the apparatus was Benito Moya, the union's treasury undersecretary. In 1959, Moya fled from a café in the center of Buenos Aires when a bomb he was about to plant in the offices of the SIAM–Di Tella corporation exploded, killing two bystanders.[70] Vandor attempted to distance himself from this incident and similar ones, but communicated with Moya and his collaborators through another important UOM leader, Avelino Fernández.[71] One of the most famous members of the apparatus was Armando Cabo, whose career in the UOM dated back to the 1940s. Cabo was reported to have been involved in Eva Perón's plan to organize workers' militias, and claimed to have played a major role in an unsuccessful effort to organize an armed resistance during the 1955 coup. After Perón's overthrow, Cabo and Moya collaborated in Peronist bomb and sabotage squads.[72] Described by Norberto Imbelloni, one of his close collaborators, as "a man who knew how to shoot very well," Cabo was present in the Avellaneda café where Rosendo García, head of the UOM's Avellaneda local and a long-standing ally of Vandor's, was assassinated in May 1966. According to Rodolfo Walsh, an investigative journalist who "disappeared" in 1977, the police were less than thorough in their investigation of the assassination, which they attributed to left-wing UOM dissidents—two of whom were also killed—sitting across the café from Vandor, García, Cabo, and Imbelloni. Walsh's examination of the physical evidence led him to conclude that García was killed by a bullet fired from Vandor's table. In the months prior to his assassination, García had been mentioned as a potential Peronist vice-gubernatorial candidate in the 1967 elections in Buenos Aires province, and Walsh suggests, but does not confirm, that Vandor was becoming irritated with the increasingly high profile of his former right-hand man.[73]

Once in control of the UOM, Vandor projected his power throughout Peronist unionism by imposing his hegemony on the "62 Organizations." Formed in September 1957, the "62" was an intermittent assembly of "notable" Peronist union leaders that coordinated the activities of Peronist-led unions in the CGT and other fora. The "62" was loosely organized; not until April 1990, 33 years after its birth, did it acquire legal status as a civil entity.[74] As late as the mid 1980s, the "62" owned no buildings, had no budget, published no official newspaper; and had no legal status.[75] It had a set of bylaws, but as one union leader put it, "few know about them and no one respects them." Decisions in the "62" have typically been made by "consensus," to the extent that if a vote is taken, "the decisions are usually disregarded."[76] The "62" in 1986 had a 19-member executive board that presided over occasional plenary sessions involving about 100 unionists from around the country, but lacked established procedures for leadership rotation. Between 1957 and 1995, the "62" had only two leaders, Augusto Vandor (1957–69) and Lorenzo Miguel (1969–95), both secretaries-general of the UOM.

Underlying Vandor's ability to dominate the "62" was the unparalleled capacity of his union, the Unión Obrera Metalurgica, to mobilize large numbers of workers for socially significant collective action. The UOM's mobilizations tended to be socially significant because the union held sway over large numbers of workers, and because many of them were employed in dynamic sectors of the economy, where local interruption of production was likely to have a ripple effect throughout the entire economy.[77] Moreover, it was fairly easy for UOM leaders to mobilize metalworkers. The union organized enough big factories that a dozen phone calls could put tens of thousands of workers into the streets, and the fact that most of these big factories were located in the Buenos Aires and Rosario metropolitan areas minimized the logistical problems of mobilization, facilitated the development of a sense of collective power, and gave the UOM's mobilizations widespread publicity.[78] The UOM workforce, although diverse, was by no means exceptionally heterogeneous, and because most metalworkers were Peronists, ideological affinity between the UOM's leadership and rank and file was closer than for many other unions. The UOM was also highly cohesive at the leadership level. Unlike the leaders of most other large unions, Vandor never faced strong competition from within his own organization; dissident Peronists were no more successful than communist militants at making headway against him.[79] Furthermore, the UOM was among the richest unions in Argentina, not just because of its size, but also because its members' wages were higher than average for industrial unions belonging to the "62." Table 1 compares the power resources of the UOM with those of the four other largest unions in the "62."

To state the underlying proposition more formally, Vandor was able

TABLE 1

The Five Largest Unions in the "62 Organizations," ca. 1965

Union/Industry	Number of members[a]	Workers in industrial sectors organized by union[b]	Workers covered by contracts signed by union[c]	Does union organize a "dynamic" industry?[d]	Does union organize a major export industry?[e]
UOM/Metals	125,700	277,063	275,000	Yes	No
AOT/Textiles	101,000	115,164	140,000	No	No
FGPIC/Meat Packing	55,000	46,850	50,000	No	Yes
ATE/State Workers	101,000	—	—	No	No
UOCRA/Construction	32,200	—	250,000	No	No

Union/Industry	Does permanent rather than seasonal employment prevail in industry?[e]	Was mid-1960s union leadership fairly cohesive?[e]	Average hourly wage in pesos of workers in industry[f]	Percentage of work force in Greater Buenos Aires region[f]	Average number of workers in biggest plants in industry[f]
UOM/Metals	Yes	Yes	94	61	496
AOT/Textiles	Yes	No	72	79	538
FGPIC/Meat Packing	Yes	No	77	33	1,746
ATE/State Workers	Yes	No	—	—	—
UOCRA Construction	No	No	—	—	—

SOURCES: [a]Documentación e Información Laboral, *Nucleamientos sindicales*, number of members reported by union to CGT in 1966 (figures checked by the ministry of labor).

[b]McGuire, "Peronism Without Perón," app. 2, calculated from INDEC, *Censo nacional económico, 1964*.

[c]*Informes Laborales*, various issues, 1963–66.

[d]Coded according to Oficina de Estudios para la Colaboración Económica Internacional, *Argentina económica y financiera*, 180.

[e]Coded according to author's evaluation.

[f]McGuire, "Peronism Without Perón," app. 2, calculated from INDEC, *Censo nacional económico, 1964*.

NOTE: The figure under "average number of workers in biggest plants in industry" represents the *average plant size* in the *industrial sub-sector* in the *geographical region* (city of Buenos Aires, Greater Buenos Aires, or rest of country) that, among all the subsectors within regions organized by the union, had the *largest average plant size*. Because important unions like the metalworkers and textile workers organized thousands of tiny workplaces as well as dozens of huge factories, a simple measure of overall average plant size would understate their capacity for mobilization. In 1964, for example, the UOM metalworkers' union organized industrial subsectors in which the average plant employed only nine workers. The UOM's capacity for socially significant worker mobilization derived, however, from its organization of a few dozen big plants employing hundreds or even thousands of workers each. The figure under "average number of workers in biggest plants in industry" uses available data to approximate the average size of the big plants in each industry.

to dominate the "62" in part because his union, the UOM, was stronger in the mid 1960s on two key dimensions of union power—capacity to mobilize and significance of mobilization—than any of the other four largest unions in the "62": the textile workers (AOT), meat packers (FGPIC), state workers (ATE), or construction workers (UOCRA). The textile workers were employed in comparably large plants (an Alpargatas plant in the federal capital at one time had more than 10,000 workers)[80] and a larger percentage of textile workers than metalworkers were employed in the Greater Buenos Aires region. However, there were twice as many metalworkers as textile workers in Argentina, and the textile industry was a traditional one, whose forward and backward linkages were less important to Argentina's overall economic health than were those of the UOM. The AOT's capacity to compete with the UOM for control of the "62" was further impeded by the union's lower wage levels (and hence more modest financial resources) and especially by struggles among rival factions of union leaders, which were often fierce.[81]

There were only about half as many meat packers as textile workers in Argentina, and although meat-packing plants were larger on average than those in the metal or textile industries, they were not as heavily concentrated in the Buenos Aires area. Meat packing was Argentina's most heavily export-oriented industry. Because meat packers' strikes could deal a severe blow to Argentina's capacity to generate foreign exchange, the FGPIC held a strategic economic and, to some extent, political position.[82] However, the meat-packing industry's insertion into the international market cut both ways in terms of the FGPIC's power. Declining European demand for Argentine beef and fluctuations in international meat prices created ongoing problems of plant closings, suspensions, and dismissals in the industry, all of which reached crisis proportions in 1964.[83] By creating a tenuous employment situation, the crisis in the meat-packing sector reduced the capacity of the FGPIC to mobilize its workers for purposes other than last-ditch defensive job actions like occupations of factories on the verge of closing permanently. The FGPIC was thoroughly Peronist at both the leadership and base levels, but because the union's notables were unusually widely dispersed along the confrontation-negotiation spectrum, struggles among Peronist union leaders for control of the FGPIC tended to be bitter and protracted.[84]

Among the largest nonindustrial unions in the "62" were the state workers' ATE and the construction workers' UOCRA. ATE organized a hodgepodge of sectors, from shipyards and coal mines to public hospitals and government ministries. This internal diversity, coupled with the geographic dispersion of its membership, diminished ATE's capacity for effective collective action. Furthermore, several important ATE leaders, including Alberto Belloni, were non-Peronists.[85] The construction workers' UOCRA also had problems of workplace dispersal. Although it organized some industrial workers (e.g., those who produced portland cement), many of its members were employed temporarily, as reflected in the low ratio of dues-paying UOCRA members to workers covered by the union's collective contracts (Table 1). Although primarily Peronist, UOCRA included a strong communist contingent. Rubens Iscaro and other Communist Party leaders controlled UOCRA from 1955 until 1959, when the union was put under government trusteeship. A Peronist list won the March 1960 "normalizing" election and all subsequent elections during the 1960s, but the Communists insisted that these results were obtained by fraud. Strong communist influence in UOCRA reduced its clout in the "62," as did conflict among different factions of Peronists in the union, which was often heated.[86]

The UOM's unparalleled strength not only gave Vandor primacy in the "62," but also helped him influence the composition of other union leaderships. As a telephone workers' leader put it, "Vandor carried a lot of weight: many leaders of other unions were his creations. When they stood for election in their unions, he provided them with all the logistical support they needed: money, propaganda, cars, posters, and so on. And they won."[87] A leader of the noodle makers' union described a similar scenario.

Beyond the metalworkers' union, Vandor represented, through the "62 Organizations," the real political power of Peronism. . . . Because of the power he wielded, a cloud of incompetents, adventurers, and corruptibles began to circulate around him, enjoying the shadow of that fruitful tree. . . . They buzzed around him, giving him no rest, and I saw a few of them, who would later judge him harshly, imploring him . . . to convert them into leaders. Back then they were his friends, because they were looking for labor ministry inspectors who could be influenced, or because they needed the metalworkers' printing press to issue election material. Or else they wanted Vandor to persuade some rival leader to give way to them.[88]

The strength of the UOM thus helped Vandor control the "62" directly, by giving him financial, organizational, and prestige resources that other "62" unionists could not match, and indirectly, by allowing him in certain cases to determine who those other "62" unionists would be. Reinforcing this structural basis of Vandor's control of the "62" were political and personal factors. On the political side, Vandor's "punch and bargain" strategy placed him squarely between more conciliatory and more combative unionists, putting him in a strategic position to speak for the union movement as a whole.[89] On the personal side, Vandor could rely on his intimidating personality to silence opponents. A "62" plenary session in late 1965 provides a good example of Vandor's ability to intimidate. In late October 1965, Perón sent a letter to his followers in Argentina authorizing Framini to denounce the "bad apples" in the union movement—a thinly veiled reference to Vandor and his followers.[90] Framini planned to read the letter aloud at a "62" plenary session scheduled for 4 November 1965.[91] The textile workers' leader had spent long periods in prison and in the rough-and-tumble of the Peronist resistance, and he was hardly a shrinking violet. Battle-hardened though Framini was, however, Vandor had the more intimidating personality. The meeting took place, but the letter-reading did not.

Vandor, in addition to his [stronger] organization [the UOM], had a stronger personality [than Framini]. He was a tougher guy. I was at the great "62" plenary . . . in the last months of 1965, after the Avellaneda conference. This was when Perón had given instructions in a letter to challenge Vandor's leadership—he said, "Vandor is the most loyal of those who have betrayed me." Alonso and Framini were there. Olmos was with us, in a minority. The top leadership of the "62" met: Framini, Gallo of FOETRA, Alonso, Racchini, Izetta, Santillán of FOTIA, Coria. . . . When they came out, they sat at the table. It was time to read the letter Perón had sent to Framini. Framini and Vandor were there. Vandor said to Framini, "Well, the plenary session is starting. Do you have something to say"? Framini was going to say something, but he remained silent. Next to me was the FOTIA leader Sánchez. He got up, and Vandor said, "What do you want, my friend?" Sánchez sat down without saying any of the things he had told us he was going to say. And on the other side, Loholaberry, the assistant secretary-general of the textile workers, said, "I'd like the floor." Vandor got up and walked over to him, stopping right beside him. "What were you going to say"? "No, no, I don't want to talk." And that was the end of the plenary session.[92]

Controlling the "62" was not the same as controlling the entire labor movement. In the early and mid 1960s, 40 to 50 percent of Argentina's reported union members belonged to labor organizations outside the "62" (Table 2). Yet the Independent group, to which most of the non-"62" unions belonged, was less powerful than these numbers suggest, primarily because of deep-seated differences among and within its constituent unions. Profound differences had also existed among factions of the "62" during the Frondizi period, but after the March 1962 coup, the conciliatory integrationist current had disappeared and the combative hard-liner faction had begun to disintegrate.[93] By October 1963, when Illia became president, the "62" was firmly under the control of Vandor and his allies. Attesting to the cohesiveness of the organization, the representatives from the "62" on the CGT directive council would hammer out their differences in private before arriving at meetings of the confederation's leadership board.[94] The Independents, by contrast, displayed no such cohesiveness. Although they had an informal organization something like the "62," with a secretary-general and a convening board,[95] it was sharply divided between "hard-liners" (militant anti-Peronists) and "soft-liners" (who were more inclined to cooperate with the "62"). Angel Bono, head of the brotherhood of railway engineers (La Fraternidad), and Francisco Pérez Leirós, the leader of the federal capital municipal workers, were prominent among the hard-liners.[96] The "soft-line" Independents included Armando March, leader of the federal capital commercial employees' union, who was viewed in the early 1960s as the single most important Independent leader. Although March was a socialist who advised the Illia government and often criticized the "62," he had a close relationship with Vandor and distanced himself from the hard-line anti-Peronists in the CGEC, the confederation of retail employees' unions throughout the entire country.[97] Even more willing to cooperate with the "62" was Fernando Donaires of the paper workers, who was a de facto ally of Vandor's, although his union remained outside the official Peronist grouping.

In addition to being split into hard-liners and soft-liners, many Independent unions were divided internally. Vertical divisions, pitting one set of leaders and loyalists against another, were pronounced in the railway workers' Unión Ferroviaria and the commercial employees' CGEC, the two largest unions outside the Peronist "62." In October 1963, the CGEC leadership was said to consist of "two brands of Peronism, three of Socialism and three of Radicalism."[98] In May 1966, 11 members of the Unión Ferroviaria's leadership council backed its Radical president, Antonio Scipione; 13 backed its Peronist vice president, Lorenzo Pepe; and 7 backed an important communist leader of the union, Víctor Vásquez.[99] The strength of Radicals and Communists in the Unión Ferroviaria kept it from exercising influence in the CGT proportional to its status in the early 1960s as Argentina's largest union.[100] Horizontal divisions, pitting a union's leaders against significant numbers of its members, also plagued many Independent and nonaligned unions. Especially in the late 1950s and early 1960s, many unions led by non-Peronists had mostly Peronist members.[101] To represent such workers, Peronist unionists created a National Union of Authentically

TABLE 2
Number of Reported Members in Unions Belonging to Various Groups, 1960–1966

Group	1960	1963	1966
"62 Organizations"	1,304,500	1,266,900	98,400
"62 Leales" (pro-Vandor)			408,350
"62 de Pie" (anti-Vandor)			417,700
MUCS (communist)	155,000	43,100	18,100
Independents	970,214	839,600	392,600
Nonaligned	15,000	—	489,600
"32 Organizations"	90,900	24,400	2,000
TOTAL	2,535,614	2,174,000	1,826,750
Percentage in "62"	51%	58%	50%

SOURCE: Documentación e Información Laboral, *Nucleamientos sindicales.*

Peronist Workers, led by the UOM luminary Avelino Fernández and controlled behind the scenes by Vandor.[102] The predominance of Peronist workers in many unions led by non-Peronists reduced the effectiveness of the chain of command within those unions, limiting their leaders' capacity to mobilize.

Non-Peronist unions were weakened not only by their heterogeneity and internal cleavages but also by the de facto alliance between their most powerful constituent, the Federación Argentina de Luz y Fuerza (FATLyF), and the "62." Real power within FATLyF, which organized workers in electrical generating plants, lay with its federal capital affiliate, the Sindicato de Luz y Fuerza–Capital. In early 1965, this affiliate included about 30,000 of the approximately 55,000 workers covered by collective contracts in the power industry.[103] Luz y Fuerza–Capital was in many ways Argentina's most impressive labor organization. Its annual income of about $7,500,000 (in 1965 U.S. dollars) enabled it to go far beyond most other unions in providing pensions, medical assistance, insurance and credit cooperatives, discount stores, libraries, tourism facilities, and recreation and cultural centers. In addition, the union initiated housing projects, provided domestic and foreign scholarships for members and their families, ran an extensive training institute for union leaders, published a biweekly 64-page magazine, conducted a regular radio show, and once produced a television program to publicize its successes. Luz y Fuerza–Capital signed Argentina's most sophisticated and progressive collective contracts, complete with profit-sharing clauses and union representation on the boards of directors of each of the three huge enterprises (two state-owned, one a joint venture between Swiss and Italian capital) that oligopolized power generation in the Greater Buenos Aires area.[104] The leaders of Luz y Fuerza–Capital were noted for administrative talent, and the union conducted its internal elections in an exemplary manner. Although the same leadership cohort, dominated by Juan José Taccone and Luis Angeleri, remained in power throughout the 1960s, elections during the decade were invariably contested, with 87–94 percent of eligible voters casting ballots, and with the incumbent leadership receiving 70–80 percent of the vote. Unparalleled benefits to members combined with competent leadership and internal democracy to keep union membership high. More than 90 percent of those eligible to join Luz y Fuerza–Capital did so.[105]

Several factors gave Luz y Fuerza–Capital power disproportionate to the size of its membership, including the power-generation industry's productive and oligopolistic character (which gave the union its huge financial resources), its strategic economic position (which threatened serious damage in the event of a strike), and its large plants located in a narrow geographical area (which made the union's members easier to mobilize). These resources were augmented by the union's high level of membership participation, as well as by its reputation as a model of administrative competence—a quality held in high esteem in the mid 1960s, especially by the military officers who successfully cultivated the union's support for the 1966 coup. Although Luz y Fuerza remained outside the "62," most of its leaders were Peronist.[106] Luis Angeleri, a Luz y Fuerza unionist who served as the CGT's press secretary from January 1963 to May 1966, almost always voted with the "62" bloc.[107] The Luz y Fuerza leader Francisco Prado, the CGT's secretary-general from May 1966 to March 1967, was handpicked by Vandor to run the confederation. Paradoxically, the refusal of Luz y Fuerza to join the "62" was a big advantage for Vandor, who could comply with requests that non-"62" unions be represented on the CGT directive council by agreeing to divide its posts equally between "62" and non-"62" unions—provided that Luz y Fuerza was counted among the latter.

At stake in the lopsided struggle between the "62" and Independents was control of the CGT, Argentina's umbrella union confederation. Since its formation in 1930, the CGT has been the country's single most important labor organization. Unlike the "62," which operated in part as an informal faction in the workers' central, the CGT had legal status, formal procedures for leadership selection and internal governance, and regular sources of revenue, including dues from affiliated unions.[108] A formally nonpartisan organization from 1930 to 1950, the CGT became an official branch of the Peronist movement from 1950 to 1955 and a shadow entity under government trusteeship from 1955 to 1961. In the latter year the Frondizi government returned it to a commission of 20 unionists, who "normalized" the confederation by organizing a January 1963 congress at which new statutes were approved (including a new declaration of formal nonpartisanship) and new leaders elected. By 1964, the CGT included almost all of Argentina's important unions, with the exception of SMATA (representing garage mechanics and motor-vehicle assembly workers) and some single-factory unions that the Frondizi government had authorized in 1960–61.[109] From 1961 onward, the CGT organized general strikes, mass demonstrations, and factory-occupation campaigns; participated with government and employer representatives in a minimum-wage council; represented Argentine unions at the annual meeting of the International Labor Organization; lobbied legislators, cabinet officials, and the president; and organized public education and propaganda campaigns.

According to the CGT's 1963 statutes, the confederation's main leadership organ was an 8-member secretariat at the head of a 20-member directive council. Each was formally responsible to a larger representative body known as the central confederal committee, but the statutory powers of this committee were ambiguous and it operated essentially in a rubber-stamp fashion. Formal sovereignty over the confederation was vested in the CGT congress, which had the statutory right to elect the directive council. In fact, however, union "notables" chose four of the seven 1961–67 CGT leadership boards without even the formal participation of the congress. In the other three cases, the "notables" drew up a single list of candidates behind the scenes and invited the delegates to the congress to vote for or against it. It was within these cliques of "notables" that Vandor exercised power. Multiple regression analysis has shown that closeness to Vandor was second only to membership size as a determinant of a union's likelihood of being represented on the CGT leadership board, outweighing affiliation with the "62," economic resources, and other measures of underlying union strength.[110]

Between March 1961, when the CGT emerged from government trusteeship, and May 1967, when the confederation began to split into left-wing and right-wing factions, Vandor appeared on a CGT leadership organ only once—on the March 1961 provisional commission that received the confederation from government trusteeship. Nonetheless, Vandor exercised decisive behind-the-scenes influence on the CGT by making sure that its key positions went to his close allies. Although numerical parity often existed between the "62" and Independents on the CGT directive councils (Table 3), such equivalence was merely formal. CGT leaders like Donaires and Angeleri, while not formally members of the "62," often voted with the Peronists on important issues, and non-"62" unions were plagued more than their "62" counterparts by vertical and horizontal cleavages that weakened their position in the CGT's internal debates. Moreover, Vandor made sure that the CGT's key leadership posts, the secretary-generalship and union/interior secretariat (which organized relations between the national CGT and its regional affiliates), remained in the hands of his close collaborators. In these ways, the real power of the "62" (and thus of Vandor) in the CGT exceeded both the proportion of "62" leaders on the CGT leadership organs and the proportion of total union members in "62" unions.

Vandor thus exercised decisive power within three key union organizations: the UOM, the "62," and the CGT. This power put him in an unparalleled position to challenge Perón for the right to act as the main power broker for the Peronist vote. Peronism in the early 1960s included politicians as well as unionists, but no politician had the resources to pose a challenge comparable to Vandor's. To establish this claim it will suffice to review the power resources available to the four main groups of Peronist politicians of the era: (1) Perón's immediate entourage and personal delegates; (2) so-called "orthodox" Peronist politicians publicly committed to following Perón's orders; (3) neo-Peronist politicians who claimed continuity with the Peronist political tradition but declared independence from Perón's personal supervision; and (4) the leaders of insurrectionary currents and guerrilla groups who claimed to be acting on behalf of Perón and the Peronist movement.

The only power resource available to Perón's immediate entourage and personal delegates was the confidence and trust that Perón placed in them. Perón's personal delegates John William Cooke, Oscar Albrieu, Héctor Villalón, and Gerónimo Remorino disappeared from the scene as soon as the exiled leader decided that their usefulness had been exhausted. The financier Jorge Antonio enjoyed a more durable relationship with Perón, but never acted independently of him. The orthodox Peronist politicians involved in Perón's coordinating and supervisory council and in the shadow Partido Justicialista—includ-

Representation of Union Groups on the CGT Directive Council, 1961–1967

	Mar. 1961	Jan. 1963	June 1964[a]	Jan. 1965[a]	May 1966[b]	Oct. 1966[b]	May 1967[c]
"62 Organizations"	10	10	14	14	3	8	13
Indep./nonaligned	10	10	6	6	4	12	7
Communists	0	0	0	0	1	0	0
TOTAL	20	20	20	20	8	20	20

[a] In June 1964, the CGT leadership board was reshuffled to replace hard-line Independent leaders who had resigned in the wake of the "62"-inspired factory-occupation campaign. These hard-line Independents also boycotted the leadership board elected at the January 1965 CGT congress.

[b] In February 1966, anti-Vandor Peronists led by José Alonso, the CGT secretary-general, were expelled from the CGT leadership board. In May 1966, pro-Vandor Peronists and non-Peronist labor leaders formed a provisional directorate that excluded the anti-Vandor Peronists. The anti-Vandor Peronists were also absent from the leadership board elected at the November 1966 CGT congress.

[c] All major sectors of the union leadership were represented on the provisional committee that took control of the CGT in May 1967. Of the thirteen Peronist leaders represented on the committee, six were from the pro-Vandor sector, six were from the anti-Vandor sector, and one was not aligned with either sector.

ing Carlos Lascano, Alberto Iturbe, and Delia Parodi—were somewhat more autonomous from Perón, in part because Vandor was able to co-opt them. Their only conceivable source of independent power would have been control of state resources after winning elective office, but as long as they proclaimed loyalty to Perón, they were banned from running.

The leaders of the neo-Peronist parties—Juan Bramuglia, Rodolfo Tecera del Franco, Felipe Bittel, Vicente Saadi, Alberto Serú García et al.—were often allowed to compete for legislative, provincial, and municipal posts. In provinces like Jujuy, Chaco, and Neúquen, they dominated the electoral scene and enjoyed steady access to the financial resources of the provincial administrations. However, all were vulnerable to accusations of "betraying the movement," and the most successful neo-Peronist parties were located in poor, remote, and sparsely populated provinces, far from the country's center of political gravity. By contrast, the neo-Peronist parties operating in the greater Buenos Aires area, like the Unión Popular and Partido Laborista, were never allowed to take control of executive office, in part because anti-Peronist elites considered the Buenos Aires provincial government too important to turn over to the Peronists. Thus deprived of state resources with which to counteract the unions' financial and organizational strength, the metropolitan neo-Peronist parties were soon colonized by Vandor and his allies.

The leaders of Peronism's insurrectionary current—John William

Cooke, Joe Baxter, and others—played a prominent role in the movement until the Peronist resistance collapsed. After January 1959, they still surfaced occasionally to make statements to the press or to engage in bomb-planting and other "direct action" measures, but they never succeeded in winning the allegiance of large sectors of the rank and file or in forging alliances with other sectors of the Peronist leadership. Perón never repudiated the armed groups and self-proclaimed revolutionaries who acted in his name, but it was not until the end of the 1960s that this current began again to gain ground in the Peronist movement.

Unlike the Peronist political personnel, the Peronist union leadership, in which Vandor came to exercise undisputed hegemony, enjoyed enormous power resources. Although the CGT was placed under government trusteeship in 1955 and was not returned to the union leaders until 1961, the individual unions were permitted to function freely for most of the 1955–66 period. As collective bargaining agents, as handlers of members' grievances against employers, as centers of some workers' social lives, and as providers of health care, education, and training, the unions played a much more salient part in the lives of urban workers—the core supporters of Peronism—than did the neo-Peronist parties or the shadow Partido Justicialista. When neo-Peronist parties presented candidates for provincial and legislative offices in 1962 and 1965, the unions, at least in the major metropolitan areas, did more to get out the vote—supposedly a core function of the political parties—than did the neo-Peronist parties themselves. In addition, as we have seen, the unions enjoyed a regular and substantial income, whereas the Peronist political personnel had no steady source of financial resources. In 1958, Oscar Albrieu, then an "orthodox" Peronist politician, had to ask Vandor for money to pay his expenses when Perón requested that he tour the country to see how Peronists were responding to the order to vote for Frondizi.[111]

In contrast to the Peronist politicians, Perón himself still had formidable resources: his continued mass appeal and his ability, even after a decade in exile, to sway millions of supporters with a letter from Madrid. However, he was hampered in his increasingly explicit struggle with Vandor by his absence from Argentina and by the military-enforced ban on parties that responded to his personal directives. Vandor, by contrast, was on the scene, and there was little the military could do, without resorting to unacceptably high levels of repression, to prevent him from organizing and financing mass strikes, mobilizations, publicity campaigns, and get-out-the-vote drives. In many respects, the struggle for the right to act as the main power broker for the Peronist vote came down to Perón's personal appeal versus Vandor's organization. The next chapter analyzes how this struggle unfolded during the government of Arturo Illia, and how the resolution of this struggle in favor of Perón contributed to the collapse of a regime that, although not democratic, was certainly more competitive than the one that replaced it.

Chapter 5

Vandor Versus Perón

During Arturo Illia's 1963–66 presidency, Peronist union leaders and neo-Peronist politicians tried to build a political party autonomous from Perón. Augusto Vandor, the leader of the powerful metalworkers' union, spearheaded the initiative. Vandor's party-building project reflected long-standing tensions between union leaders, who wanted to improve their access to policy making, and Perón, who favored direct, plebiscitarian links between himself and his followers. Vandor's project was also an attempt to carve out a more autonomous role for union leaders in the Peronist movement; as such, it recalled Cipriano Reyes's fight against Perón's order to dissolve the Partido Laborista, Luis Gay's resistance to Perón's efforts to install a more manipulable CGT secretary-general, and the emergence of more independent leaders in many unions during the waning years of Perón's presidency. What distinguished Vandor's project from these earlier challenges was that it went much farther before collapsing, partly because Vandor had gained unprecedented power in the labor movement and partly because, by 1963, many Peronists had come to doubt Perón's capacity, and even will, ever to return to Argentina.[1] This chapter explores the rise and fall of Vandor's party-building project. It argues that Vandor's initiative brought Peronism closer to party institutionalization than at any time in its previous history; that Perón himself, reluctant to be converted into a symbolic figurehead, undermined the project with the help of anti-Vandor factions of the Peronist union leadership; and that the failure of Vandor's party-building efforts helped to precipitate the 1966 coup.

Vandor's Party-Building Project Gathers Momentum

By October 1963, when Illia assumed the presidency, many military officers and UCRP leaders favored relaxing the ban on Peronism.[2] The weakening of proscription without eliminating it was a worst-case scenario for Perón. If the ban were softened, the exiled leader might find himself watching from Madrid while neo-Peronist politicians and Vandor's unionists competed for legislative seats and provincial and municipal posts, increasing their resources every time they won. In an apparent bid to prevent this eventuality, Perón tried to make Peronism seem as confrontational as possible—just as he had done prior to the 1962 election, when he had nominated Framini and himself to contest the governorship and vice-governorship of Buenos Aires. In September 1963, Perón assigned Framini and two Peronist politicians tied to Héctor Villalón, a shadowy figure identified with Peronism's extreme left, to a commission charged with reorganizing the Partido Justicialista (PJ), Peronism's "orthodox" party label, which was still without legal status. These choices were obviously not designed to relieve the worries of anti-Peronists who feared that the movement might turn to the left, and they are hard to interpret as anything other than an attempt to undermine Vandor's incursions into the political wing of Peronism by provoking the party's continued proscription at a time propitious for its admission to the electoral arena. Rubén Sosa, one of the politicians appointed to the PJ reorganizing commission, reported that Perón had given the commission instructions to "destroy the official structure of Vandorism and break the union hegemony of the UOM."[3]

Perón's ploy failed. When Villalón alluded disparagingly to the UOM leadership, Vandor pulled his union out of the "62" and asked Perón to expel Villalón's supporters from the PJ reorganizing commission. Perhaps sensing that Villalón and his allies lacked the political weight to confront Vandor, Perón agreed to replace them with individuals closely allied with the metalworkers' chief. Ostensibly to conform to pending legislation requiring internal party democracy, the restructured commission thereupon immediately announced its intention to rebuild the PJ "from the bottom up," depriving Perón of any specific role in the choice of party leaders. The shadow PJ completed a membership drive and in June 1964 held primary elections for delegates to a congress charged with selecting the party leadership. Vandor and Framini backed competing lists of delegates, and Vandor's list won a decisive victory. Although the congress acclaimed Perón as the PJ's titular head, Alberto Iturbe, a Peronist politician allied with Vandor, assumed day-to-day control of the organization.[4] As one newsweekly put it, the PJ's indirect primary elections showed that

Augusto Vandor achieved what seemed impossible: to create a true workers' party without a class-based ideology and respectful of legality, while putting himself in a virtually unassailable position for the day when Perón, willingly or not, cedes the leadership of Justicialism. As opposed to what had happened when Framini was in the first rank, the [men's] political and women's [political] wings [of the Peronist movement], "softened" by Vandor, seem to have accepted unreservedly the hegemony of the unions in composing the lists [of candidates for party posts].[5]

A crucial event in Vandor's rise to prominence was the May/June 1964 CGT factory-occupation campaign, the culmination of the confederation's *plan de lucha* (battle plan), launched that January. During a one-month period (the occupations took place on eight separate days), workers seized thousands of factories throughout the country, sometimes taking employers and managers hostage. The authorship of the *plan de lucha* is not conclusively known. Framini attributed it to José Alonso, whereas Miguel Gazzera of the pasta makers' union said that he, Vandor, and Amado Olmos thought it up.[6] The weight of the evidence suggests that Vandor was the key figure behind the initiative. The techniques used to occupy the factories recalled the ones Vandor used to coordinate strikes in the UOM, and Vandor authored the actual text of the plan de lucha resolution.[7]

Although the factory-occupation campaign in one sense "put into question the regime of private property," its underlying aim was not to challenge capitalism but to warn the Illia government, and implicitly any military or civilian successor regime, of the dangers involved in ignoring the demands of the top Peronist union leaders.[8] Nominally, the aim of the campaign was even more modest: to force the Illia government to grant price controls, higher pensions, programs to combat unemployment, a new minimum-wage law, amnesty for those (including Perón) accused of political crimes, and the removal of restrictions on Peronist electoral participation.[9] Peronists had a real gripe in the case of proscription, but the unionists advanced the economic complaints with more bombast than they deserved. Illia's economic policies were understandably shortsighted: after winning the presidency with only 25 percent of the vote, the new president subordinated the goal of tackling the country's underlying economic problems to the immediate challenge of broadening his political support base by promoting short-term economic growth. Promote short-term growth he did, however, and to the special benefit of workers. The economy grew 10.4 percent in 1964 and 9.1 percent in 1965, while real wages rose 12.0 percent in 1964 and 8.4 percent in 1965. Meanwhile, the share of wages and salaries in the national income increased from 38.2 percent in 1963 to 39.8 percent in 1965.[10]

The trend in economic and labor conditions was thus hardly such as to motivate a huge factory-occupation campaign. But as is frequently the case with strikes, conditions that reduce the motivation for labor protest at the same time increase the opportunity for such protest. Economic growth tends to be associated with improved material welfare for workers, reducing the motivation to strike. But because employers have more resources when times are good, an expanding economy permits union leaders to predict with more confidence that a strike will succeed. Moreover, because striking workers become harder to replace as economic growth absorbs the unemployed, union leaders risk less in calling a strike.[11] In a permissive political climate such as prevailed throughout the Illia presidency (when there were fewer legal or effective restrictions on the right to strike than at any time in Argentine history, save for the Alfonsín presidency), and with union leaders intent on making themselves a "power factor" in society, increased opportunity prevailed over diminished motivation, and the plan de lucha went forward.

The CGT's demands may have been far from extreme, but the same could not be said for the deadline it set for meeting them. In January 1964, just five weeks after announcing the demands, the CGT leaders called a meeting to denounce the government's inaction and approved a two-stage plan de lucha to rectify the situation. The first stage would involve "preparation, organization, and agitation." If the CGT saw no "concrete results" by the end of February 1964 (barely six weeks away), the second stage of the plan, consisting of successive waves of workplace occupations, would be put into effect during March.[12] Government concessions allowed the March deadline to pass without incident, but at a meeting of the CGT leadership on 1 May, Vandor's allies pushed through a proposal to begin the occupations on 18 May.[13] The Independents, who favored a delay, began to boycott the CGT, and for the next two years, the confederation was run exclusively by the "62."

A few days before the occupations were due to begin, CGT Secretary-General Alonso announced the procedures for carrying them out, which, in the view of Raúl Bisio and Héctor Cordone, "resembled nothing so much as a gigantic military operation." Alonso announced that

The CGT secretariat will decide on what day and at what time the occupations will be put into effect. The secretaries-general of the unions will know 24 hours in advance, but the factory delegates and workers will not be informed until they arrive for work. The CGT secretariat will also decide the duration of the occupations, during which there will be no work whatsoever in the affected plants. The CGT will report on the occupations a few hours after they have ended.[14]

The "62" leaders said that secrecy was required to avoid tipping off the police, but Bisio and Cordone note that it also served to prevent combative base-level militants from appropriating the takeovers for their own purposes.[15] In the event, the occupations, which lasted from three to eight hours, were carried out under strict discipline. Incidents of violence were rare, although workers sometimes prevented plant managers and other personnel from leaving the premises, especially in metalworking factories.[16] The first three waves of occupations included only two or three instances where workers took actions not decreed by the CGT, like refusing to return to work when so instructed by the union leadership. At the end of each scheduled day of occupations, the CGT reported the number of takeovers, and some of the large industrial unions, like the metalworkers and textile workers, named specific factories as having been occupied.[17]

The scope of the factory-occupation campaign is a matter of some controversy. On 22 May 1964, the first day of the campaign, the CGT declared that 800 plants had been occupied. By contrast, "union sources" reporting to the newspaper *Clarín* put the number at 490, the employers' association ACIEL gave a figure of between 120 and 180, and the interior ministry announced that 121 factories had been occupied. When the campaign was over, the CGT announced that 11,000 factories had been taken by a total of 3,913,000 workers, whereas the government put the number of occupations at 2,361 and did not estimate the number of participants.[18] The government may have underestimated the number of occupations, but the CGT clearly overestimated them. Its figures invariably exceeded the ones provided by union sources to *Clarín*, which were themselves greatly exaggerated. As Table 4 shows, in several economic sectors, there were many more reported factory occupiers than workers employed in the industry.

TABLE 4
*Analysis of Data on Number of Workers Participating in 1964
CGT Factory-Occupation Campaign*
(economic sectors reporting 10,000 or more workers involved only)

Sector	Union	Factories reported occupied	Workers reported involved	Workers employed in industry	Avg. plant size implied by union figures	Avg. plant size in 1964 econ. census	Avg. number of workers in biggest plants in industry
Metals	UOM	1,449	426,000	277,063	294	9	496
Textiles	AOT	1,135	278,000	115,164	245	19	538
Construction	UOCRA	738	76,700		104		
Automobiles	SMATA	148	62,500	91,229	422	4	1,439
Light/Power	FATLyF	226	51,100		226		
Oil (Private)	FASP	145	50,000	6,000	345	95	682
Rubber	FOCAA	124	49,000	12,131	395	6	18
Wood	USIMRA	192	34,000	44,372	177	3	30
Glass	SOIVA	93	28,700	9,725	309	17	88
Vegetable Oil	FOEIAAP	89	24,300	9,554	273	41	75
Meat Packing	FGPIC	19	20,000	46,850	1,053	45	1,746
Ports	SUPA	4	20,000		5,000		
Wine	FOEVA	52	19,500	17,885	375	10	54
Post Office	FOECyT		16,500				
Food	FTIA	16	16,500	45,770	1,031	22	66
Paper	FOEPCQA	72	16,100	22,598	224	21	93
Telephone	FOETRA	41	16,000		390		
Shoes	UTICRA	205	15,800	19,976	77	7	83
Ceramics	FOCRA	77	15,500	8,056	201	22	32
Garment	FONIVA	27	15,200	32,643	563	4	21
Grain Silos	URGA	250	15,000		60		
Dairy	ATILRA	18	12,000	19,037	667	4	13
Chemical	FATIQA	120	11,600	21,530	97	14	61
Oil (State)	SUPE	41	10,000	20,000	244	229	682

SOURCES: *Factories reported occupied* and *Workers reported involved* calculated from Bisio and Cordone, "La segunda etapa," 60, 64–65, 69–70, 76–77, 79, citing figures supplied by "union sources" to *Clarín*. *Workers employed in industry* calculated from INDEC, *Censo nacional económico, 1964;* for a chart showing which unions organized which sectors, see McGuire, "Peronism Without Perón," 309. *Average plant size implied by union figures* calculated by dividing the number of workers reported involved by the number of factories occupied. *Average plant size in 1964 economic census* calculated by dividing the number of workers employed in sector by the number of establishments in sector (the number of establishments was calculated from INDEC, *Censo nacional económico, 1964,* in a manner analogous to *Workers employed in industry*). *Average number of workers in biggest plants in industry* calculated from INDEC, *Censo nacional económico, 1964,* by the method described in note to Table 1 in Chapter 4.

Some factories were seized more than once, but multiple takeovers cannot account for the size of the discrepancy between reported factory occupiers and actual workers employed, which averaged 2 to 1 in textiles and metals, 3 to 1 in glass and vegetable oils, 4 to 1 in rubber, and 8 to 1 among private-sector petroleum workers. Moreover, the average workplace employed fewer than 10 people in many industries, including rubber, wood, metals, and automobiles (SMATA organized repair shops as well as assembly plants). In these industries, only a minority of the industry's personnel worked in factories large enough to be worth occupying.

Employers' associations denounced the plan de lucha, but their criticism was directed less at the unions' decision to go ahead with it than at the government's failure to repress it more energetically.[19] In fact, Martín Oneto Gaona, president of the Argentine Industrial Union (UIA), is reported to have said during the occupations that "our relations with workers have never been better."[20] Researchers at an institute for the study of labor affairs were informed by an executive that "regarding the plan de lucha, the worker-employer opposition is only formal, and a worker-employer front is more possible now than ever before." One executive knew of owners and managers who had given snacks to the workers occupying their factories, and others indicated that in some factories, management had been informed beforehand about the occupations and had assisted the workers in carrying them out.[21]

The main target of the factory-occupation campaign was not employers, but the government.[22] Precisely what the aim of the campaign was with respect to the government is, however, a matter of some dispute. Its stated goal was to win concrete changes in policy, but some writers suggest that the goal was a broader one. Peter Snow has argued that the campaign was launched to show the "intrinsic weakness" of the Illia government, and Gary Wynia has suggested that the Peronist union leaders intended the occupations to "immobiliz[e] the Radical government" as part of a campaign to "undermin[e] Illia's authority at every turn, quite aware of where their efforts would lead."[23] Independent unionists accused the "62" of "trying to create a climate of chaos and violence in order to provoke an eventual coup,"[24] and Angel Bono, a vigorously anti-Peronist leader of the locomotive engineers' union, "charged that one of the Peronistas' goals was the overthrow of the government."[25] In a 5 June 1964 speech at the Campo de Mayo military base, General Alejandro Lanusse stated that he "would not hesitate to characterize the CGT plan de lucha as union subversion."[26] Almost thirty years later, when a reporter noted to Lanusse that the 1966 coup had occurred at a time of social and economic stability, Lanusse replied "don't forget the climate of instability in the factories at the time."[27]

It is probable that the Peronist union leaders who organized the factory-occupation campaign did so with differing aims with respect to the government. Alonso's may well have been the most extreme. As the factory occupations were being carried out, Alonso made a speech in which he asked: "What are the armed forces protecting at this moment? Hunger, misery, unemployment, fraud, privilege? What borders, what rights, what freedoms are they defending? . . . We must break the structures that are strangling us and the shackles that stop us from moving forward."[28] Alonso's incendiary statement certainly supports the interpretation of the Independent unionists interviewed by Bisio and Cordone in the late 1970s, who reportedly "were united in agreeing that the idea of overthrowing the government was present from the beginning." Yet the "62" unionists interviewed by Bisio and Cordone "expressed a more moderate and nuanced view of the issue."[29] Indeed, a preponderance of evidence seems to suggest that the aim of most "62" leaders was not specifically to provoke a coup, but to demonstrate to the Illia government that institutions would have to be designed to give the CGT permanent input into policy.[30] Then, if a coup did occur—with or without the consent or connivance of the "62," and owing or not to the government's failure to create such institutions—the armed forces, by virtue of having witnessed the factory-occupation campaign, would already have received a similar message.

Whatever its precise aims, the effect of the plan de lucha was seriously to undermine the government's authority. The way Illia dealt with the occupations contributed to the perception of government weakness. Instead of calling on the police to repress them, the government brought charges of instigating criminal activity against approximately 150 members of the CGT's directive board and central confederal committee who had voted to begin the occupations.[31] Illia's tepid response showed characteristic respect for the rule of law, but only irritated those who called for much firmer action against what they viewed as subversion. The factory occupations had moderate aims, but their methods could be interpreted as a "revolutionary exercise" that "could easily evolve toward something far worse than the existing impediments to capital accumulation."[32] The commanders-in-chief of the armed forces viewed the CGT's tactics as threatening enough to put the army on a state of alert.[33] For the moment, however, the armed forces "appeared to be determined to preserve the full force of the constitution, and no immediate problem from this quarter was foreseen." Reinforcing this perception, General Juan Carlos Onganía, the army commander-in-chief, spent much of the factory-occupation period on a trip to Taiwan, Japan, and the United States.[34] In the long run, however, the factory occupations helped create a climate of instability propitious for the June 1966 military coup.

Apart from its effects on the long-term stability of the Illia government, the plan de lucha helped to consolidate Vandor's stature in the Peronist movement. Gazzera calls the factory-occupation campaign "the pinnacle of Vandor's reign"; Alain Rouquié argues that it "enabled the Vandorists to regain control over the whole of Peronist unionism"; Bisio and Cordone view it as part of a strategy that "implied a demand for greater independence from Perón"; and Juan Carlos Torre asserts that "with respect to Perón . . . [the factory-occupation campaign] was directed toward demonstrating the capacity of the union movement to formulate independent political goals." [35] The plan de lucha also may have enabled Vandor to win support from rank-and-file workers who credited the action with inducing the government to pass a minimum-wage law and to impose price ceilings. [36]

The growing strength of the Vandorist current, now highlighted by the success of the plan de lucha, was among the factors that led to Perón's decision to recoup the limelight by announcing his impending return to Argentina. On 2 December 1964, Perón attempted to return to Buenos Aires via Rio de Janeiro. When the Brazilian authorities sent his airplane back to Madrid in response to a request from the Illia government, Perón ordered his followers to launch "all-out war [against the government] by all means and at every moment." Vandor and his allies, whom some accused of deliberately scuttling the return by announcing the plan in advance, thereupon launched their version of "all-out war" by resolving to support the participation of Peronist candidates in the national deputy elections scheduled for March 1965. [37] Perón's return to Madrid seemed to demonstrate that he would never be allowed to resume an active role in Argentine political life. Some sort of "Peronism without Perón" now seemed inevitable. Vandor's comment on the failure of Operation Return was reported to have been: "Farewell to arms; it's time for elections." [38]

The legal status of the Partido Justicialista was still indeterminate at the time of Perón's attempted return, but a month later, on 7 January 1965, the elections court in the federal capital formally recognized the party and ruled that it could present candidates for all offices in all provinces. The verdict was appealed, and on 26 February 1965— only two weeks before the elections—the national elections court overturned the lower court's decision and forbade the PJ to present candidates for national deputy seats. [39] In denying recognition to the PJ, the national elections court wrote that the party was marked by a "thoroughgoing submission to a leadership of totalitarian characteristics" and ruled that it was a mere appendage of the banned Partido Peronista directed by the "self-proclaimed Peronist residing in Madrid."[40] These alleged characteristics of the PJ contravened Article 23 of the new Statute of Political Parties, promulgated on 11 January 1965, which outlawed parties subject to "personal concentration of power."[41] With the PJ outlawed, Vandor and his allies migrated to the neo-Peronist Unión Popular.

By the March 1965 national deputy elections, neo-Peronist parties were enjoying a resurgence. Although the Unión Popular had boycotted the July 1963 elections, when both Perón and Vandor had called for blank ballots, candidates from other neo-Peronist parties had received 7 percent of the national deputy vote, and there was speculation that they would be able to triple their gains in March 1965.[42] Moreover, neo-Peronist leaders had bolstered their parties' chances of retaining legal status by distancing themselves ever more explicitly from Perón. They criticized the past Peronist government for its authoritarian characteristics, portrayed Perón as a leader whose time had passed, and even helped the UCRP design and secure the passage of the Political Party Statute under which the PJ was outlawed in February 1965.[43] In an interview with the newsweekly *Primera Plana*, Oscar Albrieu, a leader of the neo-Peronist Partido de la Justicia Social, distinguished "the myth that drives the masses" from "the doctrine that orients the work of the leaders and directs it toward constructive action," and stressed the need to update the party program in accordance with the doctrine. Even more boldly, Albrieu asserted that

state authoritarianism does not belong to the essence of the Justicialist doctrine. It may have been a revolutionary necessity of the Peronist government or a professional deformity of Perón, who is a military man. The errors of Peronism derive from this state authoritarianism, and are easily correctable should there arise another chance to govern. . . . Perón has been out of the country for nine years, disoriented by the misinformation he receives from interested parties both within and outside of the movement. It is necessary to accept the manner in which Peronism has organized itself in accordance with the law, as long as it becomes a democratic and solidly structured party with a federalist sensitivity and possibilities for dialogue.[44]

As in 1962—but this time without Framini or the hard-liners, who advocated blank ballots—Vandor "rented" the legal Unión Popular label in exchange for his powerful electoral machine and an agreement to intersperse Unión Popular politicians with his own handpicked nominees. Also as in 1962, Perón faced a done deed and had little choice but to give his belated blessing to the strategy. Jorge Antonio, his personal secretary, explained lamely that Perón viewed taking part in the March 1965 elections as one of the "forms of struggle" he had demanded after the Illia government blocked his return.[45] Once again, the Unión Popular campaign was organized and financed primarily by the "62." Unionists close to Vandor received the top national deputy candidacies from the federal capital and the province of Buenos Aires,[46] and the "62," now fully controlled by Vandor, also decided which members of Peronism's political wing would run.[47] On 14 March 1965, the Unión Popular won 31 percent of the vote, the governing UCRP 30 percent, and other neo-Peronist parties 7 percent (no other party won more than 7 percent).[48] The strong showing by the Unión Popular seemed to indicate that Peronism's electoral success now depended as much on Vandor's organization as on Perón's mass appeal.

Vandor's Party-Building Project Encounters Resistance

The March 1965 elections represented a turning point in the struggle between Vandor and Perón. The election of Vandor's UOM ally Paulino Niembro to head the Peronist bloc in the chamber of deputies antagonized leaders of the newly banned PJ, several of whom demanded that Vandor's collaborators resign from the PJ leadership board. As one of them put it, "Perón keeps providing the votes, the Unión Popular its label, and Vandor the candidates; this can't continue."[49] The CGT became another source of resistance to Vandor's party-building project. Since January 1963, when Vandor had engineered his appointment as CGT secretary-general, Alonso had controlled (and greatly improved) the confederation's technical, administrative, and propaganda apparatuses. The Unión Popular's impressive showing in the March 1965 elections made it clear, however, that the CGT would henceforth have to share the stage as the main pole of Peronist opposition to the Illia government. Alonso and his CGT allies were not prepared to relinquish their position without a challenge. Just one day after the March 1965 elections, the CGT's weekly bulletin, instead of trumpeting the Peronist electoral victory and exploring the possibilities of legislative participation, issued a thinly veiled call for military intervention in a cover essay entitled "Anecdote of the Lion."

Although the military still has not issued any *planteos* [demands backed by the implicit threat of a coup in the case of noncompliance], the government has not lost a single one of its ministers. It hopes to retain them in spite of the great horrors that are taking place. However, this time the lion may eat the entire cabinet. . . . the way things are going, the only favor for which we would thank the government would be the unification of those whose mission it is to produce the [fusion] of the country with those in charge of watching over it. . . . Perhaps this time the lion will know how to act and will possess the know-how to produce the historical event that the entire people is intuiting. Without the people it is impossible to govern.[50]

The rift between Vandor and his former protégé deepened in the ensuing weeks, especially after Alonso released the draft version of a CGT pamphlet entitled "Toward a Change of Structures." After criticizing Argentina's social, economic, and political situation, the document disparaged the notion that political parties (not excepting the PJ or Unión Popular) could do anything to solve the country's problems.[51] The authors of the pamphlet included members of the CGT secretariat, CGT technical and research personnel, and representatives of some affiliated unions[52]—but not Vandor or his allies in the "62," who protested that they had found out about the document in the newspapers.[53] At a CGT assembly in late March 1965, Alonso proclaimed that the "Change of Structures" pamphlet "filled a gap that had not been covered by any political party." Vandor replied that the PJ had presented a complete program prior to the 1965 elections.[54] When the pamphlet was finally released in late June 1965, its tone had not been greatly altered, and the Peronist deputies from the "62" expressed their dismay. As one of them put it,

Those guys [Alonso and his allies in the CGT] still have this mania for announcing great wars against the government, which . . . they can't carry out. Also, do you know why they don't consult us? Don't they know they could force us into a parliamentary confrontation we don't want right now? What's happening is, they think the unions depend on the CGT. They haven't noticed that it's the CGT that depends on the unions.[55]

Disregarding Alonso's implicit opposition to his party-building initiative, Vandor and his allies moved to strengthen the incipient party's organizational base. To this end, Vandor and a group of neo-Peronist leaders proposed in July 1965 that the Unión Popular merge with eight other neo-Peronist parties under a single party label. Foreshadowing a 1987 proposal by Peronism's renewal sector, the party's draft charter argued that direct or indirect primary elections should replace the *tercio* system whereby the men's, women's, and union branches of the Peronist movement were each entitled to nominate one-third of the candidates for party leadership posts, national deputy seats, and other positions allocated on a proportional basis.[56] Actually, until the 1993 quota law imposed a women's *tercio* on all parties, Peronist candidates had never been nominated according to this scheme. In 1951, often hailed a peak year of female representation in the national legislature, women made up only 20 of 149 Peronist deputy candidates and only 5 of 30 Peronist senate candidates.[57] The Unión Popular provided for a *tercio* system in its 1955 statutes, but never actually distributed its candidacies in this fashion.[58] Vandor's proposal to eliminate the *tercio* system nonetheless posed a symbolic challenge to Peronism's character as a "movement" under Perón's plebiscitarian leadership. Not surprisingly, Perón rejected it. According to Serú García,

Perón rejected the agreement because he said that it was nothing more than an intellectual, conceptual, on-paper type of agreement; that unity had to be affective, heart-to-heart. . . . when the letter [from Perón rejecting the accord] was being read I was sitting next to Delia Parodi, and she said something like 'But what does the old man want? Does he want us to hug and kiss?' Because we couldn't do any more than we did. He said we had to reach fundamental unity, spoke of sentiments, the unity of hearts, what do I know. So what were we to do? We accepted the idea of Perón, naturally.[59]

To shore up his position, Perón dispatched his wife, Isabel, to Argentina in October 1965 on a mission of "peace and conciliation," the real purpose of which was to remind Peronists that he still intended to play an active role in the movement. Vandor and his allies countered by offering to chaperone Isabel's visit. Isabel managed to evade them for a few days, but Gerónimo Izetta and Ramón Elorza, two of Vandor's closest union allies, caught up with her and wound up escorting her on a tour of the Argentine interior, during which she enjoyed the "protection" of a dozen union bodyguards. In the presence of such companions, it is not surprising that Isabel received few pledges of support from local Peronist leaders.[60]

Open conflict between Vandor and Perón erupted a few weeks after Isabel's arrival. On 22 October 1965, about 250 delegates from neo-Peronist parties, the PJ, and the "62" met in a union hall in Avellaneda to discuss what to do about Isabel's visit. Preparations for the meeting were very disorganized. Vandor helped put together an agenda but never made it to the actual session, which began just before midnight. During the meeting several delegates accused Jorge

Antonio, Perón's personal secretary, and Enrique Güerci, a Peronist national deputy estranged from Vandor and his allies, of conniving with the Illia government to foment discord between Isabel and the local Peronist leadership. As the night wore on, denunciations grew more heated. "Loyalty is not obsequiousness," the oil workers' leader Cavalli exclaimed. "Loyalty is not genuflection," declared the neo-Peronist deputy Juan Luco. Toward the end of the meeting, the neo-Peronist deputy Alberto Serú García, in collaboration with Adolfo Cavalli, drew up and received unanimous approval for a seven-point declaration that affirmed "absolute solidarity with General Juan D. Perón" and declared "sympathy for Señora Isabel Martínez de Perón's mission of peace and conciliation," but pointedly expressed "devotion to the memory of Eva Perón, the irreplaceable standard-bearer for the country's humble people." It also "repudiated any pact between government officials and those who claim falsely to represent [Peronism]" and, most adventurously, affirmed an intention "to promote the immediate institutionalization of the Peronist movement . . . from the bottom up, through a clean democratic process in absolute conformity with the reiterated wishes of General Juan D. Perón."[61] The last clause seems disingenuous. As a weekly magazine commented, "Not a shred of political decision-making power would remain in [Perón's] hands if the party were controlled by leaders chosen, in accordance with the law, through internal elections."[62]

In implicitly refusing to recognize the right of Perón's delegates to negotiate independently with the government, in making an indirect but invidious distinction between Eva and Isabel, and in announcing their intention to create a political party "from the bottom up," Vandor and the neo-Peronists had come close to breaking explicitly with Perón. When asked if he intended to declare his independence from the exiled leader, Vandor is reported to have replied, "We are confronting Perón in order to save Perón." Although Vandor denied ever having uttered such a phrase,[63] his union and political enemies repeatedly invoked it against him. In any case, the Avellaneda declaration provoked an angry response from Perón. In a letter to retired General Arnaldo Sosa Molina, Perón referred to Vandor as an "incorrigible ambitious person who wants to go farther than his capacity permits."[64] In a letter to Framini, Perón issued a scathing condemnation of Vandor and his allies: "Although these tough little birds think they're so savvy, they haven't noticed that they're bringing on their own downfall. These suckers think I'm dying and have already begun to fight over my clothing, but I'm still strong enough to form a new Peronist movement if necessary. Then we'll see how many stay with them."[65]

The Avellaneda declaration sharpened intra-Peronist polarization and led to a realignment in the Peronist union leadership. Amado Olmos, representing what a newsweekly called the "left wing" of Vandorism, had once advocated forming a "workers' party," but after the Avellaneda declaration, he registered his opposition to Vandor's party-building project. "I don't agree with the great party strategy. I don't agree that we should continue to fight for the governorships," Olmos announced. Olmos reportedly came out against the party-building project because he felt it would marginalize Perón entirely, and because he recognized that the neo-Peronists, historically the most conservative sector of the movement, would play a key role in the new organization.[66] Olmos's defection, coupled with Alonso's growing independence and Perón's increasingly explicit opposition, made Vandor's position more precarious. Yet Vandor still controlled the UOM, the country's strongest union; the "62 Organizations," of which he was reelected secretary-general in November 1965; and the CGT, from which he was about to expel Alonso. In addition, most of the Peronist deputies owed their seats to Vandor, who also retained influence in the shadow PJ and in the neo-Peronist Unión Popular. He would need all of these resources to confront the challenges he faced over the next six months.

Factions in the Peronist Union Leadership, 1963–1966

Open rebellion in the union leadership broke out on 18 January 1966, when Framini, Alonso, Olmos, and several prominent hard-liners took out a newspaper advertisement entitled "De pie junto a Perón" ("Standing Up Beside Perón"). Without referring to the metalworkers' chief by name, the advertisement denounced Vandor for challenging Perón's leadership: "Nobody who calls himself a Peronist can seriously affirm . . . that it is 'necessary to confront Perón in order to save Perón.' . . . Those who think that the time is ripe to disobey Perón and to follow their personal ambitions, to form their own political organization—who do they think they are?"[67]

Vandor responded to this attack by expelling from the "62" all of the unions whose representatives had signed the advertisement. In response, the ousted unionists held what they described as a "legitimate plenary" of the "62" and in turn expelled the metalworkers' chief for "distorting . . . Peronist doctrine, for refusing to recognize Juan Perón as Chief of the Movement, and for trying to set himself up as chief."[68] Alonso added his own critique, accusing Vandor of "trying to run the CGT from the racetrack" (a reference to Vandor's favorite pastime) and for being a *"caudillito* who tries to manipulate the movement for his own ends."[69] For the first time in its eight-year history, the "62 Organizations" formally split. The anti-Vandor faction adopted the name "62 de Pie Junto a Perón" (after the title of the newspaper advertisement) while the pro-Vandor faction called itself "62 Leales a Perón" ("62 Loyal to Perón"). The conflict in the "62" immediately spilled over into the CGT. On 2 February 1966, the 13 Vandorists on the 20-member CGT secretariat voted to expel Alonso as the confederation's secretary-general. Named to replace him was Fernando Donaires, head of the paper workers' union, who was nominally an Independent but actually one of Vandor's closest allies. Violence soon erupted between the pro- and anti-Vandor factions. Within two weeks of the formation of the "62 de Pie," an armed group had occupied the headquarters of a Vandorist group, a huge firecracker had exploded near Vandor's usual table at the San Isidro racetrack, and a bomb had gone off at a CGT office in Avellaneda controlled by Rosendo García, Vandor's protégé in the UOM.[70]

The "62 de Pie," although united in opposition to Vandor, had little else in common. The group's key leaders spanned the full range of the Peronist ideological spectrum. Alonso represented the Falangist right of Peronist unionism, Framini the ideological blank slate of unconditional allegiance to Perón, Olmos the dissident left wing of the pragmatic Vandorist current, and the hard-liners the insurrectionary left of Peronism as a whole. This ideological smorgasbord soon produced centrifugal forces that threatened to destroy the fledgling group. On 25 March 1966, the "62 de Pie" held its first national meeting in Tucumán, home of the militant sugar workers' federation FOTIA. The meeting was disrupted by boisterous conflict between left- and right-wing factions, but a compromise was finally reached under which four of Alonso's allies, three of Framini's, and three hard-liners were named to the "62 de Pie" leadership council. Because Framini's allies could align themselves with either of the other factions, they held the balance of power on the leadership council.[71] Perón could take some comfort in this arrangement because the prominent role of the Framini faction reduced the likelihood that the organization would fall under the control of the potentially more autonomous Alonso right or hard-liner left. In an effort to characterize the "62 de Pie" as an organization beholden to FOTIA and the extreme left of Peronist unionism, Vandor took out a newspaper advertisement entitled "62 de Pie Junto al Trotskismo."[72] In fact, however, the program ratified at the Tucumán congress represented a victory for the right. Despite efforts by left-leaning unionists to include some "insurgent" paragraphs, the program concluded only with calls for more progressive taxation, for the breakup of large landholdings, for the nationalization of the banking system, and for a tax on uncultivated land.[73]

The split in the "62" was a critical event in the struggle between Vandor and Perón. By showing that an important part of the Peronist union leadership was unwilling to go along with Vandor's challenge, it shifted the terms of the struggle between Perón and the metalworkers' chief. What the journalist Mariano Grondona had recently termed a struggle between charisma and organization had now become a struggle between charisma *plus* organization on one side, and organization by itself on the other. At stake in the struggle was nothing less than the incipient institutionalization of Peronism as a political party and Vandor's hegemony over Peronist unionism. It was these issues —not attitude toward the Illia government, structural rifts between unions from different economic sectors, or ideological conflict—that divided Peronist unionism in the mid 1960s. Because other analyses have reached different conclusions,[74] and because disputes over party institutionalization and turf battles among union leaders returned to fragment Peronist unionism in later decades, it is worth delving more deeply into the nature of the rift in the "62 Organizations."

Conventional wisdom holds that the issue of cooperation with the government in office was the main source of factional conflict in the Peronist union leadership throughout the post-1955 era. Although willingness to cooperate with the government was the main issue dividing Peronist union leaders under the 1958–62 Frondizi government, and although it again became a central divisive issue during the 1966–70 Onganía period and the 1989–95 Menem administration,[75] no faction of the Peronist union leadership favored cooperating with the Illia government. Vandor and the "62 Leales" were no more willing to cooperate with Illia than were the heterogeneous factions in the "62 de Pie." It was Vandor who played the key role in organizing the 1964 factory-occupation campaign, the heaviest single blow that the unions struck against the Illia government. Opposition to Illia was even fierce among the Independent and nonaligned unions outside the "62." The light and power workers, paper workers, auto workers, and pasta makers all participated in the factory-occupation campaign, and each of these non-"62" unions remained in a de facto alliance with Vandor until the end of the Illia period. The retail clerks and civil service workers, whose non-Peronist leaders had refused to participate in the factory-occupation campaign, joined the opposition in May 1966 after Illia vetoed a law that would have made it more difficult for employers to impose layoffs.[76] The only unionists who favored cooperating with Illia were the most anti-Peronist leaders in the Independent group, including Antonio Scipione of the railway workers, Angel Bono of the locomotive engineers, and Francisco Pérez Leirós of the Federal Capital municipal workers. The rest of the Independent and nonaligned unions were almost as fierce as their Peronist counterparts in opposing the UCRP government.

If the issue of cooperation with the government did not distinguish the "62 Leales" from the "62 de Pie," what about differences in the types of economic sectors organized by the respective groups? Arturo Fernández suggests that "the unions led by Vandor corresponded to the more dynamic industrial sectors (metals, petroleum, glass, and later automobiles), whereas 'anti-Vandorism' emerged in unions pertaining to 'vegetative' industries, as well as to tertiary and service activities."[77] Similarly, Eduardo Viola has argued that "the Vandorist effort was opposed by a minority faction of Peronist unionism, tied to the most backward industrial sectors and linked organically to reproducing Perón's plebiscitarian leadership."[78] The "62 de Pie" helped Perón protect his leadership, but it was not a minority faction of Peronist unionism, nor did it draw its affiliates disproportionately from the most backward industrial sectors. In fact, the "62 de Pie" organized about the same number of unions and of unionists as did the "62 Leales," and the economic base of the unions in the "62 de Pie" was almost exactly the same along most plausibly relevant dimensions as that of the unions in the "62 Leales." As Table 5 shows, the proportion of industrial (manufacturing, extractive, construction) as opposed to nonindustrial (service, transport, public utility) unions was similar in each group. So was the proportion of dynamic versus traditional-sector unions within the manufacturing subsector of industry.[79] Neither group had more than one or two public-sector unions, and each group organized about twenty unions with a combined membership of about 400,000. The non-Peronist Independent and non-

TABLE 5

Distribution of Unions Across Economic Variables Hypothesized to Underlie
the February 1966 Split in the "62 Organizations"

	62 Leales	62 de Pie	Other 62	Non-62
Unions in group	20	21	12	40
Total membership	408,350	417,700	98,400	902,300
Private ownership	18	20	11	28
Public ownership	2	1	1	12
Nonindustrial	4	5	5	32
Industrial	16	16	7	8
Traditional industry	12	13	5	5
Dynamic industry	4	3	2	3

NOTE: Total membership figures and information about which unions belonged to which group are taken from Documentación e Información Laboral, *Nucleamientos sindicales*. Unions reporting fewer than 800 members in 1966 are excluded from all figures except those for total membership. Industrial unions were classified as "traditional" or "dynamic" according to Oficina de Estudios para la Colaboración Económica Internacional, *Argentina económica y financiera*, 180. Mining and construction unions are categorized as pertaining to the traditional industrial sector.

aligned groups, by comparison, included a much higher proportion of service and public-sector unions. Economic factors thus distinguished Peronist from non-Peronist unions, but not "62 Leales" from "62 de Pie" unions. In 1968, by contrast, economic factors (public vs. private, industrial vs. service, traditional vs. dynamic manufacturing) clearly distinguished the Peronist unions in the "CGT de los Argentinos" from those in the rival "CGT–Azopardo."[80]

Thus, neither attitude toward the government nor economic cleavages take us very far toward explaining the lines along which the "62" split. A more nuanced view of the rift requires an examination of the five major currents that made up the Peronist union leadership during the Illia period. Four of the five currents were associated respectively with the four most famous Peronist union leaders of the day: Augusto Vandor (head of the metalworkers' union and of the "62" prior to its split in January 1966), José Alonso (head of the garment workers' union and, prior to his expulsion in January 1966, of the CGT), Amado Olmos (head of the private hospital workers' union), and Andrés Framini (head of the textile workers' union). The fifth current comprised the so-called hard-liners (*duros*), whose most important representatives included Jorge DiPasquale of the pharmaceutical workers and Ricardo de Luca of the shipyard workers.

The Vandorist and hard-line factions, which had existed since 1959, were the most cohesive. Alonso, Framini, and Olmos had distinctive and idiosyncratic ideological and programmatic views that placed them outside these groupings, but they and their followers repeatedly formed temporary alliances with either the Vandorists or the hard-liners. In January 1963, Alonso had been Vandor's handpicked choice for the CGT secretary-generalship, but after the March 1965 national deputy elections, he had rebelled against Vandor. Framini was usually aligned with the hard-liners, but he sometimes acted as an intermediary between the hard-liners and Vandor or between the hard-liners and Alonso.[81] Olmos bore an ambiguous relationship to Vandor. He was originally allied with the UOM chief, having met Vandor and his co-strategist Miguel Gazzera in prison in 1956.[82] At the beginning of Illia's presidency, the more extreme elements of the Peronist left, like the followers of Héctor Villalón, regarded Vandor, Olmos, and Gazzera as forming the leading "troika" within what it referred to as the union "bureaucracy."[83] As late as March 1965, Olmos was being referred to in the mainstream Argentine press as the "voice of the left wing of Vandorism."[84] It was not until after the October 1965 meeting in Avellaneda that Olmos abandoned the metalworkers' leader.

As is evident in the tendency of journalists to refer to them as "Vandoristas," "Alonsistas," "Fraministas," and so on, the union leader factions had a strong personalistic component. Nonetheless, the contrasts among them went beyond their personal domination by particular union notables. Each differed from the others in terms of the degree of social transformation it advocated, the role it envisioned for Perón in the day-to-day leadership of the Peronist movement, and the strategy it favored for giving Peronist unionism greater access to state resources. To specify the characteristics of the rift that separated the two wings of the "62," it is necessary first to map the dimensions of cleavage among the five main union leader currents. Because it is virtually impossible to find documents in which the positions of the respective currents on these issues are expressed in pure form, the best that can be done is to scan the documentary evidence for items that (a) explicitly touch on the issues in question and (b) can be shown to have reflected the thinking of some leadership currents more than others.

To a certain extent, the leadership currents in Peronist unionism during the 1963–66 period differed in terms of the degree and type of social change each advocated. Whereas Olmos, Framini and the hard-liners advocated a fairly radical transformation of society that sometimes extended, in rhetoric at least, to explicit condemnations of capitalism, Alonso and Vandor were careful to limit their broad political demands to the implantation of a less dependent and more socially responsible version of capitalist development. This line of cleavage can be elucidated by examining the union leaders' respective positions on the issues of agrarian reform and workplace control.

The views of Olmos, Framini, and the hard-liners are synthesized in the July 1962 Huerta Grande program, named after the city in the province of Córdoba where it was presented at a national plenary session of the "62." The meeting at Huerta Grande formed part of a broader "turn to the left" that was taking place at the time within the Peronist movement. According to Framini, the initial stimulus for the leftward turn came from Perón, but the final document produced by the Huerta Grande meeting was never explicitly authorized by him. Included in the document were ten briefly worded demands, including radical calls for the "expropriation without compensation of the landed oligarchy" and for the "implantation of workers' control over production."[85] Framini, Olmos, DiPasquale, de Luca, and other hard-liners drew up the document with little input from the more conservative members of Vandor's group, which at the time included Alonso. Although Vandor presided over some of the plenary session's assemblies and sessions, few of the UOM leader's allies attended the meeting. After the Huerta Grande program was announced, moreover, the Vandorists did little to explain it to the union rank and file.[86]

The Huerta Grande demands for agrarian reform and workplace control were more radical than those envisioned by either Vandor or Alonso. An August 1963 "62" document may be taken as an expression of Vandor's personal views on these matters, for it was issued at a time when hard-liners like DiPasquale, Sebastián Borro (meat packers), and Juan José Jonch (telephone workers) were well on their way to being expelled from the "62," and when other hard-liners like Anteo Poccione (leather workers) had been won over to the Vandorist wing of the organization.[87] The document called for agrarian reform to eliminate large landholdings, but did not touch on the question of compensation and said nothing about worker control over production.[88] Vandor's views on the latter topic were revealed during a series of UOM factory occupations in 1962, during which the metalworker's chief insisted that his union intended "no collectivism" and emphasized that the factory was a "community of interests."[89] Like all of the Peronist trade union leaders, Vandor spoke frequently of "revolution," but he was careful to add that a class-based revolution was not what he had in mind. "What is necessary is revolution. It doesn't matter who makes it. . . . all social sectors [should participate in the revolution] without class prejudice. . . . I'm not in favor of a class-based movement."[90] Alonso's views on agrarian reform and workplace control were even more conservative. After coming out from under Vandor's shadow in March 1965, Alonso and some of his collaborators outlined their ideas in the "Change of Structures" pamphlet discussed above. Despite its stentorian critique of all existing "structures," the pamphlet discussed agrarian reform only in terms of a tax on potential income from under-utilized land and better utilization of "social, economic, and technical-scientific resources." It also specified that workers ideally would *share* control over production with enterprise owners and managers.[91] If the vision of social change endorsed by Framini, Olmos, and the hard-liners may be characterized as left-reformist, and if Vandor expressed a more pragmatic and compromising reformism, Alonso's policy proposals are best described as conservative and technocratic.

It would be unwise to exaggerate the ideological differences between Framini and Olmos on the one hand and Vandor and Alonso on the other. Such differences probably had as much to do with style and rhetoric as with radically different visions of what social and economic changes would be best for Argentina. Olmos, for example, who was casually labeled a "Trotskyist" by a weekly magazine, was careful to point out that he was not in favor of a "class-based party, which would be in the last instance the negation of Justicialism."[92] Olmos also argued that excluding nonlabor groups from a Peronist political party "would mean totally denying the essence of Peronism" as a multiclass alliance.[93] Far from being a Marxist, Olmos was an early example of a union leader attracted by the new social doctrine of the Catholic Church, an ideological standpoint that would come to fuller fruition in the CGT de los Argentinos created in 1968 under the typographers' leader Raimundo Ongaro, and during the 1980s in the statements and speeches of the CGT leader Saúl Ubaldini. According to one union leader who frequently collaborated with him, Olmos was a close friend of the mother of the Colombian priest-turned-revolutionary Camilo Torres.[94]

Framini's radicalism was more fiery than Olmos's, at least on a rhetorical plane. In mid 1962, Framini announced that "the nation has no way forward within the capitalist system."[95] By late 1963, journalists were characterizing Framini as a "revolutionary" and counterposing his position to Vandor's more "negotiatory" posture.[96] But considering Framini's complete loyalty to Perón and Perón's long-standing anticommunism, it is difficult to take seriously Framini's diatribes against the capitalist system. Skepticism about the depth of the AOT leader's commitment to the abolition of capitalism is reinforced by the way in which his adversaries viewed him. Framini sparked considerable resistance in the non-Peronist left, and in 1963 the more extreme "insurrectional" currents in Peronism condemned him for selling out to the "union bureaucracy."[97] Even Vandor, rather than dismissing Framini as an incorrigible leftist, merely remarked to his allies in the CGT's regional branch in La Plata: "It's impossible to have confidence in Framini: he doesn't have his own opinions; those who command him always speak through him."[98] Vandor did not specify who Framini's "commanders" might be—he had no interest in reminding his audience that Framini at the time was the union leader closest to Perón.

In addition to displaying a wide range of ideological views and programmatic aims, the five union leader currents exhibited differing attitudes toward Perón's role in the movement. Framini's willingness to do whatever Perón thought was necessary for the movement (and for Perón's capacity to keep control of it) has already been noted. Similarly, the hard-liners saw themselves primarily as a tactical weapon for Perón. "We shall offer Perón the revolutionary option if, as seems likely, negotiations with the government turn out badly," Sebastián Borro stated in August 1964.[99] Support for insurrection from Framini and the hard-liners is best interpreted as an attempt by Perón to use these segments of the union leadership to advocate spectacular but impractical solutions, as against the more pedestrian but feasible ones promoted by Vandor. By keeping alive the hope of a return to the 1946–55 polity, Framini and the hard-liners carried out Perón's work of lowering the stock of potential rivals like Vandor, whose power could only increase if the movement adopted strategies more dependent on close-to-the-ground organization. At the same time, by presenting themselves as unswerving loyalists to Perón, Framini and the hard-liners could hint to the rank and file that Vandor's ventures into the political party field called into question his own loyalty to the exiled leader. By portraying Vandor as a "traitor" to Perón, Framini and the hard-liners retained a degree of power and autonomy within Peronist unionism that they might not otherwise have enjoyed, in view of Vandor's far greater organizational resources.

If Framini and the hard-liners represented the sector of Peronist unionism most willing to follow Perón's dictates unquestioningly, Vandor represented the other end of the spectrum. The UOM leader was repeatedly accused of trying to wrest day-to-day control of the Peronist movement from Perón. Even Miguel Gazzera, a steadfast ally of the metalworkers' chief, asserted that Vandor was tricked by the politicians who surrounded him into deliberately scuttling Perón's attempt to return to Argentina in December 1964. When this effort failed, Gazzera continues, the same politicians then tricked Vandor into believing that "the time was ripe to institutionalize the Peronist movement, without Perón, of course."[100] Gazzera's assertions that Vandor was being manipulated by self-serving underlings seem rather disingenuous. The metalworkers' chief repeatedly expressed his preference for the creation of a legal Peronist party, which could not have continued to participate electorally were Perón to have functioned within it as anything more than a symbolic figurehead. One union leader who opposed Vandor is convinced that the UOM chief did in fact try hard to secure Perón's return to Argentina in 1964, knowing that he would be second-in-command if the attempt succeeded. Vandor's efforts to wrest control of the movement away from Perón only began, according to this union leader, after Perón's failed return to Argentina brought home decisively the need to look for alternative channels of political representation.[101]

Vandor repeatedly denied that he was competing with Perón for control of the movement, and Delia Parodi, one of his collaborators, rejected the notions that Vandor deliberately scuttled Perón's return or that he was trying to create a Peronism without Perón.[102] In fact, Vandor and his allies almost certainly envisioned a more oblique challenge to Perón than the usurpatory schemes that their adversaries attributed to them. Nonetheless, the underlying logic of their party-building project pointed in the direction of a greatly reduced role for the movement's founder. The tension between the explicit aims and underlying logic of Vandor's project is evident in Serú García's interpretation of it.

In my personal opinion, Vandor never had a plan involving Perónism without Perón. Peronism without Perón wasn't going to go anywhere. . . . It would have been like having Peronism without Peronists, which is what was happening then, and what is happening today [1993] more than ever. Perón, through his delegates, was becoming disconnected from the living reality of Peronism. . . . We wanted a Perón who was the leader, the chief, the principal figure of the movement. We didn't want the delegates taking advantage of Perón's charisma and prestige and acting in a practically arbitrary way, ignoring the Peronist bases. We didn't want a party independent of Perón—we weren't fools. We wanted a structured Perón, away from the principle of charisma—

which would have been hard because he utilized it very well—a Perón that responded to a political organization. . . . it was a matter of establishing a different relationship with Perón, which was hard, because the existing modality involved a relationship with a charismatic leader, and it's not easy for such a leader to change his relationship with the people.[103]

Olmos's stance toward Perón's role in the movement may have changed over time. After the Avellaneda conference of the "62" at which Vandor reportedly said, "We are confronting Perón in order to save Perón," Olmos abandoned his long-standing alliance with the metalworkers' chief, partly because, according to *Primera Plana*, he thought it would marginalize Perón entirely. This justification does not square well, however, with Olmos's previous stance toward Perón. Olmos had been the first Peronist leader to advocate forming a "workers' party," and when he ran as a national deputy candidate on the Unión Popular ticket in 1962, he reportedly said, "We want [Perón] back from exile, but as a sort of party hero, not as president. Perón is not a revolutionary."[104] It is not clear, however, whether Olmos really did change his mind on this issue in late 1965, or whether he abandoned Vandor for some other reason.

Of all the main Peronist union leaders, Alonso's view of the role Perón should play in the movement was the most ambiguous. On the one hand, Alonso tried to portray himself as a loyal supporter of Perón by being among the most bitter critics of Vandor's efforts to institutionalize Peronism as a party and by positioning himself as the most prominent figure in the "62 de Pie." In February 1966, as Vandor was busy engineering his expulsion as CGT secretary-general, Alonso condemned the metalworkers' chief for, among other things, being "the author of the slogan 'One has to be against Perón in order to save Perón.' "[105] Yet Alonso's denunciations of Vandor's "disloyalty" to Perón fit poorly with his own misgivings about the appropriateness of a "charismatic leader" undertaking to represent the interests of the trade unions. The "Change of Structures" document drawn up by Alonso and his advisers makes clear in its discussion of Argentina's "power factors" or "counterpoised groups" that Alonso was not at all in favor of a return to the situation that had prevailed under Perón, when the CGT was subordinated to the president's control.

The interests of these [counterpoised] groups cannot legitimately be delegated. Such interests, moreover, can no longer be assumed by charismatic leaders, because this does not correspond to our phase of social development. The specific and legitimate interests of the social groups are too great and derive from a very complex problematic that does not admit of delegation. Implicitly or explicitly, all [such groups] search for their own direct links to power.[106]

The most important differences between the Peronist union leader currents involved neither ideology nor attitude toward Perón's role in the movement, but rather alternative views of the *strategies* that Peronist unionism should use to advance the broad political interests of the workers. Three such methods stood out: insurrection, political party activity, and the elevation of the CGT leadership to a major policy-making role within the state. Each of the main Peronist trade union leaders was identified primarily with one of these alternatives, although each at times paid lip service to the other approaches. Framini was identified with the option of mobilizing an insurrection to restore Perón to the presidency. The textile workers' leader repeatedly expressed his confidence that "the people will be the protagonists of another October 17."[107] "We shall create the base organizations for popular mobilization," Framini announced in mid 1962, "and then organize a gigantic march on the federal capital from every site in Greater Buenos Aires."[108] In an April 1964 speech at a university in Santa Fe, Framini proclaimed the need for violent revolution: "What needs to be changed are the basics, the colonial mentality, the system. And this revolution has only one road: violence. Reality and the facts show this to be true. There is no escape."[109] DiPasquale, Borro, and the other hard-liners were even more explicit than Framini in advocating armed insurrection. "The people must oppose the regime's army of occupation with its own armed forces and [with] workers' militias, which will allow it to conquer power," they declared upon founding the Peronist Revolutionary Movement in 1964. That organization would itself assume the task of "building the structure and developing the centralized revolutionary leadership."[110]

Although Olmos advocated a more far-reaching social transformation than did Vandor, both initially agreed that workers could most effectively advance their broad political interests by electing Peronist unionists and allied politicians to top state decision-making posts. Among the major "62" leaders, Olmos had been the first strong supporter of creating a "workers' party" to participate in elections, in which the union leadership would play a "hegemonic" role, but nonlabor sectors of Peronism would also have a voice.[111] As the March 1962 elections drew near, Vandor endorsed Olmos's idea and set about colonizing the neo-Peronist Unión Popular. By November 1963, journalists specializing in labor affairs were reporting that Vandor "gives the impression that he would like to see the [Peronist] movement transforming itself into a trade-union based political party not unlike the British Labour Party, which could play a full part in national political life."[112] Unlike other figures on the Peronist left, Olmos favored Unión Popular participation in the March 1965 national deputy elections.[113] But when Vandor became more explicit in asserting his independence from Perón, Olmos began to distance himself from the metalworkers' chief and his political party strategy.

Of all the major Peronist trade union leaders, Alonso was by far the most hostile not just to political parties but to the institutions of liberal democracy in general. By the end of 1964, the CGT's press organs, closely controlled by Alonso and by the CGT's press secretary, Luis Angeleri, were arguing that "liberal" political institutions devoted to the representation of individual interests were a thing of the past: "The old image of . . . liberal democracy, in which the 'political man' assumes the representation of all societal interests, is definitively exhausted. . . . The only way to turn our spent democracy into a democracy—perhaps the only democracy that is possible in these times—is [to] incorporat[e] the forces of labor into the organs of political decision."[114]

Alonso and his close collaborators advocated the establishment of new state institutions that would allow an autonomous CGT to participate directly in formulating policy. The ideal policy-making arrangements, in Alonso's view, would be corporatist ones involving society's "power factors"—the CGT, employers' associations, the Church, and the armed forces. What each of these organized groups had in common, according to Argentines who analyzed the power-factor concept, were aspirations to a national political role, a capacity to formulate independent goals, and the power to constrain policy decisions without taking overt action.[115] In its 1963–64 annual report, the CGT announced its aspiration to be recognized as such a group: "One of the goals to be achieved is to convert the pressure group into a power factor. . . . The CGT is not merely a union body. It is a national, popular, and representative entity, and those whom it represents have given it a mandate to make itself felt in whatever ways promote the happiness of the people and the greatness of the country."[116]

Consistent with his hostility to liberal democracy and his advocacy of a corporatist approach to policy making, Alonso singled out parties for special criticism and defended the notion that Peronism was a national movement, not a mere political party. In an interview with a weekly news magazine, Alonso gave the following account of the purposes of the "62 de Pie": "We're trying to redeem the authenticity of the movement, to put it back on its historical path. Vandor is making it into just another political party, into an electoral agency. While we in the CGT were struggling for solutions, they were chasing nominations. . . . We are not against elections, but elections are only anecdotes. A movement is something more than that."[117] The March 1966 Tucumán statement of the "62 de Pie" echoed Alonso's emphasis on Peronism's character as a movement and on the need to combat efforts to transform it into a party. Few statements more aptly characterize Peronism's weak party institutionalization:

Such parties as Peronists may create to participate in the electoral process are, given our character as a majoritarian movement, simple structures subordinate to the pinnacle of leadership. Our parties do not outline strategy, they follow it. They are simply instruments . . . that allow us to do battle on the electoral front—that is, on the terrain of our adversaries. . . . [The "62 de Pie"] repudiates the efforts of groups and persons who, in the name of the movement, are trying to convert [Peronism] into a mere liberal political party, with the aim of forging an electoral front with well-known enemies of Peronism and of the people.[118]

Nowhere are Alonso's views on the archaic character of political party activity and on the need to reduce politics to administration more explicitly spelled out than in an interview he gave a month before the June 1966 coup:

Everything I do these days is based on a deep-rooted conviction that elections will not resolve the country's problems. The country needs something else. Elections are simply disputes between differently labeled committees and serve only to maintain intact the current state of affairs, the present structures. And what the country needs today is to change these structures. This is something that no party can do, because the parties are organizations whose historical time has passed. By their very nature, they end up representing the petty interests of committees and never succeed in popular representation. It is necessary to create other channels for advancing the interests of the people. In the current system, the technicians, the men really equipped to assume the task of governance, can never promote themselves to a governing function through the political parties because [the parties] are designed to promote figures from the committees. . . . our entire struggle is oriented toward preserving the character of Peronism as a movement. We are fighting those who want to convert it into a party. . . . Vandor is the party, we are the movement. . . . We respect parliamentary activity and the free play of opinions; all we think

TABLE 6
Cleavages in Peronist Union Leadership, 1963–1966

	Dimension of Cleavage		
	Ideology	View of appropriate role for Perón in Peronist movement	Preferred strategy for giving unions access to state resources
Hard-liners	Left reformist	Day-to-day control of movement	Insurrection
Framini	Unclear; occasional anticapitalist rhetoric	Day-to-day control of movement	Insurrection
Olmos	Left reformist	Symbolic figurehead to Nov. 1965, then unclear	Political party to Nov. 1965, then unclear
Vandor	Pragmatic reformist	Symbolic figurehead	Political party
Alonso	Technocratic-conservative	Symbolic figurehead	CGT

is that the parties are not the most appropriate means for achieving these objectives. I don't think this point of view can be characterized as fascist.[119]

The positions of each of the main Peronist union leader currents on the issues just outlined—ideology, the role envisioned for Perón in the day-to-day leadership of Peronism, and the preferred strategy for giving unions access to state resources—are summarized in Table 6. These factors alone cannot explain the cleavage that emerged in February 1966 (with four of the currents in the "62 de Pie" and the Vandorists alone in the "62 Leales") because, as the table makes clear, the four "62 de Pie" currents differed as much among themselves on these issues as they did from Vandor.

The "four versus one" distribution of union currents across the two wings of the "62" is best explained simply by Vandor's power-enhancement interests and by the power-preservation interests of the other four currents. In fact, the alignment is precisely that predicted by the model of "balancing behavior" in Kenneth Waltz's theory of international relations (described in Chapter 1). Applying Waltz's model, one could represent Vandor (on the scene in Argentina) as the stronger great power, Perón (exiled in Madrid) as the weaker great power, and Alonso, Olmos, Framini, and the hard-liners as peripheral states. Given Vandor's enormous advantage over each of the other four union currents in power resources (such as the capacity to mobilize, finance, and intimidate), each of the other four currents came eventually to feel its survival threatened and found Perón to be a convenient rallying point. Pure power interests, expressed as predicted by the "balancing behavior" model, explain the "four against one" pattern of cleavage, which appears enigmatic from the point of view of attitude toward the government, economic interests, view of the appropriate role for Perón in the Peronist movement, and preferred strategy for giving unions access to state resources.

The Showdown: The Mendoza Gubernatorial Election of April 1966

The first electoral showdown between Vandor and Perón came in January 1966, when gubernatorial elections were held in the northwestern province of Jujuy. Vandor threw his support to candidate José Martiarena, Jujuy's incumbent governor and head of the local branch of the neo-Peronist Partido Blanco de los Trabajadores. Perón endorsed José Nasif, a leader of the provincial branch of the PJ (which had been permitted to present candidates in Jujuy). On 30 January 1966, Martiarena was reelected with 46,000 votes; Nasif received only 4,000.[120] The contest was widely viewed as a victory for Vandor and a defeat for Perón. Grondona later referred to the Jujuy election as the "first stage in the struggle" between Vandor and Perón, arguing that "Jujuy, with Martiarena's victory and the defeat of Perón's candidate, demonstrates that charisma, 'without' organization, can do nothing against the [established political] structure."[121] Martiarena's victory did not, however, give rise to a perception that Vandor had scored a decisive victory against Perón. Jujuy was poor, predominantly rural, sparsely populated, and spatially isolated from the country's major electoral districts. Moreover, Martiarena belonged to the family that had traditionally dominated the province, and Perón had not campaigned hard for the losing candidate. The real test of strength came three months later, when Vandor and Perón supported rival candidates for the Mendoza governorship.

The Mendoza gubernatorial election was scheduled for 17 April 1966. Although many expected that Emilio Jofré of the incumbent Partido Democrática (a local conservative party) had a good chance of winning, the most gripping contest was between the main Peronist candidates: Alberto Serú García of the neo-Peronist Movimiento Popular Mendocino (MPM), who was considered to be Jofré's "most serious rival," and Ernesto Corvalán Nanclares of the local PJ.[122] The contest between Serú and Corvalán was viewed as a popular referendum on the struggle between Vandor and Perón. If Serú got more votes than Corvalán, Vandor's party-building project would get a tremendous boost; if Corvalán outpolled Serú, Peronism without Perón would be doomed.

It had been known for months that Vandor would throw his support to Serú, who had become by 1966 Argentina's most visible and outspoken neo-Peronist politician. Serú had proudly claimed the distinction of being "the first rebel" against Perón, and had been one of a handful of Peronists who, disregarding Perón's order to cast blank ballots, had run successfully for a national deputy seat in July 1963. After his March 1965 reelection, Serú had grown closer to Vandor, to the point where Carlos Risso, president of the new anti-Vandor Peronist deputy bloc, characterized the Mendoza politician as the UOM chief's "main adviser." When Serú traveled to Madrid in March 1966 to try to get Perón's support for his gubernatorial candidacy, the exiled leader refused to see him. On his return, Serú made an explicit declaration of independence from Perón: "While others only wait for orders, Vandor and I agree that Peronism must act by itself, as an organized party."[123]

Corvalán Nanclares, the less well known of the two major Peronist candidates, had resigned from the MPM in late February 1966, claiming that he had been promised but later denied the party's gubernatorial candidacy.[124] After breaking with the MPM, Corvalán had gained permission to run under the provincial PJ label, and in late March 1966, he won an explicit declaration of support from Perón.[125] Corvalán was certainly the underdog: even after Perón endorsed him, he was expected to win fewer than half as many votes as Serú.[126] Many observers felt that Perón's orders no longer carried their former weight. As one editorialist commented two days before the election, "Today . . . Perón's orders seem almost as devalued as the [recently discontinued currency] *peso moneda nacional*. This is something murmured even by those in the current backing [Perón's] 'personal delegate' [Isabel]."[127]

In addition to being viewed as a showdown between Vandor and Perón, the Mendoza contest was regarded as a "trial run" for gubernatorial elections scheduled for March 1967 in the more heavily populated provinces of Santa Fe, Córdoba, and Buenos Aires.[128] A strong showing for Serú in Mendoza, an economically advanced province with just under a million inhabitants, would be taken as a sign that Vandor's candidates would do well in these similarly large and modern provinces. In an attempt to prevent Vandor from unifying the Peronist vote, the government stepped up its campaign to "revitalize the previously anemic organization of 'Isabelista' Peronism." This campaign dated from late 1965, when the government had overlooked a law against Peronist propagandizing in order to allow Isabel to campaign against Vandor.[129] As the Mendoza election approached, favors to the Isabelistas grew more specific. It took just four days for the local electoral court to approve Corvalán's request to run under the "orthodox" PJ label, ensuring that Peronism would run divided, and Corvalán was allowed the symbolic advantage of running his campaign out of the former headquarters of Mendoza's Partido Peronista.[130] The government's most audacious attempt to undermine Serú came two days before the election, when Mendoza radio and television stations were allowed to replay a recorded message by Perón urging his followers to vote for Corvalán—despite the legal ban on the broadcast of such messages.[131] In his statement, Perón announced: "The Partido Justicialista is the [label] that officially represents us. . . . we are not opposed to ex-Peronists constituting their own party and contesting elections, but that would have to be with their own names, not ours, and they'll have to run wearing their own jersey, because only the Partido Justicialista is entitled to wear the Peronist jersey."[132]

Although Corvalán benefited from the support of Perón and of the government, Serú had organizational advantages over his rival. The large provincial wine workers' union was in the Vandorist camp, and Serú's MPM was a more developed party organization than the provincial PJ. In the 1965 national deputy elections, the MPM had won 98,000 votes, compared to only 15,000 for the Mendoza PJ.[133] Moreover, Vandor and his collaborators traveled to Mendoza to help Serú, whereas no prominent member of the "62 de Pie" made a similar journey to support Corvalán.[134] At bottom, therefore, the question was whether Perón's direct appeal to individual Peronists to support Corvalán would outweigh Vandor's organizational support for Serú. Confounding expectations, it did. Corvalán won a huge upset victory over Serú, drawing 102,000 votes against only 62,000 for the favored Vandorist candidate. The Partido Democrática's candidate, Jofré, with 129,000 votes, was assured of winning the governorship when the provincial electoral college met a week later. But as *Primera Plana* editorialized, Jofré's victory seemed "to pale before the evidence that Perón maintains his hegemony unscathed." Grondona put it more explicitly: "After Mendoza, the capital of Peronism is again in Madrid."[135]

Because Vandor's defeat in Mendoza foreshadowed what was likely to happen throughout the country, the balance of power in Peronist unionism shifted rapidly away from the metalworkers' chief. Several unions transferred their allegiances from the Vandorist "62 Leales" to the "62 de Pie," and the leadership council of the "62 Leales" resigned as a bloc. The Vandorists announced, albeit with some ambiguity, that they would henceforth refrain from trying to win hegemony over the political wing of Peronism.[136] A Vandorist candidate for governor of Santa Cruz withdrew in favor of Carlos Alberto Pérez Companc, a wealthy non-Peronist industrialist supported by the "Isabelistas."[137] Like Solano Lima before him, Pérez Companc was a nominee who, if elected, would have no political power base other than Perón himself. Serú's defeat in the 1966 Mendoza gubernatorial election spelled the end of Vandor's party-building project and, more generally, the collapse of Peronism without Perón.

Vandor's initiative failed for three main reasons. First and foremost, Perón's followers obeyed his orders because they continued to revere the exiled leader. This reverence derived from a partly idealized, partly accurate memory of how much better his 1946–55 government had been than previous and subsequent governments, and from the fact that the Peronist identity focused on Perón himself rather than on party or ideology. Moreover, the fact that Perón was not dead, but still sending messages from exile, meant that the personalistic movement he led was less susceptible to routinization than it would otherwise have been. Second, although Vandor's organizational resources did much to offset Perón's continued personalistic appeal, they were not as well developed in Mendoza as they were in the Greater Buenos Aires region. Data from Mendoza's sixteen departments show that Corvalán actually did better in urban areas than in rural ones[138] — perhaps because Perón's radio message was easier to hear, or hear about, in the cities. Third, Perón had a greater advantage in popular appeal than Vandor had in organization. On the one hand, survey data showed that only 4 percent of Peronists chose Vandor as a leader they "particularly admired."[139] On the other hand, by the time of the Mendoza elections, Perón was doing better and better on the organizational front. By early 1966, Perón had gained the support of the "62 de Pie" and of important segments of the PJ and Unión Popular. Many secondary

Peronist unionists and politicians stood to lose prominence if Vandor gained hegemony—including Alonso and Olmos, both of whom had suggested at one time or another that the unions would be better off if Perón became a symbolic figurehead. Just as peripheral states often throw in their lot with a distant great power when a closer one poses a more immediate threat, subaltern Peronist union and party leaders looked to the distant Perón to protect them from Vandor's more immediately threatening party-building project.

The Defeat of Vandor's Party-Building Project and the 1966 Coup

General Onganía began to organize pro-coup sentiment as early as April 1965, when he instructed his collaborators to draw up a plan "in case a power vacuum occur[s] and the army ha[s] to take charge of the government." This directive should be interpreted in light of Onganía's mid 1964 decision *not* to draw up such a plan because, as he put it, "once they begin to study the problems of government, they will be tempted and excited by the solutions and will want to replace the government so as to put them into effect." [140] Illia's army secretary, retired General Ignacio Avalos, threatened to resign when he found out about the directive, reasoning that its existence implied that Onganía was not fully committed to the constitutional order. Avalos's advisers persuaded him to stay on, but in October 1965, when Onganía authorized a high military appointment without seeking Avalos's approval, the army secretary did resign. To replace him, Illia chose an active-duty general, Eduardo Castro Sánchez, who thereby acquired formal political authority over Commander-in-Chief Onganía, his military superior. On hearing of Castro Sánchez's appointment, Onganía resigned, astonishing and dismaying defense ministry officials, who had received no objection from Onganía after informing him that an active-duty general might be named to the post. [141] Onganía's resignation "gave the *golpistas* a banner, a cause, and a presidential candidate." [142]

Although broader factors contributed to the June 1966 coup, and although pro-coup sentiment began to build at least a year before the Mendoza election, Vandor's defeat played an important role in sealing the fate of the Illia government. In so doing, it provides a particularly telling example of how difficult it is to maintain civilian rule in the absence of a political party conduit for the interests and demands of a powerful and politicized trade union movement. The demise of Vandor's project should not be exaggerated as a cause of the June 1966 military coup, but neither should it be disregarded.[143] The UCRP officials who decided in December 1965 that the Illia government was already doomed were overly pessimistic. Among the 29 top officers they listed as favoring a coup (only 6 were said to oppose one) were generals Nicolás Hure, Cándido López, and Alejandro Lanusse.[144] Hure and López, however, are cited elsewhere as having opposed intervention right up until the day it occurred,[145] and Lanusse, whose support for the coup was considered essential, was also apparently undecided at the time of the UCRP report. When asked whether the decision to intervene was made days or years before the coup, retired General Tomás Sánchez de Bustamante, also listed as pro-coup, gave the following response.

I think the decision was made the day they [the pro-coup officers] won over Lanusse. Because without Lanusse, it would have been hard for them to have done it. . . . [Q?: When did they win over Lanusse?] . . . I think they won Lanusse over about fifteen or twenty days before [the coup]. It was a long process. . . . it had been going on since 1964 . . . since 1965 the Commander of the Fifth Army Corps, General [Osiris] Villegas, had been an enthusiastic supporter of the idea that intervention was necessary . . . but among we commanders, General López, Cándido Adolfo López, didn't agree that the army had to intervene right up to the day of the coup. There was no unanimity, but as always happened, the most decisive take the initiative.[146]

Other evidence also supports the contention that the demise of Vandor's project was an important part of the process that led to the decision to make the coup. In a 1989 interview, General Onganía stated that the victory of Perón's candidate in the April 1966 Mendoza elections was a factor (*un dato*) in the armed forces' decision to launch a coup two months later.[147] On several occasions between October 1965 and April 1966, the press reported that officers were meeting with Vandor and others to negotiate "acceptable" Peronist candidates for key gubernatorial elections scheduled for 1967.[148] If these military officers were already committed to a coup, it is hard to explain why they engaged in such negotiation. Moreover, the contention that only the date of the coup had yet to be decided after mid 1965 accords poorly with the following statements by top military officers a few days after the Mendoza election:[149]

The results of the election clarify the choice available to the armed forces: to reach an agreement on [1967 gubernatorial] candidacies, it will now be necessary to negotiate with Perón, Isabel Perón, Andrés Framini, and the Trotskyites of FOTIA. The illusion has definitively vanished that everything can be settled in conversations with [Unión Popular leader] Rodolfo Tecera del Franco or with Vandor.[150]

The Mendoza elections have been a brutal warning to all of the political architects. With Pocho's [Perón's] victory over the neo-Peronists, it's now perfectly clear that they [the neo-Peronists] won't get anywhere in the province of Buenos Aires.[151]

Moreover, it was not until a few weeks before the coup that key political actors stopped acting as if they believed civilian rule would continue. Augusto Vandor, for example, had long been aware that a coup was possible, but his active support for neo-Peronist candidates in January and April 1966 suggests that he did not yet perceive a coup to be inevitable. Similarly, if Perón, the anti-Vandor sectors of Peronist unionism, or the Illia government had perceived a military coup to be inevitable, it would not have been reasonable for them to invest so much time and effort in thwarting Vandor's project. The Mendoza election effectively ruled out the most promising scenario for continued civilian rule. With Vandor's defeat, the military realized that they now had no one with whom to negotiate "acceptable" Peronist candidates for the 1967 gubernatorial elections. By eclipsing this scenario, Vandor's defeat help set the stage for the June 1966 coup. General Sánchez de Bustamante supported this interpretation in a 1989 interview:

The electoral solution, to be a political solution, needs to have a reasonable measure of legitimacy. This measure could have been achieved to some extent without Peronism, but not against Peronism, because to the extent that Peronism took a coherent, majority position against the solution, it stripped [that solution] of legitimacy. But to the extent that it had an acceptable presence, for example, through the provincial neo-Peronist parties, or through a cordial and friendly unionism, this legitimacy would have been an ingredient that would have allowed things to move forward.[152]

Another common view of the 1966 coup also stands in need of revision. It is often asserted that the "Peronist union leadership" actively promoted military intervention.[153] Some Peronist union leaders certainly did. José Alonso had been in contact with the military since 1964, when officers seeking to clarify the intentions behind the factory-occupation campaign turned to the CGT secretary-general after discovering that Vandor—whom they recognized as the real power behind the scenes—was in seclusion with his wife, who had suffered a miscarriage.[154] The military stepped up these contacts in December

1965, when high-ranking army officers held separate interviews with Alonso (who reportedly left the best impression), Vandor, and two other union leaders. The case that some Peronist unionists supported or resigned themselves to the coup is also bolstered by other evidence. In March 1966, top army officers, making a rare visit to a union hall, dined fraternally with top members of the union leadership in a ceremony honoring Col. Jorge Leal, who had just returned from an expedition to the South Pole.[155] Vandor's close collaborator Paulino Niembro reported in a 1981 interview that "our only recourse was to get close to the military," and that "the labor movement advanced in solidarity with the coup."[156] Onganía invited Peronist union leaders to his inauguration, and both factions of the "62" sent messages of support to the new military rulers.[157]

Peronist union leaders nonetheless had more diverse and nuanced attitudes toward the June 1966 coup than is often recognized. Moreover, some union leaders who decided to go along with the coup, including Vandor, did so later and less enthusiastically than is often thought. As late as September 1965, Vandor took the floor at a CGT meeting to condemn the *golpismo* of certain military officers.[158] Moreover, his contacts with military officers in the months prior to the Mendoza election were reportedly directed toward negotiating Peronist candidacies in the 1967 gubernatorial elections, not toward arranging the terms for Peronist participation in a future military government.[159] Illia's trade secretary Bernardo Grinspun provides further evidence that Vandor remained committed to the electoral route until quite late. After Illia signed a decree in February 1966 strengthening labor ministry oversight of union elections, Vandor contacted Grinspun to propose a deal. In exchange for the right to name the labor ministry officials in charge of supervising union elections, Vandor offered to put Rosendo García on a neo-Peronist ticket for governor of Buenos Aires. If García ran, and if Vandor's rivals proposed a competing candidate, Peronism would run divided, allowing the UCRP to win the election and reducing the chance of a coup. Grinspun conveyed Vandor's offer to Illia, who rejected it on the grounds that the democratization of union elections was nonnegotiable. In Grinspun's view, Vandor opted to go along with a coup only after the deal fell through.[160]

Grinspun's perception that Vandor decided to support a coup only very late in the game is corroborated by Serú García, who reports that "the night we lost the [April 1966 Mendoza gubernatorial] election, Vandor . . . told me, in the manner of one giving consolation, never mind, this isn't going to last, because we're going to give the green light to General Onganía."[161] This statement suggests that Vandor was waiting for the results of the election before deciding whether to cooperate with the coup, and although it does not entirely preclude the possibility that he made the decision at an earlier date, an earlier decision would have been inconsistent with the effort he expended to support Serú's candidacy. Later, moreover, Vandor may even have tried to change the light from green to yellow. On the very eve of the coup, *Primera Plana* reported that "momentum seems to be gathering in the Vandorist unions for a position against the coup, and in favor of pressuring the government to accept Peronism's institutionalization and the naming of a Buenos Aires gubernatorial candidate acceptable to the armed forces . . . however, contacts with *golpista* groups have not ceased." The possibility of a coup had long been in the air, and Vandor and his allies would need friends in the officer corps if they wanted to keep control of the CGT and the major unions in the wake of a military intervention. "Let them make the coup first, then we'll decide what to do," Vandor is reported to have said. The article also described the small communist faction of unionism as "representing, together with Vandorism, the most decidedly anti-*golpista* sector of the labor movement."[162]

The same article reported that "Amado Olmos (hospital workers, Trotskyist), together with other representatives of the [Peronist] left (DiPasquale, Arias, Eyerhalde), are against the coup and have maintained contacts with other sectors who share this position." By contrast, "José Alonso, ex-secretary-general of the CGT, appears to be decidedly *golpista*." Serú reports that "Vandor participated less [in the coup] than is often believed, even though he went [to Onganía's inauguration],"[163] and William Smith has argued that although both Alonso and Vandor "hastened to welcome the end of constitutional rule," Alonso was "involved much more intimately than Vandor in pre-coup negotiations with the military," and was repaid for his support by Onganía's labor ministry, which tried in late 1966 to "tilt the balance in favor of Alonso in the upcoming [CGT] election of new national authorities." After 1966, Alonso belonged to the informal union leader group known as the "New Current of Opinion," which favored active collaboration with the Onganía dictatorship and an indefinitely long "army-people union." Vandor, by contrast, viewed Onganía's "Argentine Revolution" as only a "transition toward Republican institutions."[164]

Despite their differences of opinion regarding the 1966 coup and the subsequent military regime, Vandor and Alonso would soon make amends and join forces to resist a common adversary: the left-leaning sectors of Peronist unionism that gained control of the CGT in 1968. By mid 1969, more conservative unionists had retaken the workers' central, but neither Vandor nor Alonso would live to enjoy their triumph or to witness Perón's return. In July 1969, Vandor was assassinated by unknown assailants who made their way into the UOM building, and in August 1970, Alonso was assassinated by an unidentified group who surrounded his automobile. These killings were condemned by the military government and by sectors of Argentine society that had never before showed much sympathy for Peronism or its leaders, marking a softening of the cleavage between Peronism and anti-Peronism that had convulsed Argentine society since the 1940s. It was precisely this softening of the conflict between Peronism and anti-Peronism, provoked by the rise of a militant left, that opened the door to Perón's return to the presidency in 1973. The murders of Vandor and Alonso also signaled the beginning of a much more savage struggle between left and right, from which Argentina has not yet fully recovered.

Chapter 6

Revolution, Restoration, and Repression

Between 1966 and 1983, Argentina experienced a period of relatively mild military rule (1966-73), an elected Peronist government (1973-76), and a period of much harsher military rule (1976-83). Whereas the Aramburu and Guido governments had presented themselves as temporary solutions to the problem of excluding Peronism from government, the 1966-73 and 1976-83 military governments promised to rule indefinitely while undertaking a more thoroughgoing transformation of society. A shift in the axis of political conflict, from Peronism versus anti-Peronism to left versus right, was behind Argentina's descent into increasingly sweeping authoritarianism. Contributing to this shift was the global wave of radical thought and action in the late 1960s and early 1970s, which had a strong impact on Argentina's cosmopolitan cities, and the Onganía government's shutting down of political opposition, which helped push many, especially urban middle-class youth, to the left.

As the axis of political conflict shifted, conservatives who had come to fear revolution more than Peronist restoration acquiesced to, and even voted for, Perón's reelection as president in 1973, hoping that he could tame new guerrilla groups—including the Peronist Montoneros. When Perón died in July 1974, the presidency passed to his widow and vice president, María Estela (Isabel) Martínez de Perón, under whose government political violence and economic crisis worsened and Peronism dissolved into warring factions. In 1975, a diverse group of "antiverticalist" Peronist politicians and union leaders tried, but failed, to give the Partido Justicialista a more pivotal role in the movement. Perón's plebiscitarian legacy helped the opposing "verticalist" faction defeat this attempt to strengthen the party. The defeat of the antiverticalist project was less significant, however, than that of the other Peronist party-building projects examined in this study: its improvised character, together with the exceptionally hostile context in which it was launched, made it far less promising than the initiatives of Vandor (1962–66) or of the renewal Peronists (1984–88). Isabel Perón's government was unable to reverse the disintegration of society, and as political violence and economic crisis spiraled out of control, the military seized power in March 1976.

Led by General Jorge Videla of the army, the military junta launched a "dirty war" aimed at the physical elimination of the Argentine left and the intimidation of the rest of society. It also suppressed parties and interest groups, imposed a reactionary cultural climate, and proclaimed a new era of unbridled capitalism. The immediate effects of this radical project were the murder or "disappearance" of thousands of people, the destruction of much of the country's inefficient but vital industrial base, and the emigration of an estimated 2 million citizens, including many of the better-educated. The long-term legacy of the military regime included the physical and psychological scars of those who survived detention and torture, the bereavement of the families of those who died or "disappeared," and an economic crisis crowned by a huge foreign debt. Yet the 1969–79 years, which began with guerrilla kidnappings and murders and ended with state terror, also generated revulsion against violence and intolerance that led to a societywide revaluation of civil liberties, electoral competition, and party activity. This revaluation of what both left and right had previously disparaged as "formal" democracy helped make the post-1983 period more congenial than previous years for democratic consolidation.

From Peronism Versus Anti-Peronism to Left Versus Right, 1966–1973

Immediately after the 1966 coup, public opinion surveys showed that a plurality of Argentines were fed up with political parties and thought that things would get better under military rule.[1] Contributing to skepticism about parties was, above all, the fact that the UCRI and UCRP governments, having been elected in the context of the ban on Peronism, had democratic legitimacy only for those who felt that Perón's abuses of authority justified the electoral exclusion of his followers. But even Perón's detractors had tired of Radical governments elected in the context of proscription, which had failed to "de-Peronize" the working class or to weaken the unions. The UCRP government in particular suffered from Illia's reputation as a plodding politician, which sat poorly with the millenarian climate of the times, and from the fact that he had been elected with only 25 percent of the vote. An economic downturn in early 1966, together with a massive campaign by military personnel, business leaders, opposition politicians, unionists, and media commentators to undermine Illia's authority, took an additional toll on his support. Military intervention always stems from a combination of internal military and societal factors, but history records few examples of coups in which society's role has been so pronounced.

The other side of the public opinion findings—the expectation that things would improve under a military government—can be explained in part by the characteristics of past experiences with military rule. The 1930–32, 1943–46, and 1955–58 dictatorships had on occasion been highly repressive, but as of 1966, no military government had engaged in repression on a scale so vast as to inspire implacable opposition to any form of renewed military rule in a critical mass of citizens (that kind of shift in public opinion would not come until the 1976–83 dictatorship). Moreover, the memories that military intervention evoked in 1966 were not altogether negative. Peronists could look back on the 1943 coup as having paved the way for Perón's rise, while anti-Peronists could remember the 1955 coup as having expelled him. Neither Peronists nor anti-Peronists saw much to be gained from preserving the proscription-based civilian regime, so when officers sent encouraging signals to each camp, Peronists and anti-Peronists alike could express optimism about life under the new military government.

Called out of retirement to lead the Argentine Revolution (as the new government christened its ambitious project) was Lt. General Juan Carlos Onganía. Whereas previous military presidents had stressed the exceptionality of their regimes, Onganía announced that his would endure until the goals of the Revolution had been achieved —no matter how long it took to achieve them. Economically, Onganía's goals were to tame inflation, restore growth, and modernize industry. Politically, Onganía hoped to create an entirely new system, revolving around corporatist institutions representing society's "real power factors." Elections and political parties might play a subordinate role in the new system, but before they were allowed to resume activity, party leaders would have to show that they were interested in promoting the common good rather than narrow personal and partisan interests.[2]

To pave the way for this political rebirth, the government dissolved existing parties, prohibited the formation of new ones, abolished all legislative bodies, and dismissed the supreme court.[3] It also launched an attack on what it viewed as cultural depravity, ordering books to be burnt, nightclubs to be shut, censorship to be imposed on movies and television, and a ban to be placed on publications purveying "communist propaganda" (or, in one case, a cartoon of the president). The climax of this assault was the "Night of the Long Batons," on 29 June 1966, when police beat up dozens of students and professors occupying a building at the University of Buenos Aires. Thirty were hospitalized, 184 professors resigned, universities were placed under government trusteeship, and leading scholars and scientists emigrated. The Night of the Long Batons and other attacks on dissidents and cultural expression alienated many middle-class youths and students not only from the government and regime but also from a national and international "system" that perpetuated inequality and repression. These groups began to move in droves toward Peronism, which for many had come to symbolize resistance to the established order.[4] Joe Baxter, a future guerrilla leader, rejoiced a few days after the Night of the Long Batons: "What's happening in Argentina is stupendous! The conditions for revolution have finally appeared!"[5]

Onganía and his collaborators, who constituted what Guillermo O'Donnell has termed the "paternalist" current of the armed forces, soon discovered that not all officers shared their economic developmentalism, moderate nationalism, and goal of creating a demobilized corporatist polity. The liberal current, which had wide support in the army, even broader backing in the navy, and the allegiance of national and transnational big business, favored a minimal economic role for the state, a friendly approach to foreign capital, and an eventual return to a liberal democracy in which workers would engage in apolitical unionism. The nationalists, a third and somewhat weaker military current, mainly supported by junior army officers, favored a big economic role for the state, an arm's-length approach to foreign capital, and the formation of a military-led "movement" actively backed by workers.[6]

Onganía's March 1967 decision to overturn the ministry of the economy to Adalbert Krieger Vasena, a liberal, dampened intramilitary tensions for a time. Krieger Vasena enacted a stabilization plan involving tariff reductions, a wage freeze, voluntary price controls, tax and credit incentives to construction and heavy industry, and a large devaluation aimed at stimulating agricultural exports and attracting foreign investment. In conjunction with the devaluation, Krieger Vasena imposed a 40 percent withholding tax on agriculture and livestock exports, by means of which the state appropriated part of the foreign-exchange windfall that would otherwise have accrued to the Pampean elite. Krieger Vasena's plan produced rapid growth, lower inflation, improvement in the balance of payments, and a wave of foreign portfolio investment, with only a small decline in the real wages of industrial workers. White-collar workers and small business fared considerably less well, and export-oriented farmers and ranchers soon came out in open opposition to government economic polices. But March 1967 to May 1969 saw the most successful economic turnaround since Perón had switched course in 1952.[7]

The Onganía government's relations with the unions were rockier than its relations with industrialists or agriculture. The CGT and most union leaders, including Vandor and Alonso, initially welcomed the new regime.[8] In late 1966, however, the government decreed compulsory arbitration of strikes and announced its intention to streamline ports, railways, and sugar mills, in part by imposing layoffs. Many union leaders went into opposition, and in December 1966, the CGT, under Vandorist control, launched a general strike, which helped to unseat the government's first minister of the economy.[9] In February 1967, the unions scheduled an "action plan" to culminate in a nationwide general strike. Onganía responded by banning street demonstrations and suspending the legal status of unions the government held responsible for the CGT's "efforts to subvert social order and threaten social peace."[10] The next month, as Krieger Vasena introduced his economic plan, the government halted collective bargaining and, after granting a small pay hike, froze wages for eighteen months.

During 1967, three factions crystallized in union leadership. The participationists, or "New Current of Opinion," comprised unionists who supported Onganía's corporatist designs, backed the paternalists in their conflict with the liberals, and felt that there was nothing to be gained by an endless stream of strikes and demonstrations. The key participationist leaders included Juan José Taccone of Luz y Fuerza, Rogelio Coria of the construction workers, Adolfo Cavalli of the state petroleum workers, José Alonso of the garment workers, and Juan Carlos Loholaberry of the textile workers.[11] The Vandorists, who constituted a second faction, kept a wary distance from the government and organized occasional strikes and protests. In addition to expressing Vandor's time-honored "punch and bargain" strategy, the

Vandorist stance was aimed at containing possible radicalization of the rank and file by alternating a combative approach with attempts to negotiate bread-and-butter gains. Prominent Vandorist unions included those of the metal, meat, food, glass, and restaurant workers. A third "combative" current consisted of union leaders who expressed a variety of grievances against government policy, the military regime, and/or the capitalist system, and called for a frontal assault on one or more of these targets. The combative leaders came from unions that had been hit hard by government policies (civil servants, state workers, railway workers, telephone workers, sugar workers), from unions and union locals in the interior of the country, especially in Córdoba, and from the typographers' union, led by Raimundo Ongaro.[12]

In March 1968, the CGT held a congress to elect a new leadership. The participationists did not attend, and the Vandorists withdrew after a commission gave voting rights to delegates from unions intervened by the Onganía government, most of whom belonged to the combative current. The largely combative unionists who remained at the congress elected Ongaro secretary-general of what came to be known as the CGT de los Argentinos. The Vandorists held a rival congress in the official CGT building on Calle Azopardo, resulting in the formation of the CGT–Azopardo. Although Perón, following his traditional strategy of backing the weaker faction, threw his support to the combative CGT de los Argentinos, Vandor's energetic campaigning and Ongaro's peculiar leadership caused one union after another to defect to the CGT–Azopardo. The fate of the CGT de los Argentinos was sealed on 24 June 1969 when Vandor flew to Madrid and, after a decade of conflict with the exiled leader, won Perón's support for his CGT–Azopardo in exchange for a pledge of loyalty. Four days later an unidentified group of assassins murdered Vandor in the UOM headquarters, triggering a cycle of violence that would last more than a decade.[13]

The collapse of the CGT de los Argentinos was offset by a burgeoning of combative unionism in the interior of the country and especially in Córdoba, Argentina's third-largest city. Several conditions made Córdoba ripe for a radicalization of union protest. First, Córdoba had a long-standing tradition of radicalism, and Peronist leaders in the area had a long-standing tradition of challenging the hegemony of their counterparts in the Buenos Aires area. Second, many of the province's workers were employed in huge, foreign-owned vehicle-assembly plants located fairly close together, so collective protest was easy to organize. As a result of special authorization from the Frondizi government, moreover, many of these plants had company unions, which (together with geographical distance) freed local militants from the control of conservative national unionists and made issues like production speeds subject to collective bargaining, raising base-level involvement. Similar autonomy prevailed in the local branches of SMATA (autos) and FATLyF (power plants), which were federations of regional unions rather than tightly controlled national organizations like the UOM or AOT. Finally, many auto workers invested their wages in university educations, and most SMATA leaders in 1972 were under 30, making them receptive to the student protest of the late 1960s.[14]

The student protest that began with the Cuban revolution, accelerated with the Night of the Long Batons, and gained additional momentum with the worldwide radicalism of the late 1960s, reached a peak in May 1969, when three students were killed in clashes with police in Rosario and Corrientes. In the same month, the Onganía government allowed prices to rise on items of basic necessity and abolished the "English Saturday" that gave workers in Córdoba a full day's pay for a half-day's work. Carlos Caballero, the ultraconservative governor of Córdoba, was happy with the abolition of the English Saturday, but refused to implement another central government decree revoking a special tax levied on Córdoba's workers for the purpose of industrial promotion. Workers and students antagonized by these measures formed a column of 13,000 and marched into the center of the city. The next day, 30 June 1969, citizens occupied 150 square blocks of downtown Córdoba, using barricades, rocks, and Molotov cocktails to fend off the police. Army battalions eventually dispersed the demonstrators, but not before fourteen had been killed and the government's image of invulnerability had been shattered for good.[15]

The Cordobazo, as the episode came to be known, triggered further radicalization, especially by emboldening emerging guerrilla groups. Rural guerrillas had made a few appearances in the late 1950s and early 1960s, but none had managed to do more than seize a police station or rob a few banks. The months after the Cordobazo, by contrast, saw the appearance of six major guerrilla groups, including the Montoneros (Peronist and mostly urban) and the Ejercito Revolucionario del Pueblo (Marxist with both urban and rural operations). María José Moyano suggests that guerrilla membership peaked in 1975 at about 5,000, and her research shows that those who joined guerrilla groups were mostly male students or ex-students in their twenties, usually from middle-class or upper-class families. The guerrillas began a campaign of bombing, kidnapping, and murder, punctuated by attacks on property and seizures of police stations, military barracks, and small towns in the countryside. According to Moyano's content analysis of Buenos Aires newspapers, the guerrillas carried out 85 kidnappings and 129 murders between January 1969 and the end of the military regime in May 1973; 140 kidnappings and 481 murders between June 1973 and the end of the elected Peronist government in March 1976; and 14 kidnappings and 310 murders between March 1976 and December 1979. Claiming at first that they regarded killing as a painful necessity forced upon them by the enemies of the people, the guerrillas soon began to adopt uniforms, ranks, and a war mentality. In the mid 1970s, the Montonero leader Mario Firmenich announced (from Cuba) his willingness to "sacrifice the organization in combat in exchange for political prestige. We have five thousand cadres less, but how many masses more? This is the point."[16]

The people who were the guerrillas' main targets—police and military officers, union leaders, and executives of big corporations—turned their houses into fortresses, took a different route to work every day, and lived in perpetual fear that they or their family members might be kidnapped or killed. Some who felt threatened or saw an opportunity to settle scores organized death squads and staffed them with police and military personnel, union bodyguards, common criminals, and persons attached to the Peronist or nationalist extreme right. Police and military officers often allowed the death squads to operate unhindered, and as time went on, the official security forces came increasingly to take illegal repression into their own hands, starting in August 1972 with the murders of 16 captured guerrillas on a naval base near Trelew. According to figures from the Buenos Aires newspapers and from a report published in 1986 by the National Commission on the Disappearance of Persons, between January 1969 and May 1973, right-wing death squads and official security forces kidnapped 44 people and killed another 34. Between June 1973 and March 1976, they kidnapped 458 and killed 1,165, and from April 1976 to December 1979, they kidnapped 7,342 and killed 6,651.[17] Many of these kidnappings, especially after 1976, resulted in the victim's "disappearance," never to be seen again. In 1995, navy and army officers revealed that thousands of the "disappeared" had been drugged and thrown unconscious but alive from airplanes into the middle of the Rio de la Plata estuary so that their bodies would drift out to sea.

Violent groups came from both inside and outside Peronism. Peronist left-wing guerrillas occasionally cooperated with non-Peronist left-wing guerrillas, and Peronist right-wing death squads sometimes allied with non-Peronist right-wing death squads. Meanwhile, the vast majority of Peronists and non-Peronists alike recoiled from the violence of both sides. As the division between left and right became more pronounced, the Peronism–anti-Peronism conflict receded into the background. For the next ten years, Argentina was torn by a new and much more deadly dispute between the self-proclaimed vanguard of "national socialism" on the left and the self-proclaimed defenders of "Western and Christian civilization" on the right. Exacerbating the polarization generated by political kidnappings and murders was the increasingly radical tone of labor protest (particularly in Córdoba and in the industrial belt southeast of Rosario), sequels to the Cordobazo in other cities, and the election of Salvador Allende, a socialist, as president of Chile. These events increased the sense of profound fear, or of giddy elation, that capitalism was about to be overthrown.

In the unions, participationists and Vandorists (now without their murdered leader) coalesced in response to the threat from below and tried to ride the wave of protest by adopting a more confrontational stance toward the government. Onganía replied by granting concessions, including wage increases and a law that gave union leaders control of vast health insurance funds (*obras sociales*) generated by worker and employer contributions. These concessions combined with the Cordobazo, guerrilla activity, labor protest, and Krieger Vasena's resignation to destroy business confidence. Direct foreign investment dried up, and small business and agrarian interests, which had previously been quiescent despite being left out of Krieger Vasena's plan, used their sectoral organizations to launch an all-out attack on the government's economic policies. When Onganía insisted on pursuing his corporatist agenda despite the growth of opposition to it both within and outside the armed forces, his military opponents, led by the army's commander-in-chief, Alejandro Lanusse, forced him to resign in June 1970.[18]

To replace Onganía, the commanders-in-chief chose General Roberto Levingston, a little-known officer who had spent the late 1960s in Washington, D.C. Despite having little clout of his own (he owed his appointment to the stalemate between Onganía's paternalists and Lanusse's liberals), Levingston tried, against the wishes of the military junta, to create a "movement" to extend the Argentine Revolution into the indefinite future. In late 1970, Levingston surprised his military colleagues by announcing that he planned to stay on as president for four or five more years. He then handed the ministry of the economy to Aldo Ferrer, a left-of-center nationalist, who gave local firms preferential access to credit and state contracts and used wage hikes and public works projects to stimulate demand. These measures antagonized big business and failed to gain the support of smaller nationally owned firms or of the CGT, which launched a succession of general strikes as inflation and guerrilla activity escalated. Levingston's goal of creating a nationalist movement intrigued Oscar Alende, who controlled what was left of the UCRI, but antagonized Perón and Balbín. In November 1970, Perón and Balbín took a historic step toward reconciliation by forming a coalition called La Hora del Pueblo, in which the leaders of several smaller parties also participated, to demand a return to democracy. The growth of opposition cost Levingston momentum, and when a second social explosion rocked Córdoba in March 1971, the military junta deposed him.

Levingston's successor as president was General Alejandro Lanusse, a member of the liberal faction in the armed forces. Shortly after taking office in March 1971, Lanusse repealed the laws suppressing party activity, appointed Arturo Mor Roig, a UCR leader, as minister of the interior, and scheduled elections for March 1973. In a decision that marked a political watershed, he then ended the ban on Peronist political activity by signing a decree-law that gave the Partido Justicialista the right to contest the 1973 elections. At the same time, however, he promulgated a separate decree-law that had the effect of preventing Perón (as well as Lanusse himself) from running for president.

Had Illia legalized the PJ while maintaining the ban on Perón, Vandor's party-building project would have gotten a big boost. In the early 1970s, however, union leaders were in no position to assume a hegemonic role within the Peronist movement. The four most important unionists of the 1955–66 era had disappeared from the scene: Olmos had died in a car accident in 1967, Framini had lost the AOT's internal elections in 1968, Vandor had been assassinated in 1969, and Alonso had been assassinated in 1970. Their successors were under fire from all sides: from dissident unionists, who were taking control of union locals around the country; from guerrilla groups, who attacked them physically as well as verbally; from Peronist university students, who were making a successful bid for greater power; and from Perón himself, who sought to minimize his dependence on the financially and organizationally autonomous union leadership by giving pride of place in the Peronist electoral campaign to the movement's left and youth sectors.

With his own candidacy proscribed, Perón picked his personal delegate, Héctor Cámpora, to be the presidential candidate of his newly formed electoral coalition, the Frente Justicialista de Liberación (FREJULI). Although dominated by the newly legalized PJ, FREJULI also included Frondizi's MID and several smaller parties and party factions. Perón's choice of his personal delegate to be FREJULI's presidential candidate was another blow to the union leaders, who had never regarded Cámpora as a serious political figure and were suspicious of him because two of his sons were active in the Peronist left. The left and youth sectors of Peronism were, by contrast, overjoyed with Perón's choice, and continued to read their own aspirations into Perón's ambiguous statements, some of which bordered on explicit endorsement of guerrilla violence.[19] Angered and dismayed by Cámpora's nomination, the unions virtually pulled out of the electoral campaign.[20] Perón made youth an official fourth "branch" of the Peronist movement, thereby reducing the proportion of deputy seats and party posts offered to unionists. No union leader was nominated for any of Argentina's 23 governorships, and the "union bureaucracy" was targeted along with the military regime in the slogans and chants of Peronism's left and youth sectors, which set the tone of the electoral campaign.[21]

After his tough battle with Vandor in the 1962–66 period, Perón could hardly have been displeased by the rise of the left and youth sectors, which were noisier than the unions but easier to manipulate. Moreover, after nearly two decades of union hegemony in the day-to-day operation of Peronism, the return to elections created unprecedented opportunities (candidacies and party leadership posts) both for Perón's circle of intimates and for old-line Peronist politicians not tarred by, or since forgiven for, association with neo-Peronist parties. The emergence of all these sectors (each of which, like the Peronist union leadership, included a multitude of internal factions) as power contenders enabled Perón to restore his plebiscitarian leadership by playing them off against one another. Perón thrived on this tactical web-spinning. Secure in power, as in the early 1950s, Perón became withdrawn and disengaged; it was only during periods of uncertainty that he applied himself enthusiastically to the tasks of leadership.

The 1973 elections also represented a turning point for Radicalism. When a 1972 court decision gave the Unión Cívica Radical del Pueblo (UCRP) the exclusive right to use the UCR label, Alende's Unión

Cívica Radical Intransigente (UCRI) changed its name to the Partido Intransigente (PI). By 1973, then, the UCR of the 1946–55 era had split into three offshoots: the UCR (former UCRP), the PI (former UCRI), and Frondizi's MID (which had split away from Alende's UCRI in 1963). Each survived into the 1990s, with the UCR becoming a major party (along with the PJ), the PI a minor left-wing party, and the MID a minor right-wing party. In November 1972, the newly reconstituted UCR, which would clearly pose the most serious challenge to Cámpora in the March 1973 presidential election, nominated its presidential candidate in a direct primary election. The contest pitted the venerable but uncharismatic Ricardo Balbín, who had run unsuccessfully for president in 1952 and 1958, against his former protégé Raúl Alfonsín. Hailed during the Illia government as the future "Argentine Kennedy," Alfonsín would likely have been the UCRP candidate for Buenos Aires governor in 1967 had the 1966 coup not intervened.[22] The definitive break between Alfonsín and Balbín had come in 1968, when Alfonsín had begun to reach out to leftist political parties, union leaders, and student groups in an effort to rally support against the military government. While Balbín helped to found the Hora del Pueblo coalition, Alfonsín joined the more frontally oppositional Encuentro Nacional de los Argentinos, which included the Partido Comunista, as well as leftist factions of other parties, in an alliance modeled loosely on Allende's Unidad Popular coalition in Chile.[23]

Much of Alfonsín's support came from the Junta Coordinadora Nacional, formed in 1968 by UCR student activists "to transform Radicalism's bureaucratic and electoralist structure into a movement fit to confront the dictatorship." Claiming that an irreconcilable antagonism existed between "the Argentine people on one side and an antinational oligarchic-monopolistic-imperialist ensemble on the other," the Coordinadora's language expressed the climate of the times, stood out against Balbín's moderate reformism, and harked back to the movementist elements in the Radical tradition.[24] In preparation for his bid for the Radical nomination, Alfonsín formed his own party faction, the Movimiento de Renovación y Cambio, with which the Coordinadora formed a loose alliance. Balbín eventually outpolled Alfonsín in the primary election, but Alfonsín made a strong showing that foreshadowed his rise in the early 1980s to the presidency of the UCR and eventually of the nation.[25] After becoming president, Alfonsín appointed Coordinadora members to high government posts, prompting conservative civilian and military leaders to contend that his administration was "leftist."

When the presidential contest took place in March 1973, Cámpora won an overwhelming victory with 49.6 percent of the vote to Balbín's 21.3 percent. Francisco Manrique, a former official of the Lanusse government, came in third with 15 percent, and two other conservative candidates won 2 and 3 percent respectively. Alende won 7 percent as the candidate of a leftist coalition centered around his Partido Intransigente (ex-UCRI), and three other leftist candidates split the remaining 2 percent. In addition to the presidential contest, the FREJULI coalition won 142 of the 243 national deputy seats, 45 of the 69 senate seats, and all of the provincial governorships.[26] Several factors contributed to the FREJULI landslide. First, since 1966, the Peronists had made important inroads into student and youth sectors that had never before supported them. Second, although Cámpora and Balbín were equally uncharismatic candidates, the Peronist nominee ran under the slogan "Cámpora to the presidency, Perón to power," which enabled him to call on the prestige of the exiled leader. Third, the UCR (ex-UCRP) had softened its traditional anti-Peronist stance, causing hardline anti-Peronists to support conservative candidates and fragmenting the non-Peronist vote. Fourth, it is likely that many conservative voters cast their ballots for Perón, regarding him as the candidate best equipped to control the popular mobilization.[27] Fifth, and most important, the Peronists, proscribed for the past eighteen years by the armed forces, had impressive antimilitary credentials, whereas the Radicals were handicapped by Mor Roig's presence in the unpopular Lanusse government.[28]

Perón's Return and Peronist Party-Building, 1973–1976

Despite his landslide victory, Cámpora's presidency did not last long. On 25 May 1973, the day he was inaugurated, thousands of militants congregated outside prisons and demanded the release of guerrilla leaders. Cámpora consented so fast that several common criminals were set free in the confusion. Shortly thereafter, Cámpora emulated Illia's tepid response to the CGT's 1964 factory-occupation campaign by doing nothing while students, hospital workers, and public employees occupied universities and workplaces for more than a week.

A perception that things were getting out of control took a tragic turn for the worse on 20 June 1973, when at least thirteen, and perhaps hundreds, died in a clash between left- and right-wing Peronists who had gathered to greet Perón on the highway between the Ezeiza airport and downtown Buenos Aires. On July 13, Cámpora and Vice President Vicente Solano Lima resigned, and the presidency passed to Raúl Lastiri, a nephew of Perón's shadowy personal secretary José López Rega, who as president of the chamber of deputies was constitutionally next in the line of succession.[29]

One of Lastiri's first acts was to announce that new presidential elections—with Perón allowed to run—would be held in September 1973, and that the winner would take office in October 1973. Perón and the UCR leader Ricardo Balbín, who by 1973 had established a cordial personal relationship, both seem to have favored a "national unity" ticket that would have made Perón the presidential candidate and Balbín the vice-presidential nominee. But under pressure from unionists and from the reactionary cabal surrounding José López Rega, Perón eventually chose his wife Isabel as the vice-presidential candidate.[30] The Perón/Perón ticket won 62 percent of the vote, with Balbín winning 24 percent and Francisco Manrique, the conservative candidate, 12 percent. Perón benefited from the votes of defectors from both the left and right, the former with nowhere else to go, and the latter hoping that he could rein in the guerrillas.

Perón's actions had contributed decisively to the destruction of the Partido Laborista, to the weakness of the original Partido Peronista, and to the failure of Vandor's party-building project. But during his second presidential period, which began in October 1973 and ended with his death in July 1974, Perón showed more sympathy for the institutionalization of the newly legalized PJ. In a May 1974 speech, Perón announced his intention to resign as chief of the Peronist movement so as to focus his waning energies on the presidency. Shortly thereafter he began to emphasize the need to strengthen the PJ and to transfer its leadership to leaders committed to the institutionalization of political democracy.[31] It is not clear how seriously he meant his instructions to be taken, however: during the 1946–55 period, he had talked about "organizing" the movement while actively encouraging its disorganization. In any event, Perón's death left the PJ as weakly institutionalized as the Partido Peronista had been two decades earlier.

Although Perón ultimately did little during his 1973–74 presidency to promote the institutionalization of a Peronist party, he did more to promote the institutionalization of a party system (i.e., the infusion with value of the principle of party competition through free elections). From 1955 to 1966, most parties had played the military card when it suited them, conniving for coups in the hope that a military government would somehow shift the balance of political forces in their favor. Sectors of the UCRP promoted military intervention prior to the ouster of the UCRI government in 1962, the UCRI welcomed the UCRP's overthrow in 1966, and several Peronist union leaders encouraged the 1966 coup.[32] During the Onganía government, however, Perón and Balbín began to recognize a common interest in restoring civilian rule and in combating the insurrectionary left. In their *La Hora del Pueblo* agreement of 1970, Balbín in effect agreed to support an end to proscription, Perón in effect agreed to refrain from overexploiting incumbency, and both demanded that the military government call free elections. But after Perón returned to the presidency in 1973, the warming of relations between Peronism and Radicalism may in some ways have obstructed the institutionalization of a party system. As Marcelo Cavarozzi has noted, Balbín's policy of "constructive opposition" to the Peronist government, which in practice meant supporting its every action for fear that criticism would invite a coup, was not propitious for the institutionalization of party competition, because it left little space for an opposition stance that could serve as a governing platform after the next elections.[33]

On 1 July 1974, Perón died of a heart attack and was replaced by his widow, Vice President Isabel Martínez de Perón. Isabel Perón's political inexperience, coupled with Perón's advocacy of party institutionalization in the weeks before his death, opened up political space for the PJ to assume a more significant role in mediating between unions and the state. Suggesting that it might assume such a role, the new party leadership under Diulio Brunello had forged close ties with a faction of Peronist union leaders led by Adelino Romero, head of the textile workers' union and secretary-general of the CGT. Romero's "moderate" faction of unionists, according to Eduardo Viola, "had an attitude of openness toward the political parties. . . . they maintained a close alliance with the new Partido Justicialista elite led by Brunello and showed tolerance toward the radicalized sectors of Peronism, intending perhaps to integrate them institutionally. Doubtlessly influenced by Perón's positions in May and June [1974], the moderates were thus oriented toward the consolidation of the democratic regime."[34]

Romero's "moderate" faction of Peronist union leaders favored democratization, a more significant role for the PJ, conciliation of the Peronist left, and support for a government-sponsored social pact aimed at controlling inflation through wage and price guidelines.[35] Two other Peronist union leader factions, which Viola terms "Vandorists" and "Lopezreguistas," had very different orientations. The leader of the "Vandorist" group was Lorenzo Miguel, who had become head of the UOM and "62 Organizations" after Vandor was assassinated in June 1969. Unlike Romero's moderates, Miguel's faction was hostile to the Peronist left, wanted to dispense entirely with the mediation of the PJ, and sought to exercise hegemony directly through the state (in this respect Miguel's position actually resembled Alonso's much more than Vandor's). The "Lopezreguistas" were union followers of José López Rega, Perón's minister of social welfare. A Rasputin-like figure who dabbled in the occult, López Rega was the real power behind the scenes during the first year of Isabel's presidency. Identified with Peronism's extreme right, López Rega helped to organize a group of death squads known as the Argentine Anticommunist Alliance (AAA) and was known to have special admiration for the political regimes created by Gadhafi in Libya and Kim Il-Sung in North Korea.[36] The Lopezreguista faction of Peronist union leaders, in Viola's view, "shared with the Vandorists an aversion toward political parties . . . and was oriented in the direction of a totalitarian regime based on Isabel's plebiscitarian leadership."[37]

At the time of Perón's death, Romero's moderates held the upper hand in Peronist unionism. At the July 1974 CGT congress, Romero was reelected as the confederation's secretary-general, although Miguel's faction managed to occupy important subaltern posts. But when Romero died suddenly of natural causes, Miguel's faction filled the power vacuum and, forging an alliance of convenience with López Rega and his followers, embarked on a successful campaign to dismantle the social pact (which Romero had favored preserving) and to displace the left-leaning Peronists who occupied several provincial governments and some lower-level union posts.[38] With most important policy initiatives now coming either from the national executive controlled by López Rega or from Miguel's "62 Organizations," the PJ and its parliamentary bloc were effectively marginalized as important political actors. The alliance of convenience between Miguel's unionists and López Rega followers, which lasted only from July 1974 to July 1975, but sufficed to derail the incipient party-building project of "moderate" unionists and PJ politicians, recalled the alliance of convenience among mutually hostile factions of union leaders in the "62 de Pie" that had helped Perón defeat Vandor's party-building project in 1966. It also resembled the situation of 1987–89, when another coalition of union leaders previously antagonistic to one another (the "Group of 15") rallied behind Menem to thwart the party-building project organized by Peronism's renewal sector.

The marginalization of the PJ was thrown into stark relief when the fragile alliance that tied Miguel and the "62" to López Rega and his cohort broke down. In late 1974, as inflation (previously moderated by the now-abandoned social pact) began to rise, the economic teams chosen by Isabel and López Rega began to implement stabilization plans with increasingly harsh consequences for workers' real incomes. In July 1975, without a glance toward the PJ leadership or its congressional bloc, the CGT, now dominated by Miguel and the "62," launched a two-day general strike (the first ever against a Peronist government), forcing Isabel Perón to jettison López Rega and his cronies. Miguel's unionists were totally unprepared, however, to govern a country in the midst of a severe social and economic crisis. In this context, political space opened up for the most promising opportunity since Perón's death to make the PJ an important vehicle of political action.[39] Best equipped to seize this opportunity was a budding "antiverticalist" faction of Peronism. Organized around a Peronist congressional bloc formed just prior to the July 1975 general strike and led by the Santa Fe senator Italo Luder, PJ vice-president Angel Robledo, and Buenos Aires governor Victorio Calabró, the antiverticalists were dedicated in the short term to wresting power from the López Rega faction and in the medium term to engineering Isabel's resignation from the presidency and to replacing her with a more experienced Peronist leader. The more traditional "verticalist" faction, led by Lorenzo Miguel and his allies in the "62," were equally dedicated to ousting the López Rega group, but favored Isabel's continuation as president. Viola describes the differences between the two groups as follows:

For the verticalists, Peronism was above all a movement revolving around a charismatic leader and structurally based on unionism. . . . For the antiverticalists, Peronism could only survive historically to the extent that it clearly assumed the form of a party, detached itself from its authoritarian traditions, and stopped trying to center itself around a plebiscitarian leadership that had not existed since Perón's death. [The antiverticalists] represented an updated Peronism that credited political democracy and the party system as a fundamental locus for interest articulation and for the formulation and implementation of state policies.[40]

The cleavage between the verticalists and antiverticalists did not correspond directly to a rivalry between unionists and politicians. Miguel's verticalists had many allies in congress, and the antiverticalists included a "Group of 8" unionists, among them Ramón Elorza of the restaurant workers, Juan Racchini of the soft-drink workers, and Ricardo de Luca of the naval engineers.[41] Most important, the antiverticalist luminary Victorio Calabró, in addition to being governor of Buenos Aires, was a top leader of the metalworkers' union—second-in-command, in fact, to Lorenzo Miguel, the most prominent representative of the verticalist faction. That Miguel and Calabró, both top leaders of the UOM, were the key leaders respectively of the verticalists and antiverticalists testifies to the continued centrality of the metalworkers' union in the Peronist movement.

Citing exhaustion, Isabel decided in September 1975 to take a leave of absence from the presidency. Italo Luder, the antiverticalist president of the senate, replaced her for the interim. Luder immediately set about putting his own stamp on the office, making cabinet changes that favored the antiverticalists. Miguel and his allies retaliated, accusing Luder of being a traitor to the Peronist heritage, of trying to wrest the presidency from Isabel, and of forging ties with the extreme left of the movement. Crucial to the verticalist counterattack was the support of a group of eleven Peronist governors led by Carlos Menem of La Rioja, "a fanatic for plebiscitarian leadership who imagined himself to be the heir of [the nineteenth-century La Rioja caudillo] Facundo Quiroga."[42] In the face of opposition from the verticalist faction, Luder retreated from the challenge and returned to his senate seat when Isabel announced in mid-October that she intended to resume the presidency. The last stage of the antiverticalist collapse came in November 1975, when Miguel expelled Calabró from the UOM, the "62," and the PJ.[43] Luder's decision to step aside and Calabró's expulsion represented the defeat of the Peronist faction with the best hope of restoring confidence in the economy, of taming the less extreme groups on the Peronist left, and of denying state resources to the right-wing death squads.[44]

The verticalists defeated the antiverticalists primarily because Perón, despite his eleventh-hour statements exhorting his followers to strengthen the PJ, had ruled in a plebiscitarian style whose legacy gave formidable political resources to Isabel and to the Peronist leaders who exercised power through her. As Pablo Kandel and Mario Monteverde point out, this legacy enabled the verticalist faction to form and to maintain itself long enough to restore Isabel to the presidency.

Between the determined antiverticalists and the committed verticalists were the undecided, some of whom spoke with Lorenzo Miguel to discover his motives for supporting Isabel. "What bothers me is the question of to whom we will pass the baton should the señora leave" was his response. Actually, the same argument was repeated time and again: Someone with the last name of Perón is the only guarantee of Justicialist unity. It was also expressed in this variant: Who would dare to expel from the government someone whose last name is Perón? Typical Argentine slyness was evident in a witticism popular in political circles: That woman protects herself by carrying a last name.[45]

One point of similarity between the 1963–66 and 1973–76 experiences is thus the role played by Perón's plebiscitarian legacy in shifting power toward factions of Peronist unionism that opposed a greater role for party activity. During the 1963–66 period, the banner of personal fealty to Perón (partly contrived in the cases of Alonso and Olmos) served as an indispensable rallying point for anti-Vandor factions of Peronist unionism that would otherwise have been at each others' throats. The coalescence of these factions, which could not have occurred without the issue of loyalty to Perón, played a crucial role in undermining Vandor's party-building project. During the 1973–76 period, the banner of fealty to Perón's designated heir, Isabel, sealed the fate of the antiverticalist party-building project. Although Miguel and the verticalists had the support of a majority of top union leaders even without trying to portray themselves as the most ardent "defenders of the faith," the minority antiverticalist faction of Peronist unionism posed a significant challenge to Miguel and his allies by winning the support of most of the important Peronist politicians at a time when those politicians had become much more important than they had been during Illia's government. Where Perón's plebiscitarian legacy played a role was in persuading many of these politicians, Luder above all, to agree to support Isabel's return to the presidency, rather than arguing for her resignation. With the politicians shifting from the antiverticalist camp to a more neutral position, hard-line antiverticalists in the unions, like Calabró, lost out to the verticalists. At this point, the "62" achieved undisputed hegemony in Isabel Perón's government. But the mounting economic crisis and political violence, together with their own lack of preparation for this protagonistic role, prevented the "62" leaders from enjoying the fruits of their success.

In mid-March 1976, as violence and inflation spiraled out of control, a majority of the CGT directive council voted down a proposal to issue a statement supporting the Peronist government and the constitutional order.[46] A few days later, the Peronist government was overthrown in a military coup.

Peronism Under Military Rule, 1976–1982

On 24 March 1976, the armed forces replaced the civilian government with a military junta and announced the beginning of the "Proceso de Reorganización Nacional." One of the first acts of the military government led by General Jorge Videla was to unleash a campaign of terror unprecedented in modern Argentine history. By the end of military rule in December 1983, at least 8,960 people had "disappeared" and thousands of others had been killed outright.[47] The military rulers explained the kidnap and murder of thousands of Argentine citizens as the unavoidable cost of a "dirty war" against leftist subversion. But as the military itself recognized, only a small proportion of the victims actually belonged to terrorist groups. General Iberico St. Jean described the strategy succinctly: "First we'll kill the subversives, then their collaborators, then . . . their sympathizers, then . . . those who remain indifferent, and finally we'll kill the timid." In a war of this sort, errors were unavoidable. According to General Luciano Menéndez, "We are going to have to kill 50,000 people: 25,000 subversives, 20,000 sympathizers, and we will make 5,000 mistakes."[48] The junta's policy toward the press provides telling insight into the use of state terror as a political weapon. Strict censorship was imposed on the day of the coup, but was repealed a month later. The lifting of censorship was among the most chilling decisions the military ever made. Between March 1976 and August 1980, 68 journalists who (intentionally or not) portrayed the regime unfavorably "disappeared," and another 36 were killed outright. In the face of uncertainty about what was permitted and what was forbidden, the press, with the partial exception of the English-language *Buenos Aires Herald*, was silenced more completely than it would have been had censorship existed.[49]

Ironically, Argentina's military rulers were preoccupied with legal forms. All told, they enacted more than 1,500 laws, more than any other government in modern Argentine history. Moreover, the military were careful, according to an Americas' Watch report, to replace more than 80 percent of the country's judges.[50] From the outset, however, the military began to violate not only the most elementary tenets of civilized existence, but also the laws under which it claimed to be operating. In its antisubversive campaign, the military made use of two decrees inherited from Isabel Perón's government, each issued at a time when López Rega was calling the shots: a November 1974 state-of-siege declaration, which permitted the suspension of constitutional rights, and a February 1975 decree that ordered the army to conduct "whatever military operations may be necessary to neutralize or annihilate the action of the subversive elements acting in the province of Tucumán," a decree that was later extended to the rest of the country.[51] During the 1985 human rights trials, a long debate emerged over the meaning of the word *annihilate*, although strangely the prosecution failed to argue that to annihilate "the action of the subversive elements" is one thing and to annihilate the alleged subversives is another. Even supposing these decrees gave legal sanction for the physical repression of armed guerrillas, fewer than 20 percent of those whom the military kidnapped and executed were in fact armed guerrillas, and none received the death penalty that the military were careful to institute in June 1976.[52] There was certainly never any attempt to justify legally the torture of thousands of captives, the theft and ransacking of their property, the sale of children born in captivity, or the military's steadfast refusal to produce or divulge the whereabouts of the "disappeared." Moreover, in a particularly blatant violation of the principle of military hierarchy, the official armed forces spawned a secret antisubversive apparatus in which junior officers often gave orders to their nominal superiors.[53]

To make sure that subversion would never return, the new military government announced its intention to eliminate once and for all the economic crises, social institutions, and ideological contamination to which subversion was attributed. It suspended political party activity, purged the universities, put the CGT under government trusteeship, outlawed strikes, and imprisoned hundreds of politicians and union leaders. It also enacted a long-term economic plan, directed by José A. Martínez de Hoz, the civilian minister of the economy, aimed at replacing state spending, inefficient industry, and trade restrictions with a free-market economic model based on agricultural exports, in which Argentina was believed to hold a comparative advantage. The new model was intended not only to reduce the budget deficits and foreign-exchange shortages to which the country's economic crises were attributed, but also to reduce the size, and hence the power, of the industrial working class, which the government saw as a driving force behind the country's economic and political instability.[54] The economic model would thus provide for the long-term demobilization of the social sectors whose short-term quiescence was assured by harsh repression. Despite the disruption entailed by these radical changes, the results of the economic model, measured by overall economic growth and inflation, were not, at first, altogether negative. Although GDP stagnated in 1976 and fell almost 4 percent in 1978, it rose 6 percent in 1977 and almost 7 percent in 1979. Meanwhile, inflation declined from 443 percent in 1976 to 160 percent in 1979. Wages, consumer-goods production, hours worked in industry, and formal-sector employment fell dramatically, but the government viewed this deterioration as the inevitable concomitant of rationalizing the country's productive structure.[55]

By 1979, the military government was rather pleased with itself. In a few short years, it had won what it considered to be a "war" against subversion, rid the country of allegedly corrupt politicians, embarked on a radical transformation of the social and economic structure, and hosted a World Cup in soccer, which Argentina conveniently won. From this position of self-confidence, the military began to think about laying the groundwork for a return to civilian rule. In 1979, General Albano Harguindeguy, Videla's interior minister, began a series of interviews with "notable" Argentine citizens to sound out prospects for the creation of a civilian-led "Movement of National Opinion" (MON), whose mission would be to continue Martínez de Hoz's neo-liberal economic policies and to anchor the future civilian-run polity in "the Christian conception of life and the traditions of our culture." The MON was to draw its leaders from conservative provincial parties and its votes from Peronist and Radical defectors. As a formula for a return to civilian rule, the MON was an aggressive, positive project initiated from a position of confidence. However, it also included defensive elements. Even at this early stage, the military recognized that its main problem would be to insulate itself from prosecution for human rights abuses. Accordingly, civilian politicians would have to refrain from questioning anything the military had done in the war against subversion. They would also have to let military officers participate in the cabinet and in a security council that would oversee all policies relating to matters of internal defense. Finally, electoral activity would not resume until 1984 or 1987 and would be carefully staged, with local and legislative elections preceding national and presidential contests.[56] Had the MON scheme come to fruition, Argentina's transition would have resembled the military-controlled ones in Brazil and Chile, both of which gave rise to civilian regimes constrained by military tutelage.

Prospects for the MON diminished, however, as the economy deteriorated. By the end of Videla's term in office (March 1981), it was clear that the economic plan was in need of revision. Wage cuts, reduced import tariffs, and an increasingly overvalued peso had depressed demand for domestically produced goods, driving industries into bankruptcy and contributing to the collapse of dozens of financial institutions. In the watershed year of 1981, real per capita GDP declined 7.3 percent and industrial production dropped 15.2 percent.[57] Meanwhile, the overvalued peso led to a huge rise in imports and permitted middle-class Argentines to go on spending sprees abroad. The need to finance the resulting balance-of-payments deficit, profligate weapons purchases, and gargantuan borrowing by state-owned corporations (which, far from being privatized, became military officers' private fiefdoms) caused the foreign debt to rise $16.8 billion in a fourteen-month period: from $8.5 billion in December 1979 to $25.3 billion (42 percent of GDP) in March 1981.[58]

Although unionists of the left (including the Peronist left) were the prime targets of the anti-labor repression, many right-of-center "62" leaders were also caught in the crackdown. Lorenzo Miguel was arrested on the day of the coup, and Oscar Smith of the light and power workers, a "62" leader who escaped the initial wave of arrests, "disappeared" in 1977. Miguel displayed remarkable fortitude during his two and a half years in prison, earning the respect of his fellow prisoners by not breaking down under brutal interrogation. While others gave in to despair, Miguel, an amateur artist, spent days in his cell painting canvasses.[59] Meanwhile, despite ferocious repression of journalists and workers alike, newspapers recorded 90 strikes and stoppages during Videla's presidency.[60] At the leadership level, a group of second-line unionists, including Saúl Ubaldini (beer workers) and Roberto García (taxi drivers), formed a "Group of 25" in 1977 to coordinate labor action, which at first was largely defensive but soon adopted a more combative profile. This combativeness alienated Jorge Triaca (plastics workers) and other members of the original "25," who seceded and formed a new faction, the Comisión de Gestión y Trabajo (GyT), in April 1978. The members of GyT came to regard the "25" as outmoded Peronist intransigents, too short-sighted to cooperate with the government's market-oriented economic policies and dangerously vulnerable to "leftist subversion."[61]

Whereas Ubaldini and García remained in the "25" and organized general strikes against the dictatorship in 1979 and 1982, Triaca and GyT forged cordial relations with the military. They opposed general strikes, refrained from antigovernment statements, and maintained a friendly dialogue with military leaders both on and off the job.[62] The incipient rapport between GyT and the military worried Lorenzo Miguel, who shared GyT's conservative and conciliatory stance but realized that the astute and urbane Triaca might use his access to government favors to convert himself into a powerful rival. Hence, upon his release from house arrest in 1980, Miguel went against the grain of his own ideological and programmatic instincts and threw his support to the more left-leaning and combative "25." It would not be the last time the wily "62" chief would subordinate ideology and program to an interest in preserving his power and autonomy against a budding challenger.

In 1980, Miguel and his close collaborators joined the "25" in a clandestine CGT. Just out of prison, Miguel had the final say in picking the confederation's secretary-general. The "25" suggested its own Hugo Curto, a young UOM leader with a high profile in the combative grouping. Diego Ibáñez and Lesio Romero, Miguel's long-time allies, suggested Fernando Donaires, a more conciliatory figure of their own generation. When Miguel declined to choose between the two candidates, Ibáñez suggested Saúl Ubaldini, a "nice guy whom everybody likes." As a secondary official in the fermentation branch of the relatively minor beer workers' union, Ubaldini in 1980 was a little-known unionist who could not pose an immediate threat to the "62" chief's behind-the-scenes hegemony. Miguel agreed to the compromise candidate, all parties accepted the choice, and Ubaldini obtained the post he would keep for the next decade.[63] Meanwhile, Triaca sought and obtained the military government's consent to form his own CGT. Because the military allowed Triaca's confederation to operate out of the official CGT building on Calle Azopardo, it came to be known as the CGT–Azopardo. Ubaldini's confederation was called the CGT–Brasil, also after the street on which its headquarters were located.

The "25" began to protest Martínez de Hoz's economic policies as early as April 1979, when they called a partly successful general strike.[64] By March 1981, Argentina's major business organizations, the Sociedad Rural and Unión Industrial, had joined the unions in decrying an economic policy that benefited nobody except financial speculators, the military-industrial complex, and companies benefiting from the state's pharaonic construction projects.[65] Spearheading protest against human rights abuses were the Mothers of the Plaza de Mayo. On 30 April 1977, fourteen women whose children had been kidnapped assembled in front of the government house in downtown Buenos Aires, demanding to know where their children were. From that day forward, the Mothers circulated in the same place every Thursday at 3:30 P.M. They survived the disappearance of one of their leaders in December 1977, and their membership grew to 5,000 as additional women joined in search of relatives who had disappeared.[66] International human rights organizations, including the OAS Inter-American Commission for Human Rights and Amnesty International, also spoke out against the human rights violations. U.S. President Jimmy Carter cut off military aid to Argentina and sent an emissary to Buenos Aires to investigate claims of disappearances and lobby for the release of prisoners.

Given the military's tight-lipped position that every aspect of the dirty war had been necessary to save the country from Marxist terrorists, national and international criticism of human rights abuses, even as it saved lives, promoted a siege mentality that reinforced the armed forces' internal cohesion. After 1980, however, military cohesion began to break down. The deepening economic crisis contributed to this erosion, but even more important was the "success" of the dirty war itself. By late 1977, the guerrilla groups had been defeated, and recorded kidnappings in which the victims were presumed killed dropped from 3,485 in 1976 to 2,544 in 1977 to 830 in 1978 to 148 in 1979.[67] Without a war climate to submerge them, personal disputes, interservice rivalries, differences over economic policy, and conflicting views about how to structure a future civilian regime bubbled to the surface. The upwelling of internal differences raised the stakes of the presidential succession scheduled for March 1981. In September 1980, Videla indicated that he wanted General Roberto Viola, commander-in-chief of the army since May 1978, to succeed him as president. Viola supported a shift to more expansionary economic policies and was willing to hold a dialogue with political party and union leaders from the pre-1976 period. These positions put him at odds with navy officers, who had traditionally supported free-market economic policies and who felt that it was now an admiral's turn for the presidency.

They also generated resentment from army hard-liners, who wanted no political opening and harbored deep hostility to the great majority of pre-1976 politicians, whom they regarded as self-interested hacks whose corrupt and demagogic practices had created a climate for Marxist subversion. Although Videla finally mustered enough army support to push through Viola's nomination, the new president began his term amid the smoldering resentment of other officers.[68]

Immediately on taking office in March 1981, Viola began to lay the groundwork for a transition to a civilian rule. On the crucial issue of immunity from prosecution for human rights violations, Viola stated categorically that "a victorious army is not investigated."[69] However, he did not share the hard-liners' maximalist goal of creating a brand-new political party to perpetuate free-market economic policies and a reactionary cultural climate under a future civilian regime. Viola made clear from the outset that he was willing to negotiate the terms of a transition with established politicians and union leaders, including Peronists. Although he never announced an electoral timetable, a plausible scenario involved Viola's transfer of the presidency when his term ended in 1984 to a civilian supported by both the armed forces and the leaders of the major political parties.[70] The shift in emphasis from the Videla/Harguindeguy dialogue with the minor conservative parties to the Viola dialogue with Peronism and Radicalism paralleled the similar shift in 1971, when General Levingston's dalliance with Oscar Alende, the leader of the UCRI (soon to be rechristened the Partido Intransigente), gave way to General Lanusse's "Great National Accord" with the major parties, which ultimately failed in its efforts to prevent Perón's return to the presidency and to halt the rise of the revolutionary left.[71]

Viola's negotiations with the main political parties and with a group of conciliatory union leaders antagonized military hard-liners and fueled rumors of an impending internal coup. At the same time, his incipient liberalization triggered a resurrection of civil society that would have been very difficult to reverse, even had it not been for the Malvinas/Falklands debacle.[72] In July 1981, combative union leaders, taking advantage of a letup of anti-labor repression, called a general strike, which idled 1.5 million workers.[73] In the same month, five political parties, including the Peronists and Radicals, formed a coalition to press for more expansionary economic policies and for a swift return to civilian rule. Recognizing that Viola's days might be numbered, the leaders of the Multipartidaria, as the party coalition was known, did not embrace his transition project wholeheartedly, but neither did they refuse to participate in a dialogue with him.

A key figure in the Multipartidaria was Ricardo Balbín, the long-standing leader of the UCR. During 1980, Balbín had served as a point of contact between the major political parties and the Videla administration. Unlike his fellow Radical Raúl Alfonsín, who was one of the dictatorship's more outspoken opponents, Balbín was ready to agree to several of the military's conditions for a return to civilian rule. Crucially, he was willing to drop the issue of human rights violations during the dirty war. He was also the first political figure to assert publicly that the disappeared were dead—thereby reducing pressure on the responsible officers to come up with information about the legal status and whereabouts of their victims. Balbín also agreed that the reach of international terrorism required military participation in a future civilian cabinet and a military-led national security council to oversee matters of internal defense. Although the junta never explicitly offered Balbín the opportunity to succeed Viola, the UCR leader's availability as a possible compromise candidate helped to keep Viola's transition project afloat. In mid 1981, however, Balbín fell ill, and in September of that year he died, dealing a blow to the military's prospects for a negotiated transition. Viola's own illness, which also became apparent in September, provided the excuse for the hard-liners, led by General Leopoldo Galtieri and Admiral Jorge Anaya, to oust him from the presidency three months later.[74]

On assuming the presidency in December 1981, Galtieri broke off negotiations with the Multipartidaria and began to resurrect the maximalist strategy for a return to civilian rule. Like Videla and Harguindeguy, Galtieri hoped to use the tiny conservative provincial parties as the base for a new political force that would carry on the work of the Proceso after military rule ended. But in contrast to his predecessors, Galtieri expected to lead the new party himself. Given the economic collapse and the parties' recent resurgence, he had little chance of winning an open election. If his project were to succeed, the economy would have to improve (which meant that the military would have to remain in power for several more years) and something would have to be done to shift popular support from the revitalized opposition to the existing regime. Galtieri had plans for coping with both of these problems. His strategy in the economic sphere was to return to the Martínez de Hoz approach, which meant reconstituting the ministry of the economy (which Viola had split into five secretariats) and replacing Viola's

pragmatic economic team with a hard-line neoliberal group behind
Roberto Alemann. His strategy for winning immediate popular support was more adventurous. Partly to assure navy support for Viola's
ouster, Galtieri gave Admiral Jorge Anaya the green light for his
pet military project: a military occupation of the Malvinas/Falkland
islands, which were claimed by both Argentina and Great Britain.[75]

Although a large demonstration against military rule took place two
days before the Argentines acted, the military occupation was far from
a last-ditch defensive measure aimed at saving the regime from an
overpowering opposition. On the contrary, it was part of an offensive
project aimed at achieving several related goals. Besides settling a long-
standing international grievance, a successful occupation, Galtieri rea-
soned, would restore military cohesion and generate a "rally round the
flag" effect that would move public opinion toward support for the
regime and eventually behind a carefully groomed successor party led
by Galtieri himself. Everything depended, of course, on the occupation's success. Defeat seems inevitable in retrospect, but Galtieri never
expected that war would break out. He calculated that the British, who
did not respond militarily when Argentina placed a token force on the
nearby South Georgia islands in March 1982, would not resist when
the main force moved onto the Malvinas/Falklands. He also calculated
that the Reagan administration, which was relying on Argentine military personnel to help train the Nicaraguan Contras, would not oppose
the occupation.[76] Both of Galtieri's assumptions proved to be wrong.
Britain went to war, the United States sided with its NATO ally, troops
suffered and died, and Argentina surrendered on 14 June 1982.

The Transition to Democracy, 1982–1983

Discredited by defeat, Galtieri resigned as president and was replaced as army commander-in-chief by General Cristino Nicolaides.
As head of the most powerful service, Nicolaides named a retired
army general, Reynaldo Bignone, to the presidency. Bignone's nomination angered the air force, which had performed better in the war
than the ill-trained and frostbitten conscript army, and antagonized
the navy, which had yet to place one of its own in the presidency.[77]
In response to the army's unilateral act, the other services withdrew
from the junta for what turned out to be three months. Nonetheless,
Bignone formed a government on 1 July 1982 to administer what Nico-

laides called "an orderly, shared, and concerted transition to democracy." Political leaders interpreted this statement to mean that civilian rule would not begin until the parties agreed to refrain from investigating human rights violations, administrative corruption, or the conduct of the war.[78] Over the next seventeen months, the parties would reject three successive attempts by the commanders-in-chief to formalize such a negotiated transition.[79]

Nicolaides' plan to install a caretaker government was not the only one advanced as the Malvinas/Falklands conflict drew to a close. Deolindo Bittel, the first vice president of the shadow PJ, proposed a power-sharing arrangement in which, for at least two years, the junta would retain control of the executive branch. Raúl Alfonsín, the UCR leader, proposed a provisional civilian government to be headed, in a gesture of poetic justice, by former president Arturo Illia.[80] Bittel's proposal was not pursued, but Alfonsín's had at least one thing going for it: the climate of the times had finally caught up with Illia's political style. During his 1963–66 term, Illia's pedestrian legalism had earned him the nickname "the turtle." So out of step was Illia with the millenarian climate of the 1960s that when the military overthrew him, eleven times as many survey respondents backed the coup as opposed it. After Isabel Perón's deflated plebiscitarianism and Videla's state terror, however, pedestrian legalism clearly had much to recommend it. In retrospect, according to a 1983 poll, three times as many survey respondents approved of Illia's government as disapproved of it.[81] In the end, however, Alfonsín's proposal did not even win backing from all sectors of the UCR, and it too became a historical footnote.[82]

One reason the military insisted on excluding civilians from a role in administering the transition involved the breadth of responsibility for the dirty war. According to one estimate, some 300 to 400 high-ranking officers conceived of the antisubversive campaign, designed plans to implement it, and headed the detention centers that operated it. The kidnapping, interrogation, torture, sustained detention, and murder was carried out by another 300 to 400 lower-ranking officers, of whom about 50 are said to have engaged regularly in torture.[83] A commission charged with collecting information on disappearances implicated more than 1,300 officers in kidnapping, torture, and murder.[84] Direct involvement in the dirty war was expanded by the "Pact of Blood" system, by which high-level officers were obliged personally to execute prisoners so that all levels of the chain of command would be implicated in illegal repression.[85] Given the breadth of responsibility for the dirty war and the ever-rising tide of antimilitary sentiment, officers were determined not to give an inch to the civilian opposition.

In fact, Argentina came very close to getting exactly the kind of transition that Nicolaides had promised. Right up to Alfonsín's un-expected victory, most people assumed that Peronism would win the 30 October 1983 presidential elections. Hence, the junta made a special effort to negotiate the transition with Lorenzo Miguel and his close collaborators, who they knew would be decisive in choosing the PJ's presidential nominee. In November 1982, press reports began to cir-culate that Nicolaides had cut a deal with the metalworkers' chief that would reportedly have given Miguel's allies control of unions under government trusteeship in exchange for a promise that a future Peron-ist government would not take legal action against military officers who had abused their power.[86] Both Miguel and Nicolaides denied the existence of a pact, but others were not so sure. Angel Robledo, a would-be PJ presidential nominee who had the backing of Triaca's GyT, noted that "there are things going on that seem to confirm these reports." Rubén Cardozo of the automobile workers, a key GyT leader, stated more directly that "a military-union pact was in the making, but now that it has come to light they're denying it."[87]

The UCR presidential hopefuls Raúl Alfonsín and Fernando de la Rúa took up the issue on 25 April 1983, identifying Lorenzo Miguel, Diego Ibáñez (state petroleum workers), Rogelio Papagno (paper workers), and the Avellaneda boss Herminio Iglesias as the Peronist leaders involved in negotiating a pact with generals Nicolaides, Suárez Mason, and Trimarco.[88] Alfonsín amplified the accusation in a monthly newsmagazine, insisting that in exchange for the military manipulat-ing union elections to allow them to gain control of important unions still under government trusteeship, Miguel and his allies had agreed to use their influence to persuade the next government to refrain from prosecuting military "excesses" and "illicit acts," from reorganizing the armed forces, from altering patterns and levels of military funding and, at least during its initial phase, from making changes to the army high command.[89] After Alfonsín won the UCR presidential nomina-tion, lawyers for Miguel's "62" initiated a libel suit against him, but the UCR candidate stood by his allegations, and Miguel dropped the suit in November 1983.[90] A significant sector of public opinion believed the charges of a military-union pact, and the Peronist presidential candi-date, Italo Luder, stated publicly that he would respect the amnesty that the military had granted to all who had committed crimes in the dirty war.[91]

Had the Peronists won the elections, Argentina's transition would have been interpreted as a carefully staged, incumbent-controlled one on the Brazilian or Chilean model, not as a case of "regime collapse" as in Greece or Portugal. In any case, the Argentine dictatorship did not "collapse" after its military misadventure. It initiated the transition by a deliberate decision, produced an incumbent caretaker government, generated new attempts to create a successor regime,[92] delayed setting an election date for nine months, stayed in power for a further eight months, controlled the timing of elections, and apparently made a secret pact with the Peronists. Had Peronism won the election, as most expected would happen, the Argentine military might also have retained prerogatives it was later denied: no prosecution for human rights violations, no immediate changeover in the high command, and no cuts in the military budget. Defeat in external war is not supposed to favor an incumbent-controlled transition to a tutelary semi-democracy,[93] but the hypothetical scenario of Peronist electoral victory (which rumors of a pact actually helped to prevent) suggests that the one may not preclude the other.[94]

Seemingly in shock immediately after the surrender, citizens were largely quiescent during Bignone's first two months in office, but opposition soon began to mobilize. Beginning in September 1982, the military faced in quick succession a demonstration in support of human rights groups, a tax revolt in the Buenos Aires metropolitan area, a general strike, and a large demonstration in support of democracy.[95] Meanwhile, the approach of elections triggered a surge of party activity. By March 1983, nearly a quarter of eligible voters had joined or rejoined political parties. The PJ alone claimed more than 3 million members, about 60 percent of whom voted in the party's primary elections in August 1983. The holding of a primary in the PJ represented a democratic advance over 1973, when Perón handpicked Cámpora in the March elections and was himself the consensus candidate in September. Even in 1983, however, the Peronist primary voter had little say in choosing the PJ presidential candidate. In each electoral district (the 23 provinces plus the federal capital), party members voted in August 1983 not for an aspirant to the PJ's presidential nomination but for a list of delegates to a national PJ congress, held on 5–6 September 1983, at which the nominee was scheduled to be chosen. Voters were often unclear as to whom the candidates on the list supported as the

Peronist presidential nominee, and in any case the delegates were not bound to vote for any particular person.[96] At the PJ congress, moreover, the delegates merely voted for or against the "unity" candidate, Italo Luder, who not surprisingly won "by acclamation" what is better termed a plebiscite than an election.[97]

The real site of the PJ presidential nomination was not the Peronist primary election, but a series of meetings in early and mid 1983 between Lorenzo Miguel and a loose group of Peronist "notables" that included Fernando Donaires, Diego Ibáñez, and Rodolfo Ponce from the unions and Deolindo Felipe Bittel, Antonio Cafiero, Herminio Iglesias, Italo Luder, Raúl Matera, and Angel Robledo from the movement's political wing. Apart from Iglesias, who had his eye on the Buenos Aires governorship, each of the politicians aspired to the presidency. The Luder-Bittel ticket was reportedly decided upon between 16 and 19 July, with Miguel playing the preponderant role throughout the entire process.[98] Miguel also dominated the selection of candidates for subaltern political offices. Of the 7 PJ deputies elected from the federal capital in 1983, 2 were unionists tied closely to Miguel and 2 others were aides to the "62." Of the 31 PJ deputies elected from the province of Buenos Aires, 8 were from the "62," and the top slot on the list went to the state petroleum workers' union leader, Diego Ibáñez, one of Miguel's closest allies in the union movement. After his election, Ibáñez was named president of the 111-member bloc of Peronist deputies.[99] Besides handpicking many of the Peronist nominees, Miguel dominated the party structure. Fully 15 of the 28 members of the PJ Consejo Metropolitano, the party's highest organ in the federal capital, were either members of the "62" or nonunionists handpicked by Miguel.[100] At its September 1983 national congress, moreover, the UOM chief was chosen as first vice president of the national PJ. Because the presidency was reserved for Isabel Perón, who was refusing to discuss Peronist politics (or even to set foot in Argentina), the first vice presidency was in effect the party's most important position. As a Spanish journalist put it, "The designation of the metalworkers' chief Lorenzo Miguel as first vice president of *justicialismo* has updated the 1973 slogan 'Cámpora to the presidency, Perón to power.' Now it will be 'Luder to the presidency, Miguel to power.'"[101]

The UCR's nomination process was more transparent and vigorously contested than the PJ's. Alfonsín of the Movimiento de Renovación y Cambio was the favorite, but before being nominated, he was forced to fend off a challenge from Fernando de la Rúa of Balbín's

Línea Nacional. Unlike in Peronism, where few ideological or stylistic differences separated the contenders for the candidacy, Alfonsín was ideologically to the left of de la Rúa and favored making the UCR a more mobilizational party. Key support for Alfonsín's Renovación y Cambio faction came from the party's youth sector and from the Junta Coordinadora Nacional, and the likelihood that Alfonsín would win enabled Renovación y Cambio to win the backing the important Línea Córdoba, which supplied Alfonsín's running mate, Víctor Martínez. Alfonsín also benefited when a sector of the Línea Nacional headed by Juan Carlos Pugliese (probably the most prestigious old-line party leader after Illia died in January 1983) split away from de la Rúa.

The competition between Alfonsín and de la Rúa was much more explicit and open than the competition among the five PJ presidential hopefuls. Unlike in the PJ, the UCR presidential ticket was determined by direct popular vote, although not all districts held the primary on the same day. The UCR, like the PJ, held indirect elections for party authorities, but unlike in the PJ, it was clear to the ordinary voter whom the competing delegates would vote for when the party congress was held in July. By 17 July 1983, when voters in 20 of the 24 electoral districts had cast ballots for the presidential ticket and for delegates to the party congress, Alfonsín had 282,762 votes and 57 delegates; de la Rúa had 44,210 votes and 16 delegates, and Luis León of the Movimiento de Afirmación Yrigoyenista had 1,016 votes and 6 delegates. At this point, eleven days before the congress was scheduled to be held, de la Rúa and León withdrew their candidacies. Alfonsín became party president on July 28, and on July 31 the Alfonsín-Martínez ticket was formally proclaimed.[102]

On 30 October 1983, Alfonsín defeated Luder by 52 to 40 percent, marking the first time in history that Peronism had lost a major national election. Five factors help explain this outcome.[103] First, Peronism in its heyday had received much of its support from industrial workers, but deindustrialization between 1974 and 1983 had eroded this traditional electoral base. Second, Alfonsín made inroads into Peronism's working-class base, winning outright in a number of industrial suburbs of Buenos Aires, although not in the poorest ones. Third, Alfonsín got decisive support from the center-right, whose parties won only 3 percent of the vote in 1983 as compared to 20 percent in March 1973. A variety of reasons prompted these defections, but it is safe to assume that many center-right voters cast a strategic vote for Alfonsín as the candidate most likely to defeat the political movement that had presided over the shattering 1973–76 experience.[104] Fourth, the Radicals ran a better campaign than did the Peronists, whose image was tarred by the evident predominance in the party of widely disliked union leaders, by the backroom deals that resulted in Luder's nomination, by well-substantiated rumors of a union-military pact, and by an election-eve campaign rally at which the Buenos Aires gubernatorial candidate Herminio Iglesias set fire to a coffin inscribed "U.C.R." This ill-conceived gesture was carried on national television and did not sit well with a population exhausted by more than a decade of violence and intolerance. Finally, and perhaps most important, the Radicals, and Alfonsín in particular, presented the image of a party concerned with formal democracy, tolerance, and human rights, while Peronism continued to portray itself as the party of nationalism, intransigence, and populism. In the wake of the devastation of the past decade, many Argentines not firmly committed to either party were simply more receptive to what the Radicals had to offer.

Chapter 7

The Rise and Fall of Renewal
Peronism

Raúl Alfonsín inherited a changed socioeconomic structure
when he took office on 10 December 1983. Only financial
interests and recipients of state contracts had gained from the military's economic policies. The agricultural sector had shown a mixed
performance: soybean and oilseed exports had risen, but regional agriculture, especially sugar, had struggled. Most branches of industry
had stagnated, and vehicle, machinery, and basic metals production
had plunged. The 1985 economic census showed a 4 percent gain in
overall manufacturing employment between 1973 and 1984, but recorded huge job losses in the bastions of industrial unionism: in factories with more than 500 workers, employment fell from 341,816 in
1973 to 244,438 in 1984.[1] Meanwhile, the growth of the urban informal
sector gave Argentina for the first time a large "reserve army of labor,"
and emigration, proletarianization, and unemployment took a toll on
small proprietors, white-collar employees, and professionals.

In addition to a changed socioeconomic structure, Alfonsín inherited a huge economic crisis. By 1983, per capita GNP had fallen 15
percent in three years, the foreign debt had risen $40 billion in seven
years, and inflation had reached an annual rate of 400 percent. After
1983, exacerbating these inherited problems, interest on the foreign
debt skyrocketed, world prices for grain declined, and capital flight
continued. The shortfall in grain prices, together with capital flight,
actually represented more of a drain on the Argentine economy than
payment of interest and principal on the foreign debt.[2] The June 1985
Austral plan—based on wage and price controls, a ban on printing
money to finance the fiscal deficit, higher prices for public services, and
the introduction of a new currency—activated underutilized industrial capacity and kept inflation under 10 percent a month for the

next two years. By mid 1987, however, the Austral plan had unraveled because of union pressure for wage increases, business pressure for easier credit and higher prices, and the government's inability to make major spending cuts.[3] In the end, Alfonsín was unable to resolve the economic problems he faced. During his five-and-a-half-year presidency, real wages dropped 50 percent, unemployment and underemployment doubled, and high but fairly constant inflation turned into accelerating hyperinflation.[4]

A severe economic crisis such as Argentina experienced during the 1980s poses at least two major challenges to democratic consolidation: it raises the stakes of distributive conflict and exposes the regime to criticism that the governments it produces are incapable of dealing with urgent problems. Making the situation even more precarious, Alfonsín made a concerted effort to curb military power.[5] In March 1985, he transferred the trials of military leaders accused of human rights violations from military to civilian courts.[6] In addition, he made significant cuts in the military budget, reduced the size of the armed forces, removed a number of industries from military jurisdiction, and refused to "vindicate" the dirty war as having saved the country from communism.

The attempt to curb military power and to bring human rights violators to justice provoked armed rebellions by military factions in April 1987, January 1988, and December 1988. The aim of these rebellions was not to overthrow the government but to force the resignation of army commanders who in the rebels' eyes had failed to defend their subordinates against prosecution for human rights violations, budget cuts, or an overall loss of prestige.[7] Although the rebellions were not explicitly aimed at installing a new military regime, they sufficed to cause Alfonsín to backtrack on the human rights trials. In December 1986, the government to introduced a "full stop" bill that set a 60-day deadline for initiating further prosecutions, and in April 1987, it sent congress a "due obedience" bill that exempted all officers at or below the rank of lieutenant colonel from prosecution for human rights violations on the grounds that they had been "just following orders."[8] Congress quickly passed both bills into law. Asked whether he would do anything different with the military issue if he could govern again from 1983 to 1989, Alfonsín responded: "No one who accepted Argentine democracy would have had many alternatives. They would have had to work more or less the way I did. There are more than 10,000 documented disappeared. There could have been a disastrous relationship between the relatives of the disappeared and those who were accused of making them into victims. The trials of those responsible pacified the country."[9]

Despite the economic crisis and the restiveness of the military, conditions at the outset of Alfonsín's presidency were probably more favorable for democratization, and for the institutionalization of a Peronist party, than at any previous time in the country's history. For the past three decades, Peronist party-building initiatives had always had to contend with the possibility, and eventually with the reality, that military intervention would bring them to an abrupt halt. In 1983, for the first time in 50 years, there was reason to believe that a military coup was no longer on the horizon. Defeat in external war, human rights violations, and gross economic mismanagement had discredited military rule. Except on the extreme right, moreover, the main justifications for past coups had lost credibility. The armed left had been mercilessly crushed, and "international communism" was far less threatening than it had been in the wake of the Cuban revolution. Some people still harbored strong anti-Peronist feelings, but the intense and widespread anti-Peronism that had helped to trigger the 1955, 1962, and 1966 coups had become greatly attenuated—mostly by the emergence of a deadlier battle between left and right, but also by Juan Perón's death, Isabel Perón's retirement, and the experience of interparty cooperation in the Hora del Pueblo and Multipartidaria coalitions.

Besides the impression that democracy would last for a long time, a second factor propitious for Peronist party institutionalization was the evolution of public opinion toward more solid support for parties and politicians. The main reason for this shift in opinion was that alternative political actors now looked decidedly worse. From 1930 to 1980, many Argentines believed that corporatist arrangements, plebiscitarian leaders, or military officers could govern the country better than party politicians. Revaluation of parties proceeded unevenly after this low point, but by the early 1980s, rule by party politicians, even unfairly elected ones like Illia, looked better in retrospect than deflated plebiscitarianism under Isabel Perón or state terror under Videla. Survey data show how attitudes toward parties had changed. In June 1967, only 20 percent of urban Argentines thought that the "general situation would improve" if "political parties were reestablished," and in July 1968, less than 20 percent felt that "political parties [should run] the country in the manner they did prior to June 27 [1966]."[10] By 1984,

84 percent of survey respondents were evaluating parties in "positive" terms, and in 1988, despite the worst economic crisis in modern Argentine history, the figure remained high at 63 percent.[11]

Also boosting the chances for Peronist party institutionalization was, paradoxically, the resurgence of Radicalism during the 1983 electoral campaign. Despite its movementist roots (and branches), the UCR had always been considered Argentina's consummate political party. Over the years, the prestige of "parties" had come to depend, in certain measure, on whether the UCR was perceived as capable of winning a fair election and producing a good government. To many Argentines, Radicalism's weak electoral performance under Perón, acquiescence in the proscription of Peronism, and reluctance to seize the torch when the 1973–76 government crumbled suggested that the UCR was both electorally impotent and unfit to govern. Alfonsín's 1983 presidential campaign helped to reverse these perceptions. By energetically promoting human rights and open political competition, by recognizing Peronism as a legitimate electoral competitor, and by speaking out against the alleged union-military pact, Alfonsín managed simultaneously to demonstrate reasonably inspiring leadership, to diminish his party's association with the proscription of Peronism, and to portray the UCR as a viable alternative to the PJ. The resurgence of Radicalism increased the prestige of all parties, giving antiparty sentiments a much less congenial audience than they had received in previous years. Moreover, Perón's death had deprived antiparty sentiments of their single most compelling exponent.

A final factor propitious for the PJ's institutionalization was its loss of the 1983 presidential election. Deprived of strongholds in the national executive, the PJ and Peronist legislative bloc loomed much larger as vehicles for political influence, and as sources of prestige and patronage resources, than would have been the case had Luder won the presidency. The most likely scenario for a Luder presidency would have been behind-the-scenes rule by Lorenzo Miguel's faction of the Peronist union leadership, perhaps under some form of military tutelage. Consider what happened when Peronism regained control of the national executive in 1989: the PJ was relegated to a role far more marginal than it had played at any time during Alfonsín's presidency. One might argue that Luder, a ponderous and deliberate lawyer, lacked the charisma that Menem employed to form a direct, affective link between himself and his supporters, and that the PJ would therefore have played a more important role during a hypothetical Luder presidency than it did during Menem's. Yet the PJ was a much more fragile organization in 1983, after seven years of military repression, than in 1989, after six years of legal opposition. Luder's inability to emulate Menem's plebiscitarian style might have favored the institutionalization of the PJ, but that advantage would have been offset by the more fragile party structures that existed in 1983 as compared to 1989.

The Rise of Renewal Peronism

The brunt of the blame for Peronism's defeat fell directly on Lorenzo Miguel, who had exercised enormous influence in choosing the Peronist nominees and in orchestrating their electoral campaigns. Opposition to Miguel's leadership broke into the open in December 1984, when the PJ held a congress to elect a new leadership. Before the congress convened, Miguel and Herminio Iglesias, the Avellaneda boss, concocted a "unity" list, which the delegates in attendance would be invited to vote for or against. The unity list included Isabel Perón as party president, the Santa Fe governor José María Vernet as first vice president, Lorenzo Miguel as second vice president, and Herminio Iglesias as general secretary.[12] Into the Teatro Odeón in Buenos Aires, which contained 420 seats, crushed 656 delegates, 60 armed security guards, and more than 200 of the outgoing leadership's "special invitees," mostly members of *barras bravas* (gangs) known for making trouble at soccer games. Once the proceedings began, Peronists known to be at odds with the existing leadership, notably Carlos Menem, were spat upon and punched. Amid the deafening roar of the barras bravas and the bone-jarring thud of huge drums beaten by UOM toughs equipped with lengths of sand-filled rubber hose, someone grabbed a microphone and announced that it was time to ratify the unity list by acclamation. At this point 414 delegates walked out, leaving only 240 in the auditorium.[13]

In February 1985, delegates who had walked out of the Teatro Odeón held a meeting of their own at Rio Hondo in the province of Santiago del Estero. The meeting marked an important change in Peronism's public image, which had reached a spectacular low at the Teatro Odeón congress. As one reporter put it, "Peronism [at Rio Hondo] succeeded in holding a congress where no one punched anyone else, no one was denied the right to speak, and journalists were allowed to cover the proceedings. . . . some *justicialistas* saw it as the Peronist movement's most important political event of the past ten years."[14] The delegates chose Isabel Perón as party president, the San Luis senator Oraldo Britos as first vice president, the "25" union leader Roberto García as second vice president, and the Córdoba politician José Manuel de la Sota as general secretary. (A few days later, Isabel Perón resigned the presidency of both wings of the party.) The congress at Rio Hondo marked the birth of renewal Peronism (Peronismo Renovador); its adversary, the Miguel-Iglesias faction, came to be known as orthodox Peronism (Peronismo Ortodoxo).

What distinguished renewal from orthodox Peronism was, above all, political style and leadership composition. The renewal Peronists called for new party leaders and more open procedures for selecting candidates. Their key figures included urbane politicians and intellectuals, provincial notables with clientelistic followings, and unionists from the "25." The orthodox wing favored the PJ's tradition of behind-the-scenes accords on political strategy and on candidates. It featured Lorenzo Miguel's "62 Organizations," Herminio Iglesias's supporters, some provincial notables of its own, and—in a bizarre twist—a few ex-Montoneros. In July 1985, the orthodox wing tried to get the renewal sector to participate in a "Unity Congress" in Santa Rosa, La Pampa, but only a few renewal Peronists took up the offer. The congress named Isabel Perón as party president (despite her having resigned the office), the Catamarca governor Vicente Saadi as first vice president, the GyT unionist Jorge Triaca as second vice president, and the incumbent Herminio Iglesias as general secretary. This lineup amounted to an all-star cast of the Peronist figures most annoying to the renewal faction.

The national deputy elections in November 1985 were the first real showdown between the competing wings of the party. The timing of the elections, which took place at the height of the Austral plan's success, helped the UCR beat the Peronists by a fairly wide margin, 43 to 35 percent. In the province of Buenos Aires, however, where the renewal and orthodox wings of the PJ ran separate lists of candidates, the renewal sector, despite coming in second to the UCR, outpolled the orthodox sector by a margin of 3 to 1. The renewal sector sent ten deputies to congress, including the "25" leaders Osvaldo Borda (rubber workers) and José Rodríguez (automobile workers), whereas the orthodox wing sent only three, including Herminio Iglesias and Jorge Triaca (plastics workers). Although two years would pass before the renewal sector assumed formal control of a unified PJ apparatus, the November 1985 legislative elections marked the effective demise of the orthodox wing under Lorenzo Miguel's hegemony.

Political Conflict in Peronist Unionism

On 17 December 1983, exactly one week after taking office, Alfonsín submitted to congress new legislation aimed at making union elections fairer and union leaderships less monolithic. The bill included provisions designed to improve the ministry of labor's ability to oversee union elections, to reduce the number of signatures needed to put an opposition list on the ballot, to limit union leaders to two consecutive three-year terms, and to give 33 percent of secretariat positions to any runner-up list that won more than 25 percent of the vote.[15] In addition to its general aim of democratizing the unions, the legislation had more partisan objectives. One group of government advisers headed by Alfonsín's chief of staff, Germán López (who had not forgotten his experience as labor undersecretary from 1963 to 1966), envisioned the union reform bill as a way to divide and weaken the unions to the point where they could not challenge government policy initiatives. Another group, in which leaders of the Coordinadora played a prominent role, felt that the new election rules would give the UCR a chance to gain a foothold in the unions, duplicating its recent success in appealing for workers' votes the industrial suburbs of Buenos Aires. In moving aggressively to widen the UCR's support, the Coordinadora was trying to create a "third historical movement" to succeed those led by Yrigoyen and Perón.[16]

During the 1983 UCR primary, the Coordinadora had given Alfonsín's candidacy a mobilizational and plebiscitarian dimension that had harked back to the days of Yrigoyen. Although retaining the party's traditional emphasis on civil liberties and democracy, the Coordinadora advocated mass mobilization, tried to challenge Peronism in the unions and working-class neighborhoods, and stressed that democracy was not just an end in itself, but also a prerequisite for social justice. While still a candidate and in the first year of his presidency, Alfonsín had touched repeatedly upon the "third historical movement" theme promoted by the Coordinadora. The plebiscitarian strand of Alfonsín's leadership was accentuated in 1984, when UCR leaders suspended a clause in the party constitution that barred elected officials from holding party positions (allowing Alfonsín to stay on as head of the party while serving as president of Argentina), and again prior to the June 1985 Austral plan, when extraparty technocrats replaced old-time party stalwarts in the ministry of the economy.[17] Alfonsín's movementism differed, however, from Perón's or Yrigoyen's. Partly because of his personal predilections and partly because of the "climate of the times," Alfonsín's early years as president were tinged with plebiscitarianism, but did not display the hegemonic vocation or eclectic view of appropriate roads to power that had colored the movementism of his predecessors.

Peronist union leaders closed ranks to confront Alfonsín's union reform bill, which Raúl Amín of the auto workers characterized as a "social-democratic prescription that the ultra-left will take advantage of."[18] Ending the three-year split between the CGT–Brasil and CGT–Azopardo, Ubaldini and Triaca merged their rival confederations under a four-member collegial leadership—from which Miguel and his allies, discredited by the Peronist electoral defeat, were excluded.[19] The newly unified CGT immediately formed a six-member commission to advise the PJ deputies on how to combat the union reform bill in congress[20]—a promising development from the point of view of the party's institutionalization. The legislation passed easily in the chamber of deputies, where the Radicals had a majority, but ran into trouble in the senate, where they did not. The upper house in 1984 included 21 senators from the PJ, 18 from the UCR, 2 each from provincial parties in San Juan, Corrientes, and Neuquén, and 1 from Frondizi's MID. With the support of the senators from Neuquén and the MID, the PJ gave the Radicals their first congressional setback, defeating the bill by a 24 to 22 margin. A weaker version of the legislation, with no provision for minority-list participation in union secretariats, finally passed in July 1984.

Although the July 1984 union reform law gave the traditional Peronist leadership more control over union elections and administration than the Radicals had hoped, it helped to democratize the unions. A survey of 37 major union elections in 1984 and 1985 revealed that fully 78 percent had involved competition between two or more lists, up from 32 percent in 1973–76 and 44 percent in 1965–68.[21] The main beneficiary of this competition turned out to be the combative and left-leaning "25." By 1986, unionists affiliated with the "25" had won competitive elections in three of the country's largest unions—the retail clerks (408,000 members), railway workers (143,000), and state workers (86,000). Bolstered by these victories—and encouraged by the perceived mandate from public opinion that the renewal sector had won in the 1985 national deputy elections—the "25" leaders began to found regional subsidiaries around the country. Their goal was to convert their group into the organized expression of Peronist unionism in the renewal branch of the PJ, in the same sense that the "62"—which still claimed to be the "political arm of Peronist unionism" as a whole—had in fact been reduced to the organized expression of Peronist unionism in the decaying orthodox branch. Although the "25" had never formally resigned from the previously all-encompassing "62," they refused to attend the meetings of Miguel's organization or to occupy the seats he held open for them on its leadership board.[22]

Propitious for the PJ's institutionalization was that the "62" and "25" each saw the party as an important vehicle for interest representation. But apart from this appreciation of the party's importance and a common allegiance to Peronism, the "62" and "25" had little in common. Besides backing different wings of the party, the union leader factions disagreed about how much power unionists should wield in the party organization. Whereas the "62" tried to dominate the orthodox wing, the "25" ceded leadership to the professional politicians in the renewal wing. Renewal Peronism's three original "referents"—Antonio Cafiero, Carlos Grosso, and Carlos Menem—were all politicians, underscoring the fact that the 1983 electoral defeat had convinced most of the renewal Peronists, including the "25," that a Peronism conspicuously subordinated to union leaders would be unable to attract many middle-class votes. A comparison of national deputy lists shows that the "62" controlled the orthodox wing more than the "25" controlled the renewal wing. In 1983, when Lorenzo Miguel called the shots in drawing up the lists of national deputy candidates from the federal capital and Buenos Aires, he placed several "62" unionists in choice positions. In 1987, by contrast, when the renewal sector called the shots, the "25" unionists were fewer in number and were placed in more precarious slots.[23]

Also distinguishing the "62" from the "25" was a huge ideological and programmatic gulf. Whereas Lorenzo Miguel announced that he was "anti-Marxist and anti-leftist" and opposed to "foreign ideologies" including "social democracy,"[24] the "25" used the language of the left to denounce "transnational capitalism" and U.S. foreign policy:

The development of the crisis at the international level and the consequent recomposition of the balance of forces at the backbone of the new transnational order has made us the chosen victims of financial interests and the World Bank—impregnable bulwarks of a transnational capitalism that has reinforced its plan of domination over three-quarters of the planet's population. . . . [W]e respect the principle of nonintervention and are vigilant in defense of the right to self-determination that today, unfortunately, is placed in jeopardy by the hegemonic interest of imperialism in the Central American region and by the recent bombing of the Republic of Libya.[25]

Programmatic differences between the factions were also manifested in competing views about the conflict in Nicaragua. Argentine military personnel had stopped training the Nicaraguan Contras by the time Alfonsín took office, but the Nicaragua issue remained ideologically charged. From the ranks of the "25," the ATE (state workers) leaders Víctor De Gennaro and Germán Abdala publicly endorsed a newspaper advertisement condemning the decision by the U.S. congress in July 1986 to approve $100 million for the Contra war.[26] Perhaps uniquely among Latin American unionists of equal stature, the "62" stood distinctly to the right on the Nicaragua issue. A "62" leader who also served as a national deputy in the orthodox wing of the party reported, "There are some Peronist deputies who agree with the Sandinista regime; I don't agree with them. . . . I'm not sure, but I don't think anyone in the orthodox wing agrees with the Sandinista regime."[27]

A successful 1986 bill to legalize divorce gives further evidence of the factions' programmatic differences. Seven of the nine "25" deputies voted in favor of the bill, whereas only one of the nine "62" deputies did so (the others abstained or voted no).[28] Miguel's close ally Diego Ibáñez (state petroleum workers) publicly opposed the legalization of divorce, and Jorge Triaca occupied a place on the podium in a Church-sponsored rally "to defend the family" against the divorce law.[29] A final, and critical, programmatic difference between the "25" and "62" involved the human rights issue. Key "25" leaders were vocal advocates for the families of the "disappeared." Ricardo Pérez (truckers) was the CGT's secretary for human rights, and other "25" leaders endorsed and attended human rights demonstrations.[30] The renewal Peronist deputies, "25" unionists among them, voted in 1987 against the due obedience legislation that eventually gave amnesty to military officers who, in violating human rights, had been "just following orders." By contrast, the orthodox Peronist deputies, "62" unionists among them, abstained on the due obedience bill, helping to assure its passage.[31] Moreover, the same "62" leader who opposed the Sandinistas had this to say about the human rights issue:

You have to judge the Proceso globally, not just in terms of the violation of human rights. The drop in the gross domestic product, the increase in speculation, the imprisonment of Isabel Perón are also violations of human rights. The military coup itself is a violation of the constitution and the law. We needed a global judgment, and the citizenry itself made such a judgment by voting against the Proceso. [The human rights trials] might sound good to international public opinion, but there's no political backing for them in Argentina. . . . I think [the human rights trials] have put the judiciary in the position of resolving a political issue.[32]

Thirteen General Strikes

In March 1985, the CGT co-leader Jorge Triaca was called to testify at the human rights trials. His performance did not endear him to those who favored prosecuting those who had violated human rights during the dirty war. Triaca had been imprisoned after the 1976 coup, but he testified that his experience in jail had not been particularly unpleasant. Triaca said that he had enjoyed "exemplary" treatment during his eight-month detention on a navy ship, and when asked whether he knew of any union leaders who had been killed, kidnapped, tortured, or illegally detained between 1976 and 1982, Triaca, overlooking even his own illegal detention, could remember only one, the notorious case of Oscar Smith of the light and power workers.[33] (The Comisión Nacional sobre la Desaparación de las Personas documented the disappearance of more than 2,700 workers, many of them unionists, during this period.) On hearing of this testimony, Ubaldini, a vocal advocate for the families of the disappeared, threatened to resign from the CGT leadership if Triaca failed to clarify his statements.[34] Triaca explained that his testimony had been dictated by the wording of the questions, but in the context of his reputation for having taken a conciliatory approach to the military government, many union leaders remained dissatisfied with his responses.

In addition to disagreeing on the human rights issue, Ubaldini and Triaca differed in their views about how the CGT should relate to the Alfonsín government. The latter conflict came into the open in August 1985, when the CGT launched its third general strike to protest the government's economic policies. In the days leading up to the strike, Triaca announced that if negotiations with the government took a positive turn, the strike could be suspended or canceled. Ubaldini, however, termed the protest "nonnegotiable." The strike went forward, generating a high level of absenteeism, and although a rally called in association with the strike was well attended, journalists noted that many of those who gathered to hear Ubaldini speak belonged not to unions but to leftist parties. Unionists who supported the strike implicitly ratified this characterization of the crowd by denouncing their "moderate" counterparts for "trying to pull the rug out from under Ubaldini" by, among other things, "refusing to provide buses to bring union members to the mobilization."[35] Disgruntled with what they felt was Triaca's insufficiently combative stance toward the Alfonsín government, and aware of the public scandal caused by his testimony at the human rights trials, five former GyT adherents on the CGT directive council announced after the 26 August general strike that they intended to make Ubaldini the confederation's sole secretary-general. These five union leaders—Miguel Candore (civil service), Alejo Farías (construction), Pedro Goyeneche (textiles), Rubén Pereyra (waterworks), and Aldo Serrano (light and power)—became the core of what came to be called "Ubaldinismo," a third union *nucleamiento* (current), oriented around the charismatic figure of Ubaldini and distinct from both the "25" and the "62."

At the behest of the Ubaldinistas, the CGT in September 1985 dissolved its collegial secretary-generalship and made Ubaldini its sole leader. Triaca immediately retreated to Miguel's "62 Organizations." Although Miguel had been discredited in electoral politics, he still controlled the metalworkers' UOM, Argentina's most powerful union, and held sway over orthodox Peronist union leaders and politicians. Moreover, the Alfonsín government regarded Miguel as a power broker of exceptional importance (the collective contracts signed by the UOM traditionally served as prototypes for those in other sectors of industry) and as a counterweight both to Ubaldini, from whom the Radicals expected a long stream of general strikes, and to Peronism's renewal sector, from which the Radicals expected their most formidable electoral challenge. From an ideological and programmatic standpoint, the alliance between Miguel and Triaca was more natural than previous alliances between Miguel and the "25" (1980) or Triaca and the "25" (1984). Triaca and Miguel shared with each other, but not with the "25," a conservative ideology and a propensity to negotiate with governments of all political stripes. Their rivalry was primarily a turf battle, which evaporated when Triaca could no longer pose a challenge to the metalworkers' chief.

The alliance between Triaca and Miguel crystallized a three-way polarization in the Peronist movement. Orthodox Peronism continued to be dominated by the "62," while renewal Peronism operated under the leadership of politicians allied with the "25." Although Ubaldini had been chosen as the orthodox PJ's union secretary at the

Teatro Odeón congress, and although he had helped to found the "25," he now declared neutrality in the orthodox-renewal dispute. Instead of struggling for control of the PJ, Ubaldini called repeated general strikes in an effort to make the CGT the main pole of opposition to the Alfonsín government. These differing views of which organization should spearhead the Peronist opposition were to some extent reflected in the opinions of the unionists who followed these major leaders. A survey of 400 unionists in August and September 1986 revealed that 33 percent of Ubaldinistas agreed that the CGT should be the main pole of opposition, in contrast to only 17 percent of "62" unionists and 20 percent of "25" leaders. By comparison, 60 percent of "62" unionists and 43 percent of "25" leaders felt that the PJ should be the main opposition vehicle, as compared to only 37 percent of Ubaldinistas.[36]

The three-way polarization between the "25," "62," and Ubaldinistas raised an issue relevant to democratic consolidation. Despite their differences, the "25" and "62," with their ties to competing wings of the PJ, had gained a strong stake in the continued operation of the electoral mechanisms through which party leaders gained access to legislative and, ultimately, executive posts. Although Ubaldini's personal commitment to the functioning of parties and elections was beyond serious dispute, his preferred mode of political expression—CGT general strikes and thunderous denunciations of government policies—tended to marginalize the party system and legislature as arenas of opposition. From the standpoint of democratic consolidation, what was most troubling about Ubaldini's tactics was not his advocacy of general strikes—which provided an outlet for social protest that might otherwise have taken more destabilizing forms—but his reluctance to take the party more seriously as a vehicle of opposition, which reduced his followers' stakes in the survival of electoral and legislative institutions.

The CGT called general strikes in January, March, June, and October 1986, giving Ubaldini unprecedented media exposure. As Ubaldini's star continued to rise, some major union leaders, including the "25" luminary José Pedraza (railway workers) and Triaca's ally Armando Cavalieri (federal capital retail clerks), began to drift closer to the CGT chief.[37] Overall, however, 1986 saw a hardening of differences among the three main factions of Peronist unionism. This crystallization included a solidification of the split between the "25" and Ubaldinismo. Ubaldini had been a founder of the "25" and continued to share the group's commitment to human rights, but he seemed uncomfortable with the urbane circles in which the renewal-sector politicians traveled. The son of a waiter, he had grown up in Mataderos, a working-class district of the federal capital. He had spent nine years working in meat-packing plants until, in 1970, he found a job in a factory that prepared brewers' yeast. During the next ten years, he worked his way up through the beer workers' union, joining its secretariat in 1974 and making his first notable appearance with a December 1978 speech at a dinner held by the "25." Ubaldini lived modestly. Reportedly, he did not own a car and did not know how to drive. He preferred plain talk, Sunday lunches at his mother's house, pilgrimages to the San Cayetano religious shrine, and an occasional soccer game or visit to a tango bar.[38]

Ubaldini's general strikes were ostensibly aimed at changing the government's economic policy. By the end of 1986, it was clear that the tactic was not working. At this point the "25" became more vocal in criticizing the CGT chief for neglecting long-term political strategy, which they felt required closer collaboration with the renewal-sector politicians. As the "25" leader Guerino Andreoni (retail clerks' confederation) put it: "Ubaldinismo is behind a leader; we in the "25" are behind a project. We see the debate much more from a political standpoint. . . . we might be able to achieve the same results without establishing a direct relation with politics, but it would take a much longer time."[39]

Ubaldini responded to accusations that he lacked a "project" by reminding critics that in February 1985, he and his allies, in conjunction with ten landowner, industrial, and trade associations, had produced a "Proposal for Growth with Freedom and Social Justice." This proposal, however, left much to be desired as an alternative program for government. According to the labor affairs analyst Héctor Palomino, it recommended that "the government raise wages at the same time it raises the exchange rate for exporters (which will in fact reduce wages), that it eliminate the fiscal deficit (which affects wages and employment in the public sector), that it extend credit to industry (which means cutting the incomes of workers and agricultural exporters), that it reduce taxes (which means reducing the state's ability to redistribute income) . . . that it promote regional development, increase subsidies to the provinces, etc."[40] In similar fashion, the CGT's July 1985 "26 Points" constituted a wish list of measures deemed capable, amid the worst economic crisis in Argentine history, of promoting investment, raising workers' real incomes, and increasing social spending.[41] A contributor to the renewal Peronist magazine *Unidos* called the 26 Points "irresponsible and incoherent . . . useful for a frontal clash [with the government] but not as a general political alternative."[42]

The Ubaldinista leader Miguel Candore (civil servants) readily confirmed that his current was organized around a leader rather than a "project," but questioned whether the "25" had in fact done much to design a viable alternative to the government's policies:

I'd like to see the famous political project of the "25." They've been working in politics for a while, in what is sometimes called renewal [Peronism], but not everyone in the "25" thinks alike. Guillán, who [abandoned the "25"], is not the same as Digón, nor is De Gennaro the same as Andreoni. If nothing else, this prevents them from expressing a political project. Around here we all talk about a project, but what I want to know is, where is it? We in the CGT have one goal: to strengthen Ubaldini throughout the country. . . . [We] move very cautiously in politics. But look here, we think that *el número uno*, and the referent of everything, is named Saúl Ubaldini.[43]

If the "25" had not gone far toward proposing a viable alternative, neither had the Ubaldinistas. Moreover, by the end of 1986, it was abundantly clear that the Radicals were not going to institute a populist economic program no matter how many general strikes the CGT launched. The absence of a coherent set of goals to guide the CGT's actions, coupled with Ubaldini's manifest failure to budge the government from its economic policy, raises the question of why the CGT kept calling general strikes. One reason may have been that the government, by refusing to endorse collective contracts that included wage hikes above a specified ceiling, may have unwittingly made itself, rather than employers, the main target of wage protests, thereby displacing labor protest from individual firms and industries to the national level. A more intentional variant of the displacement explanation emerges from a debate at a 1984 CGT plenary session, where several union leaders argued that centralized protest was needed to contain what was perceived to be an explosion of separate labor disputes. From this standpoint, as Gaudio and Thompson point out, the general strike strategy was designed "as an instrument of control *over* the various strata of unionism."[44] Neither variant of the displacement explanation seems particularly convincing, however. There was no shortage of smaller-scope labor protest during the heyday of the CGT general strikes. Between 1984 and 1988, ordinary strikes in Argentina (excluding nationwide general strikes) cost a yearly average of 2,721 working days per 1,000 wage and salary earners. This level of strike activity was nearly three times as high as in contemporary Italy and Spain, the most strike-prone advanced industrial countries, which averaged in the high 800s for the 1974–90 period.[45] Displacement of labor protest from the local to national level may have contributed to the general-strike strategy, but other factors were clearly also at work. One such factor may have been pressure from CGT delegations in the interior of the country.[46] Between January 1984 and May 1989, *Informes Laborales* recorded 236 strikes by workers demanding overdue paychecks, mostly sugar-mill workers, teachers, and civil servants in the poor provinces of the northwest.[47] The regional CGT delegations were obliged to demand that the national CGT take action to protest these and other serious problems, including plant closings, layoffs, and miserable wages.

All of these factors—wage guidelines that made the government the target of labor militancy, national union leaders' efforts to contain base-level protest, and pressure from workers in crisis-ridden economic sectors and regions—probably sustained the general strike approach in the face of its conspicuous failure to induce economic policy changes. It is interesting to note, however, that the general strikes also had the effect, intended or not, of allowing Ubaldini at periodic intervals to mobilize mass support behind his continued leadership of the CGT. This effect may well be part of the explanation for why the general-strike approach was maintained. As a second-rank leader of the 6,000-member beer workers' union, Ubaldini had a personal power interest in continuing the general-strike strategy. Lacking a strong organizational base of his own, Ubaldini's power resided in his combative oratory and in the public's consciousness of his militant opposition to the dictatorship. The mass demonstrations and media attention that accompanied the general strikes gave Ubaldini an indispensable forum for calling on these power resources, without which he would surely have disappeared into obscurity as a minor official in a minuscule union. Ubaldini's decision to press ahead with apparently ineffective general strikes lends support to the view that internal struggles in the Peronist union leadership not only result from, but often shape, the stances that different union leaders take toward the government.

The Emergence of the "15" and the Pact with Alfonsín

The independence of the Ubaldinistas from the "25" and "62" was underscored at the November 1986 CGT congress, at which unionists finally took legal control of the confederation for the first time since the March 1976 coup (the earlier CGT leaderships were informal arrangements, only grudgingly recognized by the government). For several weeks prior to the congress, negotiations had been taking place among the union "notables" to decide which of them would fill the twenty-one slots on a single "unity" list of candidates for the confederation's leadership board. (After the "unity" list was decided on behind the scenes, delegates to the congress would vote "yes" or "no"). During these negotiations, the Ubaldinistas participated as a separate tendency, distinct from both the "62" and "25."[48] A cursory glance at the outcome of the negotiations seems to reveal that the three factions had reached an equilibrium. Eighteen posts were divided equally among unionists clearly representing the three main factions. But a look at who occupied the remaining three positions reveals a clear advantage for the Ubaldinistas. First, Ubaldini himself, who received (as expected) the single secretary-general slot, was not counted as a member of "Ubaldinismo." Second, the new CGT treasury undersecretary, Hernán Prado, ostensibly a representative of the governing UCR, was "in the opinion of many just another Ubaldinista."[49] Third, although the last of the twenty-one posts went to Gerónimo Izetta, formally an independent but actually an intimate of Lorenzo Miguel's "62," this advantage for the "62" was offset by the fact that Juan Palacios (bus drivers), although a "62" nominee, was in 1986 one of Ubaldini's closest collaborators.[50] Similarly close to Ubaldini was José Pedraza (railways) of the "25," the CGT's new union and interior secretary, who invariably appeared to the right of the CGT leader at press conferences. Because the union and interior secretariat was the second most important in the confederation after the secretary-generalship itself (the position linked the CGT's central administration to dozens of regional CGTs around the country), Pedraza's de facto alliance with Ubaldini yielded yet another power resource for the charismatic secretary-general.

The November 1986 CGT normalizing congress represented the height of Ubaldini's influence. But there were already signs that he was heading for trouble. Foremost among these signs was Lorenzo Miguel's growing reluctance to support Ubaldini's combative stance. In July 1986, Miguel had surprised observers of the labor scene by sending a telegram to the economy minister, Juan Sourrouille, the favorite target of CGT antigovernment proclamations, to thank him for helping the metalworkers conclude a wage agreement with the industry's employers' organizations.[51] Miguel's cordial gesture came at a time when Ubaldini was denouncing "a conspiracy of silence, manipulated by official bodies, to strangle the determined demands of the workers."[52] By the time of the November 1986 CGT congress, Miguel was becoming skeptical about the CGT's strategy of incessant general strikes.[53] After two years of intense and fruitless confrontation, a new strategy seemed to be called for. The protagonist of this strategy would be a new conciliatory current, the "Group of 15." This new faction of Peronist unionism drew its members from Ubaldinismo, the "62," and the "25" alike.

For reasons of its own, the Alfonsín government had also become more sympathetic to the idea of a separate peace with the big industrial unions. First, one of the CGT's most irrefutable complaints was that many of the dictatorship's labor laws were still on the books. The UCR government had submitted new draft laws to congress, but it appeared that they would be bogged down in debate unless some Peronist deputies could be induced to go along with them.[54] Second, the Radicals saw that the renewal-sector Peronist politicians, flush with their victory over the orthodox sector, had left their union flank unguarded, and realized that a pact with conciliatory union leaders might help to isolate their electoral arch-rivals.[55] Some even hoped that such a pact, if successful, could rejuvenate the fading dream of a "third historical movement."[56] Third, now that Ubaldini had been ratified as secretary-general of a newly normalized CGT, an endless stream of general strikes seemed to be on the horizon unless something were done to undercut his influence. Moreover, the UOM had rocked the country with a tremendous wave of sectoral strikes during June 1986, accounting for 2.9 million working days lost, a 60 percent plunge in iron and steel production, and a 15 percent drop in overall industrial production.[57] Finally, intimations of military unrest (which culminated in an April 1987 military rebellion) had made the government more anxious to expand its base of support.[58] In a 1993 interview, Alfonsín stressed the strike surge and military rebellion factors in explaining his decision to seek a pact with Peronist unionism. When asked why he had decided to invite a Peronist unionist into his cabinet in March 1987, Alfonsín replied:

I had too many conflicts. We put up not just with 14 [sic] general strikes but also with thousands of strikes. It was too conflictive a situation. Also, the situation with the armed forces was getting increasingly tense. So, I wanted to calm social conflict a bit, to have the support of all the workers. And when the Semana Santa [military rebellion] occurred, the whole CGT came out to defend democracy. And that was the most important goal I sought. All of my governments have been impregnated with that fundamental objective. I did things I wouldn't have done had it not been for the fear of instability, and I didn't do things I would [otherwise] have done, because I had the obligation to consolidate democracy.[59]

For all of these reasons, Alfonsín decided to send one of his main "operators," the Coordinadora notable Enrique Nosiglia, to discuss a pact with some of the more flexible union leaders. Nosiglia's main contact was Armando Cavalieri, an ex-GyT luminary who controlled the Federal Capital section of the retail clerks' union.[60] The pact was concluded in March 1987 and marked the emergence of the "Group of 15" as a fourth Peronist union faction alongside the "62," the "25," and Ubaldinismo. Prominent figures in the "15" included Triaca, Cavalieri, and Carlos Alderete (light and power workers)—all former leaders of GyT. However, the group also drew heavily from Miguel's allies in the "62" (Ibáñez, Romero, Barrionuevo), repentant Ubaldinistas (Goyeneche, Serrano, Palacios, Zanola), and dissidents from the "25" (Rodríguez and Guillán). Lorenzo Miguel, as usual, kept his cards close to his chest. It was inconceivable that Ibáñez would have joined the "15" without Miguel's benediction, and Miguel's ideological and programmatic views fitted in much better with the "15" than with the Ubaldinistas or the "25." Miguel chose nonetheless to remain on the outskirts of the "15." Probably not coincidentally, this choice had the effect of increasing his leverage within the Peronist union leadership. From a position of formal neutrality, Miguel was well positioned to serve as a power broker between the "15" and the CGT, and would be able to save face if the pact with the government collapsed.

The "15" asserted that their main goal was to "search for new conditions of concertation in a social, economic, and political situation characterized by immobilism and crisis."[61] They clearly regarded Ubaldini's general-strike strategy as a major cause of immobilism: "eight general strikes haven't done anything, so the best thing to do is to search for another kind of relationship," a member of the "15" said.[62] The new relationship involved an exchange of resources between the "15" and the Alfonsín government. Carlos Alderete became Alfonsín's labor minister, other members of the "15" received secretarial and subsecretarial posts within the ministry,[63] and Miguel's metalworkers, Triaca's plastics workers, Ibáñez's state oil workers, Alderete's light and power workers, and Rodríguez's auto workers all got wage increases above those recommended by the government's wage guidelines. In exchange for these concessions, the government got the metalworkers to include in their collective contract—on which other contracts were traditionally modeled—a no-strike clause that would remain in effect for three months.[64] No general strikes were called during the six months that the "15" occupied the ministry of labor, and labor bills that had previously been stagnating in the chamber of deputies were pushed rapidly toward approval by an alliance of Radicals and orthodox Peronists, over renewal Peronist opposition.[65]

The coincidence between the Alfonsín government and the "15" was based on more than selective incentives, however. Whereas the Ubaldinistas and "25" demanded that the workers be given a bigger slice of the economic pie, the "15" and the government placed top priority on enlarging the size of the pie itself. According to Cavalieri, Argentina needed to "push for a new model of accumulation not centered on state investment" and to "get production moving before trying to redistribute resources that don't exist."[66] And whereas the Ubaldinistas and "25" demanded a moratorium on repayment of the foreign debt and for permanent cancellation of the part that had been contracted "illegitimately,"[67] Luis Barrionuevo (hotel and restaurant workers) asserted that "talk about a moratorium is archaic in the debtor countries. . . . a lot of old hobby-horses have ceased to be relevant at a time when we need proposals about how to escape from the crisis."[68] The economic vision of the "15" had nothing to do with the radical populism espoused by the revered Perón of 1945–48, but much to do with the sober developmentalism of the forgotten Perón of 1952–55—as well as with the policies that the Menem government would implement after 1989.

Apart from these economic differences, the political views of the "15" differed radically from those of the Ubaldinistas and "25." Triaca, Ibáñez, and most other key leaders of the "15" were ideologically quite conservative, whereas many of the "25" leaders had distinctly leftist views, albeit within the confines of Peronism's traditional anticommunism (had he been a western European unionist, Ubaldini would probably have been considered a left-wing Christian Democrat). A contrast has already been drawn between Triaca's testimony at the human rights trials and the support that Ubaldini and "25" gave to the families of the "disappeared." A parallel distinction can be made between the ways in which the union leader factions responded to Col. Aldo Rico's April 1987 military rebellion. Although not a full-fledged attempt to overthrow the government, the Easter Week rebellion, as the episode came to be known, made many fear for the stability of the democratic regime. Ubaldini's reaction to the uprising was immediately to denounce the rebellion and to call a general strike in defense of democracy (the situation was defused before the strike was to have taken place). Armando Cavalieri of the "15" responded more tepidly to the event. "These *muchachos* just want to express their lack of an important role, because they feel attacked by society. . . . [T]he military aren't trying to jeopardize the constitution. . . . these *muchachos* just want to be heard."[69] Cavalieri's remarks were denounced immediately by Guerino Andreoni of the "25."[70]

The Ubaldinistas and "25" were furious over the pact between the government and the "15." Ubaldini agreed only with great reluctance to support Alderete's appointment as labor minister, and shortly after he took office, the remaining Ubaldinistas joined forces with the "25" in the Mesa de Sindicalismo Renovador—whose name suggested that Ubaldini, after two years of staying outside party politics, had decided to retaliate against the "orthodox" faction of the party (with which most of the "15" sympathized) by endorsing the renewal sector.[71] When Alfonsín finally asked the "15" to resign from the ministry of labor in September 1987, the "25" leader José Pedraza (railway workers) thanked him for having "wiped from the labor movement this blemish that has always opted for the route of marginality and which no longer has a way back into Peronism," while Roberto Digón (tobacco employees) rejoiced in the downfall of "the ideologues of a corrupt and marginal unionism represented by the group of '15.' "[72] Digón, a founding member of the "25," summarized his view of the "15" as follows:

There have been two projects in the time that has passed since the military dictatorship. The one for which the "15" would become the main protagonist is the same as the one espoused by those who, a few years ago, were close collaborators of General Viola, and who shared a political project with [the former economy minister] Martínez de Hoz, with the captains of industry, and with officials of the United States Embassy. They sought then, and continue to seek, a small country with only twenty or thirty important firms, with neither small nor medium industry, and with space for only fifteen or so million Argentines. The "15" are nothing more than the reincarnation of the CGT–Azopardo or, going back a bit further, of the participationists during General Onganía's regime.[73]

Despite their overt antagonism, the "15" resembled the Ubaldinistas in one crucial respect: neither was deeply involved in the PJ. Whereas the "62" and "25" viewed the PJ as a useful vehicle for making a mark on politics and policy, the Ubaldinistas and "15" circumvented the party and sought to make their mark by gaining direct influence over

TABLE 7
Factional Differences in Peronist Unionism, 1983–1989

	"25"	Ubaldinistas	"62"	"15"
Favored human rights trials	Yes	Yes	No?	No
Strongly denounced 1987 military uprising	Yes	Yes		No
Favored moratorium on foreign debt	Yes	Yes		No
Opposed U.S. Central America policy	Yes	Yes	No	No
Favored legalization of divorce	Yes	Yes	No	No
Stance toward government	Combative	Combative	Mixed	Conciliatory
Party involvement	High	Low	High	Low

NOTE: Available information did not permit a definite conclusion as to the stance of the "62" toward the human rights trials. A blank space indicates that information was unavailable.

the national executive. But just as the "62" and "25" approached the party from different angles, the "15" and the Ubaldinistas used different methods to try to influence the national executive. The "15" tried to shape government policy from within, primarily by controlling the ministry of labor. Ubaldini tried to constrain government policies from without, by launching general strikes, mobilizing unionists for mass demonstrations, and denouncing the government in the mass media.

The ideological, combativeness, and party-involvement differences between the four main union leader factions of the 1983–89 period are summarized in Table 7. The classifications made in the table are general tendencies, not hard-and-fast distinctions. For example, the "15," who are classified as having a low propensity for party involvement, got involved in the PJ via deputies Ibáñez and Triaca, who worked on the collective-bargaining and union-structure legislation submitted to congress in 1987 (it should be noted, however, that both Ibáñez and Triaca were elected to congress not as members of the "15" but as members of the "62," which had a high propensity for party involvement). Moreover, the factions' cohesiveness should not be exaggerated. Tellingly, each was named after a putative number of unions or after a specific union leader—never according to a clear and consistent position on ideology, combativeness, or party involvement. Each faction experienced internal disputes and defections to other factions, reflecting the important role that personalism and opportunism have long played within the Peronist movement. Despite these caveats, union leaders, journalists, government officials, party leaders, and others all recognized that the factions existed. All key unionists and usually entire unions were identified with specific factions. Moreover, the "62" had bylaws, the "25" held a plenary session in 1986, the Ubaldinistas acted as a cohesive entity within the CGT, and the "15" met as a body with presidents Alfonsín and Menem.

The Triumph and Collapse of Renewal Peronism

Although the "15" got an initial round of big wage hikes, the government limited future increases. Frustrated, Alderete declared in early September that "the structural enemy of the ministry of labor is the [ministry of the] economy."[74] This impasse marked the end of the pact between the government and the "15." On 6 September 1987, when the Peronists trounced the Radicals in legislative and gubernatorial elections, Alfonsín announced that he wanted a "uniformly Radical cabinet." Evicted from the ministry of labor, the "15" lost their power base and ostensible reason for being. Their future looked unpromising in the CGT, where the Ubaldinistas and "25" were growling at them, and no better in the PJ, where the renewal sector was about to take over. Fortunately for their continued survival (and future hegemony), on exiting the ministry of labor, they caught a surge of popular support for the presidential candidacy of Carlos Menem. In September 1987, hours after Cafiero won the Buenos Aires governorship (regarded as a stepping-stone to a presidential nomination), posters endorsing Menem for president appeared in the outskirts of Buenos Aires. A month later, a group of orthodox Peronist politicians and governors endorsed Menem's candidacy.[75]

Born in 1930 to a Syrian immigrant family in the impoverished northwestern province of La Rioja, Menem grew up among the local elite (his family owned a wine-making business) and went to law school at the University of Córdoba. He became active in Peronism shortly after the 1955 coup, in the course of providing legal defense to political prisoners jailed by the anti-Peronist Aramburu government. He founded the Peronist Youth organization in the province of La Rioja and was a candidate for governor of the province in July 1963 until Perón ordered all Peronist candidates to withdraw from the race. In 1966, a police officer fractured Menem's collarbone with a baton blow when he attempted to place a wreath at a statue of San Martín on Peronist Loyalty Day (17 October). Elected governor of La Rioja in 1973, Menem was imprisoned on the day of the March 1976 coup and remained in detention until February 1980.[76] After being reelected to the La Rioja governorship in 1983, Menem struck up a friendly relationship with Alfonsín. During a 1984 referendum on the Beagle Channel peace treaty with Chile, Menem supported the "yes" position advocated by the Radicals rather than the abstentionist stance defended, with spectacular clumsiness, by the Peronist leaders Vicente Saadi, Herminio Iglesias, and Lorenzo Miguel (the "yes" won). For bucking the party line, Menem was reviled by the barras bravas at the PJ's tumultuous December 1984 Teatro Odeón congress, inspiring him to become one of the three "referents" of renewal Peronism. Here he was overshadowed by Antonio Cafiero, another of the "referents," and as it became clear that most renewal politicians favored Cafiero as the Peronist presidential candidate in the 1989 elections, Menem reconciled with orthodox Peronism. Menem's swashbuckling personal style and audacious disregard for convention gave him a certain amount of leeway for such politically expedient decisions. Because people expected the unexpected from him, he could mend fences with former adversaries—or reverse policy positions—without seeming irresolute or hypocritical. Menem's flamboyance, which delighted some and annoyed others, also helped him gain publicity. With his bushy muttonchop sideburns, grown in homage to Facundo Quiroga, Menem was unmistakable at parades or on television. He raced cars, played tennis until 1 A.M., and turned up at high-society parties. By November 1984, Menem's approval rating among national political figures was second only to Alfonsín's, and by mid 1986, in the working-class district of La Matanza, it stood at 75 percent, higher than Alfonsín's and double that of Cafiero.[77]

As Menem drew closer to the orthodox sector, Cafiero took control of the about-to-be-united PJ. Announcing that his September 1987 election as Buenos Aires governor was "a victory not of Peronism, but of renewal Peronism,"[78] Cafiero arrived at the December 1987 PJ congress with a "unity" list of party leaders that included himself as president, Menem (still nominally aligned with the renewal sector) as first vice president, and José María Vernet (Miguel's close ally and lame-duck president of the hitherto orthodox-controlled PJ) as second vice president. The next three slots went to renewal Peronists, including Roberto García of the "25," while the PJ's union secretariat went to José Lingeri, an Ubaldinista. The unilateral nomination of García and Lingeri by Cafiero and his allies antagonized Miguel and the "15," who demanded that "62" be allowed to retain its traditional right to determine which unionists would serve in Peronist party structures.

The exclusion of the "62" was not an oversight: Cafiero, using the windfall political capital that had accompanied his election as governor, was retaliating against "15" leaders, including Miguel's close ally Diego Ibáñez, who had backed "Menemista" candidates for seats in the Buenos Aires provincial legislature in the September 1987 elections. In many of these county-by-county contests, Cafiero's supporters had been forced to compete against lists of dissident Peronists supporting Menem as well as against the UCR.[79]

An important institutional expression of the conflict between the renewal sector and the "62" involved the time-honored tercio system, whereby Peronism's men's, women's, and union branches were each allotted one-third of the PJ's candidacies and leadership posts (after 1972, a youth sector was sometimes added as a fourth branch). The "62" liked the tercio system because the financial and organizational weakness of nonunion Peronism assured them control of nominations in the women's and men's branches of the movement as well as in the union sector. The right of the women's branch to nominate one-third of the candidates was usually ignored. Women had received about a third of the slots on the Peronist national deputy slates in 1951, and would again in 1993 and 1995, after congress passed a quota law that effectively imposed a women's tercio on all parties. In no other election, however, did Peronist women ever receive the tercio to which they were supposedly entitled. Moreover, the "62" often nominated or manipulated the candidates from the men's branch—as in 1983, when Lorenzo Miguel's intimates Luis Santos Casale and Torcuato Fino, both nonunion advisers to the "62," represented the men's branch in the PJ's national deputy delegation from the federal capital. Given the wide influence they exercised under the semifictional tercio system, the "62" were naturally annoyed when the renewal sector proposed in 1987 to change the party constitution to eliminate it. In the end, the system was not abolished completely, but the PJ's national directive council wound up reserving only 17 of 110 posts for unionists (10 were reserved for women and 10 for youth). Moreover, it was not specified that the 17 unionists would be nominated by the "62."[80] In short, the new party rules converted the tercio nominated by the "62" into a *sexto* nominated by all factions of Peronist unionism. A similar compromise on the tercio, tilted toward the renewal sector, was made in the party's federal capital branch.[81]

The ratification of the unity list at the December 1987 PJ congress marked the peak of the *renovadores'* party-building project. Already, however, there were signs that the victory would not go uncontested. In mid-October 1987, "15" and "62" unionists pulled out of the CGT leadership to protest the elimination of the tercio. Although they soon came back, Miguel warned pointedly that "the PJ without the union branch is like a body without a soul."[82] The battle lines were drawn on 1 November 1987, when Luis Barrionuevo, Jorge Triaca, and other "15" unionists formed the Mesa Sindical Menem Presidente (MSMP) to organize union support for Menem's presidential campaign. In response, the "25" and Ubaldinistas formed the Mesa Redonda de Sindicalismo Renovador to back Cafiero. Lorenzo Miguel, as had long been his custom, spent as long as possible with one foot in each camp—a tradition that both reflected and contributed to his position as the key power broker within Peronist unionism. Although the MSMP included two of Miguel's closest allies (Diego Ibáñez and the UOM stalwart Roberto Monteverde), press reports as late as February 1988 indicated that Miguel himself backed Cafiero.[83] Miguel tried to persuade Menem and Cafiero to form a unity ticket, but neither would accept the vice presidential slot. Miguel finally endorsed Menem in March 1988, when Cafiero rejected Vernet as his running mate in favor of José Manuel de la Sota, a staunch renewal Peronist.[84]

In certain respects, the contest between Cafiero and Menem recalled the implicit showdown between Vandor and Perón in the April 1966 Mendoza gubernatorial election. Like Vandor, Cafiero was backed by powerful organizations: the Buenos Aires provincial administration, the newly united PJ, and the "25" and Ubaldinista unions. Like Perón, Menem lacked support from party structures but received crucial backing from a sector of the Peronist union leadership: the "15"-dominated MSMP. And whereas Cafiero was a rather gray candidate, appealing more to middle-sector groups than to Peronism's traditional constituencies, Menem's flamboyance and plebiscitarian political style made him a more dynamic candidate with broader appeal within the movement. As Hugo Chumbita wrote of the primary campaign, "in contrast to Cafiero's formality, wordiness, and lukewarm progressivism, [Menem] summoned up an emotive and commonsensical discourse attached to the populist tradition, promising a peaceful revolution, infusing democracy with social content, and reviving the festive image of a leader in direct contact with the masses."[85]

On 9 July 1988, Peronism for the first time in history nominated its presidential candidate in a direct primary election. As in 1966, charisma triumphed over organization: Menem outpolled Cafiero by 53 to 46 percent. Menem was no Juan Perón, but made up for any relative charisma deficit with better organization. In 1966, the "62 de Pie" had never even traveled to Mendoza. In 1988, the "15" recruited funds for Menem's campaign, signed up new party members, printed campaign posters, mobilized the vote, and provided more than half of the 15,000 officials assigned to oversee the intraparty balloting.[86] As *Clarín*'s Ricardo Kirschbaum editorialized, "the big unions, that is the '15,' gave Carlos Menem the apparatus he needed to confront Cafierismo, which controlled the party's resources."[87] In the country as a whole, Menem got 130,000 more votes than Cafiero. But had it not been for Menem's margin of 141,000 votes in the nineteen districts of Greater Buenos Aires—the power base of Lorenzo Miguel and the "15"— Cafiero would probably have won.[88] In that case, the renewal sector might well have consolidated its party-building project, and Argentine politics would have taken a very different path.

Menem defeated Cafiero, not only because of his more dynamic personal style and his formidable support from the "15," but also because he managed to portray his opponent as a "social democrat" and to associate him with Alfonsín. Orthodox Peronists had long hurled the "social democrat" epithet at their renewal-sector opponents, hoping to present them as a bunch of urbane intellectuals mesmerized by an exotic leftist ideology perhaps appropriate for Sweden or Germany but alien to Argentina's national tradition. Menem's supporters also insisted that a Cafiero presidency would be indistinguishable from Alfonsín's. This claim gained credibility when, in December 1987, Cafiero and Alfonsín made a pact on legislation involving tax policy, labor law, and the allocation of central government revenue to the provinces.[89] Henceforth, the press began to talk of "Alfonsierismo" and Menem began to link his Peronist opponent with the Radical president, arguing that Cafiero would "continue the policies of Raúl Alfonsín because both are patterned by social democracy."[90] One reason Cafiero opted to reach this accord with Alfonsín, thereby associating himself with the increasingly unpopular president, was that he wanted to show support for the democratic regime at a time when the military was showing dangerous signs of unrest (a second military uprising occurred in January 1988, a month after Alfonsín and Cafiero reached their accord). Moreover, the November 1987 elections had given the Peronists control of 17 of Argentina's 22 provinces, and Cafiero worried that the new Peronist governors would find themselves in desperate financial straits unless tax revenue were channeled more expeditiously to the interior.[91]

Stepping back from specifics of the primary contest between Menem and Cafiero, the Peronist tradition of movementism and Perón's plebiscitarian legacy played a crucial role in undermining the renewal sector's party-building project. Menem's political style echoed Perón's. He thumbed his nose at procedures and conventions, felt he could get ahead without recourse to party organization, and tried to cultivate direct, affective links between himself and ordinary Peronists. The renewal sector, by contrast, emphasized formal organization and procedural correctness—themes with shallow roots in the Peronist tradition. Above all, Menem defended the notion that Peronism was, first and foremost, a national movement, not a party preoccupied with formal democracy:

We don't want to turn Peronism into just another liberal-democratic party. Why does this worry us? Because we view Peronism as an expression superior to the partyocracy [*partidocracia*]. We see it as a national liberation movement that goes beyond the formal democracy that the Europeans are trying to sell us. Of course, the fact that we are a movement doesn't mean that we shouldn't defend the party as a way of channeling the process of liberation, because in talking about a party we aren't renouncing our movementist conception of politics. The four vital branches—political, union, women, and youth—must be represented in the party leadership. To be clear, the party is part of the movement. The movement embraces, convenes, and expresses the totality of the different expressions that national liberation assumes in Argentine political life.[92]

Another factor behind the demise of the renewal sector's party-building project was Lorenzo Miguel's balancing behavior. By early 1988, the renewal sector had come to pose a fundamental threat to Miguel. The metalworkers' chief had suffered a devastating setback when Luder lost the presidential election in December 1983. Three successive defeats at the hands of the renovadores—in the September 1985 legislative elections, at the December 1987 PJ congress, and with the March 1988 nomination of de la Sota as Cafiero's running mate—put Miguel in an increasingly precarious position. At the height of its success in early 1988, the renewal sector seemed to be willing and able to rewrite the rules, outlaw the practices, and capture or defang the organizations that Miguel used to maintain his power and independence. Hemmed in by the renewal sector, Miguel threw his support to Menem, adding the organizational strength of the UOM to the fund-raising resources of the "15." Miguel's decision to opt for what seemed at the time to be the weaker side in the struggle between Cafiero and Menem recalled other instances in which the metalworkers' chief had engaged in balancing behavior. In 1980, when the military established cordial relations with the conciliatory GyT, Miguel threw his support to the excluded "25." In 1984 and 1985, as the renovadores and Ubaldini began their rise in the PJ and CGT, Miguel allied himself with the excluded Triaca. In early 1988, when Cafiero was favored to win the Peronist presidential nomination,[93] Miguel tilted toward Menem. In each case Miguel sided with the "outs" against the "ins," much as peripheral states in an asymmetrical bipolar system often forge an alliance with the weaker great power against the stronger.

The 1989 Presidential Election

After Menem won the 1988 primary, placing the "15" on the winning side, Miguel tilted back toward Ubaldini and the "25." In August 1988, Miguel joined the combative factions in a delegation that planned to meet with Alfonsín to discuss the economic situation. Ubaldini wound up going alone, but the "15," who had been excluded from the original group, decided they could get along without the metalworkers' chief. As Menem began his general election campaign, the "15" resurrected the MSMP, in which Miguel had never participated.[94] But as Miguel drifted away from the "15," he stopped short of giving full support to Ubaldini. In September 1988, when the CGT chief announced the twelfth general strike against the Alfonsín government, Miguel and the "25" (and more predictably the "15") refrained from endorsing the call. Reportedly, leaders of each of the three factions were concerned that a strike could cost the PJ middle-class votes in the upcoming elections.[95] In the last analysis, Miguel and the "25," reflecting their traditions of party involvement, were ready to do whatever it took to win the election.

Ubaldini, by contrast, had never been closely involved with the PJ. His main concern was to express (and spearhead) labor opposition to the Alfonsín government. Consequently, the 9 September 1988 general strike went forward. The rally called to accompany it was a resounding failure. Besides attracting few participants, it turned into a riot in which 76 people were injured.[96] The effect of the violence on Menem's campaign could have been disastrous, but Menem decided at the last minute to join the "15" in their decision not to appear at the mobilization.[97] Luis Barrionuevo would later report that he had warned Menem to disassociate himself from the act after his contacts in the intelligence service warned him that violence could erupt.[98] Three days later, Ubaldini declared a new general strike to protest the violence. Although the second strike had limited success, Ubaldini won the backing of the "25" and Lorenzo Miguel; once again, the "15" opposed the initiative.[99]

A final and only partially successful attempt to unite the Peronist labor leadership took place in February 1989, when unionists formed the Mesa Redonda de Sindicalismo Peronista to support Menem's candidacy. The new group included three representatives each from the "15," "25," "62," and Ubaldinismo.[100] Despite forging this tenuous alliance with the other union leader groups, the "15" began almost immediately to negotiate on their own with the country's main business associations. Even more surprisingly, the "15" arranged a meeting with Donald Knight, the U.S. embassy's labor attaché. They evidently made a good impression; Knight invited them to visit the United States "as soon as possible" to show that Peronist unionism was committed to solving Argentina's economic problems.[101] The meeting with the U.S. labor attaché represented a significant breach of Peronist tradition. Perón on assuming office in 1946 had a famous union dissident, Luis Gay, ousted from the CGT leadership on charges of collaborating with the AFL-CIO.

No group was more influential than the "15" in organizing and financing Menem's campaign. Juan José Zanola plastered downtown Buenos Aires with posters promoting Menem's candidacy and linking it to his own bid for reelection in the bank employees' union. Triaca and Cavalieri obtained campaign funds from business magnates like Carlos Bulgheroni and Amalia Lacroze de Fortabat.[102] Luis Barrionuevo, who argued that most union statutes permitted union funds to be put to campaign purposes, claimed in November 1990 to have donated the equivalent of U.S.$1 million to Menem's presidential bid.[103] (It was widely rumored that this came from his union's health and pension funds, but Barrionuevo denied it.)[104] In the end, even Ubaldini fell in behind Menem. Despite hyperinflation and mass suspensions and layoffs, Ubaldini agreed to refrain from calling a general strike before the presidential contest. As one of his allies put it, "To go by the situation and by the mood of the union leaders, we should be in the streets right now on a general strike, but we have to act, unfortunately, with due prudence. . . . we'll have the general strike on May 14 when all Argentines cast their votes for Peronism."[105] Moreover, instead of the traditional 1 May rally, which Menem feared might result in another riot, the CGT leaders settled for a celebratory lunch. A reporter described Menem as "tense and frowning" on receiving the news that 1,000 union leaders had been invited to the event. After giving a short speech, Menem left without waiting for Ubaldini to speak.[106]

As the incumbent party, the Radicals were in a tough position as the May 1989 elections approached. A November 1988 poll revealed that less than 10 percent of Argentines thought Alfonsín had done a good job at creating jobs or improving the standard of living—the problem areas to which most respondents gave highest priority.[107] Things only got worse. In January 1989, a little-known guerrilla group attacked the La Tablada army barracks, leaving dozens dead in a gun battle and in subsequent summary executions by the army. Big exporters, notably the Bunge y Born grain-exporting conglomerate, stopped selling dollars to the Central Bank, forcing the government to deplete its reserves and finally, on 6 February 1989, to halt sales of dollars entirely when the reserves were about to run out. Argentines rushed to buy dollars wherever they could, sending the austral spiraling downward and launching a process of hyperinflation. By late May, hungry people were breaking into supermarkets, and by July, inflation had reached 197 percent per month.[108] The Radical candidate, Eduardo Angeloz, tried to distance himself from Alfonsín by promising accelerated privatization, deregulation, and free convertibility, but he could not completely escape anti-incumbent sentiment. Ubaldini, by toning down his combative stance, and the "15," by raising campaign funds, helped make sure that Menem did not lose this advantage. On 14 May 1989, Menem outpolled Angeloz by 47 to 37 percent. For the "15," Menem's victory was a chance to gain access to power resources that their weakness in the CGT and PJ had long denied them. For Ubaldini, Menem's victory was Pyrrhic: only by challenging a popular Peronist president could he continue to pursue the general-strike strategy that showcased his personal charisma and reinforced his combative image.

Chapter 8

Free-Market Reform and Political Shenanigans

C arlos Menem during his first term as president enacted a set of free-market economic reforms, breaking with the nationalist, statist, and populist import-substitution model that had prevailed, in one form or another, for most of the preceding half-century. Menem jettisoned the old model, for which Peronism had traditionally been the standard-bearer, because it could be credibly linked to decades of poor economic performance, because "heterodox" efforts to fine-tune it had failed under Alfonsín, and because it had culminated in hyperinflation in mid 1989. He replaced it with a free-market one because, after the collapse of European communism and a decade of conservative rule in advanced industrial countries, he judged no alternative model more likely to overcome rampant inflation, recurrent stop-and-go cycles, and slow economic growth. Menem's reforms led to a huge increase in unemployment, but tamed inflation, spurred economic growth, and produced optimism about the country's economic future. These achievements helped him win reelection by a wide margin in 1995.

Some Peronist union leaders opposed Menem's reforms, but a majority cooperated with them. Some did so because they judged the old economic model to be fatally flawed; others cooperated because they viewed the new policies as best suited to prevent a return to hyperinflation. Some wanted to support the initiatives of a Peronist president, others were grateful for government jobs. Some wanted to enlarge their unions with workers from privatized factories, others wished to explore business opportunities opened up by privatization. Such inducements won enough cooperation that the reforms were able to go forward. As a result, union resources declined: membership fell, finances deteriorated, collective bargaining was decentralized, and restrictions were imposed on the right to strike. In 1995, after the repercussions of Mexico's devaluation halted the country's economic advance, more unionists began to favor a combative posture. By then, however, the reforms had proceeded far enough that the unions were less able to resist them.

Carlos Waisman has argued that Argentina's democratic instability during the second half of the twentieth century can be traced to an inward-looking "hothouse" capitalism that allocated resources inefficiently, and to a hypermobilized labor movement that worsened political polarization, feeding back into slow economic growth.[1] These factors did play a pivotal role in exacerbating distributive conflict. Hothouse capitalism limited the growth of resources, raising the stakes of the struggle for a share of what was left. The hypermobilized labor movement made urban workers more powerful in that struggle, which redistributed income toward the organized working class but worsened political polarization. By dismantling hothouse capitalism and by partly demobilizing the labor movement, Menem improved conditions for resource growth and paved the way for a less polarized (if in some ways more unequal) society. More resources and less polarization mean less intense distributive conflict, improving the prospects for democratic consolidation.

Democratic consolidation depends, however, not just on the intensity of distributive conflict, but also on the capacity of political institutions to organize and channel it. This capacity declined during Menem's first term in office (1989–95). Although Menem presided over fair elections, backed some legal and constitutional changes that improved the quality of democracy, and reduced the level of military contestation, he also deinstitutionalized the PJ, ruled by decree, stacked the supreme court, manipulated electoral rules, presided over an administration pervaded by corruption and incompetence, and pardoned military leaders convicted of human rights violations. By deinstitutionalizing the PJ, Menem reduced its ability to organize and channel the demands of the (now less powerful) unions; and by playing fast and loose with electoral, legislative, and judicial processes, he fostered skepticism about their fairness and relevance.

This chapter explores both sides of Menem's impact on the prospects for democratic consolidation. It (1) describes Menem's reforms and evaluates their impact on the economy and on workers; (2) accounts for the heterogeneity of union leaders' responses to Menem's reforms, for the decline in CGT general strikes, and for fluctuations in ordinary strike activity; (3) argues that the PJ became deinstitutional-ized during Menem's first term; and (4) analyzes Menem's handling of electoral, legislative, and judicial institutions. The analysis concludes that Menem's economic reforms created conditions for a reduction of distributive conflict, but that his personalistic style of rule reduced the capacity of the PJ, elections, congress, and the judiciary to organize and channel the conflict that remained.

Menem's Economic Reforms: Content and Impact

Menem's reforms were intended to make the state solvent and to make markets more efficient.[2] To make the state solvent, Menem priva-tized nearly all public enterprises, whose combined deficit during the 1980s had fluctuated between 2 and 7 percent of GDP.[3] By 1994, U.S.$24 billion worth of state companies had been sold off or converted into joint ventures, with the largest privatizations coming in the oil, tele-phone, gas, and electricity sectors.[4] By 1993, privatization had cost the jobs of 85,000 workers (out of 246,000 employed in public enterprises), but the state was no longer burdened with financing public-enterprise deficits, which had imposed costs on all Argentines. Menem also dis-missed 217,000 civil servants (110,000 from the central government and 107,000 from provincial and municipal governments), reducing over-all public employment (including state enterprises) from 2.03 million in 1989 to 1.81 million in 1992. In addition, Menem cut private-sector subsidies from U.S.$7.9 billion in 1989 to $4.4 billion in 1992, halted rail service to provinces that would not help subsidize it, and cut back on other forms of aid to deficit-ridden provincial administrations.[5]

On the other side of the fiscal ledger, Menem overhauled the tax system. As tax revenues fell during the 1980s, the Alfonsín govern-ment had come to rely increasingly on easy-to-collect but growth-inhibiting "tax handles" (e.g., export and energy taxes) rather than hard-to-collect but growth-friendly "efficient taxes" (e.g., income and value-added taxes). Menem's economic team changed this system by scrapping export taxes, raising the value-added tax and applying it to a wider range of goods and services, and imposing an income tax. Equally important, the general tax board (DGI) greatly improved its capacity to collect taxes. At a time of drastic personnel cutbacks in nearly every government agency, the DGI doubled its payroll be-tween 1990 and 1993.[6] Tax evasion summonses increased tenfold be-tween 1989 and 1992, while tax-related enterprise closings rose from

751 in 1990 to 17,739 in 1992. By 1992, the central government was collecting $U.S.24.4 billion in taxes, up from $U.S.13.7 billion two years
earlier, while greatly increasing the share of efficient taxes in total tax
revenues.[7] All told, tax and spending reforms gave the government a
small budget surplus in 1991, 1992, and 1993—remarkable in a country
whose fiscal deficit had averaged more than 12 percent of GDP from
1981 to 1984 and more than 5 percent of GDP from 1985 to 1989.[8]

To make markets more efficient, Menem cut nominal tariffs from
an average of 32 percent in the mid 1980s to an average of 10 percent in 1992, eliminated nontariff trade barriers like import licenses
(which had covered 47 percent of imports in 1986), and concluded the
Mercosur free trade agreement with Brazil, Paraguay, and Uruguay.[9]
He also enacted an October 1991 "mega-decree" that abolished import
quotas; simplified customs procedures; freed professionals to charge
whatever fees they pleased; removed restrictions on business hours;
decontrolled the prices of bread and prescription drugs; and eliminated decades-old regulatory boards for grain, meat, and other items.[10]

Menem's fiscal, trade, and regulatory reforms brought little relief
from inflation or recession until April 1991, when Domingo Cavallo,
the newly appointed economy minister, devalued the currency and
fixed the peso to the dollar at a rate of 1 to 1.[11] Cushioned by foreign reserves generated by a U.S.$8 billion trade surplus in the recession year
of 1990, Cavallo removed restrictions on currency transactions. At the
same time, congress passed a law that required the central bank to acquire an additional dollar in gold or foreign currency for every peso
added to the monetary base. To meet the demand for foreign currency
generated by free convertibility and by the need to increase reserves
in order to expand the money supply, it was imperative to give Argentines an incentive to hold pesos, as well as to attract funds from abroad.
Such an incentive was furnished by a surge in business optimism stem-
ming from the reforms that Menem had already enacted. Cavallo is
sometimes given too much credit for the success of his own economic
plan. Had it not been for Menem's earlier privatizations, civil-service
layoffs, tax-system overhaul, trade liberalization, and market deregulation, business confidence would not have been high enough to stop
a run on the dollar as soon as convertibility was established.

In the context of these prior reforms, however, the "convertibility
plan" led to an economic turnaround. Inflation plunged from 1,832
percent in 1990 to 4 percent in 1994. GNP growth averaged 8 percent
per annum in the plan's first four years—Argentina's fastest growth

of the century in any four-year period, and one of the world's highest growth rates in the first half of the 1990s. The budget ran surpluses in 1991, 1992, and 1993 and only a small deficit in 1994. International confidence in the economy soared: direct investment by U.S. corporations rose from $230 million in 1992 to an estimated $2 billion in 1994, a year in which U.S. investors also poured nearly $7 billion into Argentine stocks and bonds.[12] Privatization increased the cost and reduced the scope of public services, but most agreed that it improved them. Asked in November 1994 to compare utility and transport services before and after privatization, 40 percent of survey respondents in the Buenos Aires area said they had improved, 34 percent said they had stayed the same, and only 19 percent said they had gotten worse. Fully 64 percent said that the infamous telephone service had improved, while only 21 percent thought it had deteriorated.[13] World Bank, UNICEF, and economy ministry studies all indicated that poverty dropped and income distribution improved during the 1989–93 period.[14]

Recognition of the benefits of Menem's economic reforms should not obscure deficiencies in the ways in which some of them, particularly privatization, were implemented. Among the "seven sins of privatization" identified by the United Nations Development Programme is the use of "discretionary, non-transparent procedures which invite allegations of corruption and nepotism."[15] Such allegations, and in some cases indictments, attended virtually all major privatizations, notably those of state airline, telephone, electricity, and steel companies. A second "sin" of privatization is to attempt it in a buyer's market. The SOMISA steel plant was privatized at a time when Argentina's import tariffs were being slashed and when the world was groaning under a huge glut of steel. Jorge Triaca, the first official charged with privatizing SOMISA, valued the company at $2 billion. After Triaca was indicted for defrauding the government, his successor, María Julia Alsogaray (who was under investigation for illicit enrichment), valued the company at $450 million. In October 1992, 80 percent of the equity in SOMISA was sold to the sole bidder—the Techint conglomerate— for $152 million, with the remaining 20 percent going to the company's employees.[16] A third "sin" of privatization is to initiate it through non-consensual executive decrees, which "risks immediate conflict—and reversal after a change in government." The Menem government used a mix of legislation and decrees to undertake privatization. A 1989 law provided a legal framework for the first round of privatization, but the effect of this law was simply to give the government wide leeway to privatize the telephone, highway, railway, and maritime transport systems by decree.[17] The state-owned natural gas company was privatized by legislation in 1992, but the process can hardly be described as consensual: a "quorum" was obtained only after a Peronist deputy smuggled one of his friends into a seat reserved for an absent Peronist colleague. Discovery of the intruder led to the annulment of the vote. The bill eventually passed, but the most consensual aspect of the process was the tacit agreement among the legislators to let the transgression slide.[18] Given these irregularities in privatization processes, it is not surprising that a December 1992 survey showed much greater satisfaction with the fact than with the form of privatization in various industries.[19]

Currency overvaluation was another defect of Menem's reform program. Inflation fell dramatically after the convertibility plan was implemented, but did not disappear. Between April 1991 and December 1994, retail prices rose a cumulative 59 percent in Argentina. Because the peso-to-dollar exchange rate was fixed at 1 to 1 throughout this entire period, the peso rose approximately 40 percent against the U.S. dollar and 20 percent against a basket of currencies representing Argentina's major trading partners, encouraging imports and discouraging exports.[20] Because tariff cuts and renewed economic growth also boosted imports, and because export revenues stagnated (partly as a result of overvaluation) despite a rise in international grain prices, an $8 billion trade surplus in the recession year of 1990 became a $6 billion trade deficit by 1994 (the trade balance evened out again in 1995 as recession caused imports to decline). Overvaluation and tariff cuts also worsened unemployment, not just because cheaper consumer-goods imports put domestic manufacturers out of business, but also because cheaper capital-goods imports encouraged those who survived to substitute mechanical for human labor. Between 1991 and 1994, as real wages in manufacturing dropped 13 percent, labor productivity in manufacturing rose 33 percent.[21]

From 1991 to 1994, several infusions of capital helped to offset the current-account deficit and thus to prop up the peso. One was the flood of foreign investment and repatriated Argentine capital into the stock market, the oil sector, and the newly privatized public services. A second was new lending under the Brady Plan, which Argentina entered in 1992. A third was the foreign exchange supplied, despite the overvalued peso, by foreign visitors (4 million of whom spent a total of $4 billion in 1994).[22] Tourism might be viewed as a sustainable source of foreign exchange, but privatization is a one-shot deal, and port-folio investment and new lending are notoriously fickle. These sources of capital will have to compensate for an often big trade deficit, the need to pay interest and principal on $82 billion in foreign debt, and spending abroad by Argentines in an era of higher disposable income and overvalued currency. With Argentina running a U.S.$10 billion current-account deficit in 1994, any sustained cessation of capital in-flow had the potential to weaken the peso and increase pressure to de-value the currency or abandon convertibility.[23] This eventuality nearly came to pass in early 1995, when the ripple effects of the December 1994 Mexican peso devaluation caused several small banks to fold. A currency crisis was averted when Cavallo secured $6 billion in foreign loans, used tax hikes and public-sector pay cuts to deflate the economy, and sold a big bond issue to "patriotic" industrialists, but Argentina re-mained vulnerable to the vagaries of international financial markets.[24]

The main cost of Menem's reform program was a huge surge in unemployment. Between April 1991 and May 1995—a period of price stability and rapid GDP growth—unemployment rose from 6.9 to 18.6 percent of Argentina's economically active population. Meanwhile, underemployment rose from 8.6 to 11.3 percent.[25] The May 1995 fig-ures gave Argentina the second-highest jobless rate in Latin America after Nicaragua and were the highest since INDEC, the national statis-tical and census institute, had begun keeping track of unemployment in 1974.[26] A 1991 law for the first time in history made some categories of workers eligible for unemployment insurance, but as of late 1994, only 6.4 percent of the jobless were receiving it, and payments ranged only from U.S.$150 to $300 a month (the legal minimum wage was U.S.$550 a month).[27]

The government initially refused to acknowledge that rising unem-ployment was a cost of its economic reforms. Menem argued that the INDEC statistics exaggerated the "real" unemployment rate, but such a validity argument, whatever its merits, cannot explain why surveys using identical measurement techniques indicated a tripling of unem-ployment between April 1991 and May 1995. Cavallo argued that the abolition of military conscription in 1994, together with an influx of nontraditional job seekers attracted by new economic opportunities, increased the unemployment rate primarily by causing an explosion in the size of the labor force. He was partly right: even as unemployment rose 5.3 percent between 1991 and 1994, 515,000 new jobs were created, employment grew 8.4 percent, and the economically active population increased by 1,300,000.[28] Cavallo failed to note, however, that growth in the labor force ended in 1993, and thus cannot explain why unemployment rose from 10.7 percent in May 1994 to 18.6 percent in May 1995.[29] Moreover, Cavallo did not address the possibility that many of the nontraditional workers who entered the labor market after 1990 were not pulled by new opportunities but rather pushed by the fate of traditional breadwinners, particularly public-sector workers in interior provinces, who were being paid little, late, or not at all. Other government explanations for rising joblessness were even less convincing. Menem claimed that undocumented immigrants were taking jobs away from Argentines, but a study showed that expulsion of all immigrants who arrived in the country between 1989 and 1994 would reduce joblessness by only 0.2 percent.[30] The government also blamed the rise in unemployment on high nonwage labor costs and insufficiently "flexible" employment laws,[31] but labor costs fell and legislation became more "flexible" precisely during the time that unemployment tripled.

The main causes of the rise in unemployment were not those highlighted by the government, but rather civil-service layoffs, personnel cuts by newly privatized enterprises, increased import competition, and the replacement of human by mechanical labor. The convertibility plan contributed directly to the civil-service layoffs. By pegging the peso to the dollar, the plan tied the government's hands with respect to exchange rate and monetary policy, leaving fiscal policy as the main instrument for responding to external shocks. So in 1994, when foreign capital flows reversed after the United States raised interest rates and Mexico devalued its currency, the government was forced to choose between devaluing the peso, abandoning convertibility, or tightening the fiscal screws. Cavallo chose the latter alternative, which led to skyrocketing unemployment and riots in impoverished interior provinces, where the level of economic activity depended critically on federal revenue transfers. By mid 1995, Menem himself had come round to the view that the main causes of unemployment were "structural."[32]

Privatization, spending cuts, liberalization, and deregulation not only contributed to unemployment, but also stripped power from unions as organizations, in part by reducing union membership. In 1986, according to labor ministry data, 3,972,000 workers belonged to unions in Argentina, representing 36 percent of the economically active population and 57 percent of wage earners.[33] Evidence suggests that the number of union members subsequently fell after Menem took office. Most of the 302,000 civil servants and state-enterprise employees laid off between 1989 and 1993 belonged to unions. Moreover, tariff cuts and currency overvaluation, together with technological change and international competition, reduced employment in hitherto well-organized private-sector industries. In the steel industry, which had employed 34,000 in 1987, the privatization of the SOMISA steel plant (which cut its payroll from 12,000 to 5,500) combined with reduced steel exports (because of the world steel glut and currency overvaluation) to halve the number of steelworkers to 17,000 in 1993.[34] Union membership may also have dropped among employed workers. A December 1991 law made it easier for firms to hire temporary workers, who are notoriously difficult to unionize. By July 1993, 45,000 Argentines were working under temporary contracts, with reduced or no benefits.[35]

Menem also curtailed the power of union as organizations by restricting the right to strike. Despite thirteen general strikes and nearly 2,500 smaller strikes,[36] Alfonsín had refrained from limiting the right to strike and intervened not a single union. Menem, by contrast, balanced his enthusiasm for deregulating business with legislation aimed at restricting the right to strike. In early 1990, the government announced its intention to prohibit strikes in essential public services—those whose interruption would jeopardize life, health, freedom, or the security of individuals. Such services included, in the government's view, health care, waste disposal, education, transportation, and the administration of justice; telephone, post, and telegraph communications; and the production or delivery of water, electricity, gas, oil, or coal.[37] The strike legislation passed the senate in May 1990, although the upper house excluded transport and education from the list of essential public services (except in cases that the ministry of labor judged to be of "extreme gravity"). In the lower house, however, the bill got bogged down, in part because Peronist deputies of union extraction resisted its passage. As it became evident that the legislation would die or be gutted, Menem imposed it by decree on 17 October 1990, backdating the order by 24 hours to avoid signing it on Peronist loyalty day.[38]

Decentralization of collective bargaining was a third way in which Menem weakened unions as organizations. The labor legislation of the 1940s had made industry-level bargaining the norm in most sectors, although branch-level contracts prevailed in several industries (for example, the paper industry had one branch contract for pulp, one for cardboard, etc.) and firm-level contracts prevailed in Córdoba auto plants, Tucumán sugar mills, and other enterprises (in 1975, 167 of 613 contracts signed in Argentina were negotiated at the firm level).[39] This system changed with October 1991 "mega-decree," which included a provision that made it easier to negotiate contracts at the branch or firm levels. This provision had an immediate impact on bargaining: most of the 600 collective agreements signed in 1992 and 1993 were concluded at the branch or firm levels.[40] A 1993 bill to give full legal status to firm-level bargaining remained bottled up in congress at the end of Menem's first term, but the 1991 mega-decree remained in effect. To the extent that branch- and firm-level bargaining becomes more common, national union organizations will become less relevant.

A fourth way in which the Menem government weakened unions as organizations was by chipping away at their control of enormous welfare funds known as *obras sociales*. The obras sociales were created to provide health services to union members and their families, but they soon expanded into tourism, recreation, warehousing, legal services, libraries, technical schools, workplace cafeterias, funeral services, and life insurance. In the late 1980s, the 291 obras sociales administered wholly or partly by unions served, or were supposed to serve, 17.6 million beneficiaries—more than half the total population.[41] Union leaders have long been accused of skimming the obras sociales for personal and political purposes, but a full-scale investigation has never been launched. When Menem took office, union leaders were getting most of their funds from the obras sociales, not from dues. In the late 1980s, members of most large unions paid 2 or 2.5 percent of their monthly gross incomes in dues, but 3 percent in contributions to the union's obra social—complementing an employer contribution of 6 percent.[42] Under generous assumptions, the total yearly dues income of all Argentine unions was less than U.S.$0.8 billion in the early 1990s, whereas the 291 obras sociales managed a collective U.S.$2.6 billion annually.[43]

In 1970, to audit and channel income from solvent to insolvent obras sociales, the Onganía government created the National Institute of Social Insurance, which in 1989 changed its name to the National Administration of Health Insurance (ANSSAL). In 1991, an official of ANSSAL complained that it was difficult to audit the obras sociales because a majority of the individual funds kept no books.[44] It was clear, however, that most of them ran perpetually in the red, and by February 1991, fully 90 percent of the obras sociales had ceased to dispense services.[45] Despite its auditing responsibilities, ANSSAL was not itself a paragon of transparency. Although it controlled about U.S.$500 million annually in the early 1990s, no written rules governed its transfer of funds from solvent to insolvent unions. Its administrators, according to a World Bank study, used these funds "more for political rewards than for anything else."[46]

By 1989, the obras sociales were ripe for reform, and Menem chose to reform them by decree. In October 1991, a "mega-decree" made the tax board (DGI), rather than the individual obra social, the initial recipient of payments by workers and employees. In January 1993, another decree allowed beneficiaries of the 291 obras sociales to choose freely among the funds and permitted the obras sociales themselves to associate or merge at will. In December 1993, yet another decree reduced employer contributions by an estimated U.S.$800 million annually. As of mid 1995, however, these reforms were still precarious; because of strong resistance from union leaders, none of them had been written into law.

The Union Response to Menem's Reforms

FACTIONS IN THE UNION LEADERSHIP

Union leaders responded diversely to Menem's reforms. Some cooperated with them enthusiastically, others reservedly; some resisted them tenaciously, others tepidly; and some switched back and forth between support and opposition according to what seemed expedient for themselves and their constituencies. It might be supposed that union leaders reacted diversely to Menem's reforms because of sectoral preferences (with public-sector unionists opposing the reforms, private-sector unionists supporting them, etc.), but leaders of unions in similar sectoral situations spread themselves fairly evenly across the confrontation-cooperation spectrum. The diversity of responses might be ascribed to an astute divide-and-rule strategy by a Peronist president familiar with the intricacies of union politics,[47] but the unions were no more divided under Menem than under previous presidents. The main reason for the diversity of responses was that highly autonomous union leaders made differing decisions about how to respond to conflicting imperatives: that the reforms were imposed by a Peronist president but went against Peronist tradition; that they buried a defunct economic model but put the country on an untested development path; and that they brought benefits but also caused hardship. As always, moreover, turf battles among unionists seeking to preserve or expand their power helped explain where each wound up on the cooperation-confrontation spectrum.

Epitomizing the cooperative position was Jorge Triaca, the veteran leader of the plastics workers' union. Shortly after winning the May 1989 presidential election, Menem, encouraged by Lorenzo Miguel and Miguel Roig (the newly appointed economy minister), named Triaca as his labor minister.[48] Since the late 1970s, Triaca had been the most prominent member of the conservative and conciliatory wing of the union leadership. His relationship to the unions had begun in the mid 1960s, when his father had served as co-founder and treasurer of the plastics workers' union. It had solidified in the early 1970s, when he ascended to the union's assistant secretary-generalship—without ever having worked in a plastics factory. Fortunate to have married into a wealthy family, Triaca had acquired a huge mansion with a swimming pool in the elegant residential district of La Horqueta, a three-story chalet in the beach resort of Pinamar, a house in Miami, and fifty racehorses.[49] In appointing Triaca, Menem sent a signal that he would work harder to build good relations with business leaders than with the more combative union leaders. He also got a labor minister who was unlikely to become an alternative focus for popular support. In March 1990, among 1,000 survey respondents in the Greater Buenos Aires area, Triaca's approval rating was 7 percent (the lowest of all ministers), with 70 percent expressing disapproval, 18 percent ambivalence, and only 5 percent no opinion.[50] When Triaca was sworn in at Menem's inauguration, the crowd in the Plaza de Mayo let loose a cacophony of whistles and whooped up a chant in support of Ubaldini.[51]

To maintain a measure of balance among the factions of Peronist unionism, Menem assigned labor subsecretariats and other government posts to the hitherto combative "25" and Ubaldinista factions. He also placed the "15" luminary Luis Barrionuevo, his most trusted union ally, in control of ANSSAL, the agency that audited and shuffled money among the unions' obras sociales. Most of the union obras sociales were running deep in the red, so Barrionuevo's decisions could make a big difference to a union's finances. Having managed the obra social of the hotel and restaurant workers' union (allegations abounded that he had used its funds to help finance Menem's electoral campaign), Barrionuevo arrived at ANSSAL with some experience. He remained in this post until January 1991, two months after a fateful radio interview in which he explained that union leaders never needed to "stick their hand in the cookie jar" because the law and accounting firms they hired to perform services for their unions gave them so much money in kickbacks that they didn't need to skim the obras sociales. When asked by a caller where he himself got the money to buy a huge mansion in Villa Ballester, Barrionuevo replied, "I didn't make it working because it is very difficult to make money by working. Who around here makes money by working?"[52] This frank response led to Barrionuevo's resignation, but it made the *New York Times* and gained a lasting place in Argentine political lore.

A week before Menem took office, Barrionuevo suggested to Ubaldini that it was time for him to step down as secretary-general of the CGT. Menem did not publicly endorse the suggestion, but he and Ubaldini had already discussed whether the CGT chief might be interested in a post as labor attaché in a European embassy. Ubaldini had said he might be interested after his term expired in September 1990, but Menem indicated that the position was available immediately. The CGT chief managed to decline, but in October 1989, the rightist, conciliatory, pro-Menem "15" unionists, in astounding collaboration with the erstwhile leftist, combative, anti-Menem "25," called an extraordinary CGT congress at which they intended to replace Ubaldini with a figure less likely to try to block Menem's economic reforms. Ubaldini and his allies showed up at the congress, but sensing that they might be in a minority, they walked out and left the Menemista unionists to elect a new directive council headed by the former "25" leader Guerino Andreoni. The dissidents, led by Ubaldini and Lorenzo Miguel, occupied the official CGT building and named their own directive council (which for the first time included a woman, María Sánchez of the CTERA teachers' confederation). Whereas the Andreoni faction felt that union leaders had a duty to support Menem's policies even if they entailed some costs for workers, Ubaldini announced that "we will only help a government or a president who works for social justice."[53] Ubaldini's faction, headquartered on Azopardo Street, came to be known as the CGT–Azopardo; Andreoni's, for a similar reason, was called the CGT–San Martín.

According to *Clarín* reporters, the Menemista faction absorbed 80 percent of the "15," 75 percent of the "25," 70 percent of nonaligned unionists, 50 percent of Ubaldinismo, and 40 percent of the "62."[54] Some observers looked to economic factors to explain the new distribution of union leaders. It was noted, for example, that the opposition CGT–Azopardo attracted the leaders of the state workers (ATE), state oil workers, and telephone workers (federal capital local)—all of whose members were vulnerable to privatization or public sector layoffs. But if layoffs were the paramount consideration, it is far from clear why the leaders of the civil servants, state railway workers, or telephone workers (interior locals) should have opted for the pro-Menem CGT–San Martín. Personal power interests and habitual political styles provide a partial explanation for the distribution of more prominent unionists into pro- and anti-Menem factions. On the pro-Menem side were Triaca, who had fifteen years of experience as a union-government power broker, and Barrionuevo, who had proven finesse with the obras sociales and a large constituency because of it. Ubaldini, whose prominence in Peronist unionism rested heavily on a platform of general strikes and mass rallies, anchored down the anti-Menem faction, and Lorenzo Miguel, like a peripheral state displaying balancing behavior, leaned toward the weaker Ubaldini but maintained a fluid dialogue with both sides, maximizing his power as a go-between.

The loose Miguel-Ubaldini alliance involved benefits for both leaders. Without Miguel's support, Ubaldini's CGT might well have been dismissed as a dwindling hodgepodge of nostalgic statists, confrontational demagogues, militant human rights activists, and leftist social democrats. Without the pole of opposition formed by Ubaldini and his allies, Miguel might well have been eclipsed by Triaca and Barrionuevo, who thanks to their government posts had acquired patronage resources that not even he could match.[55] Miguel thus had an interest in maintaining Ubaldini as a pole of opposition to the government, despite his frequent laments about the CGT's lack of unity. In the time-honored "golpe y negociar" tradition perfected by Augusto Vandor, Miguel used the threat of more active support for Ubaldini to extract an ongoing stream of benefits for his union. In March 1990, when Ubaldini's CGT was on the verge of declaring a general strike against the government, Miguel elected to oppose the initiative—just as the ministry of labor decided that the metal workers' UOM, rather than the auto workers' SMATA, would represent workers in two car-parts factories.[56] In November 1990, Miguel withdrew his allies from Ubaldini's CGT—just as Barrionuevo agreed that ANSSAL would absorb a $25 million debt owed by the UOM's obra social.[57]

The big surprise in the new alignment of union leaders was the conversion of many "25" unionists, including Andreoni, Digón, García, and Pedraza, from "rabid Cafierismo to fairly enthusiastic Menemismo."[58] These unionists may simply have decided to put loyalty to a Peronist president above programmatic consistency. Some may have concluded that any strategy for confronting the economic crisis, including one starkly opposed to what they had previously stood for, beat a long stream of general strikes. Personal incentives, like Andreoni's selection to lead the CGT–San Martín, Digón's appointment to a labor secretariat, García's elevation to effective leadership of the PJ, and Pedraza's participation on a railway-privatization board, might have induced the former "25" leaders to throw in their lot with Menem.

In January 1991, Triaca resigned as labor minister in favor of labor undersecretary Rodolfo Díaz. Triaca's resignation was motivated partly by family concerns, but even his close allies confirmed that "the cabinet needed a breath of fresh air and [Triaca's] image in public opinion was not particularly good."[59] Triaca's departure from the government was brief, for he returned to public service in May 1991, this time as a government trustee charged with privatizing the SOMISA steel company. After reducing the payroll from 12,000 to 5,500, Triaca spent U.S.$5 million to purchase four floors of a Buenos Aires office building to serve as SOMISA's new headquarters. When an audit revealed that this price was 80 percent higher than almost identical adjoining premises had recently commanded, and discovered that Triaca's expenses had included "$100,000 for notary services, $200,000 in real estate commissions, $50,000 in plants and flowers, and $100,000 in payments to an architecture studio," Menem recalled the embattled ex-unionist from a yacht cruise off southern Brazil and asked for his resignation. A few days later, Triaca was charged with presumptive noncompliance with the duties of a public functionary and with possible fraud against the public administration, partly on the grounds that, contravening existing law, he had not consulted anyone else on the choice of a real estate agent or notary public (apparently violating an anti-kickback law) and had failed to ask the treasury secretary whether alternative quarters were available (the state at the time owned an estimated 2,000 empty buildings). A month after resigning as head of SOMISA, Triaca paid a $25,000 fee to join the Jockey Club, which Perón had once described as "a cave of oligarchs" and which had been ransacked by a Peronist mob in 1953. Triaca stayed at liberty on U.S.$100,000 bail, and charges against him were eventually dropped. Menem's choice to replace Triaca as interventor of SOMISA was María Julia Alsogaray, who was out on U.S.$10,000 bail while awaiting trial for irregularities in the privatization of the state telephone company.[60] In June 1995, Jorge

Triaca was seeking to return to politics and María Julia Alsogaray, whom Menem had appointed environment secretary, was preparing for the elevation of her post to cabinet status.[61]

A threat to the obras sociales at the beginning of 1992 encouraged pro- and anti-Menem unionists to try to unite the CGT. Traditionally, monthly contributions by workers and employers had gone directly into the bank accounts of the individual union-controlled obras sociales, without the intermediation of the state (except for the 10 percent that went to ANSSAL). The October 1991 "mega-decree" empowered the DGI to collect the monthly contributions and then distribute them to the individual obras sociales as it saw fit. In January 1992, the government sent congress a bill to write this practice into law. Two months later the two CGTs merged, selected a new leadership board, and scheduled a general strike. Unionists denied that the obras sociales bill had precipitated the unification of the CGT or provoked the general strike call, but when government agreed to withdraw the bill, the CGT called off the general strike.[62]

The leadership of the newly reunited confederation reflected unresolved conflict among its constituents. Instead of the traditional single secretary-general elected for a period of several years, the March 1992 CGT congress produced an unwieldy arrangement whereby the secretary-generalship was scheduled to rotate every six months among five unionists: José Pedraza (pro-Menem), José Rodríguez (pro-Menem), Oscar Lescano (independent but sympathetic to Menem), Aníbal Martínez (a Miguel ally), and Ramón Baldassini (a moderate pro-Ubaldini unionist). Lescano was chosen to head the confederation for the first six months and, as it turned out, for the next six as well. The agreement relegated Ubaldini to a more peripheral role in the CGT than at any time in the previous fifteen years. It also marginalized the most combative union leaders, including Víctor de Gennaro (state workers) and María Sánchez (teachers), who broke away from the official CGT and formed a new confederation, the Congreso de Trabajadores Argentinos (CTA), which protested not only Menem's economic reforms but also his personalistic style of rule and pardons of military leaders convicted of human rights violations.

Shorn of the combative CTA unions, the newly unified official CGT lobbied mildly for more "equity" and "solidarity" in economic policy and for a greater role for union leaders in policy formulation. "We aren't looking for unlimited power, just the place that corresponds to a weighty corporation like the labor movement—and we recognize that we ourselves are primarily responsible for having lost influence," Lescano told reporters.[63] The government turned a deaf ear to the CGT's respectful petitioning; not only did it refuse to repeal a decree limiting wage hikes to productivity gains, it also introduced new legislation limiting severance overtime and pay. In response, the CGT launched a general strike in November 1992—the only such action during Menem's first term in office. The general strike was rejected by the PJ and left parties and received only limited adherence in the interior of the country, where hardships were worst and where ordinary strike activity was most intense.

As the official CGT staked out a largely conciliatory position and the CTA an intensely combative one, Lorenzo Miguel took his usual place in the center. Miguel had joined the official CGT in 1992, but his metalworkers' union launched nine nationwide strikes that year to protest the government's policy of linking wage hikes to productivity gains. The UOM preferred a posture more combative than that hitherto taken by the CGT, and got its chance to push the official confederation in a more adversarial direction when, in March 1993, Naldo Brunelli, a leader of the metalworkers' union, replaced Oscar Lescano of the light and power workers as secretary-general of the confederation. With a UOM leader at the helm, the CGT adopted a more combative stance. As Brunelli tussled with Enrique Rodríguez, Menem's newly appointed labor minister, over pay raise limits and a bill to reduce union control over hiring and scheduling, Miguel announced that "President Menem has betrayed Justicialists with these kinds of measures, and I won't vote for him again."[64]

The CGT softened its tone as the November 1993 legislative elections approached (and as Brunelli received a slot on the PJ's list of national deputy candidates).[65] As soon as the election had passed, however, the issue of the obras sociales once again mobilized union leaders into action. In December 1993, the government announced a plan to limit employer contributions to the obras sociales, a move that the CGT leaders calculated would cost the funds $800 million annually. The proposal caused the resignation of Rodríguez, who had promised the unionists that no such proposal was planned (his replacement was José Armando Caro Figueroa, a labor lawyer who had served in the Alfonsín government). It also caused the CGT to schedule another general strike, which was promptly called off when the government agreed to discuss its proposal to limit overtime and severance pay— and when tax authorities announced that they were contemplating an investigation into the unions' finances, the accounts of the obras sociales, and the personal fortunes of several union leaders.[66]

The decision to call off the scheduled January 1994 general strike caused yet another split in the CGT. Unhappy with the decision to abandon the protest, leaders of several transport workers' unions broke away from the official CGT and formed a third confederation, the Movimiento de Trabajdores Argentinos (MTA). The MTA was not as broadly adversarial as the CTA, but the two confederations united to sponsor coordinated nationwide protest marches in July 1994 and general strikes in August 1994 and April 1995.[67] The departure of the combative transport workers to form the MTA left the official, largely pro-government CGT in the hands of the most conciliatory *super-Menemistas*, who arranged for one of their own, Antonio Cassia of the oil workers, to succeed Brunelli in March 1994. Cassia repudiated the CTA/MTA protests and participated actively in Menem's 1995 electoral campaign, but the huge rise in unemployment during the first half of 1995 convinced many hitherto conciliatory unionists that a more combative stance was in order. After Menem's re-election, accordingly, the "super-Menemist" Cassia resigned as CGT secretary-general in favor of Gerardo Martínez of the construction workers, a "moderate Menemist." Although the CGT adopted a somewhat more oppositional stance after this changeover, it remained to be seen, given the absence of a well-articulated alternative to Menem's policies and the continuing erosion of the unions' power resources, whether this stance could be translated into effective opposition.

The unions during Menem's first term in office may thus be classified into three groups, distinguished by the degree to which, and persistence with which, they supported or opposed the government. The combative faction was represented first by Ubaldini's CGT–Azopardo (1989–92), then by the leftist and broadly adversarial CTA (1992–95), and then also by the more narrowly militant MTA (1994–95). The conciliatory faction was represented first by Andreoni's CGT–San Martín (1989–92) and then by the official "Menemist" CGT (1992–95). The third "faction" was more an intermittent alliance of pragmatic union leaders, including Barrionuevo, Ubaldini, and Miguel, with significant organizational or prestige resources of their own. These unionists alternated between cooperation and combativeness according to their judgments about which stance would be most expedient for themselves and their constituencies. The factional configuration from 1989 to 1995 thus resembled those between 1958 and 1962 and between 1966

234 Free-Market Reform and Political Shenanigans

and 1970, when the stance toward the government in office had constituted the paramount line of cleavage. Intensity of participation in the
PJ, an important line of cleavage during the Illia and Alfonsín presidencies, was less important during Menem's first term, partly because
the party itself lost importance.

THE REDUCTION IN CGT GENERAL STRIKES

Although individual union leaders responded in diverse ways to
Menem's economic reforms, most were more quiescent than they had
been during Alfonsín's term in office. This quiescence was reflected in
the reduction of CGT general strikes from thirteen during Alfonsín's
presidency to one during Menem's first term (three if one includes the
CTA/MTA general strikes of August 1994 and April 1995). The main
reason for the CGT's quiescence was simply that many of its leaders
had arrived, with Menem, at the conclusion that free-market reform
was the least flawed way to tackle the country's economic problems—
and, in the long run, to improve the welfare of workers. In the view of
José Pedraza of the railway workers, Menem's reforms were necessary
because "there was no other way for the country to escape the profound crisis in which we found ourselves." According to Carlos West
Ocampo of the private hospital workers, "the wage is directly related
to the gross domestic product, to the capacity to produce, to the capacity to export, to the capacity to create wealth." In the opinion of
José Rodríguez of the auto workers, "if there is stability, if there is investment, if we're privatizing, if the companies can do business, that's
when living conditions will improve." Oscar Lescano of the light and
power workers even argued that the welfare of the country demanded
a reduction of union power: "Perón gave us everything, and successive
Justicialist [Peronist] governments allowed us excessive influence. . . .
we went beyond ourselves in the use of power and now we're paying
the price, including before society, which doesn't approve of many of
our stances."[68]

It would be ingenuous to take such statements entirely at face value,
but ridiculous to dismiss them as manifestations of false consciousness or as a cynical sellout by corrupt union bureaucrats to the enemies of the working class. After all, the reforms Menem implemented
during his first term in office had positive as well as negative effects
on the Argentine economy, and positive as well as negative effects on
workers and the poor. Far from having their preferences "betrayed,"

moreover, many workers expressed support for economic policies similar to those backed by pro-Menem union leaders. In 1985 and 1986, in the midst of Alfonsín's presidency, Peter Ranis conducted a set of two-hour open-ended interviews with 110 members of seven large unions. Among these union members, 71 percent supported privatization, mostly on the grounds that private firms were more efficient than public ones, or that the state should not be bailing out money-losing enterprises. The privatization of the state telephone company was supported even by a majority of its own employees, whose low morale reflected and aggravated the firm's notoriously poor service. One employee told Ranis: "I don't want to be a telephone worker forever. That is closer to death than to life. The state enterprises are almost designed to destroy your capacity for invention and your personality generally."[69]

People who work need not think of themselves exclusively or even primarily as workers. Hence, it should not be surprising that such people's opinions about free-market reform should coincide with those held more broadly among the Argentine population. A January 1991 survey of 1,016 Argentine citizens revealed that 61 percent supported a reduction in public employment, 68 percent backed the privatization of public enterprises, 77 percent favored a more open economy, and 82 percent advocated a reduction in public spending.[70] The opinions expressed by the workers Ranis interviewed also showed broad consistency with those held by nonunion sectors of Peronism. According to a May 1992 survey of 500 Peronist leaders, activists, and party members, "privatization" was viewed positively by 46 percent and negatively by 42 percent, while "reform of the state" was viewed positively by 69 percent and negatively by only 20 percent.[71] In short, it is unwise to exaggerate the degree to which workers or Peronists were predisposed to oppose free-market reform.[72] The CGT's mild response to Menem's policies cannot accurately be portrayed as a "betrayal" of the will of the rank and file.

A second reason for the CGT's quiescence was that Menem headed the political movement, Peronism, that most workers and union leaders supported. As several observers have noted, "Menem has an advantage with the unions similar to [the one] that Nixon had in opening up China."[73] Just as it took a Republican anticommunist to establish U.S. relations with China, it took a Peronist president to impose market-oriented policies on Argentina's predominantly Peronist labor movement. Dani Rodrik has characterized Menem's Argentina as the "most extreme example" of a "Nixon-in-China" syndrome that also prevailed in Poland under Solidarity and in Spain under the socialist Felipe González. The general principle at work, according to Rodrik, is that "it may take a labor-based government to undertake reforms that would be otherwise unacceptable to labor and other popular groups."[74] This explanation accords with views expressed by key politicians and unionists. "If I had done just 10 percent of what this government is doing, they would have hung me from a lamppost in the Plaza de Mayo," Alfonsín noted bitterly in August 1990, reflecting on Menem's reform program.[75] The unionist Oscar Lescano agreed with his former antagonist: "We called fourteen [*sic*] strikes against the Radical government for much less than is going on right now."[76]

The traumatic experience of hyperinflation is a third reason why Menem was able to impose free-market reforms without a combative response from the CGT. In July 1989, the month Menem took office, retail prices rose 197 percent—equivalent to a compounded annual rate of 50,000,000 percent. Cross-national analyses of free-market reform programs suggest that severe economic crises may create a window of opportunity for stabilization, privatization, liberalization, and deregulation. Stephan Haggard and Robert Kaufman characterize Menem's Argentina as a case in which "reform initiatives cut against the interests of followers" but "worsening economic circumstances induced a broad cross-section of the population to support efforts by the incoming government to apply shock treatment."[77] Joan Nelson concurs that "in Bolivia and Argentina . . . hyperinflation proved a watershed: the public, terrified, acquiesced in far more draconian reforms under second-round presidents" (i.e., Menem as opposed to Alfonsín, who presided over the "first round" of democratic government after the transition from authoritarian rule).[78] Elsewhere, Nelson has argued that "an acute crisis . . . above all rapid inflation or hyperinflation . . . predictably generates a strong popular desire for a take-charge government with a plausible plan to contain the emergency. Even draconian stabilization programs such as Bolivia's in 1985 can be accepted by much of the population as the painful remedy for an increasingly nightmarish situation."[79] If the crisis can be blamed on poor economic management by a peculiarly incompetent government, Nelson argues, a change in the basic economic model might encounter more resistance, but that was not the case in Argentina, where the crisis was widely viewed as the outcome of long-term deficiencies in the model.

The success of Cavallo's March 1991 convertibility plan at taming inflation and encouraging economic growth is a fourth reason why the CGT remained quiescent during Menem's first term in office. The reduction of inflation and resumption of economic growth were welcomed by many workers and union leaders, along with others. Several analysts have cited the success of Cavallo's program as a reason for the dearth of major labor protest during the 1989–95 period. According to Barbara Geddes, "in Argentina, lowered inflation was so widely welcomed that President Carlos Menem and his policies have maintained substantial support in spite of other costs."[80] This argument is seconded by Joan Nelson: "Especially after Cavallo's 'miracle' had taken hold in the second half of 1991, public opinion strongly supported the general direction of government economic policies. Many rank-and-file unionists no longer favored militant tactics."[81]

A fifth reason why the CGT refrained from intense protest under Menem's 1989–95 government was that many union leaders discovered that Menem's privatization program entailed new organizational and financial opportunities for their unions. In 1990, Menem's plans to privatize state-owned shipyards and arms factories were reported to hold out the possibility that, with the labor ministry's approval, the UOM metalworkers' union might absorb workers formerly represented by the ATE state workers' union.[82] And as Victoria Murillo has noted, many union leaders approached the privatization process in a rather entrepreneurial frame of mind. SUPE, formerly the state oil workers' union and now the union representing workers in any firm descended from the former state oil company Yacimientos Petrolíferos Fiscales (YPF), bought shares in an oil-equipment firm and purchased part of the shipping fleet formerly owned by YPF. In 1993, SUPE represented both employers and employees in a collective bargaining agreement between itself and the shipping-fleet workers (taking full advantage of Menem's labor "flexibilization" initiatives, the contract extended the probationary period for new employees and made it easier to hire temporary workers). The light and power workers' FATLyF, the best-administered major union in Argentina over the past thirty years, bought major shares in fifteen power plants around the country and opened a bank with an eye toward entering the newly privatized retirement-fund business. The railway workers' union purchased several privatized railway lines, while the retail clerks' federation arranged to market its own credit card. Leaders of both SUPE and the railway workers' union began to collect fees for administering the shares allocated to workers in privatization deals.[83] The emergence of unions as entrepreneurial organizations raises profound questions about their nature and purpose.

THE EVOLUTION OF ORDINARY STRIKES

Like CGT general strikes, ordinary strikes (those called at any level from a whole industry to a single plant) declined after Menem took office. Under Alfonsín, each quarter had included an average of 115 strikes, 1,984,708 strikers, and 4,874,247 days lost. These figures fell during the part of Menem's first term for which data are available (July 1989–December 1993) to 48 strikes, 1,345,719 strikers, and 3,789,812 days lost (Table 8). Peronist incumbency, the shock of hyperinflation, and satisfaction with the results of the convertibility plan, all of which have been widely cited as inhibiting CGT general strikes, could also serve as plausible explanations for the decline in ordinary strikes. The data, however, provide little support for these hypotheses.

If Peronist incumbency inhibited ordinary strikes as well as CGT general strikes, one would expect to see a fairly rapid drop in ordinary strike activity as soon as Menem took office, when the new president was enjoying a "honeymoon" during which even Peronist union leaders skeptical of his free-market reforms were willing to adopt a wait-and-see attitude. A similar prediction would emerge from the hyperinflationary-trauma hypothesis. The worst hyperinflation occurred between May and July 1989, just before Menem took office, and the second worst between December 1989 and March 1990, also early in Menem's presidency. If the drop-off in strike activity had been caused by the shock of hyperinflation, it would likely have come in the first few quarters of Menem's term, when the shock was presumably worst. Strike activity, however, *rose* by certain measures during the first five quarters of Menem's presidency. During this period, the mean quarterly number of strikes was lower than during the Alfonsín years (99 vs. 115), but the mean quarterly number of strikers was higher (2,737,632 vs. 1,984,708) and the mean quarterly number of days lost was much higher (8,485,366 vs. 4,874,247) (Table 8).

To explain why strike activity did not decline until more than a year after Menem took office, it seems reasonable to look beyond Peronism and hyperinflation to factors that came into play later in Menem's administration. One such factor is the March 1991 convertibility plan, which tamed inflation and restored economic growth. It is unlikely, however, that the convertibility plan made the difference: the down-

TABLE 8
Strike Activity in Argentina by Year and Presidential Period, 1984–1993

Year	Number of strikes	Number of strikers	Number of days lost to strikes	% strikes in public and mixed sectors	% strikers in public and mixed sectors	% days lost in public and mixed sectors
1984	495	8,459,192	16,521,182	52	62	66
1985	333	4,248,248	8,296,518	49	70	74
1986	582	11,236,940	23,170,963	68	66	56
1987	470	5,980,507	13,372,628	67	84	88
1988	443	7,443,344	33,593,112	75	87	95
1989	418	7,720,985	24,359,522	71	67	90
1990	326	9,970,886	32,844,016	75	87	95
1991	119	3,468,930	10,201,821	83	77	92
1992	99	4,656,536	7,208,282	71	37	53
1993	116	1,642,512	6,033,246	67	83	89
TOTAL	3,401	64,828,080	175,601,288			
Mean per year	340	6,482,808	17,560,129	35	31	19
			Means per quarter			
Entire period 1984 Q1–1993 Q4 40 quarters	85	1,697,163	4,386,251	66	72	78
Alfonsín presidency 1984 Q1–1989 Q2 22 quarters	115	1,984,708	4,874,247	63	75	80
Initial Menem presidency 1989 Q3–1990 Q3 5 quarters	99	2,737,632	8,485,366	74	66	85
Later Menem presidency 1990 Q4–1993 Q4 13 quarters	28	810,368	1,983,830	73	58	80
Menem presidency 1989 Q3–1993 Q4 18 quarters	48	1,345,719	3,789,812	74	63	83

SOURCE: Consejo Técnico de Inversiones, *La economía argentina* (yearbooks for 1984–93). On the collection and reliability of these data, see McGuire, "Strikes in Argentina."

turn in strikes did not come in the second quarter of 1991, when the plan took effect, but six months earlier, in the fourth quarter of 1990 (see figure). Menem's October 1990 ban on public-sector strikes comes to mind as a possible cause of the downturn, but if this ban had made the difference, public- and mixed-sector strike activity should have dropped more steeply than private-sector strike activity. That was not the case: comparing the five quarters of Menem's term before the ban with the thirteen quarters after it, the public-and-mixed-sector proportion of strikes fell only from 74 to 73 percent; of strikers, only from

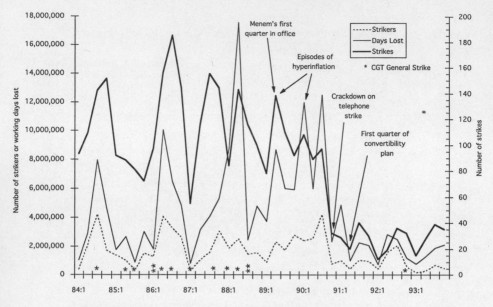

Strike Activity in Argentina by Quarter, 1984–1993

66 to 58 percent; and of working days lost, only from 85 to 80 percent (Table 8). The fairly even decline in strike activity across the public/mixed and private sectors casts doubt on the hypothesis that the ban on public-sector strikes was responsible for much of the downturn.

More important than the public-sector strike ban in reducing strike activity may well have been the defeat in September 1990 of a major strike by federal capital telephone workers protesting the privatization of the state-owned telephone company, ENTel. Widely interpreted as a test of Menem's willingness to pursue free-market reforms despite worker resistance, the telephone workers' strike might well be called a "showdown" strike. Its defeat came just prior to the drop-off in strike activity, and Menem's supporters compared it to Margaret Thatcher's defeat of the British coal miners and to Ronald Reagan's defeat of the air traffic controllers (which launched a decade of low strike activity in the United States).[84] Similarly, scholars have argued that defeats of major "showdown" strikes in 1959 and 1967 initiated periods of reduced strike activity in Argentina.[85]

Because correlation does not imply causation, the data provide only tentative support for the showdown strike explanation. Moreover, the defeat of the telephone workers' strike may have reduced strike activity only because it was inflicted by a Peronist president, or only because it came at a time when the memory of hyperinflation was fresh. It is also possible that satisfaction with the convertibility plan, or rising unemployment after 1991, kept strike activity from rising after its initial downward spike.[86] The data suggest, however, that explanations of the recent decline in strike activity should pay more attention to the defeat of a key "showdown" strike, rather than focusing exclusively on Peronist incumbency, the trauma of hyperinflation, or the economic resurgence after March 1991. The data also suggest that the causes of strikes may change significantly as one descends from huge nation-wide protests, in which political and union leader turf-battle factors are likely to be very important, to strikes in individual factories, in which such factors are far from absent, but in which bread-and-butter issues are likely to have greater incidence.[87]

The Deinstitutionalization of the Partido Justicialista

The PJ ended Menem's first term less institutionalized than it had been during Alfonsín's presidency. Menem bypassed the party in filling government posts and in picking candidates for elective offices, gave party leaders little input into government policy, and increased the isolation of the national party leadership from party members and from provincial party organizations. Union leaders maintained a degree of involvement in the chamber of deputies, but their numbers in the lower house declined. And although union chiefs continued to participate in the party's electoral campaigns, their influence over the national party leadership fell. By fostering habituation to party activity, the reiteration of internal elections in provincial PJs advanced Peronist party institutionalization during the 1989–95 period, but this trend was overshadowed by countervailing ones.

One reason for the deinstitutionalization of the PJ was its status as the incumbent party. During Alfonsín's government, when the PJ was in opposition, Peronist politicians and union leaders lacked easy access to the national executive. They were thus encouraged, by default if nothing else, to rely on the PJ and its legislators as vehicles for political influence. Under Menem, Peronist politicians and union leaders had readier access to the executive. In this situation, many shifted their attention from the party or legislative bloc toward securing executive-branch posts or toward lobbying those who did. But the deinstitutionalization of the PJ also stemmed from Menem's political style. Menem had largely ignored the party during his 1989 presidential election campaign, so he owed it no favors. At the beginning of his presidency, moreover, the PJ was still controlled by Cafiero, so to the extent that Menem gave the PJ a prominent role in his new administration, he would be sharing power with the rival renewal sector. Like Perón, moreover, Menem simply did not like parties (of the political variety) or take them seriously.

Menem's cabinet choices gave an early sign that the PJ would play a small and diminishing role in his government. "Cabinet Owe Allegiance to Menem, not Peronism" headlined the *Buenos Aires Herald* within hours of the new president's inauguration. Only three of the nine members of Menem's first cabinet could be regarded as veteran Peronists of national stature: Julio Corzo in social welfare, Italo Luder in defense, and Jorge Triaca in labor. The public works minister, Roberto Dromi, the interior minister, Eduardo Bauzá, and the chief-of-staff, Alberto Kohan, owed their appointments to personal ties to Menem. The two most prestigious ministries went to persons with no public party affiliation (Miguel Roig in economy and Domingo Cavallo in foreign affairs), while the education and justice ministry went to Antonio Salonia of the center-right Movimiento de Intransigencia y Desarrollo (MID).[88] Bauzá, Cavallo, Corzo, Luder, and Triaca had all served as national deputies, but of 49 appointees to cabinet and subcabinet positions, only 6 had held a place on the 110-member PJ national council, and two of them (Corzo and Kohan) had represented Menem's La Rioja.[89]

More astonishing than Menem's cabinet choices were his appointments to key noncabinet posts. Many of these positions went to people long considered to be Peronism's most intransigent adversaries. Alvaro Alsogaray of the conservative, promarket Unión del Centro Democrático (UCeDé) became Menem's special adviser on the foreign debt.[90] Alsogaray's daughter María Julia, another UCeDé leader, was placed in charge of privatizing two state-owned corporations, first the ENTel phone company and later the SOMISA steel plant. In August 1991, the interior minister, José Luis Manzano, appointed Adelina de Viola, another UCeDé luminary, as a "virtual vice-minister of the interior."[91] Octavio Frigerio, an MID leader whose family's anti-Peronist credentials almost rivaled those of the Alsogarays, was assigned the task of selling off parts of the state-run YPF petroleum giant, although he was forced to resign in January 1990 because of rumored links to military rebels. Manuel Roig, Menem's first economy minister, and Néstor

Rapanelli, who took over when Roig died suddenly of a heart attack, were both vice presidents of the Bunge y Born grain-trading conglomerate, Argentina's largest multinational corporation.

Menem also neglected the party as a source for recruiting governors and legislators, opting instead to give crucial candidacies to entertainment stars, sports figures, and personal associates—usually with no prior connection to the Peronist movement. In late 1991, Menem engineered the nomination of Palito Ortega, a pop singer, Carlos Reutemann, a race-car driver, and Jorge Escobar, a business executive, for the governorships of Tucumán, Santa Fe, and San Juan respectively. None of these candidates had any prior connection to the PJ, but all had impressed Menem. All won their elections, although an avalanche of criminal charges forced Escobar to resign in November 1992 (he was later reelected). Similarly, Menem imposed Avelino Porto, a conservative who promised explicitly *not* to join the PJ, as the Peronist nominee in the June 1992 senatorial election in the federal capital, contravening the wishes of the local branch of the PJ. Also against the wishes of the federal capital party authorities, Menem imposed Antonio Ermán Gonzalez in the top slot on its list of national deputy candidates in September 1993.[92] Ermán had served as economy minister from December 1989 to January 1991, but had previously been a Christian Democratic national deputy from La Rioja, where he had practiced as an accountant and developed personal ties to Menem. Having been affiliated with the PJ for only one year, he headed the local party's national deputy list despite failing to meet its requirement that all PJ–Capital candidates had to have belonged to the party for two years before standing for office.[93]

The growing role of extraparty candidates with little to recommend them apart from name recognition and a capacity to impress Menem was not a promising sign for PJ institutionalization. Some Peronist leaders seemed to prefer it this way: according to the Buenos Aires governor Eduardo Duhalde, the inclusion of extraparty figures represented a "great advance and success." In January 1992, Duhalde explicitly advocated strengthening the "movement" with extraparty figures before its consolidation as a "party." If it were up to him, he added, he would "activate the PJ only a few months before the election and would always do so expansively, allowing men of all political forces to be nominated for elected office and allowing the party electorate to vote for them in the primary election." In March 1993, Duhalde tried unsuccessfully to persuade the tennis star Guillermo Vilas to join the

PJ's list of national deputy candidates from Buenos Aires. According to reporters, the initiative was part of a long-standing effort to "pepper party lists with 'image-men,' preferably from outside the party ... who can make up for the traditional leadership's loss of credibility." Menem summarized his own attitude toward the party in January 1993: "I need the party, but I don't want it interfering in the government house, because I don't want to mix party issues and public affairs."[94]

When Menem took office in July 1989, the PJ was still in the hands of Antonio Cafiero, leader of the renewal sector. When Cafiero and other PJ leaders finally met with Menem more than a week after he became president, they "did not hide their displeasure at the fact that the newspapers had been their best source of information on [Menem's initial] decisions and appointments, in which the party had enjoyed no effective participation."[95] As a newspaper columnist editorialized on 1 September 1989:

The leader acclaimed by the Peronist masses in plebiscitarian fashion on 9 July 1988 is heading up, from the government, a conservative [project whose goal is to] reconcile the popular movement with big national and international capital. ... for a variety of reasons, including uneasiness, mistrust, and recrimination, the party cadres are not participating in the project. In fact—and this is more revealing than 50 proclamations—the committees of the defeated UCR show more life today than the basic units of the victorious Partido Justicialista.[96]

Despite their lack of input into the new administration, the PJ leaders initially took a conciliatory approach to it. "The Partido Justicialista has no reason to occupy center stage," Cafiero announced in September 1989, and in October the PJ national council endorsed Menem's controversial amnesty of military leaders involved in human rights violations, the Malvinas fiasco, and the rebellions against Alfonsín.[97] But tensions soon rose between the president and the party. In December 1989 the PJ–Buenos Aires suspended a congress after Menemists and Cafierists began slinging chairs at one another. In March 1990, Cafiero himself began to take a more critical stance toward Menem's appointments and policies, denouncing the presence of free-market conservatives in the government and referring in a speech to "the need to return to the doctrinal sources of Justicialism."[98] In April 1990, amid rumors that the government had drafted a decree suspending congress, one of Cafiero's allies in the PJ expressed concern about "a hegemonic project based on a corporatist design that envisions dispensing with political parties and even with parliament."[99]

Before the party could go beyond this level of criticism, Cafiero resigned as party president. His resignation was precipitated by the August 1990 defeat of a referendum on proposed reforms to the Buenos Aires provincial constitution, which included removal of the ban on the immediate reelection of the governor. The content of the reforms, and the process that led up to the referendum, in some ways resembled their national-level counterparts of 1994. In both reform packages, the main issue at stake was immediate reelection of the chief executive; in both cases, a pact between Peronist and UCR leaders permitted the referendum to go forward; and in both cases, the pact had the support of most major politicians.[100] The big difference was the outcome. Whereas the 1994 national constitutional reform bill passed congress by a wide margin, the 1990 Buenos Aires constitutional reform referendum went down to a lopsided defeat. The main reason for the difference was the economic climate. In early 1994, Argentina was in the midst of a promising but precarious recovery, and with polls showing that most voters supported the repeal of the ban on presidential reelection, congress passed legislation calling for the April 1994 constituent assembly. In August 1990, by contrast, Argentina was between two bouts of hyperinflation, and Cafiero was identified with the Alfonsín years, which were perceived as an unmitigated economic disaster.

Cafiero's resignation allowed Carlos Menem, the PJ's first vice president, to succeed him. As the PJ deputy bloc leader José Luis Manzano put it, Menem's first priority would be to make the party into "an instrument that will present the government with solutions, not problems."[101] In a speech at the SRA, Menem announced that the huge "no" vote had convinced him that he no longer needed to be bound by compromises, whether with the opposition or his own party. It was enough, Menem said, to form a direct link to "the people and their extraordinary wisdom."[102] As a journalist pointed out, Menem's assumption of the PJ presidency meant that he would now "have to find a balance between his conviction that the party structure is virtually meaningless and his intention to operate everything that moves in the political arena."[103] He created this equilibrium by having his brother, Eduardo Menem, a La Rioja senator, appointed as the party's first vice president. He then requested a leave of absence, whereupon Eduardo Menem, a party member only since the waning days of the 1976–83 military dictatorship, became acting president of the PJ.

By taking a leave of absence, Carlos Menem freed himself from the day-to-day burdens of running the party, but he did not give up his control over its primary patronage resource—candidacies to elective office. As the PJ–La Rioja president, Bernabé Arnaudo, put it, "Eduardo is the umbrella, Carlos is the finger." When elections rolled around, the PJ candidates would still be chosen by the "great, strong, marvelous, and heavy finger of our *conductor*."[104] Unionists were similarly convinced that in 1991, unlike in previous years, when they had exerted more influence, national deputy candidates from the province of Buenos Aires "were going to be handpicked by a gigantic finger, that of the president."[105] Even before the referendum, however, Peronist leaders were describing the PJ in terms that suggested its irrelevance. In the words of Menem's vice president, Eduardo Duhalde, "Nobody cares who the president of the party is," because "the *conductor* of the movement is Menem."[106] José Rodríguez of the auto workers' union made the same point in more colorful language: "The PJ isn't worth shit."[107]

By 1992, 86 percent of party members thought the PJ needed to increase its level of activity, and many felt that the party needed to get closer to intermediate organizations and the underprivileged.[108] That members felt disconnected from the PJ is understandable, for the party's leadership selection processes were designed to exclude them. According to its 1989 statutes, the PJ's sovereign agency was the 110-seat national council. Most of these 110 seats were spoken for: 17 went to the union branch, 10 to the women's branch, 10 to the youth branch, and 24 to provincial party presidents. The representatives from the union, women's, and youth branches were usually handpicked by cliques of notables. The provincial party presidents were usually elected by party members, but sometimes ran without opposition. The 49 "at-large" seats were supposed to be "elected by the secret and direct vote of the membership considering the Republic a single district,"[109] but no such elections ever occurred, because prior to national party congresses, notables always concocted a single list of 49 candidates, decided who the party's leaders would be, secured the congress's "general assent" for these decisions, and then declared that "the secret and direct vote of the membership" was unnecessary.

In this fashion, "general assent" at a party congress in September 1991 gave Eduardo Duhalde, José Luis Manzano, and Carlos Grosso effective leadership of the PJ, with special powers to intervene provincial party organizations, to designate candidates for elective office, and to "define the policies of a new political alliance." Also by "general assent," the congress approved retroactively the intervention of five provincial PJ leaderships over the past year and endorsed Menem's pardons of military leaders jailed for human rights violations—which party members had opposed by a 70 to 20 percent margin.[110] Another round of negotiations in January 1992 made the former "25" unionist Roberto García acting head of the party (with Menem and Duhalde on leaves of absence), and yet another in May 1993 gave the same role to Rubén Marín, governor of La Pampa. Because of the single-list system, the dearth of open elections in the women's, youth, and union branches, and the "general assent" practice by which the party congress chose the PJ national council and its top officeholders, party members had little say in selecting the national party leadership or in determining its policies.

Like party members, union chiefs had little influence over the composition or behavior of the party leadership. The presence of 17 union leaders on the PJ national council did nothing to stem the decline in the number of union deputies, which fell from 23 in 1989 to 8 in 1994 (these 8 nonetheless played an important role on the lower-house labor-legislation committee). Moreover, although Roberto García served as acting party leader from January 1992 to May 1993, his incumbency did not deter the PJ national council from condemning the November 1992 CGT general strike as baseless and nefarious in intent.[111] And although union leaders formed committees to support Peronist candidates in each of the major elections during Menem's first term,[112] such participation was not always welcomed by the party leadership. In 1993, PJ leaders advised the CGT against holding a rally in favor of a constitutional reform to permit Menem's reelection, on the grounds that it would do the reelection campaign more harm than good.[113]

Equally tenuous was the relationship between the party's provincial and national leaders. In 1995, provincial PJs held their sixth consecutive primary elections for party leaders and for gubernatorial and national deputy candidates. Party leaders in some provinces managed to concoct single lists of candidates, but most provincial PJs held contested elections.[114] These provincial elections promoted the institutionalization of the PJ by fostering habituation to party activity, but a sharp disjunction existed between the provincial PJs and the national organization. With the exception of delegates from the women's, youth, and union branches, each member of the PJ's national council formally "represented" a province. Such "representation" could be rather diffuse. It was possible to "represent" a province on the national council without holding a post in a provincial party organization, and many

248 Free-Market Reform and Political Shenanigans

council members did not hold provincial party posts.[115] It was even possible to "represent" a province in which one did not reside. In 1989, the national council included eight representatives from La Rioja, one of whom, Juan Carlos Rousselot, was the mayor of Morón—a city on the outskirts of Buenos Aires.[116] To the extent that the national council concerned itself with provincial party organizations, it was usually to intervene them. By March 1993, according to the Mendoza Peronist leader Arturo Lafalla, every provincial party organization in the country had been intervened except those of Mendoza, San Luis, and La Pampa.[117] When the national council intervened the PJ–Córdoba in December 1992, the ousted renewal Peronist José Manuel de la Sota protested that a "Stalinist methodology prevails in Justicialism, which rules out the right to dissent that must exist in a democratic party."[118] Duhalde's ability to mobilize Peronists for rallies and electoral campaigns gave him influence in Menem's inner circle, but this mobilizational capacity derived as much from his control of the Buenos Aires provincial administration as from his control of the Buenos Aires PJ.

Menem thus deinstitutionalized the PJ in part by ignoring and then capturing and subordinating a party leadership whose ties to party members, union chiefs, and provincial party presidents were in any case tenuous at best. Menem also managed to sidestep or marginalize dissent from the party's representatives in congress. One important source of such dissent emerged in early 1990, when PJ deputies from interior provinces organized a "Peronist Loyalty" faction to oppose cutbacks in federal revenue-sharing.[119] The Peronist Loyalty faction was organized around Ramón Saadi, governor of Catamarca, whose family had ruled the rugged northwestern province since 1945, using federal funds to dispense jobs and other clientelistic favors to supporters. (Prior to elections Saadi would tour poor neighborhoods handing out one shoe to each person he encountered, promising to deliver the other if he were reelected.)[120] Federal revenue-sharing contributed 93 percent of Catamarca's budget, almost 80 percent of which went to pay the 28,000 provincial employees who made up 37 percent of the province's economically active population. The Peronist Loyalty deputies might well have given Menem trouble, but the Saadi machine collapsed in 1990 when some of its members were implicated in the murder of a teenager. In April 1991, the central government intervened Catamarca and deposed Saadi, the local legislature, and all of the province's judges.[121] The collapse of the Saadi dynasty did not eliminate dissent by provincial PJ deputies and senators, but it remained relatively muted.

Other PJ legislators opposed Menem's policies for less particularistic reasons. In September 1989, eight unrepentant renewal-sector deputies from the Buenos Aires area began to protest Menem's impending amnesty of military officers accused of human rights violations. These deputies formed a "Group of Eight" to criticize the "immobilism" of the PJ and to speak out "whenever issues that may have a social impact, like the amnesty, arise." The Group of Eight advocated more fluid dialogue among the forces making up the Peronist movement, demanded the "right to disagree" with the president, indicated that the alliance with the UCeDé "strained the Peronist identity," and complained that "an in-depth discussion of the [economic] model has not yet begun."[122] The Group of Eight's supporters viewed them as stalwarts who refused to sell out to the new free-market orthodoxy; their detractors viewed them as an "intellectualized clique that represents almost nobody" and that "criticizes but provides no solutions."[123] In December 1990, when Menem pardoned the former military leaders Videla, Viola, and Massera (as well as others serving sentences for human rights violations), the Group of Eight broke with the PJ deputy bloc; shortly thereafter, its members resigned from the party itself. According to the Group of Eight luminary Juan Pablo Cafiero (son of Antonio Cafiero), "We couldn't live with a government that has fabricated a pardon, favored corruption at all levels, presided over the deterioration of [the living standards of] the popular sectors, failed to set in motion a productive revolution, and refused to accept the state as an instrument for distributing the social surplus."[124]

After breaking with the PJ, the Group of Eight joined the Frente Grande, a coalition of leftist parties. The Frente Grande won only 4 percent of the vote in the October 1993 national deputy elections, but its fortunes began to soar when, in November 1993, Menem and Alfonsín signed a pact that paved the way for the elimination of the constitutional ban on presidential reelection—and, as things turned out, for the elimination of the UCR as the main opposition party in the 1995 elections. Many who opposed Menem were angry at Alfonsín for making the constitutional reform pact, and many of them abandoned the UCR for what seemed to be the more principled and consistent opposition of the Frente Grande. With the support of disgruntled UCR voters, the Frente Grande tripled its vote share to 12 percent in the April 1994 constituent assembly election. It won outright by a huge margin in the federal capital, traditionally a bastion of the Radicals, and by a slim margin in the province of Neuquén, signaling its transition from a party confined to the Buenos Aires area to a national electoral force.

Soon to join the Frente Grande in an even larger opposition electoral coalition was José Octavio Bordón, a Peronist senator from Mendoza. Like the Group of Eight, Bordón had belonged to Peronism's renewal sector during the Alfonsín presidency. While governor of Mendoza from 1987 to 1991, Bordón had earned a reputation as a good administrator of the province's bountiful petroleum, wine, fruit, and tourism resources. More centrist than the Group of Eight, Bordón expressed a strong faith in the market and enjoyed, as of early 1993, a good personal relationship with Menem. Nevertheless, he criticized the Menem government for lacking a "social plan" to insulate the population from the effects of economic adjustment.[125] Bordón also had presidential aspirations, and in late 1993, he became the only Peronist senator to vote against the bill declaring the need for a constitutional reform that would permit Menem's reelection. After the bill passed, Bordón announced that he would challenge Menem for the PJ nomination, but in September 1994, as it became evident that Menem would prevail in such a contest, the Mendoza senator resigned from the PJ to form his own party, Política Abierta para la Integridad Social (PAIS). After the 1995 election, Menem would demand, ironically in view of his own personalistic style of rule, that Bordón relinquish his senate seat on the grounds that its rightful proprietor was the PJ, not the candidate who happened to hold it.

In late 1994, Bordón's PAIS united with the Frente Grande in an electoral coalition called the Frente del Pais Solidario (FREPASO), which also included Unidad Socialista, Democracia Cristiana, and part of the Partido Intransigente, as well as some UCR dissidents. In a direct primary election in February 1995, Bordón won the FREPASO presidential nomination, narrowly defeating the Frente Grande leader Carlos Alvarez, a former member of the Group of Eight, who by prior agreement became the vice presidential candidate. The FREPASO candidates, who had the support of the militant CTA union confederation, focused their attacks on government corruption and on the harsh effects of economic austerity on many workers and poor people. Recognizing the achievements of Menem's economic model, however, they pledged to retain its basic elements, including the pegging of the peso to the dollar. The Radical candidate, Horacio Massaccessi, the governor of Rio Negro, promised more or less the same things as Bordón, but most opponents of the government had come by 1994 to regard FREPASO as the "real" opposition. Bordón made a solid showing in the May 1995 presidential election with 29 percent of the vote, but Menem, whom most people credited with taming hyperinflation, won easily with 49 percent. Massaccessi finished a distant third with 17 percent, marking the first time in history that a UCR presidential candidate had finished lower than second in a fair election.

Under the renewal sector during Alfonsín's government, the PJ had become more institutionalized. The high point of this process came in July 1988, when party members, rather than a plebiscitarian president or a union leader clique, nominated their presidential candidate in a competitive primary election. But Carlos Menem, the winner of the primary, promptly dispensed with the services of the PJ, which was still in the hands of the renewal sector, and called instead on personal friends and unionists from the "15" to run his general election campaign. After defeating the UCR candidate Angeloz in May 1989 and taking office two months later, Menem successively ignored, captured, insulated, and marginalized the PJ organization, while stonewalling dissidents in the party's congressional delegation, many of whom ended up resigning from the PJ. By July 1995, when Menem's first term ended, the PJ was less institutionalized—infused with value—than it had been a decade earlier.

Menem and Democratic Institutions

As the members of a political community infuse a political party with value, they strengthen their stake in the survival of elections and legislatures, without which the party cannot operate effectively. Party institutionalization thus promotes democratic consolidation by giving the community's members an *instrumental stake* in the survival of democratic practices and arenas. It might be even more propitious for (or indicative of) democratic consolidation if the members of the political community were to develop a *principled commitment* to elections and congress,[126] but the contribution of party institutionalization to democratic consolidation should not be dismissed simply because it is more instrumental than principled. Indeed, an instrumental stake in democratic (or protodemocratic) arenas and procedures may well develop into principled commitment. In countries where such commitment is widespread today, parliaments emerged partly because estates found them instrumentally useful in checking monarchs, and universal suffrage emerged partly because union leaders found it instrumentally useful in securing gains for workers.

That said, principled commitment to democratic procedures and arenas is certainly propitious for (or indicative of) democratic consolidation. For such commitment to develop, people must come to view electoral, legislative, and judicial procedures as reasonably enduring, impartial, and relevant. The simple reiteration of such procedures helps convince people that they will be reasonably enduring, and reforms can be implemented to make them more impartial and relevant (such reforms, indeed, are one way in which an improvement in the quality of democracy can lead to an improvement in the stability of democracy). By these criteria, some conditions became more propitious for the development of a principled commitment to democracy during Menem's first term in office. Menem presided over six years of electoral activity, proposed or backed legal and constitutional reforms that increased the resilience, fairness, and relevance of certain democratic arenas and procedures, and reduced the level of overt military contestation. Against these credits, however, one must weigh Menem's manipulation of electoral rules, bypassing of congress with executive decrees, stacking of the supreme court, tolerance for administrative corruption, lackadaisical response to physical attacks on journalists critical of the government, and pardons of military officers convicted of human rights violations.

On the positive side of the balance sheet, Argentina between 1989 and 1995 held one constituent assembly election, two presidential elections, and three legislative elections. Moreover, the Menem government changed the penal code to give more rights to the accused and repealed the *desacato* law, which had imposed penalties on those judged to have insulted public officials. Menem also backed and promulgated the Ley de Cupos (quota law) introduced by the UCR–Mendoza senator Margarita Malharro de Torres, which required in effect that at least every third slot on a party's list of candidates for elective office be reserved for a woman. Reserving a quota of slots for women has negative as well as positive implications for the fairness of elections, but because women in 1991 held only 5 percent of Argentina's legislative seats (about average for the Western Hemisphere), and because preceding methods of configuring the lists involved party notables more than party members, the quota law probably represented a net gain for the quality of democracy.[127]

In addition to supporting these legal changes, Menem backed constitutional reforms beneficial for the quality of democracy. One such reform changed the electoral system for senators. Under the previously prevailing 1853 constitution, senators were elected by provincial legislatures for nine-year terms. Under the 1994 constitution, they will, as of 2001, be elected by direct popular vote for six-year terms. Popular election and shorter terms will make the upper house more responsive and accountable to voters.[128] The establishment of a run-off between the two presidential candidates who receive most votes (as in Brazil or France) will broaden the mandate for the chief executive and thus attenuate one of presidentialism's disadvantages for democratic stability.[129] Other positive constitutional reforms include elimination of the requirement that the president must be a Roman Catholic, more explicit definition of the conditions under which decrees of "urgency and necessity" can be issued, increased checks and balances on the nomination of supreme court justices, direct election of the mayor of the federal capital, and the creation of a body similar to Chile's Controladuría to supervise the conduct of public administration.

Menem also made some progress in reducing overt military contestation. On 3 December 1990, officers associated with Col. Mohammed Ali Seineldín launched an armed uprising against the government. Loyal officers put down the rebellion, but not before thirteen had died and several hundred had been injured. Menem's forceful response to the uprising, together with Seineldín's sentencing to life in prison, help explain why discontented officers launched no further rebellions for the next five years. But military quiescence was also fostered by Menem's decision to pardon officers convicted of human rights violations. To this extent, democratic stability (of which military quiescence is only a rough indicator) has been achieved at the price of democratic quality, which requires that the law apply equally to all: convicted criminals who have access to special power resources should not be exonerated on that account. Military prerogatives remain lower in Argentina than in Brazil or Chile, but "authoritarian enclaves" remain. For example, the state intelligence agency, SIDE, has successfully resisted attempts by legislators to find out more about its functioning. Only $5 million of SIDE's $122 million budget was itemized in 1992, and the agency claimed only four permanent employees.[130]

Although Menem presided over several elections, enacted some positive legal reforms, backed some reasonable constitutional changes, and helped to reduce military contestation, these contributions to the

quality and stability of democracy were more than offset by the negative impact of his personalistic style of rule. Although the reiteration
of elections during Menem's first term helped to foster the perception
that electoral processes would endure, Menem's penchant for fiddling
with electoral rules did little to promote the view that electoral processes were impartial or relevant. In November 1993, Menem finally
persuaded Alfonsín to support a constitutional reform that would permit incumbent presidents (including Menem) to run immediately for
reelection. The possibility of immediate presidential reelection is not
in itself inimical to democratic consolidation, but by pursuing this reform and other changes to Argentina's electoral rules in an unabash-
edly self-interested fashion, the government conveyed the impression
that electoral rules can justifiably be altered whenever such changes
benefit a popular incumbent. Menem even implied that the constitutional prohibition against immediate reelection violated his basic
political rights. In June 1992, he claimed that those who disagreed with
reelection were advocating his "proscription," and his close advisers
warned—in a veiled reference to the Illia government—that if Menem
were "proscribed," the victor in the next presidential election would
be regarded as "illegitimate," jeopardizing the constitutional order.[131]

In August 1993, the president's legal advisers, recognizing that it
would be hard to get two-thirds of the lower house to support a bill
declaring the necessity of constitutional reform, began to argue that
"two-thirds" meant two-thirds of the deputies who happened to be in
the hall when the chamber's (Peronist) authorities decided to call for
a vote, rather than two-thirds of the total of 257 deputies. Most jurists
rejected this interpretation, and the PJ senators Bordón and Cafiero announced that they would vote against any reform bill introduced without broad consensus.[132] Such consensus was achieved a few months
later when, in November 1993, Alfonsín and Menem signed the pact
that permitted the reform to go forward. Curiously, however, the new
constitution declared the threshold for avoiding a second round in the
presidential election to be 45 percent of the vote, or 40 percent with
a 10-point lead over the runner-up. It was widely believed that "the
figure [was] set lower than the customary 50% in order to accommo-
date the PJ's recent electoral performance."[133]

The Menem administration's tinkering with electoral rules went beyond the reelection issue. In October 1992, when an interior ministry
study found that the PJ would do better under a single-member plurality system for lower-house elections than under the existing multi-

member proportional system, the government announced that it was studying a bill to switch to the single-member plurality system.[134] This proposal did not flourish, but in January 1993, Menem announced that recent census results indicated that 23 seats would have to be added to the chamber of deputies, of which 11 would be assigned to the province of Buenos Aires (the district in which the PJ was strongest). Jorge Vanossi, a UCR deputy, called the proposal a "political maneuver," and the government withdrew it when an interior ministry survey showed that many Argentines agreed with him. A separate study revealed that if the size of provincial delegations were readjusted to conform to the real results of the 1990 census, only two seats would be added to the lower house—one from Mendoza and one from Rio Negro, not precisely hotbeds of Menemism.[135] The proposal to add seats to the chamber did not flourish either, but in March 1993, the government announced that it was studying the possibility of lowering the voting age to 16, opening all primary elections to voters from all parties, and replacing the existing closed-list system with one in which voters would be allowed to cross out the names of candidates for whom they did not wish to vote. A survey in the Buenos Aires area revealed that 61 percent of respondents believed that the purpose of the government's proposal was simply to help the PJ, and Francisco de Durañona y Vedia, a UCeDé deputy, complained that the government was "stretching its imagination for its own political benefit." At the same time, Duhalde announced that he favored introducing a Uruguayan-style double simultaneous vote system, in which parties could present multiple lists of candidates for elective office, with the winner being the most-voted list of the most-voted party.[136] This *ley de lemas* system, as it is known in Uruguay and colloquially in Argentina, is ideally suited to the strategy of aggregating votes by dispensing PJ candidacies to sports and entertainment stars. This barrage of proposals for self-serving electoral reform did nothing to infuse the electoral system with value.

In addition to playing fast and loose with electoral rules, Menem bypassed congress by imposing hundreds of executive orders (*decretos*) of "urgency and necessity." According to Argentine law, such orders, which are legally binding until repealed by congress or declared unconstitutional by the courts, are to be used exclusively in a "state of emergency" marked by "events out of the ordinary, exceptional situations, unpredictable circumstances, or predictable but unavoidable circumstances." By December 1993, Menem had enacted 308 such decrees, compared to about 30 in the preceding 140 years combined. One decree of "urgency and necessity" involved the donation of cement to construct a road in Bolivia.[137] The proliferation of decretos under an expansive definition of "urgency and necessity" undermined congress as an arena for processing demands.

Menem explained his profligate use of executive decrees as a response to the glacial pace of legislative activity. Although consensus takes time, and Menem can be accused of impatience, his complaint was not entirely unwarranted. Congressional votes during Menem's first term were frequently canceled for lack of a quorum, even when absenteeism was not being used as a political tactic. By mid 1991, absenteeism had grown so rampant that lower-house officers had threatened to impose a fine on any deputy who missed three consecutive legislative sessions.[138] Perhaps because they often did so little, at other times, legislators tried to do too much. On a single day in September 1992, congress passed more than 400 separate measures, including 120 laws, few of which could possibly have been subjected to extended debate or analysis—with the result, as the jurist Manuel Padilla pointed out, that their ambiguities were never clarified.[139] Other aspects of legislative behavior were also open to criticism. In 1991, a scandal broke out when senators were discovered selling the free airline tickets that were supposed to help them stay in touch with constituents.[140] Later that year, the chamber of deputies, which had just passed a somewhat stingy unemployment insurance law for workers, passed a much more generous one—for itself. According to this law, deputies who lost their seats were eligible for a two-year period to receive a monthly paycheck equivalent to half of their previous salary.[141]

Legislators may not have behaved in an exemplary fashion during Menem's first term, but their failings did not justify the profligate use of executive decrees to bypass the body entirely. Equally demure in the system of checks and balances was the judicial branch of government. In 1990 alone, Menem used decrees to restrict the right to strike in public services (although the constitution said that presidential decrees could not be used to amend existing laws, like those regulating strikes), to bar those affected by privatization from suing the state for a two-year period (although the constitution said that citizens had the right to sue the state), and to grant an amnesty to military officers awaiting trial for human rights violations (although the constitution reserved the right to grant pretrial amnesties to congress).[142] Menem's penchant for enacting such decrees gave him an incentive to acquire a more pliant judiciary. Accordingly, in April 1990, he submitted to congress a bill proposing expansion of the supreme court from five to nine members. As president, Menem would have the right to nominate the four new justices. Opposition from UCR, dissident Peronist, and minor party deputies repeatedly prevented the assembly of a quorum to consider the court-expansion bill, but one day in April, as UCR deputies were preparing to file out of the chamber to prevent a quorum, the (Peronist) officers of the lower house called a sudden voice vote. Eight seconds later, it was announced that the bill had passed. The secretary of the UCR bloc protested, to no avail, that he had been threatened at gunpoint when he attempted to check the credentials of persons, apparently not legislators, sitting in seats allotted to the Peronist bloc.[143] For the next three years, Menem had a supreme court that critics accused of abdicating its responsibilities. Rodolfo Barra, who served as the court's vice president until late 1993 (when he and two other justices resigned as part of the deal that got Alfonsín to support constitutional reform), affirmed that when the supreme court analyzed the constitutionality of a measure drawn up by a government official, it usually arrived at an interpretation "favorable to the decision" of the official who drew up the measure, because "the people voted for him."[144]

Apart from these issues involving the supreme court, there have been well-publicized irregularities involving the prosecution of Amira Yoma, the president's sister-in-law, who was acquitted on charges of drug-money laundering in September 1994. The intervention of the province of Corrientes in 1992, which was precipitated by the PJ's impending loss of the governorship, was also plagued with irregularities. Menem's own justice minister, León Arslanian, resigned in 1992 when, to fill a vacancy in an agency charged with overseeing the probity of government officials, Menem appointed an individual whom Arslanian and others regarded as unqualified. The government's manipulation of the courts not only fostered skepticism about the fairness and relevance of judicial processes, but also, according to a survey of business executives, created a perception that the courts could not be relied upon. In such circumstances, economists argue, investors will demand a higher rate of return to make up for the higher risks they feel they face.[145] Juridical insecurity thus threatens to undermine Argentina's economic gains as well as to impede its progress toward democratic consolidation.

The failings of the judicial branch go a long way toward explaining why dozens of Menem's appointees who resigned under the shadow of corruption managed to evade conviction and imprisonment. Some of the most celebrated resignations involved the labor minister Jorge Triaca (on allegations involving kickbacks during the privatization of SOMISA), the ANSSAL head José Luis Barrionuevo (in the wake of his "didn't make it working" interview), the interior minister Julio Mera Figueroa (for irregular relations with an alleged drug trafficker and suspected international terrorist), the subsequent interior minister José Luis Manzano (on charges of illicit enrichment), the PAMI retirement fund director Miguel Nazur (on charges of corruption), the subsequent PAMI director Matilde Menéndez (also on charges of corruption), presidential advisers Miguel Angel Vicco and Claudio Spaddone (on charges of defrauding the state in a powdered-milk deal), the public works minister Roberto Dromi (on charges of fraud and abuse of power), and the multifunctionary María Julia Alsogaray (on charges of illicit enrichment).

Several of Menem's in-laws serving in important government posts have also resigned amid corruption scandals. Amira Yoma, secretary of presidential audiences, resigned after being caught at Ezeiza airport with a suitcase stuffed with dollars. Karim Yoma, secretary of special affairs for the foreign ministry, resigned amid allegations that he had requested bribes from Spanish business executives. Emir Yoma, special economic adviser to the president, resigned after executives of the Swift-Armour meat packing company accused him of soliciting a bribe. Also forced to resign amid corruption or other criminal charges were a host of Peronist governors and mayors of varying proximity to Menem, including Jorge Escobar (San Luis), Carlos Mujica (Santiago del Estero), Ramón Saadi (Catamarca), and Carlos Grosso (federal capital). Alberto Lestelle, secretary of the War Against Drug Trafficking, staffed the agency with ex-members of the armed forces, people on the edge of the law, and what Clarín called gente poco recomendable, one of whom went public in November 1992 with an allegation that Lestelle had ordered him to travel to Brazil to kidnap or murder a suspected drug trafficker. Lestelle also put six of his close relatives on the payroll, used a presidential jet to take a personal vacation, and could not recall how in two years he had managed to increase his assets by $500,000 on an annual salary of $42,000.[146] Lestelle was soon indicted for illicit enrichment, but in June 1995 all charges against him were dropped.[147]

These scandals had wide repercussions. In late 1990, Peronist and opposition legislators obtained a report, apparently authored by the U.S. State Department, that included extensive information on the solicitation of bribes by members of the Menem government and that used the term *kleptocracy* to refer to a group of government officials.[148] By August 1992, survey respondents rated corruption as the most important problem facing the country.[149] In August 1993, Menem's own interior minister, Gustavo Belíz, resigned to protest what he claimed was a plot by government officials to bribe opposition deputies to support constitutional reform.[150] Such abuses reduced the quality of democracy by subordinating public to private interest, and threatened the stability of democracy by exposing the regime to accusations that it fostered corruption.

Menem's response to allegations that his appointees, advisers, and in-laws were engaging in illicit activity was to declare that Argentina suffered from a "dictatorship of the press." To cut this "dictatorship" down to size, the government proposed a variety of legal measures. In July 1992, the government withdrew a "right to reply" proposal after it was criticized by the Inter-American Press Association and others.[151] When an archbishop used a newspaper interview to criticize Menem's social policies and handling of the courts, the government issued a statement decrying "journalistic monopolies" and announced that it might be forced to take measures to "defend the freedom of the press." A wide spectrum of public figures, including Defense Minister Camillón and Foreign Minister Di Tella, regarded the statement not as a defense but as an attack on the freedom of the press.[152] In January 1995, the government submitted legislation to impose huge fines and mandatory prison sentences for libel, and to require the owner of every mass media outlet to take out U.S.$500,000 in libel insurance. When the Inter-American Press Association responded that the bill was aimed at "strangling the freedom of the press," the government withdrew it.[153] Although the government was forced to back down on each of these legal initiatives, some of its supporters developed an alternative strategy for combating the "dictatorship of the press." Between July 1989 and December 1992, according to the journalists' union leader Carlos Camaño, 139 Argentine journalists received death threats and 50 were physically attacked. Many of these journalists were critical of the government, and Camaño claimed that 65 percent of the attacks could be traced to persons with government connections.[154] Attacks on journalists continued in 1993, notably in the cases of Marcelo Bonelli (attacked while investigating Lestelle) and Hernán López Echagüe (attacked twice while investigating the recruitment of thugs for other attacks on journalists).[155]

Menem cannot be held responsible for the worst violations of human rights in Argentina since the return to democracy in 1983—the 1992 bombing of the Israeli Embassy, which killed 29 people and injured 250, and the 1994 bombing of a Buenos Aires building housing Jewish organizations, which killed 90 and injured 200. Menem condemned each atrocity in no uncertain terms and went out of his way to express solidarity with the country's Jewish community. As of mid 1995, however, no one had been brought to justice in either act. Carlos Waisman has argued that anti-Jewish terrorists have targeted Argentina in part because of the inefficiency and corruption of its security and intelligence agencies,[156] a problem that seems to have gotten worse under Menem. In April 1990, Monzer al-Kassar, a Syrian believed by Interpol and the Spanish government to be involved in drug trafficking and international terrorism, was accorded an Argentine passport in record time; Menem's sister-in-law and secretary for presidential audiences, Amira Yoma, admitted expediting al-Kassar's request.[157] When the immigration service was finally placed under government trusteeship in 1995, the interventor, Hugo Franco, declared flatly that "a mafia was operating here."[158] The rights and safety of Argentine citizens have suffered since 1989 from Menem's less-than-energetic campaign against corruption and incompetence in Argentina's intelligence and immigration agencies.

Economic Reform and Democratic Consolidation

Menem's policies from 1989 to 1995 accelerated a long-term decline in the power of the unions. This decline foreshadows a reduction in the intensity of distributive conflict, as workers and small industrialists dependent on sales to the domestic market lose their capacity to launch effective opposition to policies inimical to their short-term interests. A loss of power by the worker–small industrialist coalition (which O'Donnell has termed the "defensive alliance)[159] should diminish the intensity of overt distributive conflict by permitting big industrialists and agricultural exporters to gain hegemony. If Menem's economic reforms bear fruit, moreover, the size of the economic pie will increase, reducing the stakes, and to that extent the intensity, of distributive conflict. All other things being equal, the lighter the burden that distributive conflict places on parties, the easier it is for parties to channel such conflict through elections and congress.

It is far from assured that Menem's reforms will expand the resource base, or that the expansion of the resource base will diminish the intensity of distributive conflict. These assumptions are, however, defensible. The main problem with the optimistic scenario is that even if these assumptions hold, the ability of parties to channel distributive conflict through electoral and legislative institutions depends not only on the intensity of that conflict, but also on the degree to which parties have become institutionalized and to which electoral, judicial, and legislative processes have come to be perceived as durable, fair, and relevant. The preceding analysis of the latter factors suggests a more pessimistic scenario. Menem did, to be sure, contribute to democratic consolidation by presiding over six years of fair elections, by supporting legal and constitutional reforms that improved the functioning of certain democratic arenas and procedures, and by reducing the level of military contestation. These contributions must, however, be set against his marginalization of the Partido Justicialista, manipulation of electoral rules, profligate use of executive decrees, stacking of the supreme court, appointments of corrupt officials to vital government posts, checkered record on freedom of the press, and pardoning of military officers convicted of human rights violations. Although Menem stopped inflation, generated a measure of optimism about the country's economic future, and enjoyed military quiescence from January 1991 to July 1995, his first term in office was far from an unmixed blessing for democratic consolidation.

Chapter 9

Distributive Conflict, Party Institutionalization, and Democracy

This study has analyzed the legacy of personalist leadership, the political tactics of union leaders, and the ebb and flow of party institutionalization in the Peronist movement. These phenomena are linked to Argentina's problems in consolidating democracy. A country's ability to consolidate democracy depends in significant measure on the intensity of distributive conflict among the sectoral elites representing its most powerful class actors, and on the ability of political parties to organize and channel that conflict. The analysis thus far has focused on the latter side of this distributive conflict–party institutionalization equation. It has argued that Perón's plebiscitarianism, partly by strengthening antiparty union factions, left a legacy that impeded Peronist party institutionalization. Weak party institutionalization, in turn, encouraged Peronist union leaders to express their demands through strikes and demonstrations, contributing to a climate of instability propitious for military coups. Moreover, weak party institutionalization diminished the stake of Peronist union leaders in the survival of electoral and legislative institutions, encouraging some of them to support, or refrain from opposing, military coups. The latter consequence was more important than the former. Strikes and demonstrations can contribute to a climate of instability, but they can also serve as alternatives to more destabilizing forms of protest. What most endangers democratic stability is the perception by a critical mass of powerful union leaders that party activity is expendable. By reducing the number of influential people with an instrumental stake in the survival of electoral and legislative activity, the notion that the party is expendable strips democracy of a bulwark it would otherwise enjoy. What matters for democratic stability is not the balance between interest-group and party activity but the degree to which sectoral elites representing powerful class actors have an instrumental stake in some minimum absolute amount of party activity.

Scholars have noted that Argentina became vulnerable to democratic breakdown in the first part of the twentieth century in part because its powerful landowning class lacked enough "captive" peasant votes to establish a political party capable of winning at least a solid position in a fairly elected legislature.[1] In the absence of such a party, landowners never developed a strong instrumental stake in the survival of electoral and legislative activity. This study has advanced a parallel argument about Argentina's working class. Unlike landowners earlier in the century, workers controlled enough votes to sway presidential elections or at least to give a pro-union party a solid position in a fairly elected legislature. Throughout the twentieth century, however, most Argentine workers and union leaders shared collective identities—anarchism, syndicalism, and Peronism—in which party activity was discouraged or neglected. Consequently, workers and union leaders acquired a diminished stake in the survival of electoral and legislative activity.

In countries where unions are weak, it doesn't matter much for democratic consolidation if their ties to parties are also weak, or if the parties to which they are tied are weakly institutionalized. In Colombia, for example, unions have only weak ties to parties, but Colombia's union movement has never been strong enough to be an agent of massive strikes and demonstrations, a key member of a coup coalition, or a decisive defender of democratic institutions against a potential coup.[2] In Argentina, by contrast, unions are powerful, giving them the capacity to play each of these roles. Moreover, they are engaged in unusually intense conflict with other class actors. The first section of this chapter fleshes out the first half of the distributive conflict–party institutionalization explanation for democratic instability, first by showing that unions are more powerful in Argentina than in other Latin American countries, and then by pointing to aspects of social structure that have made conflict between unions and other class actors unusually intense in Argentina. The second section of the chapter contrasts this distributive conflict–party institutionalization explanation to alternative dependency, cultural, policy, and military explanations, and a third section uses the distributive conflict–party institutionalization perspective to assess the prospects for Argentine democracy as of the mid 1990s.

TABLE 9

Labor Force Statistics for Eight Latin American Countries in the 1980s

Country	Population 1986	Economically active population (EAP) 1986	Wage and salary earners 1980s	Urban unemployment 1985	Traditional rural employment 1980	Informal urban employment 1980	Underemployment 1980	Percentage of population in cities of 100,000+	Percentage of population in largest city
Argentina	31,014,000	11,014,000	6,949,832	5.3	6.8	21.4	28.2	57.7	32.9
Brazil	138,403,000	50,675,000	24,188,426	5.3	18.9	16.5	35.4	38.0	7.4
Chile	12,222,000	4,368,000	2,505,919	17.2	7.4	21.7	29.1	52.0	34.2
Colombia	29,310,000	9,424,000	3,521,905	14.1	18.7	22.3	41.0	42.5	14.8
Mexico	80,905,000	26,908,000	8,043,108	4.8	18.4	22.0	40.4	29.8	20.1
Peru	20,199,000	6,380,000	1,818,883	10.1	31.8	19.8	51.6	38.0	26.1
Uruguay	3,035,000	1,180,000	700,940	13.1	8.0	19.0	27.0	41.5	40.0
Venezuela	17,776,000	6,056,000	3,385,121	14.3	12.6	18.5	31.1	52.7	18.1

SOURCES: Population, EAP, Urban unemployment, Population in cities of 100,000+, Population in largest city, Wilkie and Ochoa, Statistical Abstract; Wage and salary earners, EAP times proportion of wage and salary earners in EAP as given in Mesa-Lago, La seguridad social; Traditional rural employment, Informal urban employment, Underemployment, Programa Regional del Empleo, Después de la crisis.

Union Power and Distributive Conflict in Argentina

Unions began to gain strength in Argentina around the turn of the century, and by the mid 1920s, Argentina ranked higher than Brazil, Chile, Colombia, Mexico, Peru, Uruguay, or Venezuela on several factors conducive to the development of strong unions, including factory employment, urbanization, and labor scarcity.[3] As Table 9 indicates, Argentina retained its top ranking on most of these indicators into the 1980s. Of the eight Latin American countries with the longest history of industrial and commercial development, Argentina ranked highest in the 1980s on the proportion of the population in cities of 100,000 or more, and lowest or next-to-lowest on various measures of labor surplus, including urban unemployment, traditional rural employment, and overall underemployment.[4]

Other criteria for assessing union power in various national contexts may be derived from work on advanced industrial countries by David Cameron, Walter Korpi, and John Stephens.[5] Three indicators of labor movement strength appear in the analyses of each author: union density (the unionized proportion of the labor force), organizational centralization (the fewness of national union confederations and the degree of control these confederations exercise over member unions), and political unity (the absence of major partisan or ideological rifts among leading labor organizations). Cameron, Korpi, and Stephens formulated their dimensionalities of union power with an eye to explaining such outcomes as electoral behavior, strike activity, public policy, and economic performance, but the dimensions they identified seem well suited to measuring an aspect of union power likely to affect the prospects for democratic consolidation: the degree to which unions can pose a strong challenge to the dominant classes over the distribution of wealth and income. In general, the greater the unions' power resources, the higher the level of distributive conflict. The higher this level of conflict, in turn, the more democratic consolidation will depend on whether union leaders value party activity as a way of advancing their own and their constituents' interests. If union density is high and the trade union movement is organizationally centralized and politically unified, distributive conflict will be acute, and the degree to which union leaders develop ties to well-institutionalized parties will be crucial to the prospects for democratic consolidation. If the labor movement is weak on one or more of these dimensions, distributive conflict will be more muted, and the degree to which union leaders develop ties to well-institutionalized parties will be less relevant for democratic consolidation.[6]

Union power and democratic consolidation are not necessarily at odds. Distributive conflict will be sharper in countries where unions have significant power resources, simply because the dominant classes also have significant power resources. It does not follow, however, that the sharper this distributive conflict, the harder it will be to consolidate an existing democratic regime, or to move a protodemocratic regime toward a consolidated democracy.[7] If parties are well institutionalized, they will absorb the strain that the higher level of distributive conflict places on regime stability. In certain contexts, moreover, union power may enhance indirectly the quality of democracy. As the findings of Cameron, Korpi, and Stephens all indicate, union power in rich countries is usually associated with more redistributive government policies and more egalitarian economic outcomes. Although such policies and outcomes do not logically entail improvement in the quality of democracy, they empirically promote such improvement by redistributing resources in a manner that encourages more people to participate politically in more ways, at more levels, in a more thoughtful, autonomous, and well-informed fashion. In developing countries, however, union power sometimes has ambiguous implications for the poor. Higher wages for unionized workers can mean fewer jobs for the unemployed, and low food prices can hurt even poorer rural producers.[8] Conversely, anti-inflation programs typically impose high costs on unionized workers, but may have little effect on the very poor, who tend to have benefited little from the controls, subsidies, and services that such programs target for cuts.[9] Strong unions, which seem to promote equity and poverty reduction in industrial countries, do not do so unambiguously in developing nations. Indeed, South Korea and Taiwan, with their weak labor movements, have done better at equity and poverty reduction than Argentina, Brazil, or Mexico, with their stronger labor movements.[10]

Union density—the proportion of the labor force, or alternatively of the "potentially unionizable population," that is organized into unions—is the most widely cited dimension of union power. Writing on advanced capitalist democracies, Michael Wallerstein has argued that "union density is an important—albeit not the only—determinant of union strength in the political arena as well as the market."[11] Alexander Hicks and Duane Swank, also writing on advanced capitalist democracies, have contended that high union density gives unions more resources for electoral campaigns and lobbying, more capacity to disrupt the economy, more power to extract preemptive concessions from government policy makers, and more freedom from free-rider and fragmentation obstacles to collective action.[12] In addition to being theoretically and practically important, union density, a continuous measure ranging from 0 to 100, is handy for quantitative analysis. Advanced capitalist democracies have kept records of union membership and of potentially unionizable population (each measured in a variety of ways) for more than 60 years. Writers on unions in advanced capitalist democracies have published country monographs on the minute details of what constitutes a union and who qualifies as a union member.[13]

Reliable information on union density is more difficult to obtain for Latin America. In countries where communications infrastructure is not well developed and where unions, union confederations, and labor ministries alike are often severely short of money, it is hard to undertake a census of union members. Such problems are aggravated in unions that organize thousands of tiny workplaces, as is the case with many retail trade, teachers', and rural unions, and in unions where employment undergoes severe seasonal fluctuations, as with sugar and construction workers. Moreover, unions in many countries have incentives to make their memberships appear larger than they actually are—for example, to increase their representation in the congresses of a unified labor confederation or to make the membership of one labor confederation look bigger than that of its rivals. Alternatively, or even simultaneously, unions may have incentives to make their memberships look smaller than they actually are—for example, to minimize apparent dues income and thus free up a proportion of actual dues income for uses not sanctioned by law.[14]

These data problems, along with the expansion and contraction of the respective labor movements over the years, may help explain huge discrepancies in existing compilations of union-density estimates for various Latin American countries.[15] Rather than relying on such sources, it is better to derive Latin American union-density figures from country monographs. Table 10 reports union-density figures compiled from a survey of monographs on unions in the eight countries with the longest history of urban industrial and commercial development in Latin America. The figures may not be exact and will doubtless have changed since the year in which they were registered, but they are probably not misleading as to where each country ranked on union density during the 1980s. As is clear from Table 10, Argentina ranked

TABLE 10

Union Membership and Union Structure in Eight Latin American Countries in the 1980s

Country	Union members[a]	Economically active population (EAP)[b]	Wage and salary earners[c]	Union members as % of EAP[d]	Union members as % of wage and salary earners[d]	Dominant pattern of union structure[e]	Number of peak confederations[e]	Separate public/private blue/white collar, etc., confederations[e]	Political conflict within/between peak confederations[e]
Argentina	3,972,000	11,014,000	6,949,832	36.1	57.2	Industry	Single	No	Low-Medium
Brazil	14,678,018	50,675,000	24,188,426	29.0	60.7	Local	Multiple	Not since 1977	Medium
Chile	446,194	4,368,000	2,505,919	10.2	17.8	Firm	Dominant	Not since 1984	Medium
Colombia	873,400	9,424,000	3,521,905	9.3	24.8	Firm/Craft	Multiple	No	Medium-High
Mexico	3,429,813	26,908,000	8,043,108	12.8	42.6	Industry/Local	Dominant	No	Low-Medium
Peru	860,000	6,380,000	1,818,883	13.5	47.3	Firm	Multiple	Pub/Priv	High
Uruguay	246,530	1,180,000	700,940	20.9	35.2	Industry	Single	No	Low-Medium
Venezuela	1,170,000	6,056,000	3,385,121	19.3	34.6	Local/Industry	Dominant	No	Medium

SOURCES: [a] *Union membership (in year)*: Argentina (1986), Godio and Palomino, *El movimiento sindical*, 50 (original data, membership figures submitted by unions to labor ministry in 1986). Brazil (1988), Fundação Instituto Brasilero de Geografia e Estatística, *Anuario estatístico do Brasil*, 1991, 424; figure excludes members of sindicatos comprising employers, autonomous agents, autonomous workers, and liberal professionals, but includes rural (8,314,004) as well as urban (6,364,014) wage earners belonging to sindicatos. Chile (1988), Instituto Nacional de Estadísticas (Chile), *Compendio estadístico*, 1993, 46. Colombia (1984), Botero, "Trade Unions," 119 (original data, Ministerio de Trabajo y Seguridad Social, *Segundo censo nacional sindical*, 1985). Mexico (1975), Zazueta and de la Peña, *La estructura del Congreso del Trabajo*, 389 (original data, unpublished union and government sources). Peru (1985), Haworth, "Political Transition," 213 (original data, Isabel Yepez del Castillo and Jorge Bernedo, *La sindicalización en el Perú* [Lima: Pontificia Universidad Católica, 1986]). Uruguay (1985), Gargiulo, "Uruguayan Labor Movement," 231 (original data, membership lists submitted by unions attending 3d PIT/CNT congress). Venezuela (ca. 1980), Davis and Coleman, "Political Control," 269 n. 12 (original data, Bernard Lestienne, *El sindicalismo venezolano* [Caracas: Centro Gumilla, 1981], 12).

[b] *Economically active population*: Data for 1986 from Wilkie and Ochoa, *Statistical Abstract*.

[c] *Wage and salary earners*: Data for mid 1980s. EAP times proportion of wage and salary earners in EAP as given in Mesa-Lago, *La seguridad social*.

[d] *Union density*: Computed from data in rest of table, as indicated.

[e] *Union structure and confederations*: All evaluations pertain to the mid 1980s. All evaluations done by the author; all based on various sources.

first when the denominator of the union-density quotient was the economically active population and second to Brazil (where many unionists belonged to weak rural organizations) when the denominator was the number of wage and salary earners. On various measures of organizational centralization and political unity, Argentina also ranked at the top of the list. Its unions are organized primarily on the national industrial level rather than on the provincial, municipal, craft, or enterprise levels. The country has only a single umbrella labor confederation, which includes agricultural and industrial workers, blue- and white-collar workers, and public- and private-sector workers alike. Few important unionists in Argentina have claimed to be anything but Peronist, although conflict among factions of Peronist union leaders has often been intense. In short, the characteristics of its labor force and labor organizations leave little room for doubt that Argentina has had Latin America's strongest trade unions during most of the twentieth century.

Class conflict between urban workers and industrial employers is a central feature of Argentine society, as it is of every society that has surpassed a minimal level of industrial development. What is distinctive about Argentina is that urban workers and rural landowners, who rarely interact in the workplace, also stand in a highly antagonistic relationship to each other. Because Argentina's main agricultural products, beef and grain, are land-intensive rather than labor-intensive, the country lacks a large sedentary peasantry. On the one hand, the absence of such a peasantry has diminished the salience of land reform as a political issue and has eliminated the possibility of a peasant-based social revolution. On the other hand, it has deprived Argentina of a social class that, in other countries, has been forced to absorb much of the cost of industrialization. Particularly in late-developing countries, industrial development after a certain point requires large lump-sum investments. To generate a surplus for these investments, a large number of people have to consume less than they would like, and sometimes less than they need to subsist. The Soviet Union under Stalin provides a particularly grim example of the costs of industrialization falling primarily on the peasantry, but the rural poor in Brazil and Mexico have also been forced to relinquish a portion of the surplus they might otherwise have consumed. In the absence of a politically deactivated peasantry, funds for industrialization (and for defense and administration) can come only from abroad or from a surplus that would otherwise accrue to landowners or industrial workers.

In Argentina, both of these classes are powerful and well organized. Hence, more than in most countries, industrialization in Argentina has demanded sacrifices from powerful and politicized class actors, increasing the number and intensity of demands that the party system must organize and channel if democracy is to be consolidated.[16]

A peculiarity of Argentina's ecological endowment and insertion into the world economy has accentuated the conflict between landowners and the urban working class. Argentina's main exports, grain and livestock products, are also the main items of mass consumption. The more these products are exported, the less remains for domestic consumption, which means that workers have to pay more for food. The more these products are consumed at home, the less remains to export, which means that landowners earn less foreign exchange, industrialists run short of funds to pay for imported inputs, and the state finds it harder to prop up the currency. The trade-off between food prices and foreign exchange, which is obvious to many in Argentina's literate and media-voracious population, has intensified conflict between workers and landowners.[17]

Democratic Consolidation in Argentina: Alternative Approaches

The distributive conflict–party institutionalization approach to democratic consolidation holds that a country's ability to consolidate democracy depends on the intensity of distributive conflict among the sectoral elites representing its most powerful class actors, and on the ability of political parties to organize and channel this conflict. The more intense this conflict, or the less proficient the political parties at organizing and channeling it, the weaker the chances for democratic consolidation. The less intense this conflict, or the more proficient the political parties at organizing and channeling it, the better the chances for democratic consolidation. As Adam Przeworski has argued, "if democracy is to be consolidated, distributive conflicts must be institutionalized: all major political forces must channel their economic demands through the democratic institutions and abjure other tactics."[18] Elections and legislatures are the most distinctively democratic institutions, and class actors are more likely to channel demands through them if the sectoral elites who represent them have invested resources in, and become accustomed to, expressing demands through parties.

In Argentina between 1955 and 1983, unions were unusually powerful, contributing to intense conflict over the distribution of wealth and income, but not linked to a well-institutionalized political party (or parties), leaving much of this conflict to be expressed outside the electoral and legislative systems. In this context, unions relied heavily on nonparty channels of interest expression, such as strikes, demonstrations, lobbying, mass media campaigns, and negotiation with military factions. Some of these vehicles for interest expression contributed to climates of instability propitious for military coups. Even more important, because they lacked ties to a well-institutionalized party, union leaders developed a diminished instrumental stake in the survival of the electoral and legislative institutions that parties require to be effective. Military officers thus encountered relatively weak union resistance to their attempts to overthrow these institutions, and anticipating a lack of union resistance, officers were emboldened to intervene.

The distributive conflict–party institutionalization approach coincides both with analyses that trace Argentina's problems in consolidating democracy to the intensity of conflict among its major class actors and with those that trace its problems to the weakness of its party system.[19] Within the context of the former analyses, it considers the power of Argentine workers, and of the union leaders who represent them, as one factor that has made distributive conflict particularly acute in Argentina. Within the context of the literature on the weakness of Argentina's party system, the analysis draws attention to the need to examine not only the interactions among parties (the party system), but also the characteristics of an individual political movement, Peronism, and particularly the views of plebiscitarian leaders and unionists about how expendable Peronist party organization is to achieving political power and shaping public policy. As Mainwaring, O'Donnell, and Valenzuela have pointed out, "if [parties] do not become institutionalized over time, prospects for developing effective mechanisms to express and channel interests are limited, and legitimacy and governability are likely to suffer."[20]

The distributive conflict–party institutionalization perspective on democratic consolidation shares features of Samuel Huntington's approach to political stability. Huntington argues that political stability depends on the balance between social mobilization and political institutionalization. Where social mobilization outpaces political institutionalization, political instability is likely to result. Where the two processes unfold at roughly the same pace, political stability is the probable outcome.[21] The present study, like Huntington's, attributes a political outcome (inability to consolidate democracy) partly to a disjunction between an aspect of social mobilization (the existence of powerful unions) and an aspect of political institutionalization (its absence in Peronist party organization). However, it differs from Huntington's analysis in that the outcome of interest is democracy, not stability; in that it focuses specifically on class-party ties and especially on the institutionalization of individual political parties (rather than on the institutionalization of political processes and organizations in general); and in that it defines institutionalization as infusion with value, not as adaptability, complexity, autonomy, and coherence.

The distributive conflict–party institutionalization approach may be contrasted with alternatives that focus on economic dependency, specific policy decisions at critical junctures, political culture, and the interventionist proclivities of the armed forces. These alternatives in some ways complement rather than contradict the distributive conflict–party institutionalization approach, but neither individually nor taken together do they provide a satisfactory account of Argentina's long-standing inability to consolidate democracy. Dependency and inauspicious policy choices exacerbated social conflict in Argentina, but analyses written from these perspectives generally stop short of explaining why this heightened social conflict blocked the consolidation of a democratic regime. Argentine political culture did not hamper evolution toward democracy before 1930, and it is not too different in broad cross-national perspective from political culture in Uruguay, where democracy flourished for a length of time that was impressive by European as well as Latin American standards. Military intervention can be explained in part by factors specific to the armed forces, but it has only occurred in Argentina after powerful civilian elites became exasperated with civilian political actors. A look at some of the most influential analyses written from these other perspectives reveals gaps in the explanation of the vicissitudes of Argentine democracy that the distributive conflict–party institutionalization approach helps to fill in.

The dependency approach holds that the way in which a country was, and is, incorporated into the world capitalist system is the most important factor shaping its economic and political development. A fine dependency analysis focusing specifically on Argentina is Juan Corradi's *The Fitful Republic*. In Corradi's view, Argentina's late-nineteenth-century incorporation into the world economy as a producer of agricultural exports continued to shape the country's political development long after Argentina took on the trappings of a modern society. "The resilience of the original agro-pecuarian structure," Corradi writes, "proved to be a decisive limiting factor with long-term political consequences."[22] Corradi's analysis lies within the historical-structural dependency school pioneered by Fernando Cardoso and Enzo Faletto, which emphasizes the distinctiveness of each concrete case of national dependency and stresses that international forces work their effects through partly autonomous struggles among domestic political actors. The historical-structural dependency school may be distinguished from the development-of-underdevelopment school pioneered by André Gunder Frank, which stresses processes common to all situations of dependency.[23] Both the historical-structural and development-of-underdevelopment perspectives differ in turn from what might be called the dependency-testing approach, which uses statistical techniques or systematic qualitative comparisons to seek out correlations between levels and/or types of dependency and hypothesized outcomes of dependency.[24]

Underlying the differences (and sharp polemics) among these dependency schools are the different purposes toward which each is directed. The goal of the historical-structural school, in whose tradition Corradi writes, is to highlight the distinctiveness of each dependent society; the goal of the development of underdevelopment school is to defend lawlike generalizations about dependency by illustrating their plausibility in a range of cases; and the goal of the dependency-testing school is to determine the truth or falsity of such lawlike generalizations by systematic analysis of similarities and differences among cases.[25] Like Cardoso, Corradi laments the identification of the dependency perspective with the development-of-underdevelopment and dependency-testing schools.

What had originally been a critical perspective, a fluid attempt to analyze the establishment and disestablishment of alliances between historical actors, was turned progressively into a "theory" of the international system from which changes in local social structures were derived. . . . The more systemic the approach has been, the more impoverished the resulting diagnosis. The time has come to descend from the heights of "dependency" to the concrete examination of "dependent societies," that is, to the inspection of historical modes of development, of the specific manner in which societies act upon themselves and are acted on by other, more powerful societies.[26]

Proponents of the historical-structural dependency school might well acknowledge that Taiwan, South Korea, Brazil, and Mexico—all countries that would rank high on many measures of dependency— have experienced rapid economic growth and diversification of the productive structure, progress toward the amelioration of poverty, and advances toward more democratic political forms. They might also acknowledge that Argentina's heaviest dependence on external trade and investment coincided with a period of rapid economic growth and gradual political democratization (1880–1930); that the introduction of high tariff barriers and state-led industrialization co-incided with a period of slower growth and increasingly harsh forms of authoritarianism (1930–1980); and that Canada and Australia have performed better economically and politically than Argentina despite the fact that all three countries were incorporated into the world capi-talist system at more or less the same time and in more or less the same way. Most proponents of the historical-structural dependency school would argue, however, that such broad and abstract compari-sons are ham-fisted and ahistorical. The effects of dependency on the economic and political structure, they would point out, depend on highly distinctive forms of dependency that exist in each country dur-ing a particular period of historical time—and are in any case thor-oughly mediated by partially autonomous episodes of conflict and collaboration among domestic social actors. The effects of dependency on political form, the historical-structural writers would contend, are complex, indirect, and contingent on the shifting outcomes of conflict and collaboration among social classes and class fractions both within and outside the country.

The historical-structural approach to the relationship between de-pendency and political evolution is more plausible than one based on mechanical assertions about levels of dependency and political form. There is some question, however, as to how far the historical-structural approach takes us beyond a description of various aspects of a coun-try's economic and political development, informed by the not terribly contentious proposition that the international economy has had im-portant effects on that development.[27] If a work is to be explanatory rather than descriptive, it is necessary at some point to make rea-sonably clear causal assertions of the type that seem to annoy some proponents of the historical-structural dependency school. Some such proponents might well respond that a subtle and sensitively interpre-tive historical description is as useful as any explanation that could possibly be derived from a small number of dubiously defined out-comes shaped by an enormous array of causal forces. But critics of the historical-structural school might then reiterate that the more subtle and sensitive a dependency interpretation becomes, the less it remains a dependency interpretation. In the case of Corradi's analysis, for example, they might point out that by the time the resilience of the agropecuarian structure has been linked to Argentina's political decay, it has been relegated to the status of a broad conditioning factor whose effects are mediated through processes only distally related to Argentina's specific situation of dependency. In Corradi's view:

Argentina has been built like a palimpsest of half-concluded projects. . . . With the end of a prosperous society based on agrarian exports, a new industrial structure grew, and when it faltered in turn, modern enclaves of growth developed around transnational investments. As with the accretion of strata in the history of a geological formation, none of these societal forms managed to displace the others entirely. . . . each of the successive societal forms was able to give rise to a dense network of interests and to a deeply entrenched mode of life. . . . Because each of these sectors is highly mobilized, each can defend its particular interests in an articulate manner against the others. . . . too weak to lead, each group is still strong enough to prevent any other from doing so. . . . Things return to where they started, namely, to the erratic behavior of a malfunctioning political system.[28]

The survival of the agro-export model and the power of the class to which most of its benefits accrue holds a central place in Corradi's analysis of Argentina's political decay, as it does in this study. But even if this factor alone took us a considerable distance toward explaining the vicissitudes of Argentine democracy, it would have to be recognized that the power of Argentina's landowning class is due not only to the way in which the country was incorporated into the world capitalist system but also to the extraordinary fertility of the soil of the Pampas region, to the geographical concentration of the agro-export producers, to the early resolution (as compared, for example, to Brazil) of conflicts among landowning elites, and to other factors not easily linked to dependency in any reasonably specific sense of the term. Moreover, the struggles between the landowning class and other classes, to which Corradi rightly attributes much of the responsibility for Argentina's political instability, have certainly been intensified by changes in the world economy and by Argentina's recurrent balance-of-payments crises, but they have also been sharpened by the conflict between Peronism and anti-Peronism and by other factors whose attribution to dependency would expand the meaning of the term to the point where it would no longer designate a distinctive analytical approach.

It is important to note that nondependency factors have exacerbated social conflict in Argentina, but even more important to recognize that powerful and politicized social actors locked in bitter conflict with one another do not invariably mire a country in political instability and authoritarianism. The lack of direct correspondence between level of distributive conflict and likelihood of democratic breakdown is particularly clear from the case of Sweden in the 1910s and 1920s, where workers and employers battled each other with dramatic strikes and lockouts but political parties remained valued instruments of class action. As the Swedish case suggests, even high levels of political conflict are compatible with democracy as long as political parties are recognized as important vehicles for political demands. By contrast, in Weimar Germany, Giolittian Italy, and Third Republic France, where industrial conflict was less severe than in Sweden, but where large segments of the population began in the 1920s and 1930s to disparage parties and politicians, democracy broke down. Similarly, Linz notes that the world depression of the 1930s created more unemployment in Norway and the Netherlands than in Germany or Austria, and argues that "the degree of institutional legitimacy was more decisive than the economic crisis" in determining whether democracy survived or broke down in European countries between the wars.[29] Among the various factors that may contribute to the valuation of political parties, the specific situation of dependency in which a country finds itself is not likely to loom as anything more than a broad and remote conditioning factor. Corradi's work succeeds as an insightful and provocative interpretation of Argentina's "swings between tyranny and tumult" in part because it goes beyond a dependency analysis to incorporate other factors, particularly cultural and political-institutional ones.

The types of factors to which dependency analyses call attention are, in short, better at explaining levels of distributive conflict than at explaining the degree to which political institutions are capable of organizing and channeling that conflict. A similar imbalance in explanatory power affects Carlos Waisman's *Reversal of Development in Argentina*. Waisman links Argentina's problems in consolidating democracy to specific policy decisions made by Perón, although his analysis, like Corradi's, also incorporates a range of economic, political, and cultural factors. Specifically, Waisman attributes Argentina's "failure to become an industrial democracy" to the unintended consequences of two of Perón's policies: radical protectionism for industries oriented toward the internal market, which allocated resources inefficiently and led to slow economic growth during the period after Perón's overthrow, and the creation of a state corporatist apparatus for the control of labor, which increased the mobilizational capacity of the labor movement, exacerbating real and perceived political polarization and feeding back into slow economic growth.[30]

In explaining the origins of Perón's policies, Waisman calls attention to "internal structural factors (the land-labor ratio and labor supply), the changing position of Argentina in the international system (as a consequence of depression and war), political processes (the autonomy of the state), and ideological-cognitive ones (the fear of revolution by a sector of the state elite at a crucial juncture in Argentine development)."[31] But in explaining the consequences of radical protectionism and labor corporatism for the instability and authoritarianism of the post-1955 period, Waisman focuses almost exclusively on the intervening variables of labor empowerment and economic stagnation. He argues, quite rightly, that labor empowerment and economic stagnation did much to contribute to a real and perceived situation of zero-sum politics. Such a situation, however, is a supportive but not sufficient condition for the failure to consolidate democracy. A more complete explanation for the political instability and authoritarianism of the post-1955 period requires the kind of analysis of the political sphere that Waisman employs so persuasively in tracing the origins of Perón's policies. The image of politicized class actors using powerful corporate organizations to fight for a share of an inadequately growing economic pie depicts a society experiencing high levels of distributive conflict, but does not explain why political parties proved so ineffective at organizing and channeling that conflict.

In *Reversal of Development* and other works, Waisman mentions the weakness of political parties during the post-Perón period and suggests that an increase in the power of political parties vis-à-vis interest groups would contribute to democratic consolidation in contemporary Argentina.[32] Such insights need, however, to be linked more explicitly to the theoretical framework that informs the rest of the analysis. Waisman identifies some important causes of Argentina's high levels of distributive conflict, but to get at the reasons this conflict led to political instability and authoritarianism in the post-Perón period, one would have to explain why political parties proved incapable of organizing and channeling it. That in turn would require taking fuller account of a third crucial political decision made by Perón: his creation of a weak and subservient political party incapable of surviving the post-

1955 anti-Peronist repression, and his efforts from exile to undermine the construction of a stronger Peronist party. Waisman's goal, as stated in the first sentence of his influential work, is to explain Argentina's failure to become a modern industrial democracy. This specification of what needs to be explained, however, obscures the possibility that the factors that have prevented Argentina from becoming a modern industrial society overlap with, but are not identical to, those which have kept it from becoming a stable political democracy.

Whereas Corradi emphasizes dependency and Waisman stresses specific policy decisions, a third set of explanations for Argentina's problems in consolidating democracy highlights the role of political culture. There is considerable diversity within the political culture perspective. Some analyses stress the political culture of elite groups, others the political culture of the broader population. Some suggest that Argentine political culture derives mainly from Spanish colonial rule; others view it as a product of an interaction between corporative Iberian and liberal northern European legacies. Some argue that the aspect of political culture that generates authoritarianism and political instability is contentiousness and unwillingness to compromise; others put the emphasis on a lack of commitment to democratic institutions, particularly elections.[33] It is impossible to do justice here to the diversity of arguments advanced from within the political culture perspective, but some general problems with the perspective should be pointed out. First, as Waisman has pointed out, because political culture changes more slowly than other aspects of a society, it has difficulty in explaining why Argentina was relatively prosperous, politically stable, and increasingly democratic from 1880 to 1930, and then declined economically, experienced political instability, and became increasingly authoritarian from 1930 to 1980.[34] Second, all variants of the cultural perspective would have trouble explaining why Uruguay, whose culture is not dissimilar to Argentina's, should have displayed throughout the twentieth century a degree of democracy and political stability that exceeded Argentina's and compared very favorably to that of many European nations.

Broad-based political-culture explanations for Argentine authoritarianism and political instability do not hold up well under cross-national and over-time scrutiny. To account for variation across countries and over time, proponents of such explanations would have to argue that the Iberian heritage is a sort of "spigot variable" that shuts off in some countries but not in others, and at certain times but not at others.[35] It may be possible to identify factors that promote or inhibit the expression of Iberian cultural inheritance, but to the extent that one is interested in accounting for cross-national differences in the political development of Latin American countries, or for changes over time in the political development of a single Latin American country, these promoting and inhibiting factors, once specified, would have to be elevated to a causal status as important as that of the Iberian heritage. Argentina, Chile, and Uruguay clearly share similarities in political development that distinguish them as a group from Denmark, Norway and Sweden; Kenya, Tanzania, and Uganda; or China, Korea, and Taiwan.[36] But whereas broad political culture explanations may well be helpful in explaining differences in political development between groups of countries, they are less useful for explaining differences within the groups—even recognizing that political culture is far from uniform throughout the Southern Cone, Scandinavia, East Africa, or East Asia.

Developments within the armed forces constitute a fourth explanation for the political instability and authoritarianism that has plagued Argentina for much of the twentieth century. Darío Cantón and Emilio Mignone have stressed the turn-of-the-century professionalization of the Argentine army and isolation of officers in Prussian-style training centers as an important building block for subsequent military intervention, and Mignone has argued that reducing the officers' isolation from the rest of society would contribute to democratic stability.[37] Robert Potash has suggested that changes within the armed forces between 1930 and 1945—the doubling in size of the officer corps, the tripling of the number of enlistees, the emergence of military-run factories, and War College training for officers—increased the post-1945 political assertiveness of military leaders and augmented their confidence in their ability to handle national affairs.[38] In explaining the implantation of bureaucratic-authoritarian regimes in Latin America in the 1960s and 1970s, Alfred Stepan and Guillermo O'Donnell have called attention to the emergence in many Latin American militaries of a national-security doctrine that focused military attention on internal rather than external threats, and of a "new professionalism" that broadened the scope of public affairs in which the military felt entitled and competent to take an interest.[39]

The proximate cause of the breakdown of civilian rule in Argentina has, indeed, invariably been a military coup. But as most of the authors cited in the preceding paragraph have themselves pointed out, the causes of these coups lie primarily with developments in the broader society and only secondarily with changes in the armed forces. Although Stepan and O'Donnell have stressed the importance of the national-security doctrine, Stepan has argued that better leadership by President João Goulart might have averted the 1964 coup in Brazil, and O'Donnell, in explaining the onset of military rule in various South American countries during the 1960s and 1970s, has placed less weight on the national-security doctrine than on broader societal factors like economic bottlenecks, the mobilization of the popular sector, and the emergence of technocratic roles.[40] Potash has argued that the six military coups against Argentine civilian governments between 1930 and 1976 were "more an indication of the failures of the civil sector to stand united in defense of constitutional government than of military lust for power."[41] For Rouquié, it is "in society as a whole, in its divisions, conflicts, and contradictions, that one must look for the origins of military power."[42] More generally, as Samuel Huntington has noted, "the susceptibility of a political system to military intervention varies inversely with the strength of its political parties . . . military coups do not destroy parties, they ratify the deterioration that has already occurred."[43] For each of these analysts, the fundamental causes of democratic breakdown lie outside the armed forces—notably in the strength of a country's political parties and in the willingness of a country's citizens to defend democracy when it comes under threat.

The objections to the four alternative perspectives just outlined can be summarized as follows. Economic dependency and Perón's policies toward industry and labor may help to explain why Argentina has experienced high levels of distributive conflict, but they are less effective in explaining why the country's political parties have been ill equipped to organize and channel it. Broad political culture perspectives may be helpful in explaining similarities between Argentina's political development and that of other countries with comparable cultural traditions, but they are less effective in explaining cross-temporal or cross-national variation among cases where political culture is roughly constant or similar. (If political culture is defined more narrowly to refer to the attitudes of sectoral elites toward the expendability of party organization, however, the present analysis may be said to have been written partly from a political-culture perspective.) Finally, the military's propensity to intervene probably depends less on factors specific to the military institution than on broader developments in society as a whole, and, in particular, on the ability of political parties to organize and channel distributive conflict.

Party Institutionalization and Democratic Consolidation in the 1990s

All of the Peronist party-building projects analyzed in this book have failed, and their failures have made it harder for Argentina to consolidate democracy. Perón's defeat of Vandor's project during Illia's government contributed to the 1966 coup, and the collapse of the antiverticalist project during Isabel Perón's administration facilitated the military intervention of 1976. Menem's victory over the renewal Peronists, culminating in his takeover and marginalization of the Partido Justicialista, extended Peronism's weak party institutionalization into the 1990s, perpetuating aspects of movementism and reducing incentives for union leaders to develop a stronger stake in the survival of electoral and legislative activity. In this situation, it is premature to suggest that, as of the mid 1990s, Argentine democracy was consolidated.[44]

Important consequences follow from the incompleteness of democratic consolidation in Argentina. Where democracy is not consolidated, its quality and stability suffer. Although an unconsolidated democracy cannot, by definition, fall short of the procedural minimum, its ability to move beyond this threshold is limited. Only after democracy has become the "only game in town," as Juan Linz characterized consolidation, does it acquire much potential to improve sustainably in breadth (with more people participating in a wider variety of ways), depth (with such participation becoming better informed, more thoughtful, and more autonomous), or range (with democratic practices spreading to subnational and nonstate institutions).[45] Moreover, unconsolidated democracies are more vulnerable to collapse than consolidated democracies. Unless democracy becomes widely accepted as the only game in town, political actors will think up contingency plans to deal with the possibility of its breakdown. Such plans embolden existing antidemocratic actors and promote the emergence of new ones.

Democracy can break down through foreign invasion, mass insurrection, a military coup, or erosion from within by an incumbent leader. In Argentina in the mid 1990s, foreign invasion and mass insurrection are unforeseeable. A military coup is possible, but three factors make it unlikely. First, the human rights violations and economic and military failures of the 1976–83 dictatorship have made most people intolerant of military intervention. Second, the collapse of communism in the Soviet Union and its allies has stripped credibility from the classic military argument that the danger of a communist takeover justifies the implantation of a military dictatorship. Third, in the climate of democratization that, despite setbacks, pervades Latin America in the mid 1990s, a military coup would make Argentina an international pariah. Memories fade, however, and the international climate is tempestuous. At best, these impediments to a military coup place Argentine democracy in what Geoffrey Pridham calls a state of "negative consolidation," in which protagonists of nondemocratic alternatives are neutralized.[46] A firmer basis for democratic stability and deepening is what Pridham calls "positive consolidation," a long-term shift in attitudes that helps to settle and legitimate democracy. Positive consolidation would benefit considerably from the institutionalization of the PJ. By giving Peronist union leaders a stronger instrumental stake in the survival of electoral and legislative activity, the institutionalization of the PJ would make democracy more resilient.

The other plausible scenario for democratic breakdown in Argentina would involve its erosion from within by an incumbent leader. In this scenario, a fairly elected head of government, or perhaps some other high-level official, would rig elections (as Juan Perón did in Argentina in 1951); allow the military or analogous actors into key policy-making positions (as Juan María Bordaberry did in Uruguay in 1973); dissolve or render impotent the legislature and judiciary (as Alberto Fujimori did in Peru in 1992); preside over widespread, severe, and systematic violations of human rights (as Vinicio Cerezo did in Guatemala after 1985); or abrogate the constitution and establish a dictatorship (as Adolf Hitler did in Germany in 1933). As of 1996, Menem had not crossed any of these lines. Although he issued self-serving proposals for electoral reform and pushed through a constitutional amendment to permit his own immediate reelection, the electoral reform proposals languished, the constitutional amendment was implemented legally, and no widespread electoral irregularities occurred during his 1989–95 presidency. Menem pardoned military officers convicted of human rights violations, publicly defended the dirty war, restored the military's role in "internal security," raised the budget of the state intelligence secretariat (SIDE), and inserted personnel from the 1976–83 military regime into several state agencies,[47] but he also quashed a military uprising, abolished the draft, and reduced the military budget. Menem ruled by decree and stacked the supreme court, but he did not close down congress or fire most of the country's judges. Menem responded lackadaisically to numerous, severe, and apparently systematic physical attacks on journalists critical of his government, but Argentina retained a free and active press during his first term in office, and extralegal violence by state-linked groups, although not entirely absent, was much less prevalent than in Brazil, Colombia, Guatemala, Mexico, or Peru.[48]

Although Menem's political shenanigans did not destroy Argentine democracy, they did little to promote its consolidation. By making electoral, legislative, and judicial procedures seem less enduring, fair, and relevant, Menem during his first term in office impeded the growth of democratic values, habits, and practices. If memories of the 1976–83 dictatorship fade, or if international conditions shift, Argentina could again become vulnerable to a military coup, or to the destruction of democracy from within by an elected president. In such a situation, a better-institutionalized PJ would serve as an important bulwark for democracy. Argentine union leaders are weaker than they were during the 1960s and 1970s, but they retain sufficient power to provide a formidable deterrent to a military coup or to a project of executive arrogation.[49] Should electoral and legislative institutions be threatened, the institutionalization of the PJ would give union leaders a stronger incentive to come to their defense. Prospects for the institutionalization of the PJ remain uncertain, however. As long as Peronism survives as a collective identity, some of its adherents will try to institutionalize its party structures, while others will defend its configuration as a plebiscitarian movement. Only if the pro-party forces win a decisive victory can democracy become consolidated in Argentina.

Reference Matter

Notes

1. Selznick, *Leadership in Administration*, 16–17.
2. Sartori, *Parties and Party Systems*, 3–4, 39–47. According to Sartori (p. 43), communist, Nazi, and fascist parties (which certainly can be effective under authoritarian regimes, although they have often been eclipsed by personalistic leaders) might better be termed "party-like organizational weapons."
3. Scott Mainwaring and Timothy R. Scully make a compelling argument that democratic consolidation in Latin America depends heavily on the institutionalization of party systems, but pay less attention to the institutionalization of individual parties. Mainwaring and Scully, "Introduction: Party Systems in Latin America."
4. Diamond and Linz, "Introduction: Politics, Society, and Democracy in Latin America," 21, 23.
5. On movementism in Argentina, see Cavarozzi, "Los partidos argentinos," and Rock, "Political Movements in Argentina." National movements like Peronism should be distinguished from social movements like the civil rights movement, just as parties as "parts" should be distinguished from totalitarian parties. Commonalities exist between the members of each of these pairings, but the differences are significant enough to make it dangerous to employ similar frameworks for interpreting their dynamics. Hence, although Peronism shares the four empirical properties of social movements identified by Sidney Tarrow (*Power in Movement*, 3–6)—collective challenge to the status quo, common purpose, solidarity, and sustained action against antagonists—it differs from, say, the U.S. civil rights movement in two important respects: it is more tightly organized (thanks primarily to its embeddedness in trade union structures) and it seeks explicitly to place its leaders in top state decision-making posts.
6. Sartori, *Parties and Party Systems*, ch. 1, esp. 26–27.
7. Guillermo O'Donnell has encapsulated some of these abuses of incumbency in the phrase "delegative democracy." See O'Donnell, "Delegative Democracy."

8. In a comparative analysis of postcommunist states in eastern Europe, Joan Nelson has noted a similar connection between party-system effectiveness and the propensity of unions to express their broad political demands through large-scale strikes. "While the evolving party systems in Poland and Hungary offered major portions of the union movement new channels for responsible participation in legislatures and governments, the failure of workable party systems to emerge in some other countries contributed to much more aggressive and disruptive patterns of direct political action. In Romania in particular, weak and ineffective government and confused and rapidly shifting party politics have perpetuated—perhaps intensified—the use of large-scale strikes to demand specific government action." Nelson, "Labor and Business Roles in Dual Transitions," 163.

9. On the general theme of veto politics leading to coups, see Valenzuela, "Democratic Consolidation," 68–69.

10. O'Donnell, *Bureaucratic Authoritarianism*; W. C. Smith, *Authoritarianism*; Manzetti, *Institutions*, chs. 7 and 8.

11. Burton, Gunther, and Higley, "Introduction: Elite Transformations and Democratic Regimes," 8–9. In the early 1960s, a number of Argentine journalists, intellectuals, and politicians took a similar approach to that of the above-mentioned authors, referring to the organizations from which these sectoral elites come as "power factors" in society. In this perspective, power factors are social actors who (1) have "permanent roots" in society, (2) are able to formulate their own goals, (3) seek to influence national decisions, and (4) have enough power to constrain policy decisions by their mere presence. Discussions of the "power factor" concept may be found in Bidart Campos, *Grupos de presión*, esp. 64–67, and Imaz, "Factores de poder." Charles Anderson's notion of "power contender" is also similar to the power factor concept. Anderson, *Politics and Economic Change*, 90–91.

12. Similar definitions of *party* are to be found in Sartori, *Parties and Party Systems*, 64; Collier and Collier, *Shaping the Political Arena*, 787; Mainwaring and Scully, "Introduction," 2.

13. Selznick, *Leadership in Administration*, 17–19, emphasis in original. For a similar view of institutionalization applied specifically to political parties, see Weiner, "Political Participation," 194.

14. Huntington, *Political Order in Changing Societies*, 12.

15. Ibid., 15.

16. Jepperson,"Institutions, Institutional Effects, and Institutionalism," 149. Peronist party organization would be poorly institutionalized according to Jepperson's definition as well, because it has played a very limited role in empowering and constraining Peronist union leaders and plebiscitarian presidents, and because such actors have considered party organization to be expendable, rather than taking it for granted.

17. Archer, "Party Strength and Weakness," 170.

18. The first phrase is taken from Diamond and Linz, "Introduction," 23;

the next three are from Canitrot and Sigal, "Economic Reform, Democracy, and the Crisis of the State in Argentina," 115, 129.

19. Mainwaring and Scully, "Introduction," 16; Mainwaring, "Brazil," 354; Conaghan, "Politicians Against Parties," 435.

20. W. B. Gallie regards democracy as an "essentially contested concept." Debates about the meaning of such concepts are, in Gallie's view, "not resolvable by argument of any kind," because the contending positions are each "sustained by perfectly respectable arguments and evidence" (Gallie, "Essentially Contested Concepts," 169). Stephanie Lawson argues convincingly, however, that treating democracy as an "essentially contested concept" requires one to accept the position that no definition of democracy is ultimately better than any other—a stance that "renders the concept of democracy practically and ethically unintelligible" ("Conceptual Issues," 190–91). For a different interpretation of the implications of Gallie's position, see Mason, "On Explaining Political Disagreement."

21. Bollen, "Political Democracy," 9–15, argues that democracy is best viewed as continuous, but that discrete (ordinal) indicators may be used to measure the degree of democracy present in an actual political system. It is not clear, however, how this solution would permit us to characterize an obviously dictatorial regime as nondemocratic.

22. This definition is based on Dahl's definition of polyarchy (*Democracy and Its Critics*, 221) as amended by Schmitter and Karl ("What Democracy Is . . . and Is Not," 81–82).

23. The concepts of breadth, depth, and range come from Cohen, *Democracy*, 8–27.

24. Linz, "Transitions to Democracy," 158. Compatible definitions of democratic consolidation may be found in Mainwaring, O'Donnell, and Valenzuela, "Introduction," 3; O'Donnell, "Transitions, Continuities, and Paradoxes," 48–49; Valenzuela, "Democratic Consolidation," 69–70; and Burton, Higley, and Gunther, "Introduction: Elite Transformations and Democratic Regimes," 3.

25. For a forceful argument that adversarial politics and an active press contribute to the satisfaction of economic needs, see Drèze and Sen, *Hunger and Public Action*, esp. 276, and Sen, "Freedoms and Needs."

26. Panebianco, *Political Parties: Organization and Power*, 50.

27. "Perón's personalism produced a permanent demotion of the party and parliamentary channels of political expression" (Cavarozzi, "Political Cycles in Argentina," 22).

28. E.g., Butler, "Charisma, Migration, and Elite Coalescence"; Horowitz, *Three Worlds of Development*, 323–26.

29. Weber, *Economy and Society*, 1112, 1132.

30. Madsen and Snow's analysis of Peronism as a charismatic movement shows more convincingly than previous studies that many of Perón's initial supporters were migrants to big cities. Madsen and Snow, *Charismatic Bond*. Most of the previous studies are collected in Mora y Araujo and Llorente, eds., *El voto peronista*.

31. See esp. Germani, *Política y sociedad*, ch. 9; Fillol, *Social Factors in Economic Development* 83; Baily, *Labor, Nationalism, and Politics*, 82; Butler, "Charisma, Migration, and Elite Coalescence," 429.

32. Halperín Donghi, "Algunas observaciones"; Kenworthy, "Interpretaciones ortodoxas"; Little, "Popular Origins of Peronism."

33. Collier and Collier, *Shaping the Political Arena*, 95–99.

34. O'Donnell, *Modernization and Bureaucratic-Authoritarianism*, 167–92.

35. Against the "impossible game" thesis, Eugenio Kvaternik has argued that no inexorable force prevented the two wings of the recently divided Unión Cívica Radical from banding together to defeat the Peronists in fair elections. From a perspective closer to the one taken here, Catalina Smulovitz has argued that no such force ruled out the "silent integration" into the political system of a Peronism less explicitly dependent on Perón. In general, as authors from Albert Hirschman to Juan Linz to Youssef Cohen have argued, one should not jump too quickly to the conclusion that difficult political or economic problems are impossible to resolve. Kvaternik, "Sobre partidos y democracia"; Smulovitz, "En busca de la formula perdida"; Hirschman, *Journeys Toward Progress*, 1–7; Linz, *Crisis, Breakdown, and Reequilibration*, 1–13; Cohen, *Radicals, Reformers, and Reactionaries*, 54.

36. Cavarozzi, "Peronism and Radicalism," 147.

37. I am indebted to Guillermo O'Donnell for suggesting that I use the term *loopholes* in this context.

38. Torre, "El proceso político interno," 62–63; Epstein, "Control and Cooptation," 458.

39. Waltz, *Theory of International Politics* 102–28. Avery Goldstein notes parallels between Waltz's balance-of-power model and the "paradox of the initially strongest" identified by William Gamson and William Riker and discussed by Barbara Hinkley. Like Goldstein's balance-of-power model of Chinese politics during the Cultural Revolution, Andrew Nathan's factionalism model of politics in the Chinese Communist Party is similar in many respects to that used here to model the factional struggles of Peronist union leaders. Goldstein, *From Bandwagon to Balance of Power*, 36; Hinkley, "Initially Strongest Player"; Nathan, "Factionalism Model," esp. 45–52.

40. Portantiero, "Clases dominantes y crisis política," 82–84; O'Donnell, "State and Alliances"; Sidicaro, "Poder y crisis," 66–70; Corradi, *Fitful Republic*, 113; W. C. Smith, *Authoritarianism*, 47.

CHAPTER 2

1. Díaz Alejandro, *Essays*, 1–3.   2. Flichman, *La renta del suelo*, 74–78.

3. Rock, *Argentina, 1516–1982*, 168.   4. Rennie, *Argentine Republic*, 120–27.

5. Waisman, *Reversal of Development*, 5.

6. Cardoso and Faletto, *Dependency and Development*, xix, 66–73; O'Donnell, "State and Alliances," 4; Bergquist, *Labor in Latin America*, 12.

7. Rock, *Argentina, 1516–1982*, 154.

8. O'Donnell, "State and Alliances," 6 and *Bureaucratic Authoritarianism*, 141.

9. Imaz, *Los que mandan*, 129–31, 242–48.

10. Schvarzer, "Estructura y comportamiento," 16. On the origins of the SRA, see M. L. de Palomino, "Tradición y poder," 20–25; Cúneo, *Comportamiento y crisis*, 33–41; Imaz, *Los que mandan*, 105–10.

11. Balestra and Ossona, *Qué son los partidos provinciales*, 61; Romero, *History of Argentine Political Thought*, 156–59; Rock, *Argentina, 1516–1982*, 130–31.

12. Duverger (*Political Parties*, 62–71). As Natalio Botana puts it, the PAN was "not an organization for mobilizing the population, but an instrument used by regional oligarchies to communicate among themselves" ("La reforma política de 1912," 237; see also Botana, *El orden conservador*, 224, 245 n. 4). On the PAN's nominations and *acuerdos*, see Rock, *Politics in Argentina*, 27 and Botana, *El orden conservador*, 66–71, 114.

13. Ferrero, "Los fraudes electorales," describes the vote-rigging techniques of the era.

14. Argentina's 1853 constitution imposed no property, income, or literacy qualifications on the right to vote. An 1857 electoral law explicitly granted suffrage to all males over 21 years of age, with the exception of illiterate deaf-mutes, clerics, felons, and low-ranking military personnel. Sábato and Palti, "¿Quién votaba?" 400, 415–16. Voter turnout in this era is discussed in ibid., 400; Cantón, *Elecciones y partidos políticos*, 45; and E. Gallo, "Argentina: Society and Politics," 378. On the expansion of the suffrage in European countries, see Bendix, *Nation-Building and Citizenship*, 112–22, and Lipset, "Radicalism or Reformism."

15. For a categorization of the conservative factions of the period, see P. Smith, *Argentina and the Failure of Democracy*, 136.

16. The first national army was created in 1862; it expanded in size and skill during the war with Paraguay (1865–70) and gradually eliminated the provincial militias. Lynch, "River Plate Republics," 355; Balestra and Ossona, *Qué son los partidos provinciales*, 61; Ferrer, "Armed Forces," 39, 66–68.

17. Cavarozzi, "Los partidos argentinos," 3–4.

18. Dahl, *Political Oppositions*, preface.

19. Rock, *Politics in Argentina*, 41–45; Snow, *Argentine Radicalism*, 9–11; Rennie, *Argentine Republic*, 185. Romero claims that workers also attended the meetings that founded the Unión Cívica Radical (*History of Argentine Political Thought*, 210). Although similar in name to secularist parties in Chile and in Europe, the UCR was not anticlerical: it even drew some who objected to the PAN's decisions during the 1880s to allow civil marriages and to end religious instruction in public schools.

20. Gallo and Sigal, "La formación," 163.

21. Quotation from Snow, *Argentine Radicalism*, 9; information on economic issues from Remmer, *Party Competition*, 89.

22. Rock, *Politics in Argentina*, 50–51.

23. Whitaker, *Argentina*, 68.

24. Romero, *History of Argentine Political Thought*, 212.

25. The printers' union grew out of a mutual aid society that had been formed in 1857. On the first strike and initial attempts to form union confederations, see Iscaro, *Historia del movimiento sindical*, 46–47 and 76–101. Employment in manufacturing, crafts, construction, public utilities, and mining rose from 167,000 in 1895 to 410,000 in 1914. Tornquist & Co., *Economic Development*, 11–13. For an overview in English of the early history of the Argentine labor movement, see Munck, Falcón, and Gallitelli, *Argentina*, 12–56.

26. In 1914, 62 percent of male employees in manufacturing, crafts, construction, public utilities, and mining were foreign-born (Tornquist & Co., *Economic Development*, 11–13). Immigrants were allowed to apply for citizenship after two years' residence in Argentina, but few chose to do so. In 1914, only 2 percent of foreign residents of Buenos Aires applied for citizenship; the figure for the rest of the country was 1 percent. Among the reasons why such a small percentage of foreign-born males sought citizenship may have been their emotional ties to the old country, coupled with the irrelevance of citizenship to economic opportunity (Germani, "Mass Immigration," 315–16). After the 1912 electoral reforms, a third disincentive to naturalization emerged: registering to vote meant registering for the draft. The new voter registration list was compiled on the basis of a list indicating who was eligible for military conscription (Ferrero, *Los fraudes electorales*, 52).

27. Walter, *Socialist Party*, 90.

28. Spalding, "Aspects of Change in Argentina," 84.

29. Oved, "El anarquismo," 260. The FOA included socialists as well as anarchists.

30. Oved, "El anarquismo," 337–39; Iscaro, *Historia del movimiento sindical*, 142–46. One of the many curious legal initiatives of the 1976–83 dictatorship was to restore the Ley de Residencia. Gallitelli and Thompson, "La situación laboral," 147.

31. Marotta, *El movimiento sindical*, 2: 71–77.

32. On Sáenz Peña's reformism see Botana, "La reforma política de 1912," 238–39.

33. Analyses of the legislative debates that preceded the reforms show that the conservative politicians thought they would win the majority almost everywhere, making them the dominant partner in a coalition government. P. Smith, "The Breakdown of Democracy," 11, 26n; see also E. Gallo, *Argentina*, 388, and Cantón, "Universal Suffrage," 12.

34. Cantón, *Elecciones y partidos políticos*, 45. The proportion of adult males (including disenfranchised immigrants) who voted rose from 9 percent in 1910 to 30 percent in 1916. Germani, *Política y sociedad*, 225.

35. Rock, *Politics in Argentina*, 55–60, 120–22, 299; Walter, *Socialist Party*, 121–22.

36. Cantón, *Materiales*, 1: 86.

37. P. Smith, "The Breakdown of Democracy," 21. To explain the absence of an electorally powerful sedentary peasantry, Smith also notes Argentina's

high level of urbanization. As early as 1914, cities over 5,000 accounted for 40 percent of Argentina's population. Remmer, *Party Competition*, 57.

38. Moore, *Social Origins*, 437; Rueschemeyer, Stephens, and Stephens, *Capitalist Development*, 163–65, 178, 270.

39. Rueschemeyer, Stephens, and Stephens, *Capitalist Development*, 287.

40. Gibson, "Conservative Electoral Movements," 21. Similar arguments may be found in Di Tella, *El sistema político*, 110 and "La busqueda," 323; Cornblit, "La opción conservadora," 638–39; P. Smith, "Breakdown of Democracy," 21; Rueschemeyer, Stephens, and Stephens, *Capitalist Development*, 197, 287.

41. Di Tella, *Latin American Politics*, 148.

42. Loveman, *Chile*, 257.

43. Zeitlin and Ratcliff, *Landlords and Capitalists*, 190–94; Scully, "Reconstituting Party Politics," 116–18. The key reform was the introduction in 1958 of a uniform single ballot printed by the government. This ballot replaced the heterogeneous ones printed by each individual party, whose distinctiveness enabled party agents at the polling place to verify that votes bought were actually cast. Also important to the decline of the electoral right, Scully argues, was the explicitly antiparty stance of the populist General Carlos Ibáñez during and after his successful 1952 presidential campaign. The phrase "competitive political system" indicates that Chile was a protodemocracy rather than a democracy for most of the 1931–73 period. Women did not win the suffrage until 1949, the Communist Party (representing about 10 percent of the electorate) was banned from 1948 to 1958, there was no effective secret ballot in many parts of the countryside until 1958, and the right to vote included a literacy qualification until 1970.

44. Abad de Santillán, *La F.O.R.A.*, 142, 228.

45. Deutsch, *Counterrevolution*, 64–65; Rock, *Politics in Argentina*, 119–55. The convener, initial vice president, and subsequent president of the Asociación de Trabajo was Joaquín de Anchorena, who was also president of the Sociedad Rural Argentina.

46. Rock, *Politics in Argentina*, 162–79; Deutsch, *Counterrevolution*, 73–79.

47. Rock, *Politics in Argentina*, 179. Estimates of the number killed during the entire week vary. Jacinto Oddone (*Gremialismo*, 295) estimated 700 dead, 2,000 injured, and 3,000 arrested; Rubens Iscaro (*Historia del movimiento sindical*, 2: 184) cites figures of 800 dead, 4,000 injured, and "thousands" arrested. These figures are toward the high end of the estimates (Walter, *Socialist Party*, 155).

48. Sofer, *From Pale to Pampa*, 44.

49. Anti-Jewish acts in the latter part of the twentieth century are described in Senkman, ed., *El antisemitismo en la argentina*. Senkman's book was published before the bombing in 1992 of the Israeli embassy in Buenos Aires, which killed 29 and injured 250, and in 1994 of a Buenos Aires building housing Jewish organizations, which killed 90 and injured 200. On the persecution of Jews during the 1976–83 dictatorship, see Timerman, *Prisoner Without a Name*, and Kaufman and Cymberknopf, "La dimension Judia en la represión."

50. Deutsch, *Counterrevolution*, 83.

51. Ibid., 112–52.

52. Iscaro, *Historia del movimiento sindical*, 2: 190–91; Marotta, *El movimiento sindical*, 3: 28–47. The most extensive treatment of the Patagonian massacre is that of Bayer, *Los vengadores*.

53. Deutsch, *Counterrevolution*, 117; Rock, *Politics in Argentina*, 193.

54. Rock, *Politics in Argentina*, 198, 223–24.

55. Collier and Collier, *Shaping the Political Arena*, 148.

56. The 1853 constitution was amended in 1949 to permit Perón to run for a second term. The rule against immediate reelection was restored in 1957, but the 1994 constitutional reform permitted Menem to run for and win a second consecutive term.

57. Gallo and Sigal, "La formación de los partidos políticos," 163; P. Smith, "The Breakdown of Democracy," 14.

58. P. Smith, *Politics and Beef*, 49.

59. Walter, "Politics, Parties, and Elections," 716; P. Smith, "Los Radicales argentinos," 812–24; Solberg, "Rural Unrest," 37–39. Despite these figures, P. Smith argues that Alvear's government was not significantly more pro-rancher than Yrigoyen's 1916–22 administration.

60. Snow, *Argentine Radicalism*, 41–44; Walter, *Province of Buenos Aires*, 76–77.

61. P. Smith, "Breakdown of Democracy," 14.

62. Walter, *Socialist Party*, 139, 215, 237.

63. Rock, *Politics in Argentina*, 243–47.

64. Senators have been chosen by provincial legislators for most of the twentieth century, except in the federal capital, where they have been chosen by popular vote. Reforms stipulating that senators should be popularly elected in all provinces were enacted under Perón in 1949 (reversed after Perón's overthrow in 1955), under General Lanusse in 1972 (reversed before the 1983 elections), and under Menem during the constitutional revisions of 1994 (to take effect in 2001).

65. Potter, "The Failure of Democracy," 104. After the 1928 elections, the senate consisted of 7 personalist Radicals, 9 antipersonalists, 9 conservatives, and 1 Socialist.

66. P. Smith, "The Breakdown of Democracy"; Potter, "The Failure of Democracy."

67. P. Smith, *Politics and Beef*, 49.

68. Whitaker, *Argentina*, 92–93; Rock, *Argentina, 1516–1982*, 224–226.

69. P. Smith, *Politics and Beef*, 137.

70. The "special section" of the police reportedly tortured prisoners (Lewis, *Crisis of Argentine Capitalism*, 119). Torture of political prisoners had earlier been reported in Mendoza and San Juan after Yrigoyen intervened those provinces in 1928 (Castello, *Historia contemporanea*, 21–22).

71. The remaining antipersonalists represented the conservative wing of the original group. Snow, *Argentine Radicalism*, 46.

72. Potash, *Army and Politics in Argentina, 1928–1945*, 80.

73. Walter, *Province of Buenos Aires*, 125, 148–49. The abuses included intimidation of opposition sympathizers by provincial police and the stuffing or stealing of ballot boxes.

74. Rouquié, *Poder militar*, 2: 22.

75. Díaz Alejandro, *Essays*, 96–97, 104–5. The degree to which the rate of industrialization accelerated in the 1930s is a matter of some debate. Merkx ("Sectoral Clashes," 90) notes that industrial employment grew six times faster annually during 1935–43 than during 1914–35, and Díaz Alejandro (*Essays*, 218) argues that 1930 marked a watershed, after which manufacturing became the crucial determinant of overall economic growth. On the other hand, Villanueva ("Economic Development," 67–72) notes that industry increased its share in the national product at about the same rate in the 1930s as it had in the 1920s.

76. W. Smith, *Authoritarianism*, 23–24.

77. Lewis, *Crisis of Argentine Capitalism*, 87.

78. Rock, *Argentina, 1516–1982*, 238.

79. Díaz Alejandro, *Essays*, 215.

80. Cornblit, "Inmigrantes y empresarios," 641–42.

81. Acuña, "Organizaciones empresariales."

82. Collier and Collier, *Shaping the Political Arena*, 59–99.

83. Figures for number of industrial workers from Lewis, *Crisis of Argentine Capitalism*, 36; for internal migrants from Germani, *Política y sociedad*, 230.

84. Figure for 1936 from Tamarin, *Argentine Labor Movement*, 135; figure for 1945 from Doyon, "El crecimiento sindical," 154.

85. CGT, *Estatutos* (1930), Article 4. On the formation of the CGT, see Tamarin, *Argentine Labor Movement*, ch. 4.

86. Tamarin, *Argentine Labor Movement*, 95–97.

87. Cantón, *Materiales*, 1: 62. At least 13 of the 43 socialist deputies in office from 1932 to 1934 were of working-class origin (Matsushita, *Movimiento obrero argentino*, 100). Even the conservative Partido Democrata Nacional during this period included a unionist in its 56-member bloc of deputies. Etcheberry, "Sindicalistas en la bancada conservadora."

88. Matsushita, *Movimiento obrero argentino*, 174; Ramicone, *La organización gremial obrera*, 66–67. Many of the new laws were poorly enforced. Ciria, *Partidos y poder*, 306–8; Bergquist, *Labor in Latin America*, 154.

89. Matsushita, *Movimiento obrero argentino*, 174.

90. Gaudio and Pilone, "El desarollo de la negociación colectiva" and "Estado y relaciones laborales."

91. Matsushita, *Movimiento obrero argentino*, 103.

92. Tamarin, *Argentine Labor Movement*, 149.

93. Matsushita, *Movimiento obrero argentino*, 245–46; Tamarin, *Argentine Labor Movement*, 162–63.

94. Matsushita, *Movimiento obrero argentino*, 171, 259.

95. Ciria, *Partidos y poder*, 305–6.

CHAPTER 3

1. On Patrón Costas's labor practices, see Rutledge, "Plantations and Peasants," 99–103.

2. Potash, *Army and Politics in Argentina, 1928–1945,* 179–97; Rouquié, *Poder militar,* 2: 15–22.

3. The implicitly pro-Axis neutrality was partly a gesture of resistance to U.S. hemispheric policy (Potash, *Army and Politics in Argentina, 1928–1945,* 186), but it also expressed ideological affinity for European fascism. A "strictly secret and confidential" GOU document issued shortly before the 1943 coup included the following passage: "The politician at the service of the monopolist, the foreign corporations, the Jewish businessman, and the thoughtless exploiter deserves his due. . . . The solution lies in the suppression of political, social, and economic intermediaries. To achieve this, the state must become the organ that regulates resources, directs politics, and makes society harmonious" (Potash, *Perón y el G.O.U.,* 202). Although "G.O.U." is often said to stand for "Grupo de Oficiales Unidos," the exact name of the organization represented by the acronym has not been conclusively determined.

4. Baily, *Labor, Nationalism, and Politics,* 75.

5. Alexander, *Juan Domingo Perón,* 158.

6. In a speech before the Stock Exchange in August 1944, Perón affirmed his anticommunism and reassured his audience about his overtures to labor. "Businessmen: Don't be afraid of my unionism. Never has capitalism been firmer than now. . . . What I want to do is organize the workers through the state, so that the state shows them the way forward. In this way revolutionary currents endangering capitalist society in the postwar [period] can be neutralized" (quoted in Rock, *Argentina, 1516–1982,* 257). Speaking at the Military College a year later, Perón expressed similar concerns to the army. "The government of the popular mass is beginning. It is a fact that the Army must accept. If we do not bring about a peaceful revolution, the people will initiate a violent one (quoted in Baily, *Labor, Nationalism, and Politics,* 85). Waisman (*Reversal of Development,* 190–206) makes a compelling argument that the elite fear of revolution was greatly exaggerated.

7. Harmonizing labor and capital was a central theme in Perón's early speeches. In May 1944, Perón announced that he sought to "suppress the struggles between classes, and to supplant them by a just agreement between workers and employers—that is to say, the people—under the sheltering justice that emanates from the state (quoted in Romero, *History of Argentine Political Thought,* 246).

8. Silverman, "Labor and Left Fascism," 120; Matsushita, *Movimiento obrero argentino,* 267.

9. Doyon, "El crecimiento sindical," 153; Silverman, "Labor and Left Fascism," 140–41, 169–70; Little, "La organización obrera," 334; Alexander, *Labor Relations,* 192–205; D'Abate, "Trade Unions and Peronism," 59; Rotondaro, *Realidad y cambio,* 174–75.

10. The significance of Perón's support for striking workers is reflected in government figures on labor disputes. In 1942 workers won only 10 percent of strikes and compromised in more than 80 percent; by 1945, they were winning 95 percent of the time. Kenworthy, "Formation of the Peronist Coalition," 162.

11. Luparia, *El grito de la tierra*, 107, 190–91; Baily, *Labor, Nationalism, and Politics*, 77; Blanksten, *Perón's Argentina*, 267; Silverman, "Labor and Left Fascism," 306–9. Quantitative analyses of aggregate electoral data indicate that the rural poor were strong supporters of Perón (Llorente, "La composición social," 394; Wellhofer, "Peronism in Argentina," 353). Intermediaries like the clergy, who supported Perón in 1946, and provincial caudillos interested in retaining the support or benign neglect of the central government, may also have induced the rural poor to vote for Perón (Sebreli, *Los deseos imaginarios*, 26, 132).

12. Silverman, "Labor and Left Fascism," 159; Alexander, *Labor Relations*, 68.

13. Baily, *Labor, Nationalism, and Politics*, 99.

14. Alexander, *Labor Relations*, 208.

15. Díaz Alejandro, *Essays*, 124; Silverman, "Labor and Left Fascism," 307.

16. D'Abate, "Trade Unions and Peronism," 59.

17. Cavarozzi, De Riz, and Feldman, "El contexto," 20.

18. Statistical series on real wages under Perón differ markedly, even though all available figures are based on government data. According to one series in which the year 1943 is assigned an index of 100, real wages in industry had risen to 104 by 1946, soared to 162 by 1949, plummeted to 129 by 1952, and increased again to 152 by 1955 (Silverman, "Labor and Left Fascism," 307). Other series for industrial and overall real wage levels during the Perón period show a similar pattern up to 1949, but then, in contrast to the Silverman series, register a slow, moderate decline from 1949 to 1955 (Díaz Alejandro, *Essays*, 124). Both series agree, however, that real wages in 1955 were at least 30 percent higher than in 1946.

19. Mainwaring, "State and the Industrial Bourgeoisie," 19.

20. Díaz Alejandro, *Essays*, 124–25.

21. Baily, *Labor, Nationalism, and Politics*, 77; Rotondaro, *Realidad y cambio*, 184.

22. Alexander, *Juan Domingo Perón*, 39.

23. Ciria, *Partidos y poder*, 107; Little, "La organización obrera," 334–35. On the role of dignity and self-respect in forming the Peronist identity, see James, *Resistance and Integration*, 25–33.

24. Cantón, *El parlamento argentino*, 56–57.

25. Rotondaro, *Realidad y cambio*, 220–21.

26. Perón, *El libro rojo*, 15.

27. See esp. Germani, *Política y sociedad*, ch. 9; Fillol, *Social Factors*, 83; Baily, *Labor, Nationalism, and Politics*, 82; Butler, "Charisma, Migration and Elite Coalescence," 429; and Madsen and Snow, *Charismatic Bond*, 47–48.

28. Murmis and Portantiero, *Estudios*. P. Smith ("Social Bases of Peronism," 67) suggests that in major urban electoral districts, " 'old' laboring groups played a more crucial political role than did internal migrants." Madsen and

Snow point out some methodological flaws in Smith's analysis and present a quantitative study suggesting that much of Perón's initial electoral support did indeed come from migrants (*Charismatic Bond*, ch. 3).

29. Halperín Donghi, "Algunas observaciones"; Kenworthy, "Interpretaciones ortodoxas y revisionistas"; Little, "Popular Origins of Peronism"; Germani, "El surgimento del peronismo." On the experiences of rural migrants in other Latin American countries, see the sources cited in Schoultz, *Populist Challenge*, 120–21 nn. 9 and 20.

30. Perón's willingness to be seen in public with Eva Duarte, whom he had not yet married, was viewed in some military circles as dishonorable (Luna, *El 45*, 275–76; Potash, *Army and Politics in Argentina, 1928–1945*, 228). Military opposition to Perón's pro-labor policies is discussed in Rouquié, *Poder militar*, 2: 60–61.

31. Kenworthy, "Formation of the Peronist Coalition," 211.

32. Page, *Perón*, 124–26.

33. Reyes, *Que es el laborismo*, 55.

34. Luna, *El 45*, 273–342; Reyes, *Yo hice el 17 de Octubre*, 203–53; Torre, "La CGT y el 17 de octubre 1945," 70–90; Kenworthy, "Formation of the Peronist Coalition," 210–11; Potash, *Army and Politics in Argentina, 1928–1945*, 262–82; James, "October 17th and 18th, 1945."

35. For a comparative analysis of this and other Latin American labor codes, see Collier and Collier, "Inducements and Constraints."

36. Alexander, *Labor Relations*, 177–79.

37. Silverman, "Labor and Left Fascism," 153.

38. On the replacement of the well-established communist-led meat-packers' union by the fledgling pro-Perón SAIC, see Reyes, *Yo hice el 17 de octubre*, 159–253; Bergquist, *Labor in Latin America*, 160–73; and Iscaro, *Historia del movimiento sindical*, 2: 262. On the replacement of the well-established communist-led metalworkers' union by the fledgling pro-Perón UOM, see Perelman, *Como hicimos el 17 de octubre*, 30, 44–45, and Matsushita, *Movimiento obrero argentino*, 162, 285. On the replacement of communist-led footwear and construction unions by pro-Perón unions, see Del Campo, *Sindicalismo y peronismo*, 184, and Alexander, *Labor Relations*, 178–79.

39. Doyon, "El crecimiento sindical," 154, 160. An alternative estimate by Walter Little ("Organized Labor and the Peronist State," 106) based on membership figures submitted by unions to the CGT gives a figure of 2,334,000 union members for 1951.

40. Doyon, "El crecimiento sindical," 154, 158. The UOM claimed 200,000 members in 1948 (CGT, *Memoria y Balance 1949*), but this figure is probably exaggerated; it is much higher than Doyon's estimate of 108,000, which is based on a combination of CGT, union, and ministry of labor sources.

41. Doyon, "El crecimiento sindical," 160.

42. Alexander, *Labor Relations*, 196; Doyon, "Conflictos obreros," 457–58.

43. Weil, *Argentine Riddle*, 157–64; Rock, *Argentina, 1516–1982*, 220–23.

44. Panaia, Lesser, and Skupch, "Las estratégias militares," 115–54; Halperín Donghi, *Argentina*, 28–29.

45. Díaz Alejandro, *Essays*, 109; Fodor, "Perón's Policies," 140–43.

46. Kenworthy, "Did the 'New Industrialists' Play a Significant Role in the Formation of Perón's Coalition, 1943–1946?" 19–21; Wynia, *Argentina in the Postwar Era*, 47–49.

47. In addition to these central government and public enterprise employees, there were 223,000 provincial and 107,000 municipal employees. Total government employment thus stood at 807,000 in 1955. Lewis, *Crisis of Argentine Capitalism*, 161, 260–61.

48. Ibid., 400–401.

49. The right to strike was not among the "Rights of the Worker" announced in February 1947 and later codified in the 1949 constitution. A common pattern for strike activity beginning around 1949 was that union leaders would reach an agreement not acceptable to the rank and file, resulting in a wildcat strike. The government would declare the strike illegal, suppress it, and then grant most of the workers' demands "from above." This pattern characterized the 1949 Tucumán sugar workers' strike and the 1951 railroad strikes. Similar sequences occurred among the meat packers, bank tellers, and dock workers. Baily, *Labor, Nationalism, and Politics*, 114, 129; Doyon, "Conflictos obreros."

50. After a construction workers' strike was settled in Rosario in 1946, workers got paid for the days they had been on strike (Cabanellas, *Derecho*, 331 n. 84). The custom of employers paying workers for days lost while on strike persisted through the 1980s. Apparently, employers as well as workers saw such payments as an element of the right to strike (author's interview with an official of the ministry of labor, 4 Sept. 1986). The jurisprudence on the issue is exceedingly confused. Some court decisions have held that workers are not entitled to be paid for days on strike, but others have granted such pay in specific instances (Cabanellas, *Derecho*, 328–47). Strike funds are not common in Argentine unions, but perhaps because back pay for days spent on strike is the rule rather than the exception, small retailers often extend credit to striking workers, who may also use soup kitchens (*ollas populares*) to help support themselves and their families while a strike is in progress.

51. Alexander, *Labor Relations*, 198. In the late 1950s, however, tanners and civil servants won court decisions granting them pay for the days they had been on strike—even though the ministry of labor had declared their strikes illegal! Cabanellas, *Derecho*, 331–32 n. 86.

52. Doyon, "La organización," 219–20; Sebreli, *Los deseos imaginarios*, 103.

53. The quotations are from a 24 Sept. 1952 speech by Perón, reprinted in Peyrou and Villanueva, *Documentos*, 260, cited in Giussani, *Montoneros*, 188–89n. The GOU, which Perón may have founded and of which he was a key member, also issued documents disparaging parties and politicians. See Potash, *Perón y el G.O.U.*, 198–201.

54. Potash, *Army and Politics in Argentina, 1928–1945*, 242, 245. For an extended analysis of the relationship between Peronism and Sabbatini's wing of the UCR, see Tcach, *Sabbatinismo y Peronismo*.

55. Ciria, *Política y cultura popular*, 150–52.

56. Pont, *Partido Laborista*, 38 (quotation); Reyes, *Que es el laborismo*, 54.

57. Partido Laborista platform reprinted in Pont, *Partido Laborista*, 134–38.

58. Torre, *La vieja guardia sindical*, 148–50.

59. Cantón, *Elecciones y partidos políticos*, 200–202; Reyes, *Qué es el laborismo*, 73–97.

60. Perón chose Hortensio Quijano of the UCR–JR as his running mate, disappointing Partido Laborista activists who had lobbied for Domingo Mercante, the son of a socialist locomotive engineer. Perón also endorsed UCR–JR over Partido Laborista leaders as nominees for governor of Buenos Aires and for president of the chamber of deputies. Kenworthy, "Formation of the Peronist Coalition," 234–39; Del Campo, *Sindicalismo y peronismo*, 242; Pont, *Partido Laborista*, 43–46.

61. Kenworthy, "Formation of the Peronist Coalition," 227.

62. Ciria, *Política y cultura popular*, 155–57.

63. Confalonieri, *Perón contra Perón*, 160.

64. One exception was the party chief Cipriano Reyes, who soon became the most visible figure in a vocal group of dissident Partido Laborista deputies. In 1948, after an attempt was made on his own life, Reyes was imprisoned without trial on charges of plotting to assassinate Perón. Except for one brief period at liberty, Reyes remained in prison until September 1955. Pont, *Partido Laborista*, 51–52; Baily, *Labor, Nationalism, and Politics*, 106–8; Ciria, *Política y cultura popular*, 157–63.

65. Little, "Party and State," 649.

66. Tcach, "Una interpretación del peronismo periférico," 14–20.

67. Perón, *Perón expone su doctrina*, 54. On the change of the party's name, see also Blanksten, *Perón's Argentina*, 335, and Ciria, *Política y cultura popular*, 156.

68. Ciria, *Política y cultura popular*, 163–65; Blanksten, *Perón's Argentina*, 336.

69. Ciria, "Peronism and Political Structures," 5–6.

70. Rotondaro, *Realidad y cambio*, 219.

71. Fraser and Navarro, *Eva Perón*, 107–9.

72. Ciria, "Peronism and Political Structures," 10.

73. Ciria, *Política y cultura popular*, 183. The 1954 charter also changed the party's name to "Movimiento Peronista."

74. Ciria, "Peronism and Political Structures," 6.

75. Interview with Oscar Albrieu, Oral History Project, Instituto Torcuato di Tella, Buenos Aires, 1972: 43.

76. Interview with Alberto Iturbe, Oral History Project, Instituto Torcuato di Tella, Buenos Aires, 1972: 49–50.

77. Interview with Delia Parodi, Oral History Project, Instituto Torcuato di

Tella, Buenos Aires, 1973: 19. Similar statements may be found in Bianchi and Sanchís, *El partido peronista femenino*, 1: 91–92.

78. Palermo, *Democracia interna*, 27 n. 26, quoting an unpublished paper by Luis A. Romero.

79. Perón, *Conducción política*, 325, quoted in Palermo, *Democracia interna*, 28 n. 27.

80. Palermo, *Democracia interna*, 28.

81. Interview with Alberto Iturbe, Oral History Project, Instituto Torcuato di Tella, Buenos Aires, 1972: 44.

82. Quoted in Carri, *Sindicatos y poder*, 35.

83. Quoted in Confalonieri, *Perón contra Perón*, 157.

84. Quoted in Little, "Party and State," 656–57.

85. Perón, *Perón expone su doctrina*, 55.

86. Quoted in Little, "Party and State," 660.

87. Little, "Party and State," 659.

88. Navarro, "Evita and Peronism," 15–23.

89. Fraser and Navarro, *Eva Perón*, 164–65; Page, *Perón*, 263.

90. Interview with Cabo in Callelo and Parcero, *De Vandor a Ubaldini*, 1: 29–30.

91. Baily, *Labor, Nationalism, and Politics*, 108–12, 139; Fraser and Navarro, *Eva Perón*, 104; Page, *Perón*, 181; Rotondaro, *Realidad y cambio*, 211.

92. Wynia, *Argentina in the Postwar Era*, 68–71.

93. Díaz Alejandro, *Essays*, 527.

94. Mainwaring, "El movimiento obrero," 521.

95. James, "Rationalisation," 377–90.

96. Doyon, "Organized Labour and Perón," 588; author's interview with a leader of the textile workers' union.

97. Interview with Vandor in *Confirmado*, 4 November 1965, 14–16.

98. Doyon, "Conflictos obreros," 450–51, Abellá Blasco, *Manual de sindicatos*, 91–92.

99. Cavazzoni, *La burocracia sindical*, 30–31; Baily, *Labor, Nationalism, and Politics*, 126–27.

100. Díaz Alejandro, *Essays*, 445.

101. *La Nación*, 9 June 1954, 1; *La Nación*, 10 June 1954, 1; *Hispanic American Report*, July 1954, 39–40; Baily, *Labor, Nationalism, and Politics*, 155–56; Correa, *Carlos Ons*, 36–41.

102. James, "Rationalisation," 383; Correa, *Los jerarcas sindicales*, 33; Correa, *Carlos Ons*, 36–41; Sebreli, *Los deseos imaginarios*, 115.

103. *Primera Plana* 12 Jan. 1965: 11; Walsh, *¿Quién mató a Rosendo?* 135; Gazzera, "Nosotros, los dirigentes," 113; Cardoso and Audi, *Sindicalismo*, 51.

104. Cavazzoni, *La burocracia sindical*, 30–31.

105. Dirección Nacional de Estadística y Censos, *Anuario Estadístico, 1957*, 143–45.

106. Little, "Electoral Aspects of Peronism"; Schoultz, "Socioeconomic De-

terminants"; Wellhofer, "Peronism in Argentina." The 1951 election took place after the constitution was amended (1949) to permit the immediate reelection of the president and after a law was passed (1947) granting suffrage to women. More than four million women voted in 1951, of whom 63.9 percent voted for Perón, a slightly higher proportion than the 62.5 percent Perón received overall.

107. Little, "Electoral Aspects of Peronism," 278–89; Rock, *Argentina, 1516–1982*, 305; Blanksten, *Perón's Argentina*, 77–86.

108. Little, "Electoral Aspects of Peronism," 305.

109. By 1950, most of the major unions had passed resolutions "demanding" that Perón run for reelection and that Eva be the vice-presidential candidate. In the same year, the CGT convened a special congress to support Perón's electoral bid, and a rally it organized to support the Perón-Perón ticket drew an estimated 250,000 people. Alexander, *Labor Relations*, 183.

110. Cantón, *Materiales*, 142 and 153.

111. Interview with Cabo in Calello and Parcero, *De Vandor a Ubaldini*, 1: 29–30. See James, *Resistance and Integration*, 49–52, for an analysis of incidents of resistance to the 1955 coup.

112. In "Did the 'New Industrialists' Play a Significant Role in the Formation of Perón's Coalition, 1943–1946?" Eldon Kenworthy argues that import-substitution industrialists benefited from, but had little input into, Perón's policies in the late 1940s. For interpretations that stress industrialists' initial support for Perón, see Merkx, "Sectoral Clashes," 94; Di Tella, "Populism and Reform," 71; and Smith, *Authoritarianism*, 28–29.

113. Cúneo, *Comportamiento y crisis*, 180–90.

114. The CGE primarily represented smaller industrialists, often from interior provinces, who benefited from government protection and subsidies. On its relationship with the government in the 1952–55 period, see Cúneo, *Comportamiento y crisis*, 200–214; and Lewis, *Crisis of Argentine Capitalism*, 172–74.

115. Mainwaring, "State and the Industrial Bourgeoisie," 14–21.

116. Skidmore, "Problems of Economic Stabilization," 160.

117. Smith, *Authoritarianism*, 26–32.

118. Cúneo, *Comportamiento y crisis*, 160–65. Perón may have backed away from land reform because he recognized that many army officers aspired to landownership or had family ties to cattle ranchers. Manzetti, *Institutions*, 362 n. 42.

119. On price incentives and credit see Wynia, *Argentina in the Postwar Era*, 70–71; on the rise in agricultural output, see Skidmore, "Problems of Economic Stabilization," 160.

120. Cúneo, *Comportamiento y crisis*, 216–21

121. Ibid., 247–49.

122. Banco de Análisis y Computación, *Relevamiento estadístico*, 96, 262; Díaz Alejandro, *Essays*, 528. On the relative success of the 1952 stabilization program, see Skidmore, "Problems of Economic Stabilization," 159–79.

123. Alexander, *Juan Domingo Perón*, 101.

124. Rouquié, *Poder militar*, 2: 103–4; Potash, *Army and Politics in Argentina, 1945–1962*, 180.

125. Page, *Perón*, 267–70, 289–95.

126. Potter, "Failure of Democracy"; P. Smith, "Breakdown of Democracy."

127. Little, "Electoral Aspects of Peronism," 278–80; Page, *Perón*, 228–29; Rock, *Argentina, 1512–1982*, 303–4; Cavarozzi, "Peronism and Radicalism," 146.

128. Corradi, "Between Corporatism and Insurgency," 121; Page, *Perón*, 293–97; Rouquié, *Poder militar*, 2: 105–6, Potash, *Army and Politics in Argentina, 1945–1962*, 172–77; Halperín Donghi, *Argentina*, 81.

129. Baily, *Labor, Nationalism, and Politics*, 206.

130. Luna, *De Perón a Lanusse*, 85; Rock, *Argentina, 1512–1982*, 315; Rouquié, *Poder militar*, 2: 106–7.

131. Page, *Perón*, 305. The situation was not resolved until 1963, when Perón, through the mediation of the La Plata Bishop Antonio J. Plaza (who later achieved notoriety as a defender of the post-1976 "dirty war"), was granted absolution by the papal nuncio in Spain. *Hispanic American Report*, April 1963, 166.

132. Potash, *Army and Politics in Argentina, 1945–1962*, 88, 95–98, 102, 166–69, 177–88.

133. Rouquié, *Poder militar*, 2: 108–10; Page, *Perón*, 306–10; Potash, *Army and Politics in Argentina, 1945–1962*, 188–90; Godio, *La caída de Perón*, 1: 28–33.

134. Potash, *Army and Politics in Argentina, 1945–1962*, 192.

135. Godio, *La caída de Perón*, 1: 96–105; Rouquié, *Poder militar*, 2: 113; Halperín Donghi, *Argentina*, 84.

136. Potash, *Army and Politics in Argentina, 1945–1962*, 195; Alexander, *Juan Domingo Perón*, 107.

137. Baily, *Labor, Nationalism, and Politics*, 160.

138. See Bergquist, *Labor in Latin America*, 135–36, on elite characterizations of the early twentieth-century working class as "un-Argentine."

139. O'Donnell, "State and Alliances"; Corradi, *Fitful Republic*, 113.

140. Halperín Donghi, *Argentina*, 105; Cavarozzi, De Riz, and Feldman, "El contexto," 16–23.

CHAPTER 4

1. Senén González and Torre, *Los sesenta dias de Lonardi*, 15, 51.

2. Pasini Costadoat, *Crisis democrática*, 54; Baily, *Labor, Nationalism, and Politics*, 174.

3. In November 1956, a federal judge used the ban on support from foreign organizations to bar the Communist Party, for the first time since its foundation in 1918, from campaigning or presenting candidates in elections (the organization itself was not outlawed). *Hispanic American Report*, Oct. 1956, 495; ibid., Nov. 1956, 547.

4. Perón, "Directiva," 46 and 49; see also Hodges, *Argentina, 1943–1976*, 43–46.

5. Potash, *Army and Politics in Argentina, 1945–1962*, 230–35.

6. James, *Resistance and Integration*, 43–100.

7. Zorrilla, *El liderazgo sindical*, 54.

8. James, *Resistance and Integration*, 271 n. 32.

9. Gorbato, *Vandor o Perón*, 12–24; 35–39; *Panorama*, Dec. 1965, 92; *Primera Plana*, 12 Jan. 1965, 11; Cardoso and Audi, *Sindicalismo*, 51; Carri, *Sindicatos y poder*, 68–69; Gazzera, "Nosotros, los dirigentes," 113; Walsh, *¿Quién mató a Rosendo?* 135.

10. Gaudio and Domenicone, "El proceso de normalización sindical," 165; *Primera Plana*, 12 Jan. 1965, 11; Cavarozzi, *Consolidación*, 74.

11. Doyon, "Organized Labour," 588; personal interview with a leader of the textile workers' union, Buenos Aires, 16 Sept. 1986.

12. CGT, *Memoria y Balance Anual: XIX Ejercicio, 1949*; *Clarín*, 28 Aug. 1970; López and Grabois, "Alonso," 2–3.

13. *Primera Plana*, 19 Dec. 1967, 48.

14. On the failed "normalizing congress" of 1957, see Rodríguez Lamas, *La revolución libertadora*, 130; Cavarozzi, "Sindicatos y política," 73–78; Iscaro, *Historia*, 336; Marischi, *Conciencia*, 41; James, *Resistance and Integration*, 75–76; Baily, *Labor, Nationalism, and Politics*, 181; Audi and Cardoso, "La CGT a sus dueños," 69–72, 76; Abellá Blasco, *Historia del sindicalismo*, 91.

15. César Tcach, in a useful article on the neo-Peronist parties in the province of Córdoba ("Neoperonismo y resistencia obrera," 65–66), has challenged the view that the Unión Popular was initially the most "orthodox" of the neo-Peronist parties. Tcach cites statements by Bramuglia implicitly criticizing Perón's leadership and notes that in January 1956, Perón instructed his followers to "expose and repudiate" as "traitors to our movement" Peronist leaders who tried to form new parties (this missive is reprinted in Perón, "Directivas," 47–48). In February 1957, Tcach might have added, Perón wrote a letter in which he referred to the neo-Peronist leaders as opportunists more interested in their careers than in the movement (Arias and García Heras, "Carisma disperso y rebelión," 99). Tcach is correct to point out that Bramuglia's Unión Popular was not subservient to Perón, but he does not indicate which neo-Peronist parties were more orthodox than the Unión Popular or explain why the Unión Popular, unlike other neo-Peronist parties, boycotted the 1957 constituent assembly elections, as Perón had instructed.

16. R. Gallo, *Balbín, Frondizi*, 53; Cavarozzi, *Sindicatos y política*, 43–45.

17. Guardo, *Horas difíciles*, 109–11; Potash, *Army and Politics in Argentina, 1945–1962*, 263–70.

18. *Hispanic American Report*, Jan. 1958, 43–44

19. Potash, *Army and Politics in Argentina, 1945–1962*, 264 n. 10. According to the neo-Peronist leader Alberto Serú García (personal interview, Mendoza, 9 Mar. 1993), Perón intended all along to order his followers to vote for Frondizi. Information on Perón's initial instructions to register the neo-Peronist parties comes from this interview with Serú and from the interview with Vicente Saadi, Oral History Project, Instituto Torcuato Di Tella, Buenos Aires, 1972, 66.

20. For arguments to this effect, see Potash, *Army and Politics in Argentina, 1945–1962*, 266; Arias and García Heras, "Carisma disperso y rebelión," 100; Page, *Perón*, 357–58.

21. These implications of the blank-balloting strategy are discussed in Prieto, *Treinta años*, 120, and in Potash, *Army and Politics in Argentina, 1945–1962*, 264.

22. Interview with Armando Cabo in Calello and Parcero, *De Vandor a Ubaldini*, 1: 31–32; interview with Juan José Taccone in Domínguez, *Conversaciones*, 70–71; James, *Resistance and Integration*, 86–87.

23. James, *Resistance and Integration*, 119–43, esp. 125–26. James Brennan argues that the Córdoba branch of SMATA, the auto workers' union, was more successful than most other unions during this period in winning concessions from management and in remaining reasonably democratic. Brennan, *Labor Wars*, 56–63.

24. Audi and Cardoso, "La CGT a sus dueños," 77.

25. These phrases are from the 1962 Huerta Grande program (reprinted in Baschetti, *Documentos*, 118) authored by the hard-line faction of the "62 Organizations."

26. Interview with Framini in Calello and Parcero, *De Vandor a Ubaldini*, 1: 53–55.

27. James, *Resistance and Integration*, 109.

28. Cavarozzi, *Consolidación*, 51–52.

29. Potash, *Army and Politics in Argentina, 1945–1962*, 356.

30. Verone, *La caída de Illia*, 28; interview with Framini in Cardoso and Audi, *Sindicalismo*, 19.

31. Perón, *Correspondencia*, 1: 90–93; Page, *Perón*, 377–78; Lamadrid, "Sindicatos y política," 27.

32. Among those who shared this opinion was Juan José Taccone of the light and power workers' union, interviewed in Domínguez, *Conversaciones*, 82.

33. Lamadrid, "Sindicatos y política," 26.

34. The Partido Justicialista had been created in 1959, but was immediately banned on the grounds that it bore "the official party name of the Peronist regime," was "a continuation of Peronism," and had demonstrated an "outspoken disposition to place [itself] at the unconditional service of an individual," evidenced in its leaders' affirmation that their "only directives came from Perón and their only objective was his return to power." See *Hispanic American Report*, Sept. 1959, 511; Potash, "Argentine Political Parties," 521; Ranis, "Peronismo," 85.

35. Cardoso and Audi, *Sindicalismo*, 16, 51; James, *Resistance and Integration*, 154.

36. Interview with Framini in Cardoso and Audi, *Sindicalismo*, 23; Gazzera, "Nosotros, los dirigentes," 119.

37. *Hispanic American Report*, Apr. 1963, 167; Arias and García Heras, "Carisma disperso y rebelión," 106–7.

38. *Hispanic American Report*, Sept. 1962, 648; Manna, "Coacción," 134.

39. Interview with Framini in Calello and Parcero, *De Vandor a Ubaldini*, 1: 53–54.

40. The Huerta Grande program is reprinted in Baschetti, *Documentos*, 116–18.

41. Interview with Framini in Calello and Parcero, *De Vandor a Ubaldini*, 1: 55.

42. Lamadrid, "Sindicatos y política," 77–85.

43. Quoted in Nosiglia, *El Partido Intransigente*, 64.

44. *Hispanic American Report*, Feb. 1963, 167.

45. Rowe, *Argentine Elections*, 17n.

46. Prieto, *Treinta años*, 231; O'Donnell, *Modernization*, 190. In the mid 1930s, Solano Lima was a cog in the political machine of Argentina's major conservative party, the Partido Democratico Nacional, which belonged to the governing Concordancia coalition. Etcheberry, "Sindicalistas en la bancada conservadora," 79.

47. James, "Unions and Politics," 296.

48. On the intricacies of the ban on Solano Lima and the subsequent calls for blank balloting, see *La Nación*, 4 July 1963, 1; *Hispanic American Report*, Sept. 1963, 613, and Oct. 1963, 718; and Snow, "Parties and Politics," 21–22.

49. Calculations based on data in INDEC, *Censo nacional económico, 1964*. For details of this analysis, see McGuire, "Peronism Without Perón," 141–43, 307–11.

50. Correa, *Carlos Ons*, 48–53.

51. James, "Rationalisation," 394–98.

52. *Compañero*, 5 Dec. 1963, 8

53. Gazzera, "Nosotros," 115; interview with Andrés Framini in Calello and Parcero, *De Vandor a Ubaldini*, 1: 52; personal interview with Alberto Serú García, Mendoza, 9 Mar. 1993.

54. Kirkpatrick, *Leader and Vanguard*, 224. Respondents were presented with a list of nine Peronist leaders, not including Perón, and asked if there were any whom they "particularly admired." In a separate survey in 1964 (methods not described), in which about 1,000 residents of Peronist neighborhoods were asked to choose whom they thought should succeed Perón as head of the movement, 30 percent supported Matera, 30 percent Framini, and only 15 percent Vandor. Gorbato, *Vandor o Perón*, 94.

55. Interview with Framini in Calello and Parcero, *De Vandor a Ubaldini*, 1: 52.

56. Interview with Vandor in *Confirmado*, 4 Nov. 1965, 14–16.

57. Personal interview with the plant manager described in the text, Buenos Aires, Feb. 1986.

58. *Confirmado*, 4 Nov. 1965, 15.

59. Correa, *Los jerarcas sindicales*, 72–73; Correa, *Carlos Ons*, 57–58.

60. James, "Power and Politics," 6. See also Gaudio and Domenicone, "El proceso de normalización sindical," 162.

61. Zorrilla, *Estructura*, 89.

62. Torre, "El proceso político interno," 13. This 98.8 percent rate of incumbent victory was, however, not significantly worse than the 98.6 percent rate in the U.S. House of Representatives in 1986. On union elections in Argentina (which in many cases became significantly more democratic during the 1980s), see also Gaudio and Domenicone, "El proceso de normalización sindical"; Epstein, "Union Election Data," James, "Power and Politics," Lucita, "Elecciones sindicales"; Correa, *Los jerarcas sindicales*, 84–90.

63. James, "Power and Politics," 8–9, 24–25; Gaudio and Domenicone, "El proceso de normalización sindical," 163–95; Palomino, "Elecciones en la UOM." The 1966 national UOM congress, attended by 198 delegates representing the union's 47 sections, is described in *Informes Laborales*, June 1966, 29.

64. Gaudio and Domenicone, "El proceso de normalización sindical," 163–64; interview with Framini in Calello and Parcero, *De Vandor a Ubaldini*, 53.

65. James, "Unions and Politics," 190–96; James, "Power and Politics," 9, 24; Walsh, *¿Quién mató a Rosendo?* 146, 149.

66. James, "Unions and Politics," 190–95, indicates that the number of votes in the federal capital UOM dropped from 25,000 in 1958 to 17,000 in 1961 (layoffs may explain part of this decline), and that the number of eligible voters, despite the inflation of the official rolls to 95,000, was probably closer to 65,000.

67. Secretaría de Estado de Trabajo, *Participación de los trabajadores en elecciones gremiales*, 12, 63, 67.

68. James, "Unions and Politics," 241–45; Walsh, *¿Quién mató a Rosendo?* 146.

69. *Primera Plana*, 2 Mar. 1965, 9.

70. Cavarozzi, "Consolidación," 76–77.

71. James, *Resistance and Integration*, 148.

72. Interview with Cabo in Calello and Parcero, *De Vandor a Ubaldini*, 1: 25–33; James, "Unions and Politics," 241–45. During the Peronist period, Cabo had served as UOM treasurer and as one of the union's delegates to the CGT's rubber-stamp legislative organ, the Comité Central Federal. *La Razón*, 22 Dec. 1956; CGT, *Memoria y Balance Anual: XIX Ejercicio, 1949*, 10.

73. Walsh, *¿Quién mató a Rosendo?* (Imbelloni quotation), 117. Imbelloni became an "orthodox" Peronist deputy in 1985, but left office after evidence emerged that in 1973 he had murdered a guard employed by the plastics workers' union. In June 1992, Imbelloni was sentenced to eight years in prison for the murder. *Clarín*, int. ed., 2–8 June 1992, 5. On García's possible candidacy for governor or vice-governor of Buenos Aires, see Gorbato, *Vandor o Perón*, 109, and *Primera Plana*, 22 Mar. 1966, 11.

74. *La Nación*, 5 Apr. 1990, 5.

75. Personal interview with a 1960s leader of the "62," 9 Sept. 1986.

76. Personal interview with a 1980s leader of the "62," 22 Sept. 1986. The bylaws are described in Sesenta y Dos Organizaciones, "Reglamentos de los cuerpos orgánicos de las 62 Organizaciones."

77. The series of national strikes launched by the UOM in June 1986 had enormous effects on the Argentine economy. Beginning with a day-long strike and continuing for twenty days with strikes of four hours a day, the metal-

workers' strike reduced basic iron and steel production from an index of 104 in May 1986 to 46 in June 1986 (1983 = 100). After the strikes ended, the index recovered to 92 in July 1986. The strikes also halted or slowed production at several auto plants (including the Renault plant in Santa Isabel, Córdoba, which this writer was visiting at the time) and reduced overall industrial production from an index of 115 in May to 99 in June, before recovering to 118 in July (1983 = 100). INDEC, *Estadística Mensual,* June 1987.

78. Although big factories accounted for a large absolute number of UOM members, small workshops also employed a significant proportion of the union's membership. In the late 1960s, the 6,000 UOM members in the province of Córdoba were dispersed among 600 workshops. Balvé et al., *Lucha de calles,* 106.

79. Correa, *Los jerarcas sindicales;* Walsh, *¿Quién mató a Rosendo?*

80. James, *Resistance and Integration,* 137.

81. Torre, "El proceso político interno."

82. For an ambitious extension of this proposition, see Bergquist, *Labor in Latin America.*

83. See any issue of *Informes Laborales* between Oct. 1963 and Oct. 1964.

84. *Compañero,* 6 Nov. 1963; *Informes Laborales,* Oct. 1963, 34–36.

85. James, *Resistance and Integration,* 128–29.

86. UOCRA elections of the 1960s are described in *La Nación,* 7 May 1965, 8; in *Informes Laborales,* Oct. 1963, 37, and June 1966, 41; and in Torre, "El proceso político interno."

87. Personal interview with a 1960s leader of the telephone workers' union, Buenos Aires, 6 Sept. 1986.

88. Gazzera, "Nosotros," 115–16.

89. Cavarozzi, *Consolidación,* 52.

90. *Confirmado,* 11 Nov. 1965, 11–12.

91. *Primera Plana,* 16 Nov. 1965, 19.

92. Personal interview with a 1960s leader of the telephone workers' union, Buenos Aires, 6 Sept. 1986.

93. *Extra,* Feb–Mar. 1966, 22.

94. Bisio and Cordone, "La segunda etapa," 46n.

95. *La Nación,* 19 Feb. 1965, 4; *Primera Plana,* 5 Apr. 1966, 13–15.

96. *Review of the River Plate,* 20 Dec. 1963. On one occasion, however, Bono acted as an intermediary between Vandor and the Illia government. Gorbato, *Vandor o Perón,* 109.

97. Audi and Cardoso, "La CGT a sus dueños," 77; *Primera Plana,* 29 Sept. 1964, 10; Cavarozzi, *Consolidación,* 24 n. 30.

98. *Review of the River Plate,* 31 Oct. 1963, 163.

99. *Primera Plana,* 17 May 1966, 14–15. Within the Unión Ferroviaria, the Peronists were strongest in the workshops where engines and cars were built and repaired (Cavarozzi, *Consolidación,* 26 n. 31). In 1965, there were 26 such workshops employing a total of 21,379 workers (Oficina de Estudios para la Colaboración Económica Internacional, *Argentina Económica y Financiera,* 218)

—enough to make the Unión Ferroviaria the country's tenth-largest industrial union.

100. Before the 1963 CGT "normalizing" congress, when the Independents were deciding which of their leaders would fill the four posts informally reserved for them on the CGT secretariat, Scipione, the Unión Ferroviaria president, was excluded because of fears that he would be under pressure from communist militants in his union, according to press reports (*Primera Plana*, 3 Feb. 1963, 12–13). Scipione's close ties to the historically anti-Peronist UCRP may also have contributed to his exclusion from the leadership board.

101. Zorrilla, *El liderazgo sindical argentina*, 57.

102. *Primera Plana*, 12 Jan. 1965, 12.

103. *Informes Laborales*, Jan. 1965, 12–13. Despite the organizational resources of Luz y Fuerza–Capital, scholars have devoted more attention to Luz y Fuerza–Córdoba, whose leaders were more leftist and combative. Roldán, *Sindicatos y protesta social*; Brennan, *Labor Wars*.

104. Pérez and Taccone, "Sindicalismo Argentino," 491–97; Taccone, *Crisis . . . Respuesta sindical*, 75–84; *Extra*, May 1966, 32–33.

105. C. Sánchez, "Estrategias y objectivos," 24–26.

106. Bisio and Cordone, "La segunda etapa," 10–11; *Panorama*, Dec. 1965, 91.

107. *Review of the River Plate*, 20 Apr. 1964.

108. On the precarious state of CGT finances during the 1960s, see McGuire, "Peronism Without Perón," 325–27.

109. On the reasons why some auto workers formed single-factory unions, see Evans, Hoeffel, and James, "Reflections on the Argentine Auto Workers," and Brennan, *Labor Wars*, 64–65.

110. McGuire, "Peronism Without Perón," 170–77.

111. Interview with Oscar Albrieu reported in Gorbato, *Vandor o Perón*, 46.

CHAPTER 5

1. See the survey in *Panorama*, Dec. 1964, 51.

2. The softening of military attitudes toward the ban on Peronism is discussed in Chapter 4; on the softening of UCRP leaders' attitudes, see *Hispanic American Report*, June 1964, 357.

3. González Jansen, *La Triple-A*, 43.

4. The information in this paragraph was compiled from *Hispanic American Report*, Sept. 1964, 651, and Nov. 1964, 841; *Informes Laborales*, Oct. 1963, 32; *La Razón*, 29 June 1964; *Primera Plana*, 7 July 1964, 8, 12 Jan. 1965, 13, and 2 June 1965, 16; and James, *Resistance and Integration*, 177–78.

5. *Primera Plana*, 7 July 1964, 8.

6. Interview with Framini in Calello and Parcero, *De Vandor a Ubaldini*, 1: 57; Gazzera, "Nosotros," 122.

7. For a description of the technique used in UOM strikes, see *Confirmado*, 4 Nov. 1965, 15. In authoring the plan de lucha resolution, Vandor collaborated with the printers' federation leader René Stordeur, an Independent, but it is

unlikely that Stordeur or other Independents had any real input into the plan de lucha. Many Independents were favorably disposed toward the UCRP government, and most leaders of the group agreed only reluctantly to the resolution. *Review of the River Plate*, 21 Jan. 1964, 87.

8. Quotation from Calello and Parcero, *De Vandor a Ubaldini*, 1: 73. O'Donnell stresses the nonrevolutionary character of the plan de lucha's goals (*Bureaucratic Authoritarianism*, 48).

9. These were among the demands that CGT secretary-general Alonso presented to Congress on 6 Dec. 1963. *Boletín Informativa Semanal de la CGT*, 2–8 Dec. 1963, 6–11.

10. Wynia, *Argentina in the Postwar Era*, 116, 121, 127.

11. Rees, "Industrial Conflict"; Levitt, "Prosperity Versus Strikes."

12. *Boletín Informativa Semanal de la CGT*, 13–19 Jan. 1964: 15, 20.

13. Bourdé, "La CGT argentine," 66–67.

14. Bisio and Cordone, "La segunda etapa," 58, 92.

15. Ibid., 58.

16. Near the city of La Plata, 2,000 meat packers clashed with police armed with dogs, water cannon, and tear gas, but no worker was killed or injured during the campaign and no unionist was imprisoned for more than a few hours. Bourdé, "La CGT Argentine," 68, 70, 74.

17. *La Nación*, 3 June 1964; *Informes Laborales*, May 1964, 34–35.

18. Bisio and Cordone, "La segunda etapa," 60–61, 81–82.

19. *Informes Laborales*, May 1964, 35; P. Sánchez, *La presidencia de Illia*, 44–46.

20. Rouquié, *Poder militar*, 2: 237.

21. *Informes Laborales*, May 1964, 36

22. Bisio and Cordone, "La segunda etapa," 89–91; Torre, *Los sindicatos*, 33.

23. Snow, *Political Forces*, 106–8; Wynia, *Argentina: Illusions and Realities*, 130–32.

24. Sánchez, *La presidencia de Illia*, 44.

25. *Hispanic American Report*, Aug. 1964, 555.

26. *Boletín Informativa Semanal de la CGT*, 22–28 June 1964, 10.

27. *Clarín*, int. ed., 9–15 Mar. 1993, 12. In the same interview, Lanusse described his crucial eleventh-hour decision to support the 1966 coup as "the greatest mistake of my life."

28. Quoted in Rouquié, *Poder militar*, 2: 237.

29. Bisio and Cordone, "La segunda etapa," 50.

30. The CGT leadership constantly expressed this demand in its *Boletín Informativa Semanal de la CGT*, e.g., 1–7 June 1964, 20–21.

31. *Boletín Informativa Semanal de la CGT*, 1–7 June 1964, 1.

32. O'Donnell, *Bureaucratic Authoritarianism*, 48.

33. Bourdé, "La CGT Argentine," 68.

34. *Hispanic American Report*, Aug. 1964, 556–57.

35. Gazzera, "Nosotros, los dirigentes," 122; Rouquié, *Poder militar*, 2: 237; Bisio and Cordone "La segunda etapa," 8–9; Torre, *Los sindicatos*, 33.

36. *Hispanic American Report*, Aug. 1964, 651.

37. *Primera Plana*, 8 Mar. 1966, 16.

38. *Primera Plana*, 22 Dec. 1964, 8

39. *Primera Plana*, 12 Jan. 1965, 13; 9 Mar. 1965, 6, 12; Justo López, *Partidos políticos*, 103–11.

40. *Primera Plana*, 2 Mar. 1965, 8; interview with Paulino Niembro in Cardoso and Audi, *Sindicalismo*, 52.

41. *Primera Plana*, 15 Mar. 1965, 10.

42. *Hispanic American Report*, June 1964, 359. Defying Perón's orders to stand down, nine senators, seventeen national deputies, and three governors had been elected under neo-Peronist labels in July 1963. Arias and García Heras, "Carisma disperso," 108–9.

43. Alberto Serú García, a national deputy from the Movimiento Popular Mendocino, played a key role in securing the passage of the government's Political Party Statute (Justo López, *Partidos políticos*, 113). Perón made no secret of his distaste for the neo-Peronist role in designing the statute (*Primera Plana*, 21 Apr. 1964, 8–10), and when Serú ran for governor of Mendoza in Apr. 1966, Perón repaid him by backing one of his rivals.

44. *Primera Plana*, 5 May 1964, 7.

45. *Primera Plana*, 2 Feb. 1965, 12–14.

46. James, "Unions and Politics," 278–300.

47. Author's interview with a 1960s leader of the telephone workers' union.

48. Ranis, "Peronismo Without Perón," 120. The Unión Popular was considered to be the "orthodox" Peronist label in the provinces where it contested elections. By this time, the definition of an "orthodox" Peronist leader in the leading periodicals had shifted from one who obeyed Perón's orders at election time (many of these "orders" had, in any case, been extracted from Perón by the unionists) to one who had supported or participated in the reorganization of the PJ, the CGT factory-occupation campaign, and the events surrounding Perón's attempt to return to Argentina. "Unorthodox" neo-Peronist parties, now defined as those that presented candidates who had not been approved by Vandor or Perón, received only 318,000 votes, as against 3,032,000 for the Unión Popular and other "orthodox" Peronist labels (*Primera Plana*, 23 Mar. 1965, 9–11).

49. Niembro's election to head the Peronist deputy bloc is discussed in *Primera Plana*, 30 Mar. 1965, 9; quotation from *Primera Plana*, 11 May 1965, 14.

50. *Boletín Informativo Semanal de la CGT*, 15–21 Mar. 1965, 1. The "lion" in this passage is a metaphor for the armed forces.

51. CGT, "La CGT en marcha," 17, 64–70.

52. *Boletín Informativo Semanal de la CGT*, 8–14 Mar. 1965, 18–22.

53. *Confirmado*, 2 July 1965, 13.   54. *Informes Laborales*, Mar. 1965, 24.

55. *Confirmado*, 2 July 1965, 12.   56. *Primera Plana*, 6 July 1965, 18.

57. For the names of the female candidates, see Bianchi and Sanchis, *El partido peronista femenino*, 100 n. 2. Ciria (in *Política y cultura popular*, 184) gives a figure of 6 female senators and 24 female deputies elected in 1951, but does not provide names or a source. Pellet Lastra (in *El congreso por adentro*, 225)

gives a figure of 6 female senators and 23 female deputies elected in 1951, and adds that in subsequent years, through 1987, women never made up more than 5 percent of either house.

58. Tcach, "Neoperonism y resistencia obrera," 67.

59. Author's interview with Alberto Serú García, Mendoza, 17 Mar. 1993.

60. *Primera Plana*, 19 Oct. 1965, 10–12; 2 Nov. 1965, 10; *Confirmado*, 21 Oct. 1965, 12; 28 Oct. 1965, 16.

61. The information in this paragraph comes from the author's interview with Alberto Serú García, Mendoza, 17 Mar. 1993, and from Dr. Serú's minutes of the Avellaneda meeting, of which he was secretary. I am indebted to Dr. Serú for giving me handwritten and typed copies of the minutes; a list of those present at the roll call; and draft and typescript versions of the final statement. In the reference to Eva Perón in the handwritten draft of the final statement, the word *irreplaceable* is emphasized. Dr. Serú confirmed that its inclusion was intended as an oblique criticism of Isabel and those who surrounded her.

62. *Primera Plana*, 9 Nov. 1965, 16.   63. *Informes Laborales*, Jan. 1966, 21.

64. *Primera Plana*, 21 Dec. 1965, 16   65. *Primera Plana*, 9 Nov. 1965, 16–17.

66. *Primera Plana*, 2 Nov. 1965, 10.   67. *Informes Laborales*, Jan. 1966, 21–24

68. *Informes Laborales*, Feb. 1966, 15.

69. *La Razón*, 2 Feb. 1966.

70. *Primera Plana*, 8 Mar. 1966, 14–16.

71. *Primera Plana*, 29 Mar. 1966, 10–11; 5 Apr. 1966, 11.

72. *Primera Plana*, 5 Apr. 1966, 11. The English translation of this title is "62 Standing Up Beside Trotskyism."

73. Reprinted in Baschetti, *Documentos*, 230. On the battle of the left to include "insurgent" paragraphs, see *Primera Plana*, 29 Mar. 1966, 11.

74. "Relations between the unions and the government were the main focus of disagreement in the [Peronist] union leadership [during the 1955–73 period], the issue from which divisions perennially flared up and which reorganized the *nucleamientos* [groups of union leaders]," Juan Carlos Torre asserts ("El proceso político interno," 62–63). "The direct result of government attempts to control organized labor in the post-Peronist years was the factionalization of the trade union movement between those willing to cooperate and those opposed," Edward Epstein writes; "loyalty to Perón" was the "nominal issue" in "the Vandor-Framini dispute of 1964 [and in] the Vandor-Alonso split of 1966," but "each dispute really dealt with the degree of union cooperation with the government which each of the contending sides advocated" (Epstein, "Control and Cooptation," 458).

75. On factional conflict in Peronist unionism under Frondizi, see Chapter 4. On factional conflict in the unions during the 1966–70 period, see O'Donnell, *Bureaucratic Authoritarianism*, 84–85 and Fernández, *Ideologías*, 2: 10–57. On factional conflict under Menem, see Chapter 8.

76. *Primera Plana*, 28 June 1966, 17.

77. Fernández, *Ideologías*, 2: 11. The author notes that the correspondence was not perfect. Munck, Falcón, and Gallitelli recognize, by contrast, that

the bifurcation of the "62" "did not represent a split between fractions of the working class but simply a quarrel between rival bureaucratic cliques" (*Argentina*, 159).

78. Viola, "Democracia e Autoritarismo," 93.

79. Broadly speaking, dynamic sectors of industry as compared with traditional sectors tend to employ more advanced technology, to be more productive per unit of labor or capital, and to be more closely connected by forward and backward linkages to the most rapidly expanding sectors of the economy. A 1966 report published by the Oficina de Estudios para la Colaboración Económica Internacional (*Argentina Económica y Financiera*, 180) lists metals, auto, paper, glass, chemicals, plastics, ceramics, and rubber as dynamic sectors. O'Donnell (*Bureaucratic Authoritarianism*, 106) lists basic metals, fabricated metals, machines and equipment, nonmetallic minerals, chemicals, and paper as dynamic sectors. He lists food, beverages, textiles, and wood as traditional sectors.

80. W. Smith, *Authoritarianism*, 340–42.

81. Framini had resigned dramatically from the PJ and "62" after Vandor's allies won the PJ's internal elections in mid 1964, but by mid 1965, he had ceased overtly to oppose the metalworkers' chief (*Primera Plana*, 6 July 1965, 18). At the March 1966 Tucumán conference of the "62 de Pie," Framini's allies linked Alonso's right to the hard-line left (*Primera Plana* 5 Apr. 1966, 11).

82. Gazzera, "Nosotros" 113.

83. *Compañero*, 30 Oct. 1963, 3.

84. *Primera Plana*, 2 Mar. 1965, 9.

85. The Huerta Grande demands are reprinted in Baschetti, *Documentos*, 118.

86. Interview with Framini in Calello and Parcero, *De Vandor a Ubaldini*, 1: 55–56. Ducatenzeiler (*Syndicats et politique*, 111) reports that Jorge DiPasquale and other hard-liners did not attend the meeting, but her information conflicts with Framini's and is not attributed to a participant in the Huerta Grande plenary session.

87. James, "Unions and Politics," 341; *Extra*, Feb.–Mar. 1966, 22.

88. James, "Unions and Politics," 313–14. Some of the other demands made in the Huerta Grande Program were also reflected in the August 1963 "62" document: the nationalization of bank deposits and of key industrial sectors, state controls over foreign trade, and the prohibition of imports that competed with national production. James (ibid., 348) argues that the demands in the August 1963 document were just as radical and more specific than those in the Huerta Grande program, but this assertion does not seem valid in the case of agrarian reform or worker control over production.

89. James, "Unions and Politics," 318.

90. Quoted in Walsh, *¿Quién mató a Rosendo?* 163.

91. CGT, "La CGT en marcha," 58.

92. The weekly magazine was *Primera Plana* (28 June 1966, 18); the quotation from Olmos is from *La Razón*, 14 July 1961.

93. Quoted in James, "Unions and Politics," 328.

94. Author's interview with a 1960s leader of the telephone workers' union.

95. Lamadrid, "Sindicatos y política," 80.

96. See, e.g., *Review of the River Plate*, 31 Oct. 1963, 163.

97. *Compañero*, 5 Dec. 1963, 3; see also the statement by the Partido de Trabajo quoted in Lamadrid, "Sindicatos y política," 83.

98. *Confirmado*, 21 May 1965, 11.

99. Quoted in James, "Unions and Politics," 346.

100. Gazzera, "Nosotros," 126–30. On Gazzera's view of Vandor's role in Perón's attempt to return to Argentina, see also Gorbato, *Vandor o Perón*, 91–93.

101. Author's interview with a 1960s leader of the telephone workers' union.

102. Gorbato, *Vandor o Perón*, 96–97.

103. Author's interview with Alberto Serú García, Mendoza, 17 Mar. 1993.

104. Quoted in Horowitz, "Election in Retrospect," 281.

105. *La Razón*, 2 Feb. 1966.

106. CGT, "La CGT en marcha," 68–69.

107. *La Razón*, 21 Apr. 1964.

108. Quoted in Lamadrid, "Sindicatos y política," 81.

109. *La Razón*, 30 Apr. 1964. Framini went on to blast the institution's rector for accepting a half-million dollar grant from the Ford Foundation, announced that the UN Economic Commission for Latin America was a servant of imperialism, and advocated Argentina's becoming a "peaceful atomic power."

110. Quoted in James, "Unions and Politics," 345.

111. Gazzera, "Nosotros," 119; *Primera Plana*, 19 Dec. 1967, 49–50.

112. *Review of the River Plate*, 11 Nov. 1963, 218.

113. *Primera Plana*, 2 Mar. 1965, 9.

114. *Boletín Informativa Semanal de la CGT*, 16–22 Nov. 1964, 15.

115. Bidart Campos, *Grupos de presión*; Imaz, "Factores de poder."

116. CGT, *Memoria y Balance, 1963–1964*, 24, 26.

117. *Primera Plana*, 29 Mar. 1966, 11.

118. Reprinted in Baschetti, *Documentos*, 230–31. By "enemies of the people," Alonso may be referring to Frondizi and his Movimiento de Integración y Desarrollo (MID). Under the Guido government, Vandor's Unión Popular and Frondizi's wing of the UCRI (which soon became the MID) forged an electoral front that was banned on the eve of the July 1963 elections. In the months and years that followed, Vandor was respeatedly accused of being a closet *frondizista* (see esp. Cairo, *Peronismo claves*, 29–52). Framini accused the Vandorists of hoping that all Peronist parties would be banned so that they could run in the 1965 legislative elections under Frondizi's party label (*La Razón*, 19 July 1964). In 1971, Perón's right-hand man Jorge Antonio alleged that Vandor, Framini, Parodi, Iturbe, and Lascano had worked out a deal to run in the 1965 elections on the MID ticket if the PJ were outlawed, and would have done so when the PJ was banned in Feb. 1965, except that Perón ordered them to use the Unión Popular label on pain of expulsion from Peronism (Rouquié, *Poder militar*, 2:

238–39). It is unlikely, however, that Vandor would have preferred an alliance with the independent-minded Frondizi, who had his own political following and organization, to one with the easily manipulable Unión Popular.

119. *Ultima Hora*, 26 May 1966, 14.

120. *Confirmado*, 16 Dec. 1965, 18; *Primera Plana*, 8 Mar. 1966, 14–15.

121. *Primera Plana*, 26 Apr. 1966, 7.

122. *La Nación*, 21 Apr. 1966, 6. A federal court had barred the PJ from contesting the March 1965 national deputy elections, but provincial courts had jurisdiction over the party's right to participate in local elections. In many interior provinces during the early and mid 1960s, such courts regularly allowed local branches of the PJ to contest elections for governor and for provincial legislative seats. It took only four days for the Mendoza courts to approve the PJ's participation in the 1966 gubernatorial election, and some suspected that the UCRP government had leaned on the Mendoza court to let the party run as a way of splitting the Peronist vote. *La Nación*, 19 Apr. 1966, 20.

123. *Primera Plana*, 22 Mar. 1966, 13.

124. Strout, *Recruitment of Candidates in Mendoza*, 37. Serú gives a very different account of the nomination controversy. According to Serú, Dr. Enrique Querubini, a veteran MPM politician, asked him for the MPM gubernatorial candidacy a few months before the election. Partly because Querubini was getting on in years, Serú assented. Shortly thereafter, another party faction offered the candidacy to Corvalán, who was then in retirement. When Corvalán accepted, Serú, worried that Querubini lacked the political weight to beat Corvalán in the primary, asked Querubini if he would be willing to step down. Querubini assented and Serú became the faction's candidate. When Serú beat Corvalán in the primary, Corvalán left the MPM to become the candidate of the local PJ. Author's interviews with Alberto Serú García, Mendoza, 9 and 17 Mar. 1993.

125. *Primera Plana*, 29 Mar. 1966, 10–11

126. *Confirmado*, 17 Mar. 1966, 14, and 31 Mar. 1966, 19; *Primera Plana*, 12 Apr. 1966, 12.

127. *La Nación*, 15 Apr. 1966, 18

128. *Confirmado*, 31 Mar. 1966, 18.

129. *La Nación*, 21 Apr. 1966, 6.

130. *Confirmado*, 31 Mar. 1966, 17; *La Nación*, 19 Apr. 1966, 20.

131. *Confirmado*, 21 Apr. 1966, 14; *Primera Plana*, 26 Apr. 1966, 16; *La Nación*, 21 Apr. 1966, 6.

132. *La Nación*, 17 Apr. 1966, 20.

133. Cantón, *Materiales*, 2: 240–41

134. *Primera Plana*, 12 Apr. 1966, 15; *La Nación* 19 Apr. 1966, 20. According to Alberto Serú García (personal interview, Mendoza, 9 Mar. 1993), those who came to Mendoza to support his candidacy included Vandor, Cafiero, Delia Parodi, Oscar Lascano, Carlos Juárez, and the UOM treasurer Lorenzo Miguel, who "brought money."

135. *Primera Plana*, 26 Apr. 1966, 7, 16.

136. *Primera Plana,* 10 May 1966, 10, 15; 17 May 1966, 14.

137. Halperín Donghi, *Argentina,* 138; *Primera Plana,* 31 May 1966, 18.

138. Cantón, *Elecciones y partidos políticos,* 206–8; Madsen and Snow, *Charismatic Bond,* 60–61.

139. Kirkpatrick, *Leader and Vanguard,* 224.

140. Both Onganía quotations are included in the memoirs of General Manuel Laprida, transcribed in Kvaternik, *El péndulo cívico militar,* 38–39.

141. Memoirs of General Manuel Laprida transcribed in Kvaternik, *El péndulo cívico militar,* 38–66. In retrospect, Laprida might well have been less surprised, because he later recalled a conversation with Onganía in August 1965 in which the army commander-in-chief had confided to him, with "a sly smile," that he had been thinking about "dos, dos, y dos"—two years as army commander-in-chief (beginning in 1963), two years of retirement, and two years in a campaign for president (memoirs of General Manuel Laprida transcribed in Kvaternik, *El péndulo cívico militar,* 133). As early as 1962, officials of the Guido government had been pushing for an Onganía presidency, if possible via the July 1963 elections (Kvaternik, *Crisis sin salvataje,* 111–13).

142. Rouquié, *Poder militar,* 2: 235. A *golpista* is someone who favors or promotes a coup.

143. "It would be useless to inspect the last six months of the Illia government for the immediate and fortuitous causes of the June 1966 coup. One would find only pretexts, not even precipitants: the fuse had been lit ten months before" (ibid., 248).

144. *Primera Plana,* 4 Jan. 1966, 17.

145. Fayt, *El político armado,* 43.

146. Author's interview with retired General Tomás Sánchez de Bustamante, Buenos Aires, 15 July 1989.

147. Author's interview with retired General Juan Carlos Onganía, Boulogne, Province of Buenos Aires, 12 July 1989.

148. *Primera Plana,* 12 Oct. 1965, 15; 11 Jan. 1966, 8; 22 Mar. 1966, 10.

149. O'Donnell ("Modernization and Military Coups," 211) argues that once the electoral strength of Peronism had been confirmed in the March 1965 deputy elections, "the major question was simply the date of the new coup d'état, not its execution or its termination of the political regime of 1955–66."

150. A "top military officer" quoted in *Confirmado,* 21 Apr. 1966, 14. FOTIA is the federation of Tucumán sugar workers' unions, controlled at the time by a leftist faction.

151. Gen. Manuel Laprida quoted in Kvaternik, *El péndulo cívico militar,* 79.

152. Author's interview with retired General Tomás Sánchez de Bustamante, Buenos Aires, 15 July 1989.

153. See, e.g., Luna, *De Perón a Lanusse,* 177; Wynia, *Argentina: Illusions and Realities,* 131; Hodges, *Argentina, 1943–1988,* 59.

154. *Primera Plana,* 12 Jan. 1965, 13.

155. *Primera Plana,* 11 Jan. 1966, 8, and 22 Mar. 1966, 9.

156. Interview with Niembro in Cardoso and Audi, *Sindicalismo,* 68–69.

157. *Informes Laborales*, July 1966, 30–32.
158. *Primera Plana*, 28 Sept. 1965, 13
159. *Primera Plana*, 11 Jan. 1966, 8.
160. Interview with Grinspun transcribed in Gorbato, *Vandor o Perón*, 109–10. Grinspun was Alfonsín's economy minister in 1984–85.
161. Author's interview with Alberto Serú García, Mendoza, 9 Mar. 1993.
162. *Primera Plana*, 28 June 1966, 20.
163. Author's interview with Alberto Serú García, Mendoza, 9 Mar. 1993.
164. W. Smith, "Crisis of the State," 1: 328; 2: 649 n. 28; 2: 651 n. 47.

CHAPTER 6

1. Snow, *Political Forces in Argentina*, 49–50. See also Turner, "Study of Argentine Politics," 93; and O'Donnell, *Bureaucratic Authoritarianism*, 39–40.
2. O'Donnell, *Bureaucratic Authoritarianism*, 58–60.
3. W. C. Smith, *Authoritarianism*, 52.
4. Moyano, "Armed Struggle in Argentina," 33–35.
5. Quoted in Giussani, *Montoneros*, 32.
6. O'Donnell, *Bureaucratic Authoritarianism*, 54–57, 172–73.
7. On the impact of Krieger Vasena's stabilization plan, see O'Donnell, *Bureaucratic Authoritarianism*, 103–38; and W. C. Smith, *Authoritarianism*, 145–49.
8. *Informes Laborales*, July 1966, 25–32, 40–50.
9. Senén González, *El sindicalismo después de Perón*, 89–90; Rotondaro, *Realidad y cambio*, 318; W. C. Smith, *Authoritarianism*, 64, 112–13.
10. O'Donnell, *Bureaucratic Authoritarianism*, 79–83; W. C. Smith, *Authoritarianism*, 113–14; Rotondaro, *Realidad y cambio*, 321–30.
11. Alonso and Loholaberry (who, with the ministry of labor's help, defeated Framini in the AOT's May 1968 internal elections) did not join the participationists until 1968 (Torre, "El proceso político interno," 43–53; Rotondaro, *Realidad y cambio*, 343). Of the 26 participationist unions in the 1969–71 period, 11 came from the "62 de Pie," 5 from the "62 Leales," and 10 from unions aligned with neither faction (DIL, *Nucleamientos Sindicales*, 37–39). That nearly half of the participationist unions came from the "62 de Pie" is another indication of the ad hoc nature of that supposedly militant body.
12. The positions of the three currents are summarized in O'Donnell, *Bureaucratic Authoritarianism*, 84–85, and W. C. Smith, *Authoritarianism*, 116–20. On the combative unions in Córdoba, see Brennan, *Labor Wars*, and Roldán, *Sindicatos y protesta social*.
13. Bra, "El Asesinato de Vandor," 75–78; Gorbato, *Vandor o Perón*, 141–65; Rotondaro, *Realidad y cambio*, 335–44; Lewis, *Crisis of Argentine Capitalism*, 402.
14. This analysis follows that of James, *Resistance and Integration*, 215–35, and Brennan, *Labor Wars*, 343–58. James puts more emphasis on the sociological factors, whereas Brennan stresses historical and cultural traditions.
15. Basic sources on the Cordobazo include Brennan, *Labor Wars*; Balvé et al., *Lucha de calles*; Delich, *Crisis y protesta social*; James, *Resistance and Inte-*

gration, 221–23; O'Donnell, *Bureaucratic Authoritarianism*, 158–60; W. C. Smith, *Authoritarianism*, 128–33, and Lewis, *Crisis of Argentine Capitalism*, 369–84.

16. Moyano, "Armed Struggle in Argentina," 172. The rest of the information in this paragraph is also taken from Moyano's dissertation, a revised version of which has been published as *Argentina's Lost Patrol*.

17. Moyano, "Armed Struggle in Argentina," 237, 245, 255. On controversies surrounding the measurement of human rights abuses in Argentina, see Brysk, "Politics of Measurement."

18. W. C. Smith, *Authoritarianism*, 165–88; O'Donnell, *Bureaucratic Authoritarianism*, 197–226.

19. O'Donnell, *Bureaucratic Authoritarianism*, 234n, 242n, 306.

20. Torre, *Los sindicatos en el gobierno*, 47–48; Senén González, *Diez años de sindicalismo*, 9–10.

21. James, *Resistance and Integration*, 242.

22. *Primera Plana*, 10 May 1966, 13.

23. M. Acuña, *De Frondizi a Alfonsín*, 2: 204–7; W. C. Smith, *Authoritarianism*, 181.

24. This discussion of the Coordinadora is based on Altamirano, "La Coordinadora" (quotations from Coordinadora documents on pages 299n and 310). The origins of the Coordinadora are described exhaustively in Leuco and Díaz, *Los herederos de Alfonsín*, 65–92.

25. Balbín got 165,140 votes to Alfonsín's 126,204 (M. Acuña, *De Frondizi a Alfonsín*, 2: 206). The now-defunct UCRP had also nominated its presidential candidates by direct primary. Prior to the 1958 elections won by the UCRI's Frondizi, Balbín won the UCRP nomination over Miguel Angel Zavala Ortíz by 187,762 votes to 132,310 (R. Gallo, *Balbín, Frondizi*, 172).

26. A 1972 decree established that senators would henceforth be elected directly rather than by the provincial legislatures and that each province would have three senators rather than two. It also provided for a two-round electoral system for president, whereby the initial first-place and second-place vote-getters would have to compete against each other in a second round unless the first-place finisher won more than 50 percent of the vote (Cámpora won just under 50 percent but Balbín conceded, precluding the need for a second round). These rules were scrapped in 1983 in favor of the previous system, but similar rules, including a two-round system for electing the president, direct election of senators (as of 2001), and three senators from each province, were reinstituted during the 1994 constitutional reform, best known for permitting the immediate reelection of the president.

27. See the surveys discussed in Turner, "Study of Argentine Politics," 96–97.

28. W. S. Smith, "Return of Peronism," 125, 140; Cavarozzi, "Peronism and Radicalism," 165–66.

29. On the Ezeiza massacre, see Verbitsky, *Ezeiza*, and Martínez, *Perón Novel*. The official death toll was 13, with approximately 400 injured (Verbitsky, *Ezeiza*, 117–18), but the Montonero leader Mario Firmenich, to whose

organization many of the dead belonged, gave a figure of 182 killed (Giussani, *Montoneros*, 235n).

30. W. S. Smith, "Return of Peronism," 133–34.

31. Viola, "Democracia e Autoritarismo," 486–87.

32. On the general theme of playing the military card, see O'Donnell, *Bureaucratic Authoritarianism*, 207–8. On the UCRP's willingness to play the military card during the Frondizi government, see Cavarozzi, "Los partidos y el parlamento," 139. On Frondizi's reaction to Illia's overthrow, see W. C. Smith, *Authoritarianism*, 64.

33. The analysis in this paragraph follows that of Cavarozzi, "Peronism and Radicalism," 152, 167.

34. Viola, "Democracia e Autoritarismo," 517.

35. See Ayres, " 'Social Pact,' " on this aspect of Perón's economic policy.

36. González Jansen, *La Triple-A*, 13–20; Viola, "Democracia e Autoritarismo," 534.

37. Viola, "Democracia e Autoritarismo," 517.

38. De Riz, *Retorno y Derrumbe*, 119–21.

39. Viola, "Democracia e Autoritarismo," 571.

40. Ibid., 574.

41. Senén González, *Diez años de sindicalismo argentino*, 48.

42. The characterization of Menem is from Viola, "Democracia e Autoritarismo," 574–75.

43. Far from being isolated in his union, Calabró had the support of numerous UOM locals in the Buenos Aires metropolitan area, but such support proved insufficient to save his political career. Senén González, *Diez años de sindicalismo argentino*, 49; De Riz, *Retorno y Derrumbe*, 141.

44. Cavarozzi, "Los partidos y el parlamento," 151.

45. Kandel and Monteverde, *Entorno y caída*, 120.

46. Interview with Miguel Unamuno in Cardoso and Audi, *Sindicalismo*, 104–5. Lorenzo Miguel was among the few top union leaders who stuck by Isabel Perón to the bitter end.

47. Number of disappearances from CONADEP, *Nunca Mas*, 16. The authors of this study note (p. 479) that the real figure is higher because many disappearances went unreported.

48. St. Jean quote from C. Acuña and Smulovitz, "¿Ni olvido, ni perdón?" 8–9; Menéndez quote from W. C. Smith, *Authoritarianism*, 232.

49. Cox, "Sound of One Hand Clapping." Figures on killings of journalists from p. 9.

50. C. Acuña and Smulovitz, "¿Ni olvido, ni perdón?" 7 n. 11, 9 n. 18.

51. López Alonso, *1930–1980*, 315. Neither international law nor the Argentine constitution gives the government unlimited powers during a state of siege. Article 23 of the Argentine constitution gives those detained during such periods the option of leaving the country, but this option was legally suspended during the 1976–83 dictatorship. See Groisman, "El 'Proceso de Reorganización Nacional,' " 63–64.

52. C. Acuña and Smulovitz "¿Ni olvido, ni perdón?" 9 n. 18. An early report on human rights abuses in Argentina estimated that fewer than 20 percent of the disappeared were members of guerrilla groups. *Latin America Political Report*, 6 Jan. 1978, cited in Rock, *Argentina, 1516–1982*, 367.

53. Osiel, "Making of Human Rights Policy," 141.

54. See Canitrot, "Discipline," 917–18, for this interpretation of the goals of the government's economic policies.

55. Figures on GDP and inflation from W. C. Smith, *Authoritarianism*, 248.

56. Quotation from González Bombal, "El diálogo político," 27; other information from ibid., 21–23, 40–44, 69–82.

57. Figures on real per capita GDP and industrial production from W. C. Smith, *Authoritarianism*, 248.

58. Rock, *Argentina, 1516–1982*, 373. According to the Stockholm International Peace Research Institute, Argentina spent up to $14.3 billion on arms purchases between 1976 and 1982 (Burns, *Land That Lost Its Heroes*, 8). The sales pitches of international banks, which found themselves awash in petrodollars after the oil price hikes of 1979, also helped boost the foreign debt to $43.5 billion by the time the military left office.

59. Cordeu, Mercado, and Sosa, *Peronismo*, 139; Beliz, *CGT*, 98; interview with Lorenzo Miguel in *Siete Días*, 19 Dec. 1984, 8–9; Aznárez and Calistro, *Lorenzo*, 220–21.

60. Falcón, "Conflicto social y régimen militar," 115.

61. Pozzi, "Argentina, 1976–1982," 120–21.

62. In 1980, for example, Triaca (founder of GyT and assistant secretary-general of the plastics workers' union) sold a property valued at U.S.$1.5 million to Partagás, a consortium of fifteen generals and three lieutenant-colonels. (Triaca explained that an inheritance from his mother-in-law had enabled him to buy the 2,150-square-meter property, which was located in a fashionable quarter of the federal capital). Rubén Furman y Guillermo Alfieri, "La mano en la trampa," *Página Doce*, 25 Nov. 1990, 4; *Clarín*, 9 July 1989, 20.

63. Beliz, *CGT*, 31–32; Cordeu, Mercado, and Sosa, *Peronismo*, 73–74.

64. Abós, *Los organizaciones sindicales*, 54–55; Pozzi, "Argentina, 1976–1982," 127–28.

65. Dabat and Lorenzano, *Conflicto malvinense*, 112–16. On the construction projects, see Simpson and Bennett, *Disappeared*, 198–203.

66. Navarro, "Personal Is Political"; Brysk, *Politics of Human Rights in Argentina*, 47–49; Membership figure from Guest, *Behind the Disappearances*, 210.

67. Yearly figures for recorded disappearances from Moyano, "Armed Struggle in Argentina," 53.

68. Pion-Berlin, "Fall of Military Rule," 64–65.

69. Quoted in Guest, *Behind the Disappearances*, 271.

70. González Bombal, "El diálogo político," 83–84.

71. O'Donnell, *Bureaucratic Authoritarianism*, 238–41; W. C. Smith, *Authoritarianism*, 178–79, 190–94.

72. On the difficulty of reversing the "resurrection of civil society" during transitions, see O'Donnell and Schmitter, *Transitions from Authoritarian Rule*, 48–56.

73. Federal police figures given in Dabat and Lorenzano, *Conflicto malvinense*, 122.

74. González Bombal, "El diálogo político," 40–44, 99–102, 112–13.

75. Fontana, "De la crisis de Malvinas," 6–7; González Bombal, "El diálogo político," 114–16; Vacs, "Authoritarian Breakdown," 28.

76. Guest, *Behind the Disappearances*, 337–40. Galtieri had impressed the Reagan administration on a tour of the United States shortly before taking office. National Security Adviser Richard Allen remarked that he posessed "a majestic personality" and Defense Secretary Caspar Weinberger was "very impressed" by Galtieri (Oscar Cardoso et al., *Malvinas*, 29). These remarks, publicized in the press, were not lost on Galtieri. In an April 1983 interview with the newspaper *Clarín*, Galtieri said that he had thought of himself "as the pampered child of the North Americans," and added "if I had known the Americans would take the position they finally adopted, we would never have invaded" (quoted in Fox and Meisler, "Buenos Aires," 14).

77. Fontana, "De la crisis de Malvinas," 16.

78. *Latin American Weekly Report*, 23 July 1982, 7.

79. The first attempt to formalize a negotiated transition came in November 1982 in the form of a fifteen-point document demanding military participation in the next government, rejecting any inquiry into the dirty war or military corruption, and prohibiting the dismissal of military-appointed judges (Verbitsky, *Civiles y militares*, 33; Fontana, "De la crisis de Malvinas," 22–23). The second involved the April 1983 "Final Document of the Military Junta on the War Against Subversion and Terrorism" (San Martino de Dromi, *Historia política*, 2: 361; Verbitsky, *Civiles y militares*, 34–35). The third attempt to negotiate an agreement involved the September 1983 "Law of National Pacification" (Fontana, "De la crisis de Malvinas," 27–31). The second and third documents represented little more than attempts to avoid prosecution for human rights violations.

80. Burns, *Land That Lost Its Heroes*, 124–25.

81. For the 1966 poll, see Turner, "Study of Argentine Politics," 93; for the 1983 survey, see Catterberg, *Argentina Confronts Politics*, 80.

82. Burns, *Land That Lost Its Heroes*, 125.

83. Osiel, "Making of Human Rights Policy," 141.

84. Fox, "Argentina: A Prosecution in Trouble," 42. Two sources close to the Alfonsín administration independently suggested the slightly higher figure of 1,500–2,000 (Moyano, " 'Dirty War' in Argentina," 267 n. 82).

85. Moyano, " 'Dirty War' in Argentina," 64.

86. *Latin American Weekly Report*, 5 Nov. 1982, 2–3.

87. CISEA, *Argentina, 1983*, 102–3. Other Peronists also believed that a pact was in the making. Carpena and Jacquelin, *El intocable*, 222–23.

88. Beliz, *CGT*, 168–69; Gaudio and Thompson, *Sindicalismo peronista*, 17. For an account that gives Herminio Iglesias the key role in the negotiations, see Cordeu, Mercado and Sosa, *Peronismo*, 111–18. Another detailed account of the alleged pact may be found in Aznárez and Calistro, *Lorenzo*, 133–38.

89. *Entrelineas*, no. 18 (May 1983), quoted in Abós, *Las organizaciones sindicales*, 148.

90. Carpena and Jacquelin, *El intocable*, 225.

91. Osiel, "Making of Human Rights Policy," 143.

92. The protagonists of these attempts included General Galtieri (Burns, *Land That Lost Its Heroes*, 104), Admiral Massera (Guest, *Behind the Disappearances*, 71–72, 346), and Brigadier General Lami Dozo (*Latin American Weekly Report*, 13 Aug. 1982, 6; 27 Aug. 1982, 1).

93. Viola and Mainwaring, "Transitions to Democracy"; Stepan, "Paths Toward Redemocratization."

94. This argument is developed in McGuire, "Interim Government."

95. Viola and Mainwaring, "Transitions to Democracy," 207.

96. Palermo, "Democracia interna en los partidos," 90 n. 69.

97. Cordeu, Mercado and Sosa, *Peronismo*, 41.

98. Ibid.

99. McGuire, "Union Political Tactics," 42.

100. Palermo, "Democracia interna en los partidos," 99–100.

101. Quoted in Aznárez and Calistro, *Lorenzo*, 151–52.

102. *Convicción*, 19 July 1983, 2; *Clarín*, 3 July 1988, 3.

103. Analysis of the reasons for the UCR victory in the 1983 elections may be found in Jorrat "Las elecciones de 1983"; Maronese et al., *El voto peronista '83*; and Mora y Araujo, "Nature of the Alfonsín Coalition."

104. A 1983 survey of Argentina's major urban centers showed that only 6 percent of upper-class respondents approved of the 1973–76 Peronist government, whereas 82 percent disapproved. On the other hand, 64 percent of upper-class respondents approved of the 1963–66 Illia government (the last time the Radicals had held the presidency), whereas only 15 percent disapproved (Catterberg, *Argentina Confronts Politics*, 80).

CHAPTER 7

1. INDEC, *Censo nacional económico, 1985*, 15. See Lewis, *Crisis of Argentine Capitalism*, 463–65, for a list of major factory closings under the 1976–83 military regime. The evolution of overall manufacturing employment under the 1976–83 military regime is a matter of some dispute. Whereas the 1985 economic census showed a slight rise between 1973 and 1984, a ministry of labor study showed a 30 percent drop in overall manufacturing employment between 1974 and 1981 (Ministerio de Trabajo, "Ocupación y producto," 31).

2. *La Nación*, 8 July 1989, 13; Schwarzer and Aronskind, "Exportaciones Argentinas: Su peor momento."

3. Manzetti and Dell'Aquila, "Economic Stabilisation"; Lewis, *Crisis of Argentine Capitalism*, 484–87.

4. W. C. Smith, "Democracy, Distributional Conflicts, and Macroeconomic Policymaking," 11, 16, 22.

5. Aguero, "Military and the Limits to Democratization," 159–62.

6. Asked in a 1993 interview whether it would have been better to transfer the trials to civilian courts earlier, when public anger at the 1976–83 juntas was more acute, Alfonsín replied "that would have been unconstitutional. Actually there are two constitutional problems, because having the trials in the military courts was itself unconstitutional, and taking them out of those courts was also unconstitutional." Author's interview with Raúl Alfonsín, New Haven, Conn., 8 Apr. 1993.

7. Norden, "Rebels with a Cause?" 10.

8. On the human rights trials and the military's response, see Osiel, "Making of Human Rights Policy"; Crawford, "Due Obedience and the Rights of Victims," Acuña and Smulovitz, "¿Ni olvido, ni perdón?" Pion-Berlin, "Between Confrontation and Accommodation" and "To Prosecute or Pardon?" and Brysk, *Politics of Human Rights in Argentina*.

9. Author's interview with Raúl Alfonsín, New Haven, Conn., 8 Apr. 1993.

10. Snow, *Political Forces in Argentina*, 50. The methodology of the surveys was not reported.

11. Catterberg, *Argentina Confronts Politics*, 56.

12. Vernet, who had worked in the UOM's Santa Fe section, was Lorenzo Miguel's close ally (Morales Solá, *Asalto a la ilusión*, 88). Miguel took the second vice presidency despite having stated publicly, in deference to his perceived responsibility for the 1983 electoral defeat, that no unionist should occupy any of the party's top four posts (*Tiempo Argentino*, 14 Sept. 1984, 6).

13. *Somos*, 21 Dec. 1984, 7–15; Leuco and Díaz, *El heredero de Perón*, 36–40.

14. Abós, *El posperonismo*, 110.

15. Gaudio and Domenicone, "El proceso de normalización sindical," 32–35.

16. Gaudio and Thompson, *Sindicalismo peronista*, 39. On the "third historical movement," see Aznar et al., *Alfonsín*.

17. Altamirano, "La Coordinadora," 315–19; Cavarozzi, "Peronism and Radicalism," 172; M. Acuña, *De Frondizi a Alfonsín*, 2: 224–25.

18. Quoted in Gaudio and Thompson, *Sindicalismo peronista*, 42. The use of "social democratic" as an epithet was popular among those who opposed the Alfonsín government and/or renewal Peronism.

19. *Informes Laborales*, Feb. 1984, 3.53.

20. Gaudio and Thompson, *Sindicalismo peronista*, 41.

21. Gaudio and Domenicone, "El proceso de normalización sindical," 66.

22. *Informes Laborales*, Feb. 1986, 3.445.

23. McGuire, "Union Political Tactics," 43–44.

24. See respectively *El Bimestre Político y Económico*, July–Aug. 1988, 37; *El Periodista*, 20–26 Sept. 1985, 11; and *El Bimestre Político y Económico*, Nov.–Dec. 1987, 29.

25. Movimiento Sindical Peronista Renovador, "Documento final," 2, 13.

26. The text of this statement was published in *La Razón*, 22 July 1986, 12. Antonio Cafiero, a key renewal politician, also sided with the Sandinistas against the Contras (*El Bimestre Político y Económico*, Sept.–Oct. 1987, 27).

27. Author's interview with a union leader from the "62," 22 Sept. 1986.

28. *Clarín*, 21 Aug. 1986, 8.

29. *Clarín*, 13 Aug. 1986, 11, on Ibáñez; *El Bimestre Político y Económico*, July–Aug. 1986, 29, on Triaca.

30. *La Razón*, 10 July 1986, 13.

31. *El Bimestre Político y Económico*, May–June 1987, 27, 36, 39.

32. Author's interview with a union leader from the "62," 22 Sept. 1986.

33. *La Razón*, 25 Apr. 1985, 14.

34. *Clarín*, 27 Apr. 1985, 12. Ubaldini during the Alfonsín presidency attended human rights demonstrations, publicly embraced the Mothers of the Plaza de Mayo, and declared opposition to the due obedience bill (*Informes Laborales*, Sept. 1985, 3.361; *El Bimestre Político y Económico*, May–June 1987, 36). In June 1988, Ubaldinista and "25" representatives issued a joint statement advocating that "the armed forces . . . subordinate themselves to the democratic system, and guarantee the people that nothing will stand in the way of the prosecution of those who, using the [military] institution, violated human rights" (*Informes Laborales*, June 1988, 3.837).

35. *Informes Laborales*, Aug. 1985, 3.352, and Sept. 1985, 3.360.

36. CEPNA, *El nuevo sindicalismo*, 73.

37. *El Periodista*, 8–14 Nov. 1985, 7.

38. *Clarín*, 15 Sept. 1985, 18–19; Morales Solá, *Asalto a la ilusión*, 71; Beliz, *CGT*, 33–35.

39. Quoted in Beliz, *CGT*, 117.

40. Palomino, "Confrontación de actores y sistemas," 15.

41. The "26 Points" are incuded as appendices to Beliz, *CGT*, and Gaudio and Thompson, *Sindicalismo peronista*.

42. Palermo, "Transformación social," 79.

43. Quoted in Beliz, *CGT*, 117–18.

44. Gaudio and Thompson, *Sindicalismo Peronista*, 99. Emphasis in original.

45. According to data compiled from newspapers by the Consejo Técnico de Inversiones, Argentina experienced 2,311 strikes between 1984 and 1988, accounting for a total of 94,563,257 days lost (both figures exclude CGT general strikes). Even if, as evidence suggests, these figures slightly overestimate the number of days lost to strikes, Argentina's strike volume during this period would still have been many times higher than that of any advanced industrial country. Strike figures for Argentina from McGuire, "Strikes in Argentina"; for other countries, *Economist*, 7 Nov. 1992, 24.

46. Gaudio and Thompson, *Sindicalismo Peronista*, 93.

47. McGuire, "Causes of Strikes in Argentina," 7, table 2.

48. *Informes Laborales*, Dec. 1986, 3.601–3.610

49. *La Nación*, int. ed., 10 Nov. 1986, 2.

50. *La Razón*, 1 Mar. 1986, 14.   51. *La Razón*, 10 July 1986, 19.

52. *La Razón*, 22 July 1986, 14.   53. *Informes Laborales*, Nov. 1986, 3.609.

54. *Informes Laborales*, Mar. 1987, 3.657.

55. *La Nación*, int. ed., 30 Mar. 1987, 4.

56. Gaudio and Thompson, *Sindicalismo Peronista*, 172.

57. Strike figures (corrected for source's overestimate of employment in metalworking industry) from *Tendencias Económicas*, June 1985, 9. Iron/steel and industrial production figures from INDEC, *Estadística Mensual*, June 1987.

58. *Apuntes*, June 1987, 2.

59. Author's interview with Raúl Alfonsín, New Haven, Conn., 8 Apr. 1993.

60. Beliz, *CGT*, 19, 182–84. Asked to confirm that Nosiglia and Cavalieri had been the main architects of the 1987 pact, Alfonsín responded that "it was a whole group of unionists, but I was mainly interested in SMATA [the auto workers' union] and Luz y Fuerza [the light and power workers' union], not so much Cavalieri. He has a certain presence but it's not with combative unionism [*sindicalismo luchador*]. I was interested in SMATA and Luz y Fuerza. I would have preferred José Rodríguez of SMATA to become [labor] minister, and if the UOM had gone along with him, it would have given me coverage that would have reduced the level of conflict." Author's interview with Raúl Alfonsín, New Haven, Conn., 8 Apr. 1993. Lorenzo Miguel and other metalworkers' leaders vetoed Rodríguez's appointment because the UOM had been struggling with SMATA for decades over who would get to represent workers in auto and auto parts factories. Had Rodríguez become labor minister, he would have acquired the authority to arbitrate such demarcation disputes.

61. *Clarín*, 7 July 1988, 6.

62. Quoted in Beliz, *CGT*, 186.

63. *Informes Laborales*, Apr. 1987, 3.673.

64. *Informes Laborales*, Mar. 1987, 3.657, and Apr. 1987, 2.127; *La Nación*, int. ed., 30 Mar. 1987, 2.

65. *El Bimestre Político y Económico*, July–Aug. 1987, 35; *Clarín*, 20 July 1987, 14.

66. *Informes Laborales*, Mar. 1989, 3.924.

67. *Informes Laborales*, June 1988, 3.837; Aug. 1988, 3.859.

68. *El Bimestre Político y Económico*, Jan.–Feb. 1989, 27–28.

69. *Informes Laborales*, May 1987, 2.1299.

70. *Informes Laborales*, Apr. 1987, 2.1258.

71. *Informes Laborales*, Mar. 1987, 3.653, and Apr. 1987, 3.673; *La Nación*, int. ed., 26 Mar. 1987, 1.

72. *Clarín*, 9 Sept. 1987, 15.

73. Beliz, *CGT*, 121.

74. *Clarín*, 4 Sept. 1987, 21.

75. Gaudio and Thompson, *Sindicalismo Peronista*, 202.

76. Beliz, *CGT*, 57–62, 118–19, 147–58; Leuco and Díaz, *El heredero de Perón*, 55–60, 71; *La Nación*, 8 July 1989, 8. On Menem's background, see also Cerruti and Ciancaglini, *El octavo circulo*, and Cerruti, *El jefe*.

77. On the 1984 poll, see Leuco and Díaz, *El heredero de Perón*, 34; a poll in

Somos, 21 Dec. 1984, 12, gave similar results. On the 1986 poll, see Leuco and Díaz, *El heredero de Perón*, 49.

78. *El Bimestre Político y Económico*, Sept.–Oct. 1987, 44.
79. Leuco and Díaz, *El heredero de Perón*, 50.
80. Partido Justicialista, "Carta Orgánica Nacional," Article 24. Of the 17 union representatives on the national directive council in mid 1989, 7 came from the "15," 5 from the "25," 4 from the Ubaldinistas, and only 1 from the pro-Miguel core of the "62" (Partido Justicialista, "Consejo Nacional").
81. Palermo, "Transformación social," 85.
82. Gaudio and Thompson, *Sindicalismo Peronista*, 201.
83. *Informes Laborales*, Jan.–Feb. 1988, 3.786.
84. Morales Solá, *Asalto a la ilusión*, 88–90.
85. Chumbita, *El enigma peronista*, 156.
86. Leuco and Díaz, *El heredero de Perón*, 45, 173.
87. *Clarín*, 3 July 1988, 3.
88. Figures from Leuco and Díaz, *El heredero de Perón*, 52.
89. *El Bimestre Político y Económico*, Nov.–Dec. 1987, 44.
90. *Clarín*, 1 July 1988, 6.
91. Morales Solá, *Asalto a la ilusión*, 84–85.
92. Quoted in Beliz, *CGT*, 201–2.
93. Cerruti and Ciancaglini, *El octavo circulo*, 12.
94. *Informes Laborales*, Aug. 1988, 3.851; Gaudio and Thompson, *Sindicalismo Peronista*, 231, 234.
95. *Latin American Weekly Report*, 22 Sept. 1988.
96. Gaudio and Thompson, *Sindicalismo Peronista*, 233–34.
97. *El Bimestre Político y Económico*, Sept.–Oct. 1988, 24.
98. Interview with Barrionuevo in Daiha and Haimovichi 1989, 63.
99. *El Bimestre Político y Económico*, Sept.–Oct. 1988, 24–26
100. *Informes Laborales*, Mar. 1989, 3.921–22.
101. *El Bimestre Político y Económico*, Mar.–Apr. 1989, 28. "We have good relations with the armed forces, with the Church, with employers, and with certain embassies. Ours is a project of power. Although they may try to knock us down, we will be there—no matter what the government," a member of the "15" commented in July 1988 (quoted in Gaudio and Thompson, *Sindicalismo Peronista*, 230).
102. Leuco and Díaz, *El heredero de Perón*, 176. Information on Zanola posters from personal observation.
103. *Bimestre Político y Económico*, Sept.–Oct. 1988, 53; *La Nación*, int. ed., 26 Nov. 1990, 4.
104. Interview with Barrionuevo in Daiha and Haimovichi, *Menem y su entorno*, 65.
105. Juan José Lingeri (waterworks) quoted in *Informes Laborales*, Apr. 1989, 3.930.
106. *Informes Laborales*, May 1989, 3.934.
107. Catterberg, *Argentina Confronts Politics*, 93, 95. Alfonsín's good–very

good rating was much higher in other areas: 62 percent on respect for human rights and 58 percent on assurance of democratic stability.

108. On the deepening economic crisis prior to the 1989 elections, see W. C. Smith, "Hyperinflation," 37–41. The yearly rise in consumer prices from August 1988 to July 1989 was 3,610 percent. W. C. Smith, "State, Market, and Neoliberalism," 45.

CHAPTER 8

1. Waisman, *Reversal of Development*, 122.
2. This characterization of free-market reforms draws on Przeworski, *Democracy and the Market*, 136.
3. World Bank, *Argentina*, 115.
4. *Economist*, "Back in the Saddle," 5; *Clarín*, int. ed., 12–19 Oct. 1993, 12.
5. Employment and subsidy figures from World Bank, *Argentina*, 211, 299, 308.
6. World Bank, *Argentina*, 6, 13, 40–46, 303.
7. *Clarín*, econ. suppl., 21 Nov. 1993, E6–7, E12.
8. Bouzas, "¿Mas alla de la estabilización y la reforma?" 7.
9. Ibid., 15. On the Mercosur free trade agreement, see Manzetti, "Political Economy of MERCOSUR."
10. *Clarín*, int. ed., 29 Oct.–4 Nov. 1991, 1, 6–7.
11. What Cavallo actually did was to make 10,000 australes, the currency in use in Apr. 1991, worth U.S.$1. The peso was not introduced until Jan. 1, 1992, when it was made equivalent to 10,000 australes.
12. *Journal of Commerce*, 12 Dec. 1994; *Buenos Aires Herald*, 5 Jan. 1995 (both via Knight-Ridder Financial News over the Internet).
13. *Clarín*, int. ed., 6–12 Dec. 1994, 12.
14. The economy ministry poverty studies are reported in *Clarín*, int. ed., 22–28 Dec. 1992, 7, and *Clarín*, econ. suppl., 15 Aug. 1993, 11. The UNICEF income distribution study is reported in Powers, "Politics of Poverty," 20, citing the summary in *Latin American Economy & Business*, Jan. 1994, 6. The World Bank poverty and income distribution study is reported in *Página 12*, 21 and 22 Sept. 1994, as summarized by Marcelo Zlotogwiazda in *Microsemanario* 168 (19–25 Sept. 1994) available over the internet at gopher://gopher.uba.ar. Montoya and Mitnik, "Evolución de pobreza," also present data showing that poverty dropped and income distribution improved during Menem's first term. This research was sponsored by the Fundación Mediterranea, to which the economy minister Domingo Cavallo belonged.
15. UNDP, *Human Development Report 1993*, 49–51.
16. *Clarín*, econ. suppl., 5 Apr. 1992, 2–5; *Clarín*, int. ed., 27 Oct. 1992, 5.
17. FIEL/CEA, *Argentina*, 145.
18. *Clarín*, int. ed., 21 Apr. 1992, 3.
19. Mora y Araujo, "Las demandas sociales," 316.
20. *Economist*, "Back in the Saddle," 6.

21. Productivity figure from *Clarín*, econ. suppl., 29 Jan. 1995, 5; manufacturing wage figure from FIEL, *Indicadores de Coyuntura: Reseña 1994*, special issue (July 1995), 21. Across the economy as a whole, real wages declined 7 percent and purchasing power fell 3 percent between 1991 and June 1995. FIEL, *Indicadores de Coyuntura*, no. 347 (July 1995): 21.

22. *Economist*, 8 Apr. 1995, 59. This figure represented a significant increase over 1992, when 3 million foreign visitors spent $3.1 billion. By contrast, tourist arrivals in Brazil fell from 2 million in 1987 to 1 million in 1991, partly because of fear of crime and AIDS. *Clarín*, int. ed., 25–31 Aug. 1992, 10; 16–22 May 1993, 13. In 1994, 2 million foreign visitors to Brazil spent $1.8 billion (*Economist*, 8 Apr. 1995, 59).

23. Foreign-debt figure for 1993 from World Bank, *Argentina*, 271; current-account-deficit figure for 1994 (third quarter) from *Economist*, 12–18 Aug. 1995, 90.

24. *Wall Street Journal*, 21 Mar. 1995, 1, 17; *La Nación*, 28 Feb. 1995. Foreign-debt figure (for 1994) from the Interamerican Development Bank, available over the internet at http://iadb6000.iadb.org/http/argentina.

25. FIEL, *Indicadores de Coyuntura*, no. 347 (July 1995): 53, 54.

26. *Latin American Weekly Report*, 27 July 1995, 326. Unemployment figures from 1974 onward may be found in Consejo Técnico de Inversiones, *La economía argentina, 1993*.

27. On law and who it covered, see *Clarín*, int. ed., 4 Aug. 1992, 3. On the proportion of workers receiving unemployment insurance and the size of their payments, see *Latin American Weekly Report*, 27 Aug. 1995, 326.

28. For Menem's claim, see *Clarín*, int. ed., 31 Jan.–6 Feb. 1995, 3; for Cavallo's interpretation, see *Latin American Weekly Report*, 16 Feb. 1995, 63 and 27 July 1995, 326, as well as *Clarín*, int. ed., 25 July–1 Aug. 1995, 6–7; for the statistics, see *Clarín*, econ. suppl., 29 Jan. 1995, 3, 5, and *Latin American Weekly Report*, 27 July 1995, 326.

29. Adolfo Canitrot in *Clarín*, econ. suppl., 23 Jan. 1995, 8–10.

30. For the claim, see *Clarín*, int. ed., 31 Jan.–6 Feb. 1995, 3; for the study see *Latin American Weekly Report*, 27 July 1995, 326.

31. *Latin American Weekly Report*, 11 Aug. 1994, 350; 26 Jan. 1995, 35; 2 Feb. 1995, 63.

32. *Clarín*, int. ed., 18 July 1995, 1, 6–7.

33. Godio and Palomino, *El movimiento sindical*, 50. Other estimates of union membership and a discussion of their reliability may be found in Feldman, "Tendencias de la sindicalización," and Lamadrid and Orsatti, "Una revisión de las medidas."

34. *Clarín*, econ. suppl., 5–11 Apr. 1992, E2–3; 5–11 Dec. 1993, E6–7.

35. *Clarín*, econ. suppl., 14 Nov. 1993, E2–3.

36. McGuire, "Strikes in Argentina."

37. FIEL/CEA, *Argentina*, 223.

38. *La Nación*, int. ed., 28 May 1990, 1; 4 June 1990, 5; 22 Oct. 1990, 1.

39. Moreno, *La nueva negociación*, 190.

40. *Clarín*, econ. suppl., 14 Nov. 1993, E2–3.

41. World Bank, *Argentina*, 74–75. Additional information on services provided by the *obras sociales* comes from *Página Doce*, 25 Nov. 1990, 4.

42. In the late 1980s, textile workers paid union dues of 2 percent of gross income; bank clerks, metal workers, and railway workers paid 2.5 percent. Dues figures from printout of computerized data furnished specially to the author by labor ministry personnel, Buenos Aires, July 1989.

43. World Bank, *Argentina*, 70. Assuming that each union member pays dues of 2 percent on monthly pay (*salario del bolsillo*) averaging $768 (the average for 15 private-sector industries and services in March 1993, according to *Clarín*, econ. suppl., 26 Sept. 1993, 8–9), the average Argentine unionist pays about U.S.$184 in dues each year. Assuming (generously) that there are 4,000,000 union members in Argentina, the total dues income collected by all Argentine unions would amount to U.S.$737,000,000.

44. *Clarín*, 4 July 1991, 9.

45. *La Prensa*, 21 Feb. 1991, 5.

46. Figure from *Página Doce*, 16 June 1989, 7; quotation from World Bank, *Argentina*, 76. On the political uses of ANSSAL funds, see also *Página Doce*, 2 July 1991, 6.

47. Adelman, "Post-Populist Argentina," 83.

48. Miguel's support for Triaca derived mainly from his reluctance to have the post go to José Rodríguez of the SMATA auto workers union, which the UOM had confronted for 25 years in demarcation disputes (of which the labor minister was final arbiter). *Redacción* 194 (June 1989): 22. On Roig's influence, see also *Clarín*, 9 July 1989, 20; on Miguel's, see also *La Nación*, int. ed., 21 Jan. 1991, 3.

49. Rubén Furman y Guillermo Alfieri, "La mano en la trampa," *Página Doce*, 25 Nov. 1990, 4; *Clarín*, 9 July 1989, 20.

50. *La Nación*, int. ed., 5 Mar. 1990, 5.

51. The author was present in the crowd.

52. *La Nación*, int. ed., 26 Nov. 1990, 2, 4; *Página Doce*, 25 Nov. 1990, 4; *New York Times*, 25 Nov. 1990, A10.

53. *Clarín*, 12 Oct. 1989, 2–4, and 15 Oct. 1989, 2–6; *Somos*, 18 Oct. 1989, 10–12; *La Prensa*, 28 Oct. 1989, 5.

54. *Clarín*, 15 Oct. 1989, 5.

55. Miguel's not inconsiderable patronage resources derived in part from "his long-term association with the entrepreneur Julio Raele, whose Instituto Cooperativo de Seguros still insures a good part of the unions' buildings, automobiles, and properties" (*Página Doce*, 25 Nov. 1990, 4). Raele also provides life insurance and burial insurance for UOM members (Carpena and Jacquelin, *El intocable*, 203–14).

56. *La Nación*, int. ed., 19 Mar. 1990, 4. Miguel's own explanation for why he opposed the general strike was that he did not wish to launch a frontal attack on the government at a time when the army commander-in-chief was in the hospital with what proved to be a terminal illness, fueling rumors of a military

330 Notes to Pages 229-36

coup. "I don't want to wind up back on the boat," Miguel said, in a reference to his 1976 imprisonment on a navy ship (*La Nación*, int. ed., 12 Mar. 1990, 3).

57. *La Nación*, int. ed., 19 Nov. 1990, 2–4; 4 Dec. 1990, 2; 24 Dec. 1990, 2.

58. *La Nación*, int. ed., 7 Aug. 1989, 2.

59. *La Nación*, int. ed., 21 Jan. 1991, 1, 3; quotation from *La Prensa*, 21 Jan. 1991, 3.

60. *Clarín*, int. ed., 17–23 Dec. 1991, 3; 14–20 July 1992, 7; *Página Doce*, 4 July 1991, 6, *Latin American Regional Reports–Southern Cone*, RS-92-01, 6 Feb. 1992, 2.

61. *Clarín*, int. ed., 6–12 June 1995, 5; 27 June–3 July 1995, 3.

62. *Clarín*, int. ed., 28 Jan.–3 Feb. 1992, 5; 24–30 Mar. 1992, 5; 30 June–5 July 1992, 1, 3; 14–20 July 1992, 3.

63. *Clarín*, int. ed., 31 Mar.–6 Apr. 1992, 5.

64. *Clarín*, int. ed., 4–10 May 1993, 6.

65. Kelsey and Levitsky, "Captivating Alliances," 9 n. 33.

66. *Página 12*, 27, 28, and 29 Jan. 1994, as summarized in *Microsemanario* 137 (24–30 Jan. 1994), available over the internet at gopher://gopher.uba.ar. In a rare endorsement of a government proposal, Ubaldini, who lived modestly, said that he approved of the tax authorities' plan to investigate the personal fortunes of union leaders. *Clarín*, int. ed., 21–27 Dec. 1993, 1, 6–7; 4–10 Jan. 1994, 1, 3.

67. *Clarín*, int. ed., 2–8 Aug. 1994, 1, 3.

68. All quotations taken from interviews with these union leaders in Grande, *El poder que no fue*, 13, 21, 76, and 91–92 respectively. For a similar statement by Jorge Triaca of the plastics workers, Menem's first labor minister, see W. C. Smith, "Hyperinflation," 41.

69. Ranis, *Argentine Workers*, 127–36. Quotation from p. 103.

70. *La Nación*, int. ed., 14 Jan. 1991, 8. Methodology not given, but the poll was conducted by Mora y Araujo, Noguera y Asociados, a reputable firm. In a September 1994 poll by Hugo Haime and Associates, 68 percent rated the government's economic plan "OK" or "good" while only 28 percent rated it "bad"; 55 percent rated the government's privatization policy "OK" or "good" while 41 percent rated it "bad" (*Economist*, "Back in the Saddle," 14).

71. *Clarín*, int. ed. 19–25 May 1992, 12.

72. Joan Nelson argues that unions usually do not attempt to block economic adjustment programs; Barbara Geddes, as well as Robert Bates and Anne Krueger, argue that unions usually do not succeed in blocking such programs. Nelson, "Poverty, Equity, and the Politics of Adjustment," 245; Geddes, "Challenging the Conventional Wisdom," 109–13; Bates and Krueger, "Generalizations," 455.

73. A U.S. embassy official quoted in Erro, *Resolving the Argentine Paradox*, 186.

74. Dani Rodrik, quoted in John Williamson, ed., *The Political Economy of Policy Reform* (Washington, D.C.: Institute for International Economics, 1994), 213. Rodrik's point is echoed by Nelson, "Poverty, Equity, and the Politics of

Adjustment," 248–49, and, specifically for the Argentine case, by G. Munck, "Critical Juncture Framework," 10.

75. *La Nación*, int. ed., 13 Aug. 1990, 3.

76. *Clarín*, int. ed., 31 Mar.–6 Apr. 1992, 5. The actual number of CGT general strikes during the Alfonsín presidency was 13.

77. Haggard and Kaufman, "Political Economy of Inflation and Stabilization," 31.

78. Nelson, "How Market Reforms and Democratic Consolidation Affect Each Other," 13.

79. Joan M. Nelson, quoted in John Williamson, ed., *The Political Economy of Policy Reform* (Washington, D.C.: Institute for International Economics, 1994), 472–73.

80. Geddes, "Challenging the Conventional Wisdom," 112.

81. Nelson, "Labor and Business Roles," 169.

82. *Página 12*, 23 Dec. 1990, 4.

83. Murillo, "Union Response to Economic Reform in Argentina," 18–22.

84. Wynia, *Argentina: Illusions and Realities*, 209–10, 223n. On the strike-dampening effect of the defeat of the air traffic controllers' strike in the United States, see Lewin, "Public Employee Unionism," 248.

85. On the 1959 defeat and subsequent decline in strike activity, see James, *Resistance and Integration*, 118–19. On the 1967 defeat and subsequent decline in strikes, see O'Donnell, *Bureaucratic Authoritarianism*, 79–83, 290; and W. C. Smith, *Authoritarianism*, 113–14, 133–35.

86. Little empirical evidence in fact supports the conventional wisdom that high unemployment is a major deterrent to strikes. Jackson, *Strikes*, 137–39.

87. For a quantitative test of this hypothesis, see McGuire, "Causes of Strikes in Argentina."

88. Michael Llanos, "Cabinet Owe Allegiance to Menem, not Peronism," *Buenos Aires Herald*, 8 July 1989.

89. *Buenos Aires Herald*, 11 July 1989; Partido Justicialista, "Consejo Nacional."

90. On the UCeDé, see Gibson, "Democracy and the New Electoral Right."

91. Economist Intelligence Unit, *EIU Country Report No. 4, 1991: Argentina*, 9.

92. *Clarín*, int. ed., 26 Nov.–2 Dec. 1991, 7; 23–29 June 1992, 3; 16–22 Feb. 1993, 6–7; 16–22 Mar. 1993, 3.

93. Partido Justicialista de la Capital Federal, "Carta Orgánica," art. 63, sec. A.

94. Quotations in this paragraph from *Clarín*, int. ed., respectively, 31 Dec. 1991–5 Jan. 1992, 5; 9–15 Mar. 1993, 5; and 12–18 Jan. 1993, 7.

95. *Clarín*, 17 July 1989.

96. J. Castro in *Cronista Comercial*, quoted in *El Bimestre Político y Económico*, Dec. 1989, 12.

97. *La Nación*, int. ed., 18 Sept. 1989, 5 (quotation); 30 Oct. 1989, 5.

98. *La Nación*, int. ed., 2 Jan. 1990, 1; 19 Mar. 1990, 1 (quotation).

99. *La Nación*, int. ed., 23 Apr. 1990, 1.

100. *Página Doce*, 4 Aug. 1990, 4; Wynia, "Argentina's Economic Reform," 60.

101. *Página Doce*, 10 Aug. 1990, 2.

102. *La Nación*, int. ed., 13 Aug. 1990, 5.

103. Gabriela Cerruti in *Página Doce*, 9 Aug. 1990, 9.

104. *Página Doce*, 26 Aug. 1990, 6.

105. Quotation from an unidentified Buenos Aires union leader, *La Nación*, int. ed., 7 Jan. 1991, 8.

106. *El Bimestre Político y Económico*, Aug. 1990, 28.

107. *La Nación*, int. ed., 12 Mar. 1990, 5.

108. *Clarín*, int. ed., 19–26 May 1992, 12.

109. Partido Justicialista, "Carta Orgánica Nacional," art. 24.

110. *Latin American Regional Reports–Southern Cone*, RS 91-08, 17 Oct. 1991, 3. Data on PJ member attitudes toward the pardon from *Clarín*, int. ed., 19–25 May 1992, 12.

111. In an unpublished document—reportedly drafted without García's participation—the PJ national council's executive board asserted that the strike "lacks motives or proposals and has hidden goals" (*Clarín*, int. ed., 3–9 Nov. 1992, 5).

112. Kelsey and Levitsky, "Captivating Alliances," 12.

113. *Clarín*, int. ed., 31 Aug. 1993, 3. For a case study of declining union influence in the PJ-Rosario, see Fernández, *Las nuevas relaciones*, 95–99 and 111–14.

114. Elections were contested in eight of the eleven provincial PJs holding primaries in March 1995 (*La Nación*, 4, 5, 13 Mar. 1995, and *Clarín*, 13 Mar. 1995, summarized in *Microsemanarios* 185 [27 Feb.–5 Mar. 1995] and 186 [6–12 Mar. 1995], available over the internet at gopher://gopher.uba.ar).

115. *Clarín*, 4 July 1991, 13.

116. Partido Justicialista, "Consejo Nacional." Charges of corruption led several times to Rousselot's suspension as mayor of Morón, but the courts repeatedly reinstated him. Rousselot originally came from Chaco.

117. Author's interview with Arturo Lafalla, president of the PJ-Mendoza (1987–91), PJ national deputy from Mendoza (1993–95), and governor-elect of Mendoza (1995), Mendoza, Argentina, 9 Mar. 1993.

118. *Clarín*, int. ed., 5–10 Jan. 1993, 6.

119. *La Nación*, int. ed., 2 Jan. 1990, 3; 12 Feb. 1990, 5; 12 Mar. 90, 5.

120. Zicolillo and Montenegro, *Los Saadi*, 88.

121. *Clarín*, 20 July 1991, 8; *La Prensa*, 25 Apr. 1991, sec. 2, 4.

122. All quotations in this paragraph from *El Bimestre Político y Económico*, Dec. 1989, 26, and Apr. 1990, 30. See also *La Nación*, int. ed., 25 Sept. 1989, 3; 5 Feb. 1990, 5; and 1 Oct. 1990, 4.

123. Quotations respectively from Leonor Casari de Alarcia, Menem's closest collaborator in the Peronist deputy delegation from Córdoba, and Carlos Brown, mayor of San Martín. *La Nación*, int. ed., 12 Feb. 1990, 3.

124. Author's interview with Juan Pablo Cafiero, San Isidro, Argentina, 3 July 1991.

125. Author's interview with José Octavio Bordón, Mendoza, Argentina, Mar. 8, 1993; Onofri, "Bordón y Gabrielli," 7–8; *Clarín*, int. ed., 8–14 Oct. 1991, 6; 3–9 Feb. 1993, 3.

126. Whitehead, "Consolidation of Fragile Democracies," 79.

127. Figures for women's representation in national parliaments from UNDP, *Human Development Report 1993*, 150–51, 195. On the Ley de Cupos, see Pellet Lastra, *El congreso por dentro*, 225–27. The internal statutes of several social democratic, labor, and green parties in western Europe include formal or informal quotas for women (Gallagher and Marsh, *Candidate Selection in Comparative Perspective*, esp. 89, 109, 123, 154, 200, and 223 n. 9), but only in Argentina are parties legally required to include such quotas. In France, a campaign to pass a law that would require each party to allocate women 50 percent of the slots on its list of parliamentary candidates gained momentum in 1993 (*New York Times*, 31 Dec. 1993, A4).

128. The 1994 constitution also increased the number of senators from each province from two to three and assigned one of the three seats to a minority party. Articles 54 and 56 of this constitution stipulated that every two years, one-third of the provinces would elect all three senators simultaneously, with two senate seats going to the party receiving most votes and one to the party receiving the second most.

129. Linz, "Perils of Presidentialism"; Mainwaring, "Presidentialism in Latin America."

130. *Clarín*, int. ed., 14–20 Jan. 1992, 6; 21–27 Apr. 1992, 5; *Clarín*, econ. suppl., 19 Dec. 1993, E1. For discussions of military contestation and military prerogatives in Argentina, Brazil, and Chile, see Stepan, *Rethinking Military Politics*; Acuña and Smith, "Politics of Arms Production"; Aguero, "Military and the Limits to Democratization"; Hunter, "Politicians Against Soldiers"; McGuire, "Interim Government"; McSherry, "Military Power"; Valenzuela, "Democratic Consolidation"; and Zaverucha, "Degree of Military Political Autonomy."

131. *Clarín*, int. ed., 2–8 June 1992, 4; 16–22 June 1992, 6–7.

132. *Clarín*, int. ed., 17–23 Aug. 1993, 5.

133. *Latin American Weekly Report*, 16 June 1994, 262.

134. *Clarín*, int. ed., 13–19 Oct. 1992, 1, 7.

135. *Clarín*, int. ed., 19–25 Jan. 1993, 6–7. Mendoza and Rio Negro were respectively the home provinces of José Octavio Bordón, the FREPASO candidate in the 1995 presidential election, and Horacio Massaccesi, the UCR candidate.

136. *Clarín*, int. ed., 23–29 Mar. 1993, 1, 6–7. On the use of the double simultaneous vote in Argentine provincial elections, see De Riz, "El debate sobre la reforma electoral."

137. Ferreira Rubio and Goretti, "Government by Decree," 15; Carey and

Shugart, "Presidential Decree Authority," esp. 11–16; *Clarín*, econ. suppl., 13 June 1993, E2–3.

138. *Página 12*, 12 July 1991, 3.

139. *Clarín*, econ. suppl., 13 June 1993, E2–3.

140. *Clarín*, int. ed., 1–7 Sept. 1992, 6.

141. *Clarín*, int. ed., 22–28 Oct. 1991, 8; 19–26 Nov. 1991, 3.

142. *Economist*, 27 Oct. 1990, 46, 50.

143. *El Bimestre Político y Económico*, June 1990, 38.

144. *Clarín*, int. ed., 27 Apr.–3 May 1993, 5.

145. *Clarín*, econ. suppl., 13 June 1993, E2–3.

146. *Clarín*, int. ed., 24–30 Nov. 1992, 7; 5–11 Jan. 1993, 3; 16–22 Feb. 1993, 7; 13–19 July 1993, 3; 20–26 July 1993, 5.

147. *Clarín*, int. ed., 20–26 June 1995, 3.

148. For the "kleptocracy" report and a synopsis of corruption scandals through 1991, see Cerruti and Ciancaglini, *El octavo círculo*, 219–81.

149. *Clarín*, int. ed., 12–18 Aug. 1992, 12.

150. *Clarín*, int. ed., 24–30 Aug. 1993, 1, 3, 5.

151. *Clarín*, int. ed., 14–20 July 1992, 4, 7; 21–27 July 1992, 5.

152. *Clarín*, int. ed., 15–21 June 1993, 1, 3.

153. *Microsemanario* 181 (Jan. 1995) available at gopher://gopher.uba.ar; *Clarín*, int. ed., 3–9 Jan. 1995, 1, and 21–27 Feb. 1995, 3.

154. *Latin American Regional Reports—Southern Cone*, RS-93-07, 9 Sept. 1993, 7.

155. U.S. Department of State, *Country Reports on Human Rights Practices for 1993*.

156. Summary of Waisman's report "Why Argentina?" (New York: American Jewish Committee, July 1994) in *Latin American Weekly Report*, 15 Sept. 1994, 414–15.

157. *Clarín*, int. ed., 19–25 May 1992, 1; 26 May–1 June 1992, 1.

158. *Clarín*, int. ed., 21–27 Feb. 1995, 5.

159. O'Donnell, "State and Alliances," 20–21.

CHAPTER 9

1. Di Tella, "La busqueda," 323; Cornblit, "La opción conservadora," 638–39; P. H. Smith, "Breakdown of Democracy," 21. For a general argument that democratic stability depends on dominant classes being represented by parties with electoral clout, see Di Tella, *El sistema político*, 110; Rueschemeyer, Stephens, and Stephens, *Capitalist Development and Democracy*, 197, 287; and Gibson, "Conservative Electoral Movements," 21.

2. On the weakness of the Colombian labor movement and of labor-party ties in Colombia, see Collier and Collier, *Shaping the Political Arena*, 673–77 (a section co-authored with Ronald Archer).

3. Collier and Collier, *Shaping the Political Arena*, 59–99.

4. These figures take no account, it should be noted, of the huge rise in

unemployment after 1991, which seriously weakened the unions, making the weakness of their ties to the PJ less of an impediment than in the past to the prospects for democratic consolidation. For most of the twentieth century, however, Argentina had low levels of open unemployment, contributing to union power and thus making the strength of union-party ties pertinent to the prospects for democracy.

5. Korpi, *Democratic Class Struggle*, 35, 183, 195–99; Cameron, "Social Democracy"; Stephens, *Transition from Capitalism to Socialism*, 49, ch. 4, 142–43.

6. Democratic consolidation is a composite of two dimensions: stability and quality. The argument made here is that a minimum of party institutionalization promotes the stability of democracy—not that a maximum of party institutionalization enhances the quality of democracy. The literature on Italian "partyocracy" and Venezuelan "partyarchy" in fact suggests that where parties nearly monopolize political representation, the quality of democracy may suffer. On Italian "partyarchy," see, e.g., Spotts and Wieser, *Italy: A Difficult Democracy*, 4–8; for a less critical view of Italian parties, see LaPalombara, *Democracy, Italian Style*, 215–18. On Venezuelan "partyarchy" and its negative effects on the quality (and even stability) of democracy, see Coppedge, *Strong Parties and Lame Ducks*, ch. 2. Andreas Schedler, in "Under- and Overinstitutionalization," argues that a golden mean of party-system institutionalization maximizes the quality of democracy.

7. A protodemocracy is a regime that does not allow, but shows unmistakable signs of moving toward, universal adult suffrage and/or unrestricted electoral competition.

8. Bates, *Markets and States in Tropical Africa*, ch. 2.

9. Nelson, "Poverty, Equity, and the Politics of Adjustment," 232.

10. McGuire, "Development Policy," 232–33.

11. Wallerstein, "Union Organization in Advanced Industrial Democracies," 481–82.

12. Hicks and Swank, "On the Political Economy of Welfare Expansion," 89–90.

13. Visser, *European Trade Unions in Figures*; Bain and Price, *Profiles of Union Growth*.

14. Torre, "La tasa de sindicalización en Argentina."

15. Union membership in Argentina as a percentage of the economically active population, which the labor ministry registered as 36 percent in 1986 (Godio and Palomino, *El movimento sindical*, 50–51), has been put at 17 percent in 1983 (Banuri and Amadeo, "Worlds Within the Third World," 178); 25 percent in 1975 (Haggard and Kaufman, "Political Economy of Inflation and Stabilization," 276); 32 percent in 1960 (Organización de Estados Americanos, *América en Cifras*); 25 percent at some point during the 1970s (U.S. National Foreign Assessment Center, *National Basic Intelligence Factbook*), and 28 percent at some time during the 1980s (U.S. Central Intelligence Agency, *World Factbook, 1992*). Discrepancies for Brazil and Peru are even greater. Many of these sources rely ultimately on reports that are compiled by labor attachés in U.S.

embassies, submitted to the U.S. Department of Labor, and released every few years by it as a "Foreign Labor Trends" booklet. These reports show little cross-national consistency on such basic matters as whether the denominator of the union-density quotient is the total of wage and salary earners or the (much larger) economically active population.

16. O'Donnell, in *Modernization and Bureaucratic Authoritarianism,* linked the need for large lump-sum investments in heavy industry to the rise of bureaucratic-authoritarian military regimes in the most modern South American countries in the 1960s and 1970s. Hirschman, Kaufman, and Serra (in Collier, ed., *New Authoritarianism in Latin America*) showed that the links between these phenomena are less clear than O'Donnell's original portrayal suggested, but in his summary of their findings, Collier notes that O'Donnell's hypothesis fits the Argentine case rather well. Moreover, Collier adds, many of the contributors to the debate over O'Donnell's hypothesis agree that "the more recent period of economic growth in Latin America has in important ways been more difficult than the initial phase of industrialization and that these new difficulties have had important political implications" (Collier, "Bureaucratic-Authoritarian Model," 380–81).

17. O'Donnell, "State and Alliances," 7.

18. Przeworski, "Games of Transition," 127.

19. A fine example of the social conflict perspective is O'Donnell, "State and Alliances"; a fine example of the weakness of the party-system approach is Cavarozzi, *Autoritarismo y democracia.* On the relationship of party system strength to the prospects for democracy, see also Mainwaring and Scully, "Introduction: Party Systems in Latin America."

20. Mainwaring, O'Donnell, and Valenzuela, "Introduction" to *Issues in Democratic Consolidation,* 10.

21. Huntington, *Political Order in Changing Societies,* esp. ch. 1.

22. Corradi, *Fitful Republic,* 50. The Spanish term *agropecuario* might better be translated as "agricultural and livestock."

23. Frank has argued, for example, that economic development has been rapid and sustained where and when peripheral regions have been relatively isolated from the world capitalist system, and slow and ephemeral where and when peripheral regions have been firmly incorporated into the world economy. These theses are advanced most explicitly in Frank, "Development of Underdevelopment." For a more detailed historical treatment of the Brazilian and Chilean cases, see Frank, *Capitalism and Underdevelopment.* The key work in the historical-structural dependency school is Cardoso and Faletto, *Dependency and Development.*

24. Chase-Dunn, "Effect of International Economic Dependence"; Evans and Timberlake, "Dependence, Inequality, and the Growth of the Tertiary"; Kaufman, Chernotsky, and Geller, "Preliminary Test of the Theory of Dependency."

25. Each of the three dependency schools corresponds to one of the three models of comparative historical research identified by Skocpol and Somers

in "Uses of Comparative History": the "historical-structural" school to what Skocpol and Somers call the "contrast of contexts"; the "development-of-underdevelopment" school to what Skocpol and Somers call the "parallel demonstration of theory"; and the "dependency-testing" school to what Skocpol and Somers call "comparative history."

26. Corradi, *Fitful Republic*, xv. In "Consumption of Dependency Theory in the United States," Cardoso attacked what he considered to be the clumsy abuse by the dependency-testing school of the finely wrought subtleties of the historical-structural perspective. For an exhaustive response to these criticisms by an unrepentant dependency tester, see Packenham, *Dependency Movement*.

27. This criticism of the dependency perspective was advanced by Bill Warren, who wrote from a Marxist standpoint, in *Imperialism: Pioneer of Capitalism*, 165–67.

28. Corradi, *Fitful Republic*, 111–13.

29. Linz, "Transitions to Democracy," 160.

30. Waisman, *Reversal of Development*, 122. For a condensed version of this argument, see Waisman, "Argentina: Autarkic Industrialization and Illegitimacy."

31. Waisman, *Reversal of Development*, 254.

32. Ibid., 285; "Argentine Paradox," 98, and "Argentina: Autarkic Industrialization and Illegitimacy," 100.

33. Dahl stresses the political culture of the broader population and a lack of commitment to democratic institutions like elections (*Polyarchy*); Wynia highlights contentious political culture and unwillingness to compromise of elites (*Argentina in the Postwar Era* and *Argentina: Illusions and Realities*); Crassweller emphasizes the political culture of the broader population and traces it to the Iberian heritage (*Perón and the Enigmas of Argentina*), and Susan and Peter Calvert underscore the political culture of the broader population, trace it to the interaction between Iberian and liberal European values, and assert that it has created both unwillingess to compromise and a lack of belief in democratic institutions (*Argentina: Political Culture and Instability*). Core works linking the Iberian heritage to authoritarianism in Latin America as a whole include Morse, "Heritage of Latin America"; Wiarda, "Toward a Framework"; and Veliz, *Centralist Tradition*.

34. Waisman, *Reversal of Development*, 95. Similar problems attend cultural explanations for the rapid economic development of South Korea and Taiwan, which began suddenly in the early 1960s (McGuire, "Development Policy," 236–38).

35. The apt phrase is from Schmitter, "Still the Century of Corporatism?" 90.

36. The similarities in Latin American political experiences are stressed by Wiarda ("Toward a Framework"). Writing in the early 1970s, Wiarda attached an adjective like *tutelary* or *guided* to many Latin American experiences with democracy.

37. Cantón, *La política de los militares argentinos*; Mignone, "Military."

38. Potash, *Army and Politics in Argentina, 1928–1945*, 283.

39. Stepan, "New Professionalism"; O'Donnell, "Modernization and Military Coups." Key works on the implanation of bureaucratic-authoritarian military regimes include O'Donnell, *Modernization and Bureaucratic Authoritarianism*; O'Donnell, *Bureaucratic Authoritarianism*; and Collier, ed., *New Authoritarianism in Latin America.*

40. Stepan, "Political Leadership"; O'Donnell, *Modernization and Bureaucratic Authoritarianism.*

41. Potash, *Army and Politics in Argentina, 1945–1962*, 381. See also Potash, "Alfonsín's Argentina," 3–4, and Di Tella, *Latin American Politics*, 148.

42. Rouquié, *Poder militar*, 2: 379.

43. Huntington, *Political Order in Changing Societies*, 409–10.

44. Acuña, "Politics and Economics," 63. Schmitter and Karl ("Types of Democracy," 58, 68) also classify Argentine democracy as consolidated, although Schmitter characterizes it elsewhere ("Consolidation of Democracy," 429) as unconsolidated.

45. Linz, "Transitions to Democracy," 158. The concepts of breadth, depth, and range are from Cohen, *Democracy.*

46. Pridham, "International Context," 168–69.

47. McSherry, "Institutional Legacies."

48. O'Donnell, "The State, Democratization, and Some Conceptual Problems"; Huggins, ed., *Vigilantism in Latin America.*

49. The phrase "executive arrogation" is from Huntington, "Democracy for the Long Haul," 9.

Works Cited

1. BOOKS, ARTICLES, MONOGRAPHS, AND
GOVERNMENT AND UNION DOCUMENTS

Abad de Santillán, Diego. *La F.O.R.A.: Ideología y trayectoria del movimiento obrero revolucionario en la Argentina.* Buenos Aires: Proyección, 1971.

Abellá Blasco, Mario. *Historia del sindicalismo: Los obreros, la economía, la política.* Buenos Aires: A. Peña Lillo, 1967.

———. *Manual de sindicatos.* Buenos Aires, 1973.

Abós, Alvaro. *Las organizaciones sindicales y el poder militar, 1976–1983.* Buenos Aires: Centro Editor de América Latina, 1984.

———. *El posperonismo.* Buenos Aires: Legasa, 1986.

Acuña, Carlos H. "Organizaciones empresariales y políticas públicas en la Argentina." In CIESU/FESUR/ICP, eds., *Organizaciones empresariales y políticas públicas.* Montevideo: FESUR/Ediciones Trilce, 1992.

———. "Politics and Economics in the Argentina of the Nineties." In William C. Smith, Carlos H. Acuña, and Eduardo A. Gamarra, eds., *Democracy, Markets, and Structural Reform in Latin America.* New Brunswick, N.J.: Transaction, 1994.

Acuña, Carlos H., and William C. Smith. "The Politics of Arms Production and the Arms Race Among the New Democracies of Argentina, Brazil, and Chile." In Lars Schoultz, William C. Smith, and Augusto Varas, eds., *Security, Democracy, and Development in U.S.–Latin American Relations.* New Brunswick, N.J.: Transaction, 1994.

Acuña, Carlos H., and Catalina Smulovitz. "¿Ni olvido, ni perdón? Derechos humanos y tensiones cívico-militares en la transición argentina." Paper prepared for the 16th International Congress of the Latin American Studies Association, Washington, D.C., 4–6 Apr. 1991.

Acuña, Marcelo. *De Frondizi a Alfonsín: La tradición política del radicalismo.* 2 vols. Buenos Aires: Centro Editor de América Latina, 1984.

Adelman, Jeremy. "Post-Populist Argentina." *New Left Review* 203 (Jan. 1994): 65–91.

Aguero, Felipe. "The Military and the Limits to Democratization in South

America." In Scott Mainwaring, Guillermo O'Donnell, and J. Samuel Valenzuela, eds., *Issues in Democratic Consolidation: The New South American Democracies in Comparative Perspective.* Notre Dame, Ind.: University of Notre Dame Press, 1992.

Alexander, Robert J. *Labor Relations in Argentina, Brazil and Chile.* New York: McGraw-Hill, 1962.

―――. *Juan Domingo Perón: A History.* Boulder, Colo.: Westview Press, 1979.

Altamirano, Carlos. "La Coordinadora: Elementos para una interpretación." In José Nun and Juan Carlos Portantiero, eds., *Ensayos sobre la transición democrática en la Argentina.* Buenos Aires: Puntosur, 1987.

Anderson, Charles. *Politics and Economic Change in Latin America.* Princeton, N.J.: Van Nostrand, 1967.

Archer, Ronald P. "Party Strength and Weakness in Colombia's Besieged Democracy." In Scott Mainwaring and Timothy R. Scully, eds., *Building Democratic Institutions: Party Systems in Latin America.* Stanford: Stanford University Press, 1995.

Arias, María F., and Raúl García Heras. "Carisma disperso y rebelión: Los partidos neoperonistas." In Samuel Amaral and Mariano Ben Plotkin, eds., *Perón: Del exilio al poder.* San Martín, Buenos Aires: Editorial Cántaro, 1993.

Audi, Rodolfo, and Oscar Raúl Cardoso. "La CGT a sus dueños." *Todo es Historia* 15, no. 167 (Apr. 1981): 62–79.

Ayres, Robert L. "The 'Social Pact' as Anti-Inflationary Policy: The Argentine Experience Since 1973." *World Politics* 28, no. 4 (July 1976): 473–501.

Aznar, Luis, et al. *Alfonsín: Discursos sobre el discurso.* Buenos Aires: FUCADE-EUDEBA, 1986.

Aznárez, Carlos, and Julio César Calistro. *Lorenzo: El padrino del poder sindical.* Buenos Aires: Tiempo de Ideas, 1993.

Baily, Samuel J. *Labor, Nationalism, and Politics in Argentina.* New Brunswick, N.J.: Rutgers University Press, 1967.

Bain, George Sayers, and Robert Price. *Profiles of Union Growth: A Comparative Statistical Portrait of Eight Countries.* Oxford: Basil Blackwell, 1980.

Balestra, Ricardo R., and Jorge L. Ossona, *Qué son los partidos provinciales.* Buenos Aires: Editorial Sudamericana, 1983.

Balvé, Beva et al. *Lucha de calles, lucha de classes: Elementos para su análisis (Córdoba 1971–1969).* Buenos Aires: Ediciones La Rosa Blindada, 1973.

Banuri, Tariq, and Edward J. Amadeo, eds. "Worlds Within the Third World: Labour Market Institutions in Asia and Latin America." In Tariq Banuri, ed., *Economic Liberalization: No Panacea. The Experiences of Latin America and Asia.* Oxford: Clarendon Press, 1991.

Bates, Robert. *Markets and States in Tropical Africa: The Political Basis of Agricultural Policies.* Berkeley: University of California Press, 1981.

Bates, Robert, and Anne Krueger. "Generalizations Arising from the Country Studies." In Bates and Krueger, eds., *Political and Economic Interactions in Economic Policy Reform.* Cambridge, Mass.: Blackwell, 1993.

Bayer, Osvaldo. *Los vengadores de la Patagonia trágica*. 3 vols. Buenos Aires: Galerna, 1972–74.

Beliz, Gustavo. *CGT, el otro poder*. Buenos Aires: Planeta, 1988.

Bendix, Reinhard. *Nation-Building and Citizenship*. 1964. 3d ed. Berkeley: University of California Press, 1977.

Bergquist, Charles. *Labor in Latin America: Comparative Essays on Chile, Argentina, Venezuela, and Colombia*. Stanford: Stanford University Press, 1986.

Bianchi, Susana, and Norma Sanchis. *El partido peronista femenino*. 2 vols. Buenos Aires: Centro Editor de América Latina, 1988.

Bidart Campos, Germán J. *Grupos de presión y factores de poder*. Buenos Aires: A. Peña Lillo, 1961.

Bisio, Raúl H., and Héctor G. Cordone. "La segunda etapa del plan de lucha de la CGT. Un episodio singular de la relación sindicatos-estado en la Argentina." MS. Centro de Estudios e Investigaciones Laborales (CEIL), Buenos Aires, 1980.

Blanksten, George. *Perón's Argentina*. Chicago: University of Chicago Press, 1953.

Bollen, Kenneth. "Political Democracy: Conceptual and Measurement Traps." In Alex Inkeles, ed., *On Measuring Democracy: Its Consequences and Concomitants*. New Brunswick, N.J.: Transaction, 1991.

Botana, Natalio. "La reforma política de 1912." In Marcos Giménez Zapiola, ed., *El régimen oligárquico*. Buenos Aires: Amorrortu, 1975.

———. *El orden conservador: La política Argentina entre 1880 y 1912*. Buenos Aires: Sudamericana, 1977.

Botero, Rocio Londoño. "Trade Unions and Labor Policy in Colombia, 1974–1987." In Edward C. Epstein, ed., *Labor Autonomy and the State in Latin America*. Boston: Unwin Hyman, 1989.

Bourdé, Guy. "La CGT argentine et les occupations d'usines de mai–juin 1964." *Le Mouvement Social* 108 (Apr.–June 1978): 53–87.

Bouzas, Roberto "¿Mas alla de la estabilización y la reforma? Un ensayo sobre la economía argentina a comienzos de las '90." *Desarrollo Económico* 33, no. 129 (Apr.–June 1993): 3–27.

Bra, Gerardo. "El asesinato de Vandor." *Todo es Historia* 23, no. 265 (July 1989): 70–78.

Brennan, James P. *The Labor Wars in Córdoba, 1955–1976*. Cambridge, Mass.: Harvard University Press, 1994.

Brysk, Alison. *The Politics of Human Rights in Argentina: Protest, Change, and Democratization*. Stanford: Stanford University Press, 1994.

———. "The Politics of Measurement: Counting the Disappeared in Argentina." In *Human Rights and Developing Countries*, ed. D. L. Cingranelli. Greenwich, Conn.: JAI Press, 1994.

Burns, Jimmy. *The Land That Lost Its Heroes: The Falklands, The Post-War, and Alfonsín*. London: Bloomsbury, 1987.

Burton, Michael, Richard Gunther, and John Higley. "Introduction: Elite Transformations and Democratic Regimes." In John Higley and Richard Gunther, eds., *Elites and Democratic Consolidation in Latin America and Southern Europe.* New York: Cambridge University Press, 1992.

Butler, David J. "Charisma, Migration and Elite Coalescence: An Interpretation of Peronism." *Comparative Politics* 1, no. 3 (Apr. 1969): 423–39.

Cabanellas, Guillermo. *Derecho de los conflictos laborales.* Buenos Aires: Editorial Omeba, 1966.

Cairo, Angel. *Peronismo claves.* Buenos Aires: Centro de Estudios Aporte, 1975.

Calello, Osvaldo and Daniel Parcero. *De Vandor a Ubaldini.* 2 vols. Buenos Aires: Centro Editor de América Latina, 1984.

Calvert, Susan, and Peter Calvert. *Argentina: Political Culture and Instability.* Pittsburgh, Pa.: University of Pittsburgh Press, 1989.

Cameron, David. "Social Democracy, Corporatism, Labor Quiescence, and the Representation of Economic Interest in Advanced Capitalist Society." In John Goldthorpe, ed., *Order and Conflict in Contemporary Capitalism.* New York: Clarendon Press, 1984.

Canitrot, Adolfo. "Discipline as the Central Objective of Economic Policy: An Essay on the Economic Programme of the Argentine Government Since 1976." *World Development* 8, no. 11 (Nov. 1980): 913–28.

Canitrot, Adolfo, and Silvia Sigal. "Economic Reform, Democracy, and the Crisis of the State in Argentina." In Joan M. Nelson, ed., *A Precarious Balance: Democracy and Economic Reforms in Latin America.* San Francisco: Institute for Contemporary Studies, 1994.

Cantón, Darío. "Universal Suffrage as an Agent of Mobilization." Buenos Aires: Documento de Trabajo, Instituto Torcuato di Tella, 1966.

———. *El parlamento argentino en épocas de cambio: 1890, 1916, y 1946.* Buenos Aires: Editorial del Instituto (Centro de Investigaciones Sociales, Instituto Torcuato Di Tella), 1966.

———. *Materiales para el estudio de la sociología política en la Argentina.* 2 vols. Buenos Aires: Editorial del Instituto (Centro de Investigaciones Sociales, Instituto Torcuato Di Tella), 1968.

———. *La política de los militares argentinos: 1900–1971.* Buenos Aires: Siglo Veintiuno Editores, 1971.

———. *Elecciones y partidos políticos en la Argentina: Historia, interpretación y balance, 1910–1966.* Buenos Aires: Siglo Ventiuno, 1973.

Cardoso, Fernando Henrique. "The Consumption of Dependency Theory in the United States." *Latin American Research Review* 12, no. 3 (1977): 7–24.

Cardoso, Fernando Henrique, and Enzo Faletto. *Dependency and Development in Latin America.* Berkeley: University of California Press, 1979.

Cardoso, Oscar R., and Rodolfo Audi. *Sindicalismo: El poder y la crisis.* Buenos Aires: Editorial de Belgrano, 1982.

Cardoso, Oscar R., Ricardo Kirschbaum, and Eduardo van der Kooy. *Malvinas: La trama secreta.* Buenos Aires: Sudamericana-Planeta, 1983.

Carey, John M., and Matthew Soberg Shugart. "Presidential Decree Authority: Toward a Theoretical Understanding." Paper prepared for the 18th International Congress of the Latin American Studies Association, Atlanta, Ga., 10–12 Mar. 1994.

Carpena, Ricardo, and Claudio A. Jacquelin. *El intocable: La historia secreta de Lorenzo Miguel*. Buenos Aires: Editorial Sudamericana, 1994.

Carri, Roberto. *Sindicatos y poder en la argentina*. Buenos Aires: Sudestada, 1967.

Castello, Antonio E. *Historia contemporanea de los argentinos*, vol. 1: *La reacción conservadora*. Buenos Aires: Abaco de Rodolfo Depalma, 1987.

Catterberg, Edgardo. *Argentina Confronts Politics: Political Culture and Public Opinion in the Argentine Transition to Democracy*. Boulder, Colo.: Lynne Rienner, 1991.

Cavarozzi, Marcelo. *Sindicatos y política en Argentina 1955–1958*. Estudios CEDES, vol. 2, no. 1. Buenos Aires: Centro de Estudios de Estado y Sociedad (CEDES), 1979.

———. *Consolidación del sindicalismo peronista y emergencia de la formula política argentina durante el gobierno frondizista*. Estudios CEDES, vol. 2, no. 7/8. Buenos Aires: Centro de Estudios de Estado y Sociedad (CEDES), 1979.

———. *Autoritarismo y democracia, 1955–1983*. Buenos Aires: Centro Editor de América Latina, 1983.

———. "Los partidos argentinos: Subculturas fuertes, sistema debil." Paper presented at the meeting of the "Political Parties and Redemocratization in the Southern Cone" project at the Woodrow Wilson International Center for Scholars, Washington, D.C., Nov. 1984.

———. "Los partidos y el parlamento en la Argentina: Un pasado de fracasos y un futuro cargado de desafios." In Hilda Sábato and Marcelo Cavarozzi, eds., *Democracia, orden político y parlamento fuerte*. Buenos Aires: Centro Editor de América Latina, 1984.

———. "Political Cycles in Argentina Since 1955." In Guillermo O'Donnell, Philippe C. Schmitter, and Laurence Whitehead, eds., *Transitions from Authoritarian Rule: Latin America*. Baltimore: Johns Hopkins University Press, 1986.

———. "Peronism and Radicalism: Argentina's Transitions in Perspective." In Paul Drake and Eduardo Silva, eds., *Elections and Democratization in Latin America, 1980–85*. San Diego: Center for Iberian and Latin American Studies, Center for U.S.–Mexican Studies, and Institute of the Americas, University of California, San Diego, 1986.

Cavarozzi, Marcelo, Liliana De Riz, and Jorge Feldman. "El contexto y los dilemas de la concertación en la Argentina actual." Paper presented at the workshop on "Labor in Contemporary Latin America: An Agenda for Research" at the Kellogg Institute of International Studies, University of Notre Dame, 28 Feb.–2 Mar. 1985.

Cavazzoni, Omar Pablo. *La burocracia sindical argentina*. Buenos Aires: Centro de Estudios y Acción Socialista, 1984.

CEPNA [Centro de Estudios Para el Proyecto Nacional]. *El nuevo sindicalismo: Opiniones y actitudes de su dirigencia media*. Buenos Aires: CEPNA, 1986.

Cerruti, Gabriela. *El jefe: Vida y obra de Carlos Saúl Menem*. Buenos Aires: Planeta, 1993.

Cerruti, Gabriela, and Sergio Ciancaglini. *El octavo circulo: Crónica y entretelones de la Argentina menemista*. Buenos Aires: Planeta, 1991.

CGT [Confederación General de Trabajo de la República Argentina]. *Estatutos*. Buenos Aires: CGT, 1930.

————. *Memoria y balance anual: XIX ejercicio, 1949*. Buenos Aires: CGT, 1949.

————. *Memoria y balance, 1963–1964*. Buenos Aires: CGT, 1964.

————. "La CGT en marcha hacia el cambio de estructuras." Buenos Aires: CGT, 1965.

Chase-Dunn, Christopher. "The Effect of International Economic Dependence on Development and Inequality: A Cross-National Study." *American Sociological Review* 40, no. 12 (Dec. 1975): 720–30.

Chumbita, Hugo. *El enigma peronista*. Buenos Aires: Puntosur, 1989.

Ciria, Alberto. *Partidos y poder en la Argentina moderna*. Buenos Aires: Editorial Jorge Alvarez, 1968.

————. "Peronism and Political Structures, 1945–1955." In Alberto Ciria et al., eds., *New Perspectives on Modern Argentina*. Bloomington: Institute for Latin American Studies, Indiana University, 1972.

————. *Política y cultura popular: La Argentina peronista, 1946–1955*. Buenos Aires: Ediciones de la Flor, 1983.

CISEA [Centro de Estudios Sobre el Estado y la Administración]. *Argentina, 1983*. Buenos Aires: Centro Editor de América Latina, 1984.

Cohen, Carl. *Democracy*. New York: Free Press, 1971.

Cohen, Youssef. *Radicals, Reformers, and Reactionaries: The Prisoner's Dilemma and the Collapse of Democracy in Latin America*. Chicago: University of Chicago Press, 1994.

Collier, David. "The Bureaucratic-Authoritarian Model: Synthesis and Priorities for Further Research." In David Collier, ed., *The New Authoritarianism in Latin America*. Princeton, N.J.: Princeton University Press, 1979.

————, ed. *The New Authoritarianism in Latin America*. Princeton, N.J.: Princeton University Press, 1979.

Collier, David, and Ruth Berins Collier. "Inducements and Constraints: Disaggregating Corporatism." *American Political Science Review* 73, no. 4 (Dec. 1979): 967–86.

Collier, Ruth Berins, and David Collier. *Shaping the Political Arena: Critical Junctures, the Labor Movement, and Regime Dynamics in Latin America*. Princeton, N.J.: Princeton University Press, 1991.

CONADEP [Comisión Nacional sobre la Desaparación de las Personas]. *Nunca más*. Buenos Aires: CONADEP, 1985.

Conaghan, Catherine. "Politicians Against Parties: Discord and Disconnection in Ecuador's Party System." In Scott Mainwaring and Timothy R. Scully, eds., *Building Democratic Institutions: Party Systems in Latin America*. Stanford: Stanford University Press, 1995.

Confalonieri, Orestes D. *Perón contra Perón*. Buenos Aires: Editorial Antygua, 1956.

Consejo Técnico de Inversiones. *La economía argentina, 1992*. Buenos Aires: Consejo Técnico de Inversiones, 1992.

———. *La economía argentina, 1993*. Buenos Aires: Consejo Técnico de Inversiones, 1993.

Coppedge, Michael. *Strong Parties and Lame Ducks: Presidential Partyarchy and Factionalism in Venezuela*. Stanford: Stanford University Press, 1994.

Cordeu, Mora, Silvia Mercado, and Nancy Sosa. *Peronismo: La mayoría perdida*. Buenos Aires: Sudamericana-Planeta, 1985.

Cornblit, Oscar. "La opción conservadora en la política argentina." *Desarrollo Económico* 14, no. 56 (Jan.–Mar. 1975): 599–640.

Corradi, Juan E. "Between Corporatism and Insurgency: The Sources of Ambivalence in Peronist Ideology." In Morris J. Blachman and Ronald G. Hellman, eds., *Terms of Conflict: Ideology in Latin American Politics*. Philadelphia: Institute for the Study of Human Issues, 1977.

———. *The Fitful Republic: Economy, Society, and Politics in Argentina*. Boulder, Colo.: Westview Press, 1985.

Correa, Jorge. *Los jerarcas sindicales*. Buenos Aires: Editorial Polémica, 1972.

———. *Carlos Ons: Un dirigente metalúrgico clasista*. Buenos Aires: Editorial Anteo, 1975.

Cox, Robert. "The Sound of One Hand Clapping: A Preliminary Study of the Argentine Press in a Time of Terror." Working Paper No. 83, Latin American Program, Woodrow Wilson International Center for Scholars, Washington, D.C, 1980.

Crassweller, Robert D. *Perón and the Enigmas of Argentina*. New York: Norton, 1987.

Crawford, Kathryn Lee. "Due Obedience and the Rights of Victims: Argentina's Transition to Democracy." *Human Rights Quarterly* 12, no. 1 (Feb. 1990): 17–52.

Cúneo, Dardo. *Comportamiento y crisis de la clase empresaria*. Buenos Aires: Pleamar, 1967.

Dabat, Alejandro, and Luis Lorenzano. *Conflicto malvinense y crisis nacional*. Mexico City: Teoria y Política, A.C., 1982.

D'Abate, Juan Carlos. "Trade Unions and Peronism." In Frederick Turner and José Enrique Miguens, eds., *Juan Perón and the Reshaping of Argentina*. Pittsburgh, Pa.: University of Pittsburgh Press, 1983.

Dahl, Robert, ed. *Political Oppositions in Western Democracies*. New Haven, Conn.: Yale University Press, 1966.

———. *Polyarchy*. New Haven, Conn.: Yale University Press, 1971.

———. *Democracy and Its Critics*. New Haven, Conn.: Yale University Press, 1989.

Daiha, Alejandra, and Laura Haimovichi. *Menem y su entorno*. Buenos Aires: Puntosur, 1989.

Davis, Charles L., and Kenneth M. Coleman. "Political Control of Organized Labor in a Semi-Consociational Democracy: The Case of Venezuela." In Edward C. Epstein, ed., *Labor Autonomy and the State in Latin America*. Boston: Unwin Hyman, 1989.

De Riz, Liliana. *Retorno y derrumbe: El último gobierno peronista*. Mexico City: Folios Ediciones, 1981.

————. "El debate sobre la reforma electoral en la Argentina." *Desarrollo Económico* 32, no. 126 (July–Sept. 1992): 163–84.

Del Campo, Hugo. *Sindicalismo y peronismo: Los comienzos de un vínculo perdurable*. Buenos Aires: Consejo Latinoamericano de Ciencias Sociales (CLACSO), 1983.

Delich, Francisco. *Crisis y protesta social: Córdoba, 1969–1973*. Buenos Aires: Siglo Veintiuno Editores, 1974.

Deutsch, Sandra McGee. *Counterrevolution in Argentina, 1900–1932: The Argentine Patriotic League*. Lincoln: University of Nebraska Press, 1986.

Diamond, Larry, and Juan J. Linz. "Introduction: Politics, Society, and Democracy in Latin America." In Larry Diamond, Juan J. Linz, and Seymour Martin Lipset, eds., *Democracy in Developing Countries: Latin America*. Boulder, Colo.: Lynne Rienner, 1989.

Díaz Alejandro, Carlos. *Essays on the Economic History of the Argentine Republic*. New Haven, Conn.: Yale University Press, 1970.

Dirección Nacional de Estadística y Censos. *Anuario estadístico de la República Argentina*. Buenos Aires, 1957.

Di Tella, Torcuato S. *El sistema político argentino y la clase obrera*. Buenos Aires: Editorial Universitaria de Buenos Aires, 1964.

————. "Populism and Reform in Latin America." In Claudio Velíz, ed., *Obstacles to Change in Latin America*. 1965. New York: Oxford University Press, 1969.

————. "La busqueda de la formula política argentina." *Desarrollo Económico* 11, no. 42–44 (July 1971–Mar. 1972): 317–26.

————. *Latin American Politics: A Framework For Analysis*. Austin: University of Texas Press, 1990.

Dix, Robert. "Democratization and the Institutionalization of Latin American Political Parties." *Comparative Political Studies* 24, no. 4 (Jan. 1992): 488–511.

DIL [Documentación e Información Laboral]. *Nucleamientos sindicales*. Buenos Aires: DIL, 1972.

Domínguez, Nelson. *Conversaciones con Juan J. Taccone*. Buenos Aires: Colihue/Hachette, 1977.

Doyon, Louise. "El crecimiento sindical bajo el peronismo." *Desarrollo Económico* 15, no. 57 (Apr.–June 1975): 151–61.

————. "Conflictos obreros durante el régimen peronista, 1946–1955." *Desarrollo Económico* 17, no. 67 (Oct.–Dec. 1977): 437–73.

————. "Organized Labour and Perón, 1943–1955: A Study in the Conflictual Dynamics of the Peronist Movement." Ph.D. diss., University of Toronto.

―――. "La organización del movimiento sindical peronista, 1946–1955." *Desarrollo Económico* 24, no. 94 (July–Sept. 1984): 202–34.

Drèze, Jean, and Amartya Sen. *Hunger and Public Action.* Oxford: Clarendon Press, 1989.

Ducatenzeiler, Graciela. *Syndicats et politique en Argentine, 1955–1973.* Montreal: Les Presses de l'Université de Montréal, 1980.

Duverger, Maurice. *Political Parties: Their Origins and Activity in the Modern State.* 1951. London: Methuen, 1964.

Economist. "Back in the Saddle: A Survey of Argentina." 26 Nov. 1994.

Epstein, Edward C. "Union Election Data as a Political Indicator." *Latin American Research Review* 11, no. 2 (1976): 160–67.

―――. "Control and Cooptation of the Argentine Labor Movement." *Economic Development and Cultural Change* 27, no. 3 (Apr. 1979): 445–65.

Erro, Davide G. *Resolving the Argentine Paradox: Politics and Development, 1966–1992.* Boulder, Colo.: Lynne Rienner, 1993.

Etcheberry, Alberto Ferrari. "Sindicalistas en la bancada conservadora." *Todo es Historia* 27, no. 314 (Sept. 1993): 74–83.

Evans, Judith, Paul Heath Hoeffel, and Daniel James. "Reflections on the Argentine Auto Workers and their Unions." In Rich Kronish and Kenneth S. Mericle, eds., *The Political Economy of the Latin American Motor Vehicle Industry.* Cambridge, Mass.: MIT Press, 1984.

Evans, Peter, and Michael Timberlake. "Dependence, Inequality, and the Growth of the Tertiary: A Comparative Analysis of Less Developed Countries." *American Sociological Review* 45, no. 4 (Aug. 1980): 531–52.

Falcón, Ricardo. "Conflicto social y régimen militar: La resistencia obrera en Argentina (marzo 1976–marzo 1981)." In Bernardo Gallitelli and Andrés A. Thompson, eds., *Sindicalismo y regimenes militares en Argentina y Chile.* Amsterdam: Centrum voor Studie en Documentatie van Latijns Amerika, 1982.

―――. "Políticas neoliberales y respuestas sindicales, 1989–1992." In Omar Moreno, ed., *Desafíos para el sindicalismo en la Argentina.* Buenos Aires: Legasa, 1993.

Fayt, Carlos. *El político armado: Dinámica del proceso político argentino 1960/1971.* Buenos Aires: Pannedille, 1971.

Feldman, Silvio. "Tendencias de la sindicalización en Argentina." *Estudios del Trabajo,* no. 2 (2d semester 1991): 79–109.

Fernández, Arturo. *Ideologías de los grupos dirigentes sindicales, 1966–1973.* 2 vols. Buenos Aires: Centro Editor de América Latina, 1986.

―――. *Las nuevas relaciones entre sindicatos y partidos políticos.* Buenos Aires: Centro Editor de América Latina, 1993.

Ferreira Rubio, Delia, and Mateo Goretti. "Government by Decree in Argentina, 1989–1993." Paper prepared for the 18th International Congress of the Latin American Studies Association, Atlanta, Ga., 10–12 Mar. 1994.

Ferrer, José. "The Armed Forces in Argentine Politics to 1930." Ph.D. diss., University of New Mexico, 1966.

Ferrero, Roberto A. "Los fraudes electorales." *Todo es Historia* 17, no. 197 (Oct. 1983): 48–64.

FIEL/CEA [Fundación de Investigaciones Económicas Latinoamericanas/Consejo Empresario Argentino]. *Argentina: La reforma económica, 1989–1991.* Buenos Aires: Ediciones Manantial, 1991.

Fillol, Tomás Roberto. *Social Factors in Economic Development: The Argentine Case.* Cambridge, Mass.: MIT Press, 1961.

Flichman, Guillermo. *La renta del suelo y el desarrollo agrario argentino.* Mexico City: Siglo Veintiuno Editores, 1978.

Fodor, Jorge. "Perón's Policies for Exports: Dogmatism or Common Sense?" In David Rock, ed., *Argentina in the Twentieth Century.* Pittsburgh, Pa.: University of Pittsburgh Press, 1975.

Fontana, Andrés. "De la crisis de Malvinas a la subordinación condicionada: Conflictos intramilitares y transición política en Argentina." Paper prepared for international seminar on "Autonomización castrense y democracia en América Latina," Santiago de Chile, 22–25 May 1985.

Fox, Elizabeth. "Argentina: A Prosecution in Trouble." *Atlantic Monthly* 255, no. 3 (Mar. 1985): 38–42.

Fox, Elizabeth, and Stanley Meisler. "Buenos Aires: The Weight of the Past." *Atlantic Monthly* 253, no. 1 (Jan. 1983): 12–16.

Frank, André Gunder. *Capitalism and Underdevelopment in Latin America.* London: Pelican Books, 1967.

———. "The Development of Underdevelopment." In *Latin America: Underdevelopment or Revolution.* New York: Monthly Review Press, 1969.

Fraser, Nicholas, and Marysa Navarro. *Eva Perón.* New York: Norton, 1985.

Fundacão Instituto Brasilero de Geografia e Estatística. *Anuario estatístico do Brasil.* Rio de Janeiro: IBGE, 1991.

Gallagher, Michael, and Michael Marsh. *Candidate Selection in Comparative Perspective: The Secret Garden of Politics.* London: Sage, 1988.

Gallie, W. B. "Essentially Contested Concepts." *Proceedings of the Aristotelian Society* 56 (1955–56): 166–98.

Gallitelli, Bernardo, and Andrés Thompson. "La situación laboral en la Argentina del 'Proceso,' 1976–1981." In Bernardo Gallitelli and Andrés A. Thompson, eds., *Sindicalismo y regimenes militares en Argentina y Chile.* Amsterdam: Centrum voor Studie en Documentatie van Latijns Amerika, 1982.

Gallo, Ezequiel. "Argentina: Society and Politics, 1880–1916." In Leslie Bethell, ed., *The Cambridge History of Latin America.* Vol. 5. Cambridge: Cambridge University Press, 1986.

Gallo, Ezequiel, and Silvia Sigal, "La formación de los partidos políticos contemporaneos: La Unión Cívica Radical, 1890–1916." In Torcuato S. Di Tella et al., eds., *Argentina, sociedad de masas.* Buenos Aires: EUDEBA, 1965.

Gallo, Ricardo. *Balbín, Frondizi y la división del radicalismo, 1956–1958.* Buenos Aires: Editorial de Belgrano, 1983.

Gargiulo, Martín. "The Uruguayan Labor Movement in the Post-Authoritarian

Period." In Edward C. Epstein, ed., *Labor Autonomy and the State in Latin America*. Boston: Unwin Hyman, 1989.

Gaudio, Ricardo, and Héctor Domenicone. "El proceso de normalización sindical bajo el gobierno radical." MS. Centro de Estudios de Estado y Sociedad (CEDES), Buenos Aires, 1986.

Gaudio, Ricardo, and Jorge Pilone. "El desarollo de la negociación colectiva durante la etapa de modernización industrial en la Argentina, 1935–1943." *Desarrollo Económico* 23, no. 90 (July–Sept. 1983): 255–86.

———. "Estado y relaciones laborales en el periodo previo al surgimiento del peronismo, 1935–1943." *Desarrollo Económico* 24, no. 94 (July–Sept. 1984): 235–73.

Gaudio, Ricardo, and Andrés Thompson. *Sindicalismo peronista—gobierno radical: Los años de Alfonsín*. Buenos Aires: Fundación Friederich Ebert, 1990.

Gazzera, Miguel. "Nosotros, los dirigentes." In Miguel Gazzera and Norberto Ceresole, *Peronismo: Autocrítica y perspectivas*. Buenos Aires: Editorial Descartes, 1970.

Geddes, Barbara. "Challenging the Conventional Wisdom." *Journal of Democracy* 5, no. 4 (Oct. 1994): 104–18.

Germani, Gino. *Política y sociedad en una época de transición: De la sociedad tradicional a la sociedad de masas*. Buenos Aires: Editorial Paidós, 1965.

———. "Mass Immigration and Modernization in Argentina." In Irving L. Horowitz, ed., *Masses in Latin America*. New York: Oxford University Press, 1970.

———. "El surgimento del peronismo: El rol de los obreros y de los migrantes internos." *Desarrollo Económico* 13, no. 51 (Oct.–Dec. 1973): 435–88.

Gibson, Edward L. "Democracy and the New Electoral Right in Latin America." *Journal of Interamerican Studies and World Affairs* 32, no. 3 (Fall 1990): 177–228.

———. "Conservative Electoral Movements and Democratic Politics: Core Constituencies, Coalition Building, and the Latin American Electoral Right." In Douglas Chalmers, Maria do Carmo Campello de Souza, and Atilio A. Boron, eds., *The Right and Democracy in Latin America*. New York: Praeger, 1992.

Giussani, Pablo. *Montoneros: La soberbia armada*. Buenos Aires: Sudamericana-Planeta, 1984.

Godio, Julio. *La caída de Perón*. 2 vols. Buenos Aires: Centro Editor de América Latina, 1985.

Godio, Julio, and Héctor Palomino. *El movimiento sindical argentino hoy: Historia, organización y neuvos desafios programáticos*. Buenos Aires: Fundación Ebert, 1987.

Goldstein, Avery. *From Bandwagon to Balance-of-Power Politics: Structural Constraints and Politics in China, 1949–1978*. Stanford: Stanford University Press, 1991.

González Bombal, Inés. "El diálogo político: La transición que no fue." Documento CEDES 61. Buenos Aires: Centro de Estudios de Estado y Sociedad, 1991.

González Jansen, Ignacio. *La Triple-A*. Buenos Aires: Contrapunto, 1986.

Gorbato, Viviana. *Vandor o Perón*. Buenos Aires: Tiempo de Ideas, 1992.

Grande, María Herminia. *El poder que no fue: CGT, 1982–1992*. Rosario[?]: Editorial Fundación Ross, 1993.

Groisman, Enrique I. "El 'Proceso de Reorganización Nacional' y el sistema juridico." In Oscar Oszlak, ed., *"Proceso," crisis y transición democrática*. Buenos Aires: Centro Editor de América Latina, 1984.

Guardo, Ricardo C. *Horas difíciles: 1955 setiembre 1962*. Buenos Aires: Ediciones Ricardo C. Guardo, 1963.

Guest, Iain. *Behind the Disappearances: Argentina's Dirty War Against Human Rights and the United Nations*. Philadelphia: University of Pennsylvania Press, 1991.

Haggard, Stephan, and Robert R. Kaufman. "The Political Economy of Inflation and Stabilization in Middle Income Countries." In Haggard and Kaufman, eds., *The Politics of Economic Adjustment*. Princeton, N.J.: Princeton University Press, 1992.

Halperín Donghi, Tulio. "Algunas observaciones sobre Germani, el surgimiento del peronismo y los migrantes internos." *Desarrollo Económico* 14 no. 56 (Jan.–Mar. 1975): 765–779.

———. *Argentina: La democracia de masas*. Buenos Aires: Editorial Paidós, 1983.

Haworth, Nigel. "Political Transition and the Peruvian Labor Movement, 1968–1985." In Edward C. Epstein, ed., *Labor Autonomy and the State in Latin America*. Boston: Unwin Hyman, 1989.

Hicks, Alexander, and Duane Swank. "On the Political Economy of Welfare Expansion." *Comparative Political Studies* 17, no. 1 (Apr. 1984): 81–119.

Hinckley, Barbara. "The Initially Strongest Player: Coalition Games and Presidential Nominations." *American Behavioral Scientist* 18, no. 4 (Mar.–Apr. 1975): 497–512.

Hirschman, Albert. *Journeys Toward Progress: Studies of Economic Policy-Making in Latin America*. 1963. New York: Norton, 1973.

Hodges, Donald C. *Argentina, 1943–1987*. Albuquerque: University of New Mexico Press, 1988.

Horowitz, Irving Louis. "The Election in Retrospect." In Richard R. Fagen and Wayne A. Cornelius Jr., *Political Power in Latin America: Seven Confrontations*. Engelwood Cliffs, N.J.: Prentice Hall, 1970. Published originally as "Storm over Argentina," *The Nation*, 31 Mar. 1962, pp. 281–82.

———. *Three Worlds of Development: The Theory and Practice of International Stratification*. New York: Oxford University Press, 1972.

Huggins, Martha K., ed., *Vigilantism and the State in Modern Latin America: Essays on Extralegal Violence*. New York: Praeger, 1991.

Hunter, Wendy. "Politicians Against Soldiers: Contesting the Military in Post-authoritarian Brazil." *Comparative Politics* 27, no. 4 (July 1995): 425–43.

Huntington, Samuel P. *Political Order in Changing Societies*. New Haven, Conn.: Yale University Press, 1968.

———. "Democracy for the Long Haul." *Journal of Democracy* 7, no. 2 (Apr. 1996): 3–13.

Imaz, José Luis de. "Factores de poder y grupos de presión en la sociedad argentina actual." *Boletín Informativa Semanal de la CGT*, no. 84 (19–25 Oct. 1964): 18–26.

———. *Los que mandan (Those Who Rule)*. Albany: State University of New York Press, 1970.

INDEC [Instituto Nacional de Estadística y Censos]. *Censo nacional económico, 1964*. Buenos Aires: INDEC, 1965.

———. *Censo nacional económico, 1985: Industria manufacturera. Resultos definitivos, primera etapa*. Buenos Aires: INDEC, 1988.

Instituto Nacional de Estadísticas (Chile). *Compendio estadístico, 1993*. Santiago de Chile: Ministerio de Economía, 1993.

Iscaro, Rubens. *Historia del movimiento sindical*. Vol. 2. Buenos Aires: Editorial Fundamento, 1973.

Jackson, Michael P. *Strikes*. New York: St. Martin's Press, 1987.

James, Daniel. "Power and Politics in Peronist Trade Unions." *Journal of Interamerican Studies and World Affairs* 20, no. 1 (Feb. 1978): 3–36.

———. "Unions and Politics: The Development of Peronist Trade Unionism, 1955–1966." Ph.D. diss., University of London, 1979.

———. "Rationalisation and Working-Class Response: The Context and Limits of Factory Floor Activity in Argentina." *Journal of Latin American Studies* 13, no. 2 (Nov. 1981): 375–402.

———. "October 17th and 18th, 1945: Mass Protest, Peronism and the Argentine Working Class." *Journal of Social History* 22, no. 2 (Spring 1988): 441–61.

———. *Resistance and Integration: Peronism and the Argentine Working Class, 1946–1976*. Cambridge: Cambridge University Press, 1988.

Jepperson, Ronald L. "Institutions, Institutional Effects, and Institutionalism." In Walter W. Powell and Paul J. DiMaggio, *The New Institutionalism in Organizational Analysis*. Chicago: University of Chicago Press, 1991.

Jorrat, Jorge Raúl. "Las elecciones de 1983: ¿Desviación o realineamiento?" *Desarrollo Económico* 26, no. 101 (Apr.–June 1986): 89–120.

Justo López, Mario. *Partidos políticos: Teoría general y régimen legal*. Buenos Aires: Cooperadora de Derecho y Ciencias Sociales, 1965.

Kandel, Pablo, and Mario Monteverde. *Entorno y caída*. Buenos Aires: Editorial Planeta Argentina, 1976.

Kaufman, Edy, and Beatriz Cymberknopf. "La dimensión judia en la represion durante el gobierno militar en la Argentina, 1976–1983." In Leonardo Senkman, ed., *El antisemitismo en la Argentina*. 2d ed. Buenos Aires: Centro Editor de América Latina, 1989.

Kaufman, Robert, Harry Chernotsky, and Daniel Geller. "A Preliminary Test of the Theory of Dependency." *Comparative Politics* 7, no. 3 (July 1975): 303–30.

Keck, Margaret E. *The Workers' Party and Democratization in Brazil.* New Haven, Conn.: Yale University Press, 1992.

Kelsey, Sarah, and Steven Levitsky. "Captivating Alliances: Unions, Labor-Backed Parties, and the Politics of Economic Liberalization in Argentina and Mexico." Paper prepared for the 18th International Congress of the Latin American Studies Association, Atlanta, Ga., 10–12 Mar. 1994.

Kenworthy, Eldon. "The Formation of the Peronist Coalition." Ph.D. diss., Department of Political Science, Yale University, 1970.

————. "Did the 'New Industrialists' Play a Significant Role in the Formation of Perón's Coalition, 1943–1946?" In Alberto Ciria et al., *New Perspectives on Modern Argentina.* Bloomington: Latin American Studies Program, Indiana University, 1972.

————. "Interpretaciones ortodoxas y revisionistas del apoyo inicial del peronismo." *Desarrollo Económico* 14, no. 56 (Jan.–Mar. 1975): 749–63.

Kirkpatrick, Jeane. *Leader and Vanguard in Mass Society: A Study of Peronist Argentina.* Cambridge, Mass.: MIT Press, 1971.

Korpi, Walter. *The Democratic Class Struggle.* London: Routledge, 1983.

Korpi, Walter, and Michael Shalev. "Strikes, Industrial Relations and Class Conflict in Capitalist Societies." *British Journal of Sociology* 30, no. 2 (June 1979): 164–87.

Kvaternik, Eugenio. "Sobre partidos y democracia en la Argentina entre 1955 y 1966." *Desarrollo Económico* 18, no. 71 (Oct.–Dec. 1978): 409–31.

————. *Crisis sin salvataje: La crisis político-militar de 1962–63.* Buenos Aires: Ediciones del IDES, 1987.

————. *El péndulo cívico militar: La caída de Illia.* Buenos Aires: Editorial Tésis, 1990.

Lamadrid, Alejandro. "Sindicatos y política. El gobierno Guido." MS. Centro de Estudios de Estado y Sociedad (CEDES), Buenos Aires, 1986.

Lamadrid, Alejandro, and Alvaro Orsatti. "Una revisión de las medidas sobre tasa de sindicalización en Argentina." *Estudios del Trabajo,* no. 2 (2d semester 1991): 135–59.

LaPalombara, Joseph. *Democracy, Italian Style.* New Haven, Conn.: Yale University Press, 1987.

Lawson, Stephanie. "Conceptual Issues in the Comparative Study of Regime Change and Democratization." *Comparative Politics* 25, no. 2 (Jan. 1993): 183–205.

Leuco, Alfredo, and José Antonio Díaz. *Los herederos de Alfonsín.* Buenos Aires: Sudamericana/Planeta, 1987.

————. *El heredero de Perón: Menem, entre Dios y el Diablo.* Buenos Aires: Planeta, 1989.

Levitt, Theodore. "Prosperity Versus Strikes." *Industrial and Labor Relations Review* 6, no. 2 (Jan. 1953): 220–26.

Lewin, David. "Public Employee Unionism and Labor Relations in the 1980s: An Analysis of Transformation." In Seymour M. Lipset, ed., *Unions in Transi-*

tion: Entering the Second Century. San Francisco: Institute for Contemporary Studies, 1986.

Lewis, Paul H. *The Crisis of Argentine Capitalism.* Chapel Hill: University of North Carolina Press, 1990.

Linz, Juan J. *The Breakdown of Democratic Regimes: Crisis, Breakdown, and Re-equilibration.* Baltimore: Johns Hopkins University Press, 1978.

——. "The Perils of Presidentialism." *Journal of Democracy* 1, no. 1 (Winter 1990): 51–69.

——. "Transitions to Democracy." *Washington Quarterly* 13, no. 3 (Summer 1990): 143–64.

Lipset, Seymour Martin. "Radicalism or Reformism: The Sources of Working-Class Politics." *American Political Science Review* 77, no. 1 (Mar. 1983): 1–18.

Little, Walter. "Organized Labor and the Peronist State, 1943–1955." Ph.D. diss., University of Glasgow, 1972.

——. "Electoral Aspects of Peronism, 1946–1954." *Journal of Interamerican Studies and World Affairs* 15, no. 3 (Aug. 1973): 267–84.

——. "Party and State in Peronist Argentina, 1945–1955." *Hispanic American Historical Review* 53, no. 4 (Nov. 1973): 644–62.

——. "The Popular Origins of Peronism." In David Rock, ed., *Argentina in the Twentieth Century.* Pittsburgh, Pa.: University of Pittsburgh Press, 1975.

——. "La organización obrera y el estado peronista, 1943–1955." *Desarrollo Económico* 19, no. 75 (Oct.–Dec. 1979): 331–76.

Llorente, Ignacio. "La composición social del movimiento peronista hacia 1954." In Manuel Mora y Araujo and Ignacio Llorente, eds., *El voto peronista: Ensayos de sociología electoral argentina.* Buenos Aires: Sudamericana, 1980.

López, Ricardo, and Roberto Grabois. "Alonso: Los participacionistas y la penetración imperialista en los sindicatos argentinos." Buenos Aires: Peronismo y Liberación, 1970.

López Alonso, Gerardo. *1930–1980: Cincuenta años de historia argentina.* Buenos Aires: Editorial de Belgrano, 1982.

Loveman, Brian. *Chile: The Legacy of Hispanic Capitalism.* New York: Oxford University Press, 1979.

Lucita, Eduardo. "Elecciones sindicales y autorganización obrera en Argentina." *Cuadernos del Sur* no. 3 (1985): 5–53.

Luna, Félix. *El 45: Crónica de un año decisivo.* Buenos Aires: Editorial Jorge Alvarez, 1969.

——. *De Perón a Lanusse, 1943/1973.* Buenos Aires: Editorial Planeta, 1972.

Luparia, Carlos H. *El grito de la tierra: Reforma agraria y sindicalismo.* Buenos Aires: La Bastilla, 1973.

Lynch, John. "The River Plate Republics." In Leslie Bethell, ed., *Spanish America After Independence.* Cambridge: Cambridge University Press, 1987.

Madsen, Douglas, and Peter G. Snow. *The Charismatic Bond: Political Behavior in Time of Crisis.* Cambridge, Mass.: Harvard University Press, 1991.

Mainwaring, Scott. "The State, Political Crisis, and Regime Breakdown: Peronism, 1952–1955." M.A. thesis, Yale University, 1975.

Mainwaring, Scott. "El movimiento obrero y el peronismo, 1952–1955." *Desarrollo Económico* 21, no. 84 (Jan.–Mar. 1982): 515–30.

———. "The State and the Industrial Bourgeoisie in Perón's Argentina, 1945–1955." *Studies in Comparative International Development* 21, no. 3 (Fall 1986): 3–31.

———. "Presidentialism in Latin America." *Latin American Research Review* 25, no. 1 (1990): 157–79.

———. "Brazil: Weak Parties, Feckless Democracy." In Scott Mainwaring and Timothy R. Scully, eds., *Building Democratic Institutions: Party Systems in Latin America*. Stanford: Stanford University Press, 1995.

Mainwaring, Scott, Guillermo O'Donnell, and J. Samuel Valenzuela, "Introduction." In Mainwaring, O'Donnell, and Valenzuela, eds., *Issues in Democratic Consolidation: The New South American Democracies in Comparative Perspective*. Notre Dame, Ind.: University of Notre Dame Press, 1992.

Mainwaring, Scott, and Timothy R. Scully. "Introduction: Party Systems in Latin America." In Scott Mainwaring and Timothy R. Scully, eds., *Building Democratic Institutions: Party Systems in Latin America*. Stanford: Stanford University Press, 1995.

Manna, Antonio. "Coacción y coalición: Peronismo y partidos políticos, 1962–1963." In Samuel Amaral and Mariano Ben Plotkin, eds., *Perón: Del exilio al poder*. San Martín, Buenos Aires: Editorial Cántaro, 1993.

Manzetti, Luigi. *Institutions, Parties, and Coalitions in Argentine Politics*. Pittsburgh, Pa.: University of Pittsburgh Press, 1993.

———. "The Political Economy of MERCOSUR." *Journal of Interamerican Studies and World Affairs* 35, no. 4 (Winter 1993–94): 101–41.

Manzetti, Luigi, and Marco Dell'Aquila. "Economic Stabilisation in Argentina: The Austral Plan." *Journal of Latin American Studies* 20, pt. 1 (Jan. 1988): 1–26.

Marotta, Sebastián. *El movimiento sindical argentino, su genesis y desarrollo*. 3 vols. Buenos Aires: Lacio, 1960, 1961, 1970.

Marischi, Vicente, ed. *Conciencia y organización en el mundo sindical*. Buenos Aires: Ediciones del Calicanto, 1968.

Maronese, Leticia, Ana Cafiero de Nazar, and Victor Waisman. *El voto peronista '83*. Buenos Aires: El Cid, 1985.

Martínez, Tomás Eloy. *The Perón Novel*. New York: Pantheon Books, 1988.

Mason, Andrew. "On Explaining Political Disagreement: The Notion of an Essentially Contested Concept." *Inquiry* 33, no. 1 (Mar. 1990): 81–98.

Matsushita, Hiroshi. *Movimiento obrero argentino, 1930–1945*. Buenos Aires: Hyspamerica, 1986.

McGuire, James W. "Peronism Without Perón: Unions in Argentine Politics, 1955–1966." Ph.D. diss., University of California, Berkeley, 1989.

———. "Union Political Tactics and Democratic Consolidation in Alfonsín's Argentina, 1983–1989." *Latin American Research Review* 27, no. 1 (1992): 37–74.

———. "The Causes of Strikes in Argentina, 1984–1991." Working Paper No. 49, Institute of Industrial Relations, University of California, Berkeley, 1992.

———. "Interim Government and Democratic Consolidation: Argentina in Comparative Perspective." In Yossi Shain and Juan J. Linz, eds., *Between States: Interim Governments in Democratic Transitions*. Cambridge: Cambridge University Press, 1995.

———. "Development Policy and Its Determinants in East Asia and Latin America." *Journal of Public Policy* 14, no. 2 (Apr. 1995): 205–42.

———. "Strikes in Argentina: Data Sources and Recent Trends." *Latin American Research Review* 31, no. 3 (1996): 127–50.

McSherry, J. Patrice. "Military Power, Impunity and State-Society Change in Latin America." *Canadian Journal of Political Science* 25, no. 3 (Sept. 1992): 463–88.

———. "Institutional Legacies of Military Rule in Argentina." Paper prepared for the 19th International Congress of the Latin American Studies Association, Washington, D. C., 28–30 Sept. 1995.

Merkx, Gilbert W. "Sectoral Clashes and Political Change: The Argentine Experience." *Latin American Research Review* 4, no. 3 (Fall 1969): 89–114.

Mesa-Lago, Carmelo. *La seguridad social y el sector informal*. Programa Regional del Empleo para America Latina y el Caribe, Investigaciones sobre empleo No. 32. Santiago: Organización Internacional de Trabajo, 1990.

Mignone, Emilio. "The Military: What Is to Be Done?" *NACLA Report on the Americas* 21, no. 4 (July–Aug. 1987): 15–24.

Ministerio de Trabajo de la Nación. "Ocupación y producto en la industria manufacturera argentina, 1976–1983." Ministerio de Trabajo de la Nación, Dirección Nacional de Recursos Humanos y Empleo, 1983.

Montoya, Silvia, and Oscar Mitnik. "Evolución de la pobreza y la distribución del ingreso en Argentina." *Novedades Económicas* 17, no. 172–73 (Apr.–May 1995): 7–12.

Moore, Barrington. *Social Origins of Dictatorship and Democracy: Lord and Peasant in the Making of the Modern World*. Boston: Beacon, 1966.

Mora y Araujo, Manuel. "The Nature of the Alfonsín Coalition." In Paul Drake and Eduardo Silva, eds., *Elections and Democratization in Latin America*. San Diego: Center for Iberian and Latin American Studies, University of California, San Diego, 1986.

———. "Las demandas sociales y la legitimidad de la política de ajuste: El programa de reforma económica y la opinión pública argentina." In Felipe de la Balze, ed., *Reforma y convergencia: ensayos sobre la transformación de la economía argentina*. Buenos Aires: Manantial, 1993.

Mora y Araujo, Manuel, and Ignacio Llorente, eds. *El voto peronista. Ensayos de sociología electoral argentina*. Buenos Aires: Editorial Sudamericana, 1980.

Morales Solá, Joaquín. *Asalto a la ilusión: Historia secreta del poder en la Argentina desde 1983*. Buenos Aires: Planeta, 1990.

Moreno, Oscar. *La nueva negociación: La negociación colectiva en la Argentina*. Buenos Aires: Fundación Friederich Ebert, 1991.

Morse, Richard. "The Heritage of Latin America." In Louis Hartz, ed., *The Founding of New Societies*. New York: Harcourt, Brace & World, 1964.

Movimiento Sindical Peronismo Renovador. "Documento final dado por el primero plenario nacional del Movimiento Sindical Peronismo Renovador (M.S.P.R.)." MS. Carlos Paz, Provincia de Córdoba, 1986.

Moyano, María José. "Armed Struggle in Argentina 1969–1979." Ph.D. diss., Yale University, 1991.

———. "The 'Dirty War' in Argentina: Was It a War and How Dirty Was It?" In Hans Werner Tobler and Peter Waldmann, eds., *Staatliche und parastaatliche Gewalt in Lateinamerika*. Frankfurt am Main: Vervuert Verlag, 1991.

———. *Argentina's Lost Patrol: Armed Struggle, 1969–1979*. New Haven, Conn.: Yale University Press, 1995.

Munck, Gerardo. "The Critical Juncture Framework and Argentina: The Menem Revolution in Comparative Perspective." Paper prepared for the 1994 Annual Meeting of the American Political Science Association, New York, 1–4 Sept. 1994.

Munck, Ronaldo, with Ricardo Falcón and Bernardo Gallitelli. *Argentina: From Anarchism to Peronism*. London: Zed, 1987.

Murillo, M. Victoria. "Union Response to Economic Reform in Argentina." Paper prepared for conference on "Inequality and New Forms of Popular Representation," Columbia University, New York, 3–5 Mar. 1994.

Murmis, Miguel, and Juan Carlos Portantiero. *Estudios sobre los orígenes del peronismo*. 1971. Buenos Aires: Siglo Veintiuno Editores, 1984.

Nathan, Andrew J. "A Factionalism Model for CCP Politics." *China Quarterly*, no. 53 (Jan.–Mar. 1973): 34–66.

Navarro, Marysa. "Evita and Peronism." In Frederick Turner and José Enrique Miguens, eds., *Juan Perón and the Reshaping of Argentina*. Pittsburgh, Pa.: University of Pittsburgh Press, 1983.

———. "The Personal Is Political: Las Madres de Plaza de Mayo." In Susan Eckstein, ed., *Power and Popular Protest: Latin American Social Movements*. Berkeley: University of California Press, 1989.

Nelson, Joan M. "Poverty, Equity, and the Politics of Adjustment." In Stephan Haggard and Robert R. Kaufman, eds., *The Politics of Economic Adjustment*. Princeton, N.J.: Princeton University Press, 1992.

———. "How Market Reforms and Democratic Consolidation Affect Each Other." In Nelson, ed., *Intricate Links: Democratization and Market Reforms in Latin America and Eastern Europe*. New Brunswick, N.J.: Transaction, 1994.

———. "Labor and Business Roles in Dual Transitions: Building Blocks or Stumbling Blocks?" In Nelson, ed., *Intricate Links: Democratization and Market Reforms in Latin America and Eastern Europe*. New Brunswick, N.J.: Transaction, 1994.

Niño, Carlos Santiago. "Transition to Democracy, Corporatism, and Presidentialism with Special Reference to Latin America." In Douglas Greenberg et al., eds., *Constitutionalism and Democracy: Transitions in the Contemporary World*. New York: Oxford University Press, 1993.

Norden, Deborah L. "Rebels with a Cause? The Argentine Carapintadas."

Paper prepared for the 1990 Annual Meeting of the Midwest Political Science Association, Chicago, 5–7 Apr. 1990.

Nosiglia, Julio E. *El Partido Intransigente*. Buenos Aires: Centro Editor de América Latina, 1983.

Oddone, Jacinto. *Gremialismo proletario argentino*. Buenos Aires: La Vanguardia, 1949.

O'Donnell, Guillermo. "Modernization and Military Coups: Theory, Practice and the Argentine Case." In Abraham F. Lowenthal, ed., *Armies and Politics in Latin America*. New York: Holmes & Meier, 1976.

———. "State and Alliances in Argentina, 1956–1976." *Journal of Development Studies* 15, no. 2 (Oct. 1978): 3–33.

———. *Modernization and Bureaucratic Authoritarianism: Studies in South American Politics*. Berkeley: Institute of International Studies, University of California, Berkeley, 1979 [1973].

———. *Bureaucratic Authoritarianism: Argentina, 1966–1973, in Comparative Perspective*. Berkeley: University of California Press, 1988.

———. "Transitions, Continuities, and Paradoxes." In Scott Mainwaring, Guillermo O'Donnell, and J. Samuel Valenzuela, eds., *Issues in Democratic Consolidation: The New South American Democracies in Comparative Perspective*. Notre Dame, Ind.: University of Notre Dame Press, 1992.

———. "Delegative Democracy." *Journal of Democracy* 5, no. 1 (Jan. 1994): 55–69.

———. "The State, Democratization, and Some Conceptual Problems." In William C. Smith, Carlos H. Acuña, and Eduardo A. Gamarra, eds., *Latin American Political Economy in an Age of Neoliberal Reform: Theoretical and Comparative Perspectives for the 1990s*. New Brunswick, N.J.: Transaction, 1994.

O'Donnell, Guillermo, and Philippe C. Schmitter. *Transitions from Authoritarian Rule: Tentative Conclusions About Uncertain Democracies*. Baltimore: Johns Hopkins University Press, 1986.

Oficina de Estudios para la Colaboración Económica Internacional. *Argentina económica y financiera*. Buenos Aires: OECEI, Dirección de Planificación y Estudios, 1966.

Onofri, José Esteban. "Bordón y Gabrielli: Comparación y perspectivas." MS. Unión Comercial y Industrial de Mendoza, Mendoza, Dec. 1991.

Organización de Estados Americanos. *América en cifras*. Washington, D.C.: Organización de Estados Americanos, 1965.

Osiel, Mark. "The Making of Human Rights Policy in Argentina: The Impact of Ideas and Interests on a Legal Conflict." *Journal of Latin American Studies* 18, pt. 1 (May 1986): 135–78.

Oved, Iaacov. *El anarquismo y el movimiento obrero en Argentina*. Mexico City: Siglo Veintiuno, 1978.

Packenham, Robert. *The Dependency Movement: Scholarship and Politics in Development Studies*. Cambridge, Mass.: Harvard University Press, 1992.

Page, Joseph. *Perón: A Biography*. New York: Random House, 1983.

Palermo, Vicente. "Democracia interna en los partidos: Las elecciones parti-
darias de 1983 en el radicalismo y el justicialismo porteños." Buenos Aires:
Ediciones del IDES, 1986.

———. "Transformación social: Partido y sindicatos." *Unidos* 11 (1989): 75–87.

Palomino, Héctor. "Elecciones en la UOM; un espejo de la normalización sindical." *El Bimestre Político y Económico* 4, no. 19 (Jan./Feb. 1985): 2–6.

———. "Confrontación de actores y sistemas: Los sindicatos en los primeros
años de gobierno constitucional." MS. Centro de Investigaciones Sobre el
Estado y la Administración (CISEA), Buenos Aires, 1987.

Palomino, Mirta L. de. *Tradición y poder: La sociedad rural argentina, 1955–1983.*
Buenos Aires: Centro de Investigaciones Sociales Sobre el Estado y la Administración (CISEA), 1988.

Panaia, Marta, Ricardo Lesser, and Pedro Skupch. "Las estratégias militares
frente al proceso de industrialización, 1943–1947." In Marta Panaia et al., *Estudios sobre los orígenes del peronismo/2.* Buenos Aires: Siglo Veintiuno Argentina, 1973.

Panebianco, Angelo. *Political Parties: Organization and Power.* Cambridge: Cambridge University Press, 1988.

Partido Justicialista de la Capital Federal. "Carta orgánica." Photocopy. Buenos
Aires, 1986.

Partido Justicialista. "Carta Orgánica Nacional." Photocopy. Buenos Aires,
1987.

———. "Consejo Nacional." Photocopy. Buenos Aires, 1989.

Pasini Costadoat, Emilio. *Crisis democrática y Argentina futuro.* Buenos Aires:
Ediciones Pasini Costadoat, 1969.

Pellet Lastra, Arturo. *El congreso por dentro.* Buenos Aires: Sainte Claire, 1992.

Perelman, Angel. *Como hicimos el 17 de octubre.* Buenos Aires: Ediciones Coyoa-
cán, 1961.

Pérez, Félix, and Juan José Taccone. "Sindicalismo Argentino." In Torcuato S.
Di Tella and Tulio Halperín Donghi, eds., *Los fragmentos de poder.* Buenos
Aires: Editorial Jorge Alvarez, 1969.

Perón, Juan D. *Perón expone su doctrina.* Buenos Aires: Ediciones Nueva Era,
1947.

———. *Conducción política.* Buenos Aires: Escuela Superior Peronista, 1951.

———. "Directivas generales para todo los Peronistas" [Jan. 1956]. In Roberto
Baschetti, ed., *Documentos de la resistencia peronista, 1955–1970.* Buenos Aires:
Puntosur, 1988.

———. *El libro rojo de Perón.* Buenos Aires: A. Peña Lillo, 1973.

———. *Correspondencia.* Vol. 1. Buenos Aires: Corregidor, 1983.

Peyrou, Alejandro, and Ernesto E. Villanueva, eds. *Documentos para la historia
del Peronismo.* Buenos Aires: Carlos Pérez, 1969.

Pion-Berlin, David. "The Fall of Military Rule in Argentina, 1976–1983." *Journal of Interamerican Studies and World Affairs* 27, no. 2 (Summer 1985): 55–76.

———. "Between Confrontation and Accommodation: Military and Government Policy in Democratic Argentina." *Journal of Latin American Studies* 23, no. 2 (May 1991): 543–71.

Pont, Elena Susana. *Partido Laborista: Estado y sindicatos*. Buenos Aires: Centro Editor de América Latina, 1984.

Portantiero, Juan Carlos. "Clases dominantes y crisis política en la Argentina actual." In Oscar Braun, ed., *El capitalismo argentino en crisis*. Buenos Aires: Siglo Veintiuno, 1973.

Potash, Robert A. "Argentine Political Parties, 1957–1958." *Journal of Interamerican Studies* 1, no. 4 (Oct. 1959): 515–24.

———. *The Army and Politics in Argentina, 1928–1945: Yrigoyen to Perón*. Stanford: Stanford University Press, 1969.

———. *The Army and Politics in Argentina, 1945–1962: Perón to Frondizi*. Stanford: Stanford University Press, 1980.

———. *Perón y el G.O.U.* Buenos Aires: Editorial Sudamericana, 1984.

———. "Alfonsín's Argentina in Historical Perspective." University of Massachusetts at Amherst Program in Latin American Studies Occasional Paper No. 21. 1988.

Potter, Anne L. "The Failure of Democracy in Argentina, 1916–1930: An Institutional Perspective." *Journal of Latin American Studies* 13, no. 1 (May 1981): 83–109.

Powers, Nancy. "The Politics of Poverty in Argentina in the 1990s." Paper prepared for the 18th International Congress of the Latin American Studies Association, Atlanta, 10–12 Mar. 1994.

Pozzi, Pablo A. "Argentina, 1976–1982: Labour Leadership and Military Government." *Journal of Latin American Studies* 20, pt. 1 (May 1988): 111–38.

Pridham, Geoffrey. "The International Context of Democratic Consolidation: Southern Europe in Comparative Perspective." In Richard Gunther, P. Nikiforos Diamandouros, and Hans-Jürgen Puhle, eds., *The Politics of Democratic Consolidation: Southern Europe in Comparative Perspective*. Baltimore: Johns Hopkins University Press, 1995.

Prieto, Ramón. *Treinta años de vida argentina, 1945–1975*. Buenos Aires: Editorial Sudamericana, 1977.

Programa Regional del Empleo para America Latina y el Caribe. *Después de la crisis: Lecciones y perspectivas*. Documento de Trabajo PREALC 250. Santiago: Organización Internacional de Trabajo, 1984.

Przeworski, Adam. *Democracy and the Market: Political and Economic Reforms in Eastern Europe and Latin America*. New York: Cambridge University Press, 1991.

———. "The Games of Transition." In Scott Mainwaring, Guillermo O'Donnell, and J. Samuel Valenzuela, eds., *Issues in Democratic Consolidation: The New South American Democracies in Comparative Perspective*. Notre Dame, Ind.: University of Notre Dame Press, 1992.

Przeworski, Adam, and Michael Wallerstein. "The Structure of Class Conflict in Democratic Capitalist Societies." *American Political Science Review* 76, no. 2 (June 1982): 215–38.

Ramicone, Luis. *La organización gremial obrera en la actualidad: Apuntes para la historia.* Buenos Aires: Editorial Bases, 1963.

Ranis, Peter. "Peronismo Without Perón: Ten Years After the Fall, 1955–1965." *Journal of Interamerican Studies* 8, no. 1 (Jan. 1966): 112–28.

———. *Argentine Workers: Peronism and Contemporary Class Consciousness.* Pittsburgh, Pa.: University of Pittsburgh Press, 1992.

Rees, Albert. "Industrial Conflict and Business Fluctuations." *Journal of Political Economy* 60, no. 5 (Oct. 1952): 371–82.

Remmer, Karen L. *Party Competition in Argentina and Chile: Political Recruitment and Public Policy, 1890–1930.* Lincoln: University of Nebraska Press, 1984.

Rennie, Ysabel. *The Argentine Republic.* New York: Macmillan, 1945.

Reyes, Cipriano. *Qué es el laborismo.* Buenos Aires: Ediciones R.A., 1946.

———. *Yo hice el 17 de octubre.* Buenos Aires: GS Editorial, 1973.

Rock, David. *Politics in Argentina, 1890–1930: The Rise and Fall of Radicalism.* Cambridge: Cambridge University Press, 1975.

———. *Argentina, 1516–1982: From Spanish Colonization to the Falklands War.* Berkeley: University of California Press, 1985.

———. "Political Movements in Argentina: A Sketch from Past to Present." In Mónica Peralta Ramos and Carlos H. Waisman, eds., *From Military Rule to Liberal Democracy in Argentina.* Boulder, Colo.: Westview Press, 1987.

Rodríguez Lamas, Daniel. *La revolución libertadora.* Buenos Aires: Centro Editor de América Latina, 1985.

Roldán, Iris M. *Sindicatos y protesta social en la Argentina, 1969–1974. Un estudio de caso: El Sindicato de Luz y Fuerza de Córdoba.* Amsterdam: Centrum voor Studie en Documentatie van Latijns Amerika, 1978.

Romero, José Luis. *A History of Argentine Political Thought.* Stanford: Stanford University Press, 1963.

Rotondaro, Rubén. *Realidad y cambio en el sindicalismo.* Buenos Aires: Pleamar, 1971.

Rouquié, Alain. *Poder militar y sociedad política en la Argentina.* French ed., 1978. 2 vols. Buenos Aires: Emecé, 1982.

Rowe, James W. *The Argentine Elections of 1963: An Analysis.* Washington, D.C.: Institute for the Comparative Study of Political Systems, 1964.

Rueschemeyer, Dietrich, Evelyne Huber Stephens, and John D. Stephens. *Capitalist Development and Democracy.* Chicago: University of Chicago Press, 1992.

Rutledge, Ian. "Plantations and Peasants in Northern Argentina: The Sugar Cane Industry of Salta and Jujuy, 1930–1943." In David Rock, ed., *Argentina in the Twentieth Century.* Pittsburgh, Pa.: University of Pittsburgh Press, 1975.

Sábato, Hilda, and Elias Palti. "¿Quién votaba en Buenos Aires? Práctica y teoría del sufragio, 1850–1880." *Desarrollo Económico* 30, no. 119 (Oct.–Dec. 1990): 395–424.

Sánchez, Carlos H. "Estrategias y objectivos de los sindicatos argentinos." MS. Instituto de Economía y Finanzas, Facultad de Ciencias Económicas, Universidad Nacional de Córdoba, 1973.

Sánchez, Pedro. *La presidencia de Illia*. Buenos Aires: Centro Editor de América Latina, 1983.

San Martino de Dromi, María Laura. *Historia política argentina, 1955–1988*. 2 vols. Buenos Aires: Astrea, 1988.

Sartori, Giovanni. *Parties and Party Systems: A Framework for Analysis*. Cambridge: Cambridge University Press, 1976.

Schedler, Andreas. "Under- and Overinstitutionalization: Some Ideal Typical Propositions Concerning New and Old Party Systems." Working Paper No. 213, Helen Kellogg Institute for International Studies, University of Notre Dame, Mar. 1995.

Schmitter, Philippe C. "Still the Century of Corporatism?" In Frederick B. Pike and Thomas Stritch, eds., *The New Corporatism: Social-Political Structures in the Iberian World*. Notre Dame, Ind.: University of Notre Dame Press, 1974.

———. "The Consolidation of Democracy and the Representation of Social Groups." *American Behavioral Scientist* 35, no. 4–5 (Mar.–June 1992): 422–49.

Schmitter, Philippe C., and Terry Lynn Karl. "What Democracy Is . . . and Is Not." *Journal of Democracy* 2, no. 3 (Summer 1991): 75–88.

———. "The Types of Democracy Emerging in Southern and Eastern Europe and South and Central America." In Peter M. E. Vollen, ed., *Bound to Change: Democracy in East-Central Europe*. New York: Institute for EastWest Studies, 1992.

Schoultz, Lars. "The Socioeconomic Determinants of Popular-Authoritarian Electoral Behavior: The Case of Peronism." *American Political Science Review* 71, no. 4 (Dec. 1977): 1423–46.

———. *The Populist Challenge: Argentine Electoral Behavior in the Postwar Era*. Chapel Hill: University of North Carolina Press, 1983.

Schwarzer, Jorge. "Estructura y comportamiento de las grandes corporaciones empresarias argentinas, 1955–1983." Centro de Investigaciones Sociales Sobre el Estado y la Administración (CISEA), Buenos Aires, 1990.

Schwarzer, Jorge, and Ricardo Aronskind. "Exportaciones Argentinas: Su peor momento." *El Bimestre Político y Económico* 35 (Sept.–Oct. 1987): 21–25.

Scully, Timothy R. "Reconstituting Party Politics in Chile." In Scott Mainwaring and Timothy R. Scully, eds., *Building Democratic Institutions: Party Systems in Latin America*. Stanford: Stanford University Press, 1995.

Sebreli, Juan José. *Los deseos imaginarios del peronismo*. Buenos Aires: Legasa, 1985.

Secretaria de Estado de Trabajo. *Participación de los trabajadores en elecciones gremiales*. Buenos Aires: Secretaría de Estado de Trabajo, Dirección Nacional de Recursos Humanos, Departamento Socio-Económico, Division de Estadísticas Sociales, 1969.

Selznick, Philip. *Leadership in Administration: A Sociological Interpretation*. Evanston, Ill.: Row, Peterson, 1957.

Sen, Amartya. "Freedoms and Needs." *New Republic* 210, no. 3 (10–17 Jan. 1994): 31–38.

Sesenta y Dos Organizaciones. "Reglamentos de los cuerpos orgánicos de las 62 Organizaciones." MS. Buenos Aires, n.d.

Senén González, Santiago. *El sindicalismo después de Perón.* Buenos Aires: Editorial Galerna, 1971.

———. *Diez años de sindicalismo argentino: De Perón al Proceso.* Buenos Aires: Ediciones Corregidor, 1984.

Senén González, Santiago, and Juan Carlos Torre. *Ejército y sindicatos: Los sesenta dias de Lonardi.* Buenos Aires: Editorial Galerna, 1969.

Senkman, Leonardo, ed. *El antisemitismo en la Argentina.* 2d ed. Buenos Aires: Centro Editor de América Latina, 1989.

Sidicaro, Raúl. "Poder y crisis de la gran burguesía agraria." In Alain Rouquié, ed., *Argentina, hoy.* Mexico City: Siglo Veintiuno, 1982.

Silverman, Bertram. "Labor and Left Fascism: A Case Study of Peronist Labor Policy." Ph.D. diss., Columbia University, 1967.

Simpson, John, and Jana Bennett. *The Disappeared: Voices from a Secret War.* London: Robson Books, 1985.

Skidmore, Thomas. "The Problems of Economic Stabilization in Postwar Latin America." In James M. Malloy, ed., *Authoritarianism and Corporatism in Latin America.* Pittsburgh, Pa.: University of Pittsburgh Press, 1977.

Skocpol, Theda, and Margaret Somers. "The Uses of Comparative History in Macrosocial Inquiry." *Comparative Studies in Society and History* 22, no. 2 (Apr. 1980): 174–97.

Smith, Peter H. "Los Radicales argentinos y la defensa de los intereses ganaderos, 1916–1930." *Desarrollo Ecónomico* 7, no. 25 (Apr.–June 1967): 795–829.

———. *Politics and Beef in Argentina.* New York: Columbia University Press, 1969.

———. "The Social Bases of Peronism." *Hispanic American Historical Review* 52, no. 1 (Feb. 1972): 55–73.

———. *Argentina and the Failure of Democracy.* Madison: University of Wisconsin Press, 1974.

———. "The Breakdown of Democracy in Argentina, 1916–1930." In Juan J. Linz and Alfred Stepan, eds., *The Breakdown of Democratic Regimes: Latin America.* Baltimore: Johns Hopkins University Press, 1978.

Smith, Wayne S. "The Return of Peronism." In Frederick C. Turner and José Enrique Miguens, eds., *Juan Perón and the Reshaping of Argentina.* Pittsburgh, Pa.: University of Pittsburgh Press, 1983.

Smith, William C. "Crisis of the State and Military-Authoritarian Rule in Argentina, 1966–1973." 2 vols. Ph.D. diss., Stanford University, 1980.

———. *Authoritarianism and the Crisis of the Argentine Political Economy.* Stanford: Stanford University Press, 1989.

———. "Democracy, Distributional Conflicts, and Macroeconomic Policymaking in Argentina, 1983–89," *Journal of Interamerican Studies and World Affairs* 32, no. 2 (Summer 1990): 1–42.

———. "State, Market, and Neoliberalism in Post-Transition Argentina: The

Menem Experiment." *Journal of Interamerican Studies and World Affairs* 33, no. 4 (Winter 1991): 45–82.

———. "Hyperinflation, Macroeconomic Instability, and Neoliberal Restructuring in Democratic Argentina." In Edward C. Epstein, ed., *The New Argentine Democracy: The Search for a Successful Formula*. Westport, Conn.: Praeger, 1992.

Smulovitz, Catalina. "En busca de la formula perdida: Argentina, 1955–1966." *Desarrollo Económico* 31, no. 121 (Apr.–June 1991): 113–24.

Snow, Peter G. *Argentine Radicalism: The History and Doctrine of the Radical Civic Union*. Iowa City: University of Iowa Press, 1965.

———. "Parties and Politics in Argentina: The Elections of 1962 and 1963." *Midwest Journal of Political Science* 9, no. 1 (Feb. 1965): 1–36.

———. *Political Forces in Argentina*. 1st ed. Boston: Allyn & Bacon, 1971.

Snow, Peter G., and Luigi Manzetti. *Political Forces in Argentina*. 3d ed. Westport, Conn.: Greenwood, 1993.

Sofer, Eugene F. *From Pale to Pampa: A Social History of the Jews of Buenos Aires*. New York: Holmes & Meier, 1982.

Solberg, Carl. "Rural Unrest and Agrarian Policy in Argentina, 1912–1930." *Journal of Interamerican Studies* 13, no. 1 (Jan. 1971): 18–52.

Spalding, Hobart. "Aspects of Change in Argentina, 1890–1914." Ph.D. diss., University of California, Berkeley, 1965.

Spotts, Frederic, and Theodor Wieser. *Italy: A Difficult Democracy*. Cambridge: Cambridge University Press, 1986.

Stepan, Alfred. "The New Professionalism of Internal Warfare and Military Role Expansion." In Alfred Stepan, ed., *Authoritarian Brazil: Origins, Policies, and Future*. New Haven, Conn.: Yale University Press, 1973.

———. "Political Leadership and Regime Breakdown: Brazil." In Juan J. Linz and Alfred Stepan, eds., *The Breakdown of Democratic Regimes: Latin America*. Baltimore: Johns Hopkins University Press, 1978.

———. "Paths Toward Redemocratization: Theoretical and Comparative Considerations." In Guillermo O'Donnell, Philippe C. Schmitter, and Laurence Whitehead, eds., *Transitions from Authoritarian Rule: Comparative Perspectives*. Baltimore: Johns Hopkins University Press, 1986.

———. *Rethinking Military Politics: Brazil and the Southern Cone*. Princeton, N.J.: Princeton University Press, 1988.

Stephens, John. *The Transition from Capitalism to Socialism*. Urbana: University of Illinois Press, 1979.

Strout, Richard Robert. *The Recruitment of Candidates in Mendoza Province, Argentina*. Chapel Hill: University of North Carolina Press, 1968.

Taccone, Juan J. *Crisis . . . Respuesta sindical*. Buenos Aires: Luz y Fuerza, 1971.

Tamarin, David. *The Argentine Labor Movement, 1930–1945: A Study in the Origins of Peronism*. Albuquerque: University of New Mexico Press, 1985.

Tarrow, Sidney. *Power in Movement*. New York: Cambridge University Press, 1994.

Tcach, César. "Una interpretación del peronismo periférico: El partido peronista de Córdoba, 1945–1955." Documento CEDES 54. Buenos Aires. Centro de Estudios de Estado y Sociedad, 1990.

———. *Sabbatinismo y Peronismo: Partidos políticos en Córdoba, 1943–1955.* Buenos Aires: Editorial Sudamericana, 1991.

———. "Neoperonismo y resistencia obrera en la Córdoba libertadora, 1955–1958." *Desarrollo Económico* 36, no. 137 (Apr.–June 1995): 63–82.

Timerman, Jacobo. *Prisoner Without a Name, Cell Without a Number.* New York: Random House, 1981.

Tornquist, Ernesto, & Co. *Economic Development of the Argentine Republic in the Last Fifty Years.* Buenos Aires: Ernesto Tornquist & Co., 1919.

Torre, Juan Carlos. "La tasa de sindicalización en Argentina." Buenos Aires: Centro de Investigaciones, Instituto Torcuato Di Tella, 1972.

———. "El proceso político interno de los sindicatos en Argentina." Buenos Aires: Centro de Investigaciones Sociales, Instituto Torcuato Di Tella, 1974.

———. "La CGT y el 17 de octubre 1945." *Todo es Historia* 10, no. 107 (Mar. 1976): 70–105.

———. *Los sindicatos en el gobierno, 1973–1976.* Buenos Aires: Centro Editor de América Latina, 1983.

———. *La vieja guardia sindical y Perón: Sobre los orígenes del peronismo.* Buenos Aires: Sudamericana, 1990.

Turner, Frederick. "The Study of Argentine Politics Through Survey Research." *Latin American Research Review* 10, no. 2 (1975): 73–94.

UNDP [United Nations Development Programme]. *Human Development Report 1993.* New York: Oxford University Press, 1993.

United States. Central Intelligence Agency. *The World Factbook, 1992.* Washington, D.C.: Central Intelligence Agency, 1992.

———. Department of State. *Country Reports on Human Rights Practices for 1993.* Washington, D.C.: Government Printing Office, 1994.

———. National Foreign Assessment Center. *National Basic Intelligence Factbook.* Washington, D.C.: National Foreign Assessment Center, 1977.

———. *National Basic Intelligence Factbook.* Washington, D.C.: National Foreign Assessment Center, 1980.

Vacs, Aldo. "Authoritarian Breakdown and Redemocratization in Argentina." In James M. Malloy and Mitchell A. Seligson, eds., *Authoritarians and Democrats: Regime Transition in Latin America.* Pittsburgh, Pa.: University of Pittsburgh Press, 1987.

Valenzuela, J. Samuel. "Democratic Consolidation in Post-Transitional Settings: Notion, Process, and Facilitating Conditions." In Scott Mainwaring, Guillermo O'Donnell, and J. Samuel Valenzuela, eds., *Issues in Democratic Consolidation: The New South American Democracies in Comparative Perspective.* Notre Dame, Ind.: University of Notre Dame Press, 1992.

Veliz, Claudio. *The Centralist Tradition in Latin America.* Princeton, N.J.: Princeton University Press, 1979.

Verbitsky, Horacio. *Ezeiza.* Buenos Aires: Editorial Contrapunto, 1985.

———. *Civiles y militares: Memoria secreta de la transición*. Buenos Aires: Editorial Contrapunto, 1987.

Verone, Mario Antonio. *La caída de Illia*. Buenos Aires: Editorial Coincidencia, 1985.

Villanueva, Javier. "Economic Development." In Mark Falcoff and Ronald H. Dolkart, eds., *Prologue to Perón: Argentina in Depression and War, 1930–1943*. Berkeley: University of California Press, 1975.

Viola, Eduardo José. "Democracia e autoritarismo na Argentina contemporânea." Ph.D. diss., Universidade de São Paulo, 1982.

Viola, Eduardo José, and Scott Mainwaring. "Transitions to Democracy: Brazil and Argentina in the 1980s." *Journal of International Affairs* 38, no. 2 (Winter 1985): 193–219.

Visser, Jelle. *European Trade Unions in Figures*. Boston: Kluwer, 1989.

Waisman, Carlos H. *Reversal of Development in Argentina*. Princeton, N.J.: Princeton University Press, 1987.

———. "Argentina: Autarkic Industrialization and Illegitimacy." In Larry Diamond, Juan J. Linz, and Seymour Martin Lipset, eds., *Democracy in Developing Countries: Latin America*. Boulder, Colo.: Lynne Rienner, 1989.

———. "The Argentine Paradox." *Journal of Democracy* 1, no. 1 (Winter 1990): 91–101.

Wallerstein, Michael. "Union Organization in Advanced Industrial Democracies." *American Political Science Review* 83, no. 2 (June 1989): 481–501.

Walsh, Rodolfo. *¿Quién mató a Rosendo?* 1969. Buenos Aires: Ediciones de la Flor, 1985.

Walter, Richard J. *The Socialist Party of Argentina, 1890–1930*. Austin: Institute of Latin American Studies, University of Texas, Austin, 1977.

———. "Politics, Parties, and Elections in Argentina's Province of Buenos Aires, 1912–42." *Hispanic American Historical Review* 64, no. 4 (Nov. 1984): 707–735.

———. *The Province of Buenos Aires and Argentine Politics, 1912–1943*. Cambridge: Cambridge University Press, 1985.

Waltz, Kenneth N. *Theory of International Politics*. Reading, Mass.: Addison-Wesley, 1979.

Warren, Bill. *Imperialism: Pioneer of Capitalism*. London: Verso, 1980.

Weber, Max. 1922. *Economy and Society*. Berkeley: University of California Press, 1980.

Weil, Felix. *Argentine Riddle*. New York: John Day, 1944.

Weiner, Myron. "Political Participation: Crisis of the Political Process." In Leonard Binder et al., *Crises and Sequences in Political Development*. Princeton, N.J.: Princeton University Press, 1971.

Wellhofer, E. Spencer. "Peronism in Argentina: The Social Base of the First Regime." *Journal of Developing Areas* 11, no. 3 (Apr. 1977): 335–56.

Whitaker, Arthur P. *Argentina*. Englewood Cliffs, N.J.: Prentice-Hall, 1964.

Whitehead, Laurence. "The Consolidation of Fragile Democracies: A Discussion with Illustrations." In Robert A. Pastor, ed., *Democracy in the Americas: Stopping the Pendulum*. New York: Holmes & Meier, 1989.

Wiarda, Howard. "Toward a Framework for the Study of Political Change in the Iberic-Latin Tradition: The Corporative Model." *World Politics* 25, no. 3 (Jan. 1973): 206–35.

Wilkie, James A., and Enrique Ochoa, eds. *Statistical Abstract of Latin America*. Vol. 27. Los Angeles: UCLA Latin American Center Publications, University of California, 1989.

World Bank. *Argentina: From Insolvency to Growth*. Washington, D.C.: World Bank, 1993.

Wynia, Gary. *Argentina in the Postwar Era*. Albuquerque: University of New Mexico Press, 1978.

———. "Argentina's Economic Reform." *Current History* 90, no. 553 (Feb. 1991): 57–60, 83–84.

———. *Argentina: Illusions and Realities*. 2d ed. New York: Holmes & Meier, 1992.

Zaverucha, Jorge. "The Degree of Military Political Autonomy During the Spanish, Argentine, and Brazilian Transitions." *Journal of Latin American Studies* 25, no. 2 (May 1993): 283–99.

Zazueta, César, and Ricardo de la Peña. *La Estructura del Congreso del Trabajo: Estado, trabajo, y capital en México*. Mexico City: Fondo de Cultura Económica, 1984.

Zeitlin, Maurice, and Richard Ratcliff, *Landlords and Capitalists: The Dominant Class of Chile*. Princeton, N.J.: Princeton University Press, 1988.

Zicolillo, Jorge, and Néstor Montenegro. *Los Saadi. Historia de un feudo: del 45 a María Soledad*. Buenos Aires: Legasa, 1991.

Zorrilla, Rubén. *Estructura y dinámica del sindicalismo argentino*. Buenos Aires: La Pléyade, 1974.

Zorrilla, Rubén. *El liderazgo sindical argentina: Desde sus orígenes hasta 1975*. Buenos Aires: Siglo Veinte, 1983.

2. PERIODICALS

Apuntes (Buenos Aires, Documentación e Información Laboral), 1987
El Bimestre Económico y Político (Buenos Aires, CISEA), 1983–90
Boletín Informativa Semanal de la CGT (Buenos Aires, CGT), 1963–65
Buenos Aires Herald (Buenos Aires), 1989
Clarín (Buenos Aires), 1963–93
Clarín, edición internacional (Buenos Aires), 1991–94
Compañero (Buenos Aires), 1963
Confirmado (Buenos Aires), 1965–66
Convicción (Buenos Aires), 1983
Economist (London), 1990–95
Economist Intelligence Unit Country Report: Argentina (London), 1991
Estadística Mensual (Buenos Aires, INDEC), 1987
Extra (Buenos Aires), 1966

Hispanic American Report (Stanford), 1954–64
Indicadores de Coyuntura (Buenos Aires, FIEL), 1995
Informes Laborales (Buenos Aires, DIL), 1963–89
Latin American Weekly Report (London), 1982–88
Latin American Regional Report: Southern Cone (London), 1991–93
La Nación (Buenos Aires), 1954–66
La Nación, edición internacional (Buenos Aires), 1989–95
La Prensa (Buenos Aires), 1991
La Razón (Buenos Aires), 1956–85
Mirador (Buenos Aires, SOIVA Glass Workers' Union), 1985
New York Times (New York), 1990–93
Página 12 (Buenos Aires), 1990–93
Panorama (Buenos Aires), 1963–64
El Periodista (Buenos Aires), 1985–89
Primera Plana (Buenos Aires), 1963–67
Redacción (Buenos Aires), 1989
Review of the River Plate (Buenos Aires), 1963–64
Siete Días (Buenos Aires), 1984–85
Tendencias Económicas (Buenos Aires, Consejo Técnico de Inversiones), 1985
Tiempo Argentino (Buenos Aires), 1984
Ultima Hora (Asunción), 1966
Wall Street Journal (New York), 1995

3. ORAL HISTORY ARCHIVE, INSTITUTO TORCUATO DI TELLA, BUENOS AIRES

Transcripts of interviews with:

Albrieu, Oscar (1972)
Iturbe, Alberto (1972)
Parodi, Delia (1973)
Saadi, Vicente (1972)

Index

In this index an "f" after a number indicates a separate reference on the next page, and an "ff" indicates separate references on the next two pages. A continuous discussion over two or more pages is indicated by a span of page numbers, e.g., "57–59." *Passim* is used for a cluster of references in close but not consecutive sequence.

Bus drivers and union (UTA), 83, 87, 201
Business associations, *see* Employers' associations
Business confidence, 159, 219, 257
Business leaders, 2, 5f, 154, 159f, 185f. *See also* Industrialists
Business, big, 160
Business, small, 53, 159f, 185, 302

Caballero, Carlos, 157
Cabo, Armando, 66, 70, 83, 98, 307
Cafieristas, 211, 229, 244
Cafiero, Antonio, 182, 249, 315; during Alfonsín presidency, 21, 193, 207–13, 324; during Menem presidency, 242, 244f, 249, 254
Cafiero, Juan Pablo, 249
Calabró, Victorio, 167, 319
Camaño, Carlos, 259
Cameron, David, 265f
Camillón, Oscar, 259
Cámpora presidency, 163–64
Cámpora, Héctor, 161–64, 182, 318
Canada, 274
Candore, Miguel, 196, 199
Cantón, Darío, 279
Capital flight, 185
Capitalism, perceived threat to, 159. *See also* Communism: fear of
Cardoso, Eleuterio, 87
Cardoso, Fernando Henrique, 273
Cardozo, Rubén, 180
Caro Figueroa, Armando, 232
Carter, Jimmy, 175
Carulias, Manuel, 87
Cassia, Antonio, 233
Castillo, Ramón, 46, 51
Castro Sánchez, Eduardo, 145
Catholic Church, 72–74, 133, 138, 194, 253, 291, 297, 303
Cavalieri, Armando, 197, 203, 205, 214, 325
Cavalli, Adolfo, 85, 125, 155
Cavallo, Domingo, 219, 222f, 236f, 242, 327
Cavarozzi, Marcelo, 165
Censorship, *see under* Media
Central Bank, 58, 219
Centros Independientes, 60–61

Cerezo, Vinicio, 282
CGE (Confederación General Económico), 70, 302
CGT de los Argentinos, 130, 133, 156
CGT, 6; political activities before 1955, 47, 49, 62, 66, 74–75, political activities after 1955, 21, 107, 114–20, 155, 160f, 195–202; origins, 47, 107; factionalism and splits, 48, 51, 107–8, 126, 127, 215, 231, 233; intervention of member unions, 59; legal status, 56, 81, 107–8, 200f; intervention by government, 81, 110, 171; congresses, 83–84, 107, 201f, 228, 309; structure and organization, 106–7, 123, 138, 201; finances, 106, 309; leadership, 107, 136, 150, 165, 167, 192–201 *passim*, 207–13 *passim*, 228, 231, 307, 309; regional delegations, 200f; women in, 228. *See also* "Change of Structures" pamphlet; General strikes; Plan de lucha. *See also under* Perón; Union leaders, Peronist; Vandor; Unions
CGT-Azopardo (1960s), 130, 156
CGT-Azopardo (1980s), 174, 192, 205
CGT-Azopardo (1990s), 228–29, 233
CGT-Brasil, 174, 192
CGT-San Martín, 228ff, 233
Chamber of Deputies, 43, 47, 49, 63, 68, 182, 192, 204, 254–57. *See also* Legislature. *See also under* Partido Justicialista; Union leaders, Peronist
"Change of Structures" pamphlet, 123, 133, 136
Charisma, 15–16. *See also* Menem: personalism; Perón: personalism; Peronism: charisma in
Chile, 31, 253, 258, 279; parties and political system, 6, 33, 293; social classes, 6, 38f; Allende presidency, 159, 162; democratic transition, 173, 181
Christian Democrats, 204, 243, 250
Chumbita, Hugo, 210
Church, *see* Catholic Church
Citizenship, 35, 37, 292
Civil rights movement (USA), 287
Civil service workers and union (UPCN), 129, 156, 196, 199f, 229, 299
Civil society, 176, 321

Library of Congress Cataloging-in-Publication Data

McGuire, James W. (James William)
  Peronism without Perón : unions, parties, and democracy in
Argentina / James W. McGuire.
     p.   cm.
  Includes bibliographical references (p.   ) and index.
  ISBN 0-8047-2831-3 (cloth : alk. paper)
  1. Argentina—Politics and government—1943–   .
  2. Peronism.   3. Trade-unions—Argentina—Political activity—
History.   4. Democracy—Argentina—History.   I. Title.
  F2849.M393   1997
  320.982'09'044—dc20   96-41942
                                                                CIP

⊗ This book is printed on acid-free, recycled paper.

Original printing 1997
Last figure below indicates year of this printing:
06 05 04 03 02 01 00 99 98 97